How to Do *Everything* with

Flash™ 8

Bonnie Blake
Doug Sahlin

ENTER

.JPG

.swf

LOADING

1

McGraw-Hill/Osborne

New York   Chicago   San Francisco   Lisbon
London   Madrid   Mexico City   Milan   New Delhi
San Juan   Seoul   Singapore   Sydney   Toronto

The McGraw·Hill Companies

McGraw-Hill/Osborne
2100 Powell Street, 10th Floor
Emeryville, California 94608
U.S.A.

To arrange bulk purchase discounts for sales promotions, premiums, or fund-raisers, please contact
McGraw-Hill/Osborne at the above address.

How to Do Everything with Flash™ 8

1234567890 FGR FGR 019876

ISBN 0-07-226245-1

Acquisitions Editor	Megg Morin
Project Editor	Mark Karmendy
Acquisitions Coordinator	Agatha Kim
Technical Editor	Denise Laurent
Copy Editor	Mark Karmendy
Proofreader	Paul Tyler
Indexer	Claire Splan
Composition	International Typesetting and Composition
Illustration	International Typesetting and Composition
Cover Series Design	Dodie Shoemaker
Cover Illustration	Jacey

This book was composed with Adobe® InDesign®.

For Matthew, my best boy
—Bonnie Blake

For Emily, whenever I may find her
—Doug Sahlin

About the Authors

Bonnie Blake is an award-winning designer who specializes in interactive media and motion graphics. She is also professor of multimedia design at Ramapo College of New Jersey, the author of three books, and co-author of three others including *Flash Deconstrukt* and *50 Fast Digital Video Techniques*. Her edition of *How to Do Everything with Macromedia Flash MX 2004* was an amazon.com bestseller in the computer book category. Bonnie is also the moderator and co-host of the Adobe Premiere forum for the World Wide Users Group (http://wwug.com). Stop by and say hello to her sometime.

Doug Sahlin is a Flash web designer, photographer, and videographer living in Central Florida. He is the author of 15 books including *How to Do Everything with Adobe Acrobat 7.0* and *Digital Photography QuickSteps*. When he's not busy writing books, Doug photographs clients who include artists, authors, and fashion models.

Contents at a Glance

Contents

Acknowledgments

First and foremost I would like to thank Doug Sahlin for being a great co-author, talented artist, photographer, designer, and friend. As always, it was a pleasure working with such an amazing professional.

The team at McGraw-Hill/Osborne is always supportive, helpful, and full of great advice. Special thanks to Megg Morin for believing in this book and guiding it through its successful editions. As always, Agatha Kim helped the whole process run smoothly, and our editor, Mark Karmendy, was a pleasure to work with and provided us with great comments and a keen eye for details. Thanks to our tech editor Den Laurent, our book was tested and scrutinized well; you are hands down the coolest Flash tech editor in the UK. To Mary Cicitta, thank you again for your input and research, advice, and editing. Also, many thanks to Margot Maley Hutchison for making this all possible.

Last, special thanks to my colleague, Professor Pat Keeton, for being a supportive friend, mentor, and therapist. You truly are an inspiration.

—Bonnie Blake

Kudos to my lovely and talented co-author Bonnie Blake, a.k.a. Lucy. In addition to being a connoisseur of vintage rock and roll, she's inspiration, upbeat, and always a pleasure to work with.

Special thanks to Megg Morin for spearheading yet another edition of *How to Do Everything with Flash*. Many thanks to Agatha Kim, McGraw-Hill/Osborne's tireless taskmaster for keeping the squeaky wheel greased and making sure our documents and screenshots got delivered to the proper parties. Thanks to Mark Karmendy for polishing our text to perfection. Special thanks to the very blonde and very British technical editor extraordinaire, Den Laurent, for making sure our steps were proper and for making sure we didn't tell the reader to hit ALT when we should have told them to hit CTRL. As always, thanks to Margot Maley Hutchison for handling the contractual details and making this project possible.

Thanks to my good friend Barry Murphy for being an inspiration and the man with the plan. As always thanks to my friends and relatives, especially you, Ted and Karen.

—Doug Sahlin

Introduction

Flash 8 certainly bears no resemblance to the first version of Flash I worked on way back in 1997. Unlike its predecessor, Flash 8 is truly a solid program with rich features and a sophisticated interface.

Flash 8 now ships in two versions, Flash 8 Basic and Flash 8 Professional. The basic drawing and animation features in both programs are identical, as are the simple scripting capabilities. Flash 8 Basic is an ideal solution for those needing to produce interactive animation that is of simple to medium complexity. In fact, you can even embed video clips into Flash 8 Basic files, so even though the application is "basic" it still has many features you find in the Professional version.

Flash 8 Professional does all that Flash Basic does and much more. The Flash 8 Professional user may be a web developer, programmer, video user, experienced designer, or anyone else who likes to control the more complex elements of Flash design, like scripting. A Flash "power user" would look to the Professional version for the more advanced features it offers. New and intermediate users, whether in Flash Basic or Professional, will find that this book provides a comprehensive foundation in all you need to know in Flash to get you up and running in no time. By the time you finish the first chapter of this book, you will have created your first animation. In the last half of the book, you will learn all you need to know about working with video in Flash and scripting with ActionScript to make objects and movies interact with one another and your audience.

As fun as it is to make movies in Flash, the myriad of features it offers can boggle the imagination and of course increase the steepness of the learning curve. If you don't have the luxury of spare time to learn all the features of Flash 8, this book will get you pointed in the right direction. In the chapters that follow, you'll find all the information you need about Flash 8 Basic, as well as many of the expanded features of Flash 8 Professional.

Flash is such a diverse application that it appeals to both designers and developers. Designers love the application because of the ease with which they can create compelling animations. Developers enjoy the sophisticated applications they can create, such as shopping carts, which marry animation and ActionScript to create an application that's not only functional but also fun for the end user. In this book we cater to both designer and developer. If you're a designer who has long wanted to add interactivity to your Flash designs but doesn't want to tackle the seemingly daunting task of learning ActionScript, you'll love the chapters on behaviors and timeline effects. Additionally, Flash 8 provides a Script Assist Wizard for those rookies who want to give scripting a try but need some help. With these helpful scripting features, you can easily add interactivity to your movies without knowing much about ActionScript. And for highbrow, hard-coding developers, Flash offers ActionScript 2, which is discussed in Part IV of this book.

Flash beginners will find this book perfect for their needs. With just a basic understanding of Flash and a creative spark, you can create graphics and animations that will dazzle even a more seasoned Flash user. This book focuses on getting you up and running as quickly and efficiently as possible.

In fact, we have designed this book with just that in mind. We explain the basics of Flash in simple language and show you how to put the application to work for your productions. Not only do we explain how to make interesting animations to pique the attention of your viewing audience, we also show you how to add interactivity to your Flash productions. All of the exercises in the book can be altered to fit your own projects. Take the basic recipes we provide, change the images, the colors, and—voilà!—you have an original design. After mastering the basic recipes, you can branch out and add your own creative spark to what you've learned from this book. That's when it really becomes fun. And when you have mastered this application and put a few examples of your expertise on the Internet, people may start seeking you out for your Flash services. That's when it becomes both fun and profitable.

A word of caution is in order here. Once you learn the application, you'll start thinking of new and cool ways to dazzle your viewing audience. The only problem is that these creative sparks often wake you from a sound sleep. Keep a pad and pencil by your bedside so you can jot your new idea down and get back to sleep.

Online Examples and Source Files

Throughout the book there are examples that demonstrate the various techniques that you can use in your Flash productions. You'll find these examples and source files, along with some added bonuses, at the McGraw-Hill/Osborne web site (**www.osborne.com**) for you to refer to and, in some cases, modify and customize for your own movies. These will come in handy, especially when you're trying to come to grips with the more advanced features of Flash 8. You can use the source code together with the written text to gain a comprehensive understanding of both the creative and technical aspects of Flash 8.

The Structure of this Book

There are five parts to this book. The chapter subjects are arranged in order of complexity, starting with the more basic aspects of Flash and building up to the final chapters, which introduce the program's more advanced features, such as how to work with ActionScript and how to publish Flash files. This book is organized into the following parts:

Part I: Learn the Building Blocks of Flash

Part I is designed to give you an overview of what Flash is all about, its fabulous capabilities, and the process you would use to actually build a movie in Flash. Here, your first animation comes to life, giving you a hands-on tour of Flash and the tools of the application. You'll also get an in-depth look at the Flash workspace.

Part II: Add Graphic Elements to Your Flash Movies

Part II introduces the process of creating objects in Flash and manipulating the properties of these elements. Scale, color, position, and countless other properties are covered in depth. You'll also learn about how to transform objects, and you'll get a chance to try the many special techniques you can use to create exciting visual effects. Importing and exporting vector art, bitmaps, and audio and video from today's most popular programs are also examined in detail, as is creating static, input, and dynamic text. The amazing capabilities of symbols are introduced in this section, as well as the concept of instances.

Part III: Put Your Flash Movie in Motion

Part III covers all facets of animation, including frame-by-frame animation and the tried-and-true Flash staples: shape and motion tweening. In this part of the book, you'll learn animation basics and how to put animation to work for you. Timeline effects are also introduced in Part III. And you'll find in-depth training on how to create symbols in this section, including buttons and movie clips. The chapters are peppered with step-by-step examples of projects designed to flatten your learning curve.

Part IV: Lay the Groundwork for Flash Interactivity

Part IV begins with a chapter devoted to behaviors. Behaviors are prescripted objects that let you add interactivity to a Flash production without having to write ActionScript. This makes it fairly easy for you to jump right in and immediately start adding simple interactivity to your movies. The latter chapters of this part introduce you to the powerful features of ActionScript 2. Here you'll find detailed instructions on how to use the most popular actions, along with some How To sections that show you how to use ActionScript to add items, such as a soundtrack and a field that displays the current time, to your movies.

Part V: Embellish and Publish Your Flash Movies

In Part V we provide you with an introduction to the Flash Components, which are prebuilt components that you can add to your movies to include items such as scrolling text boxes, scroll panes, windows that can be dragged and dropped, and much more. The beauty of components is that you can specify the parameters to tailor a specific component to your Flash production. The final chapter in this section shows you how to publish your Flash production in Flash's native SWF format, as well as several other formats.

Appendix: Flash Resource Guide

Check the Appendix out if you're ready to immerse yourself in Flash and take your studies to the next level. Included is a comprehensive list of Flash-related applications, technical resources, and Flash web sites.

For those readers who want to delve a little deeper into ActionScript, this Appendix is equipped with a complete list of web sites offering free source code. This is a great way to learn how other designers have created many of the cool effects you see on the Web.

Also included are learning resources, technical references, tutorials, and sites that offer audio, sound loop, and video downloads for use in your Flash movies.

Conventions Used in this Book

Flash 8 is for PC and Mac users alike. In this regard, there are certain things to keep in mind when reading this book. When shortcut keys are listed next to menu commands, the Windows version is listed first and the Mac version second. The shortcut keys themselves are abbreviated. Because the interface is nearly identical on both platforms, the screen captures were done on both Mac and Windows platforms.

Throughout the book you'll find Notes that tell you about important Flash features, as well as issues to avoid. You'll also find a liberal helping of Tips that are designed to streamline your Flash workflow. You'll find insights and interesting tidbits about Flash-related subjects in the Did You Know sidebars. We've also included a generous helping of How To sidebars, in which you'll find information on how to create elements for your Flash movies. To help users who want to become familiar with the more advanced features of Flash 8 Professional, the book includes Flash Professional sidebars, which explain the expanded features and provide information on how to use them.

Conclusion

Our goal was to produce a book that provides you with a desktop reference for the most popular Flash features, as well as to give you some real-world examples of Flash that you can use in your daily work. We sincerely hope that you will find the information in these pages helpful and entertaining. If we've done our job right, this copy will find a place near your computer and quickly become dog-eared from repeated readings.

Part I

Learn the Building Blocks of Flash

Chapter 1

Make a Flash Movie

How to...

- Make a movie
- Get set up
- Input text
- Animate text
- Add an action

If you bought this book, it's a safe bet that you're familiar with Flash and its tremendous potential as a multimedia design tool. Most likely you want to learn how to animate in Flash, save the animation, and put it up on the Web or output to video or DVD. Perhaps you want to learn how to add interactivity to your Flash movie so your viewers can press buttons and drag objects to trigger events. Or maybe you don't quite know what you want to do with it yet and you want to take it for a test run to see what its capabilities are. Whoever you are and whatever your reasons are for reading this book, one thing has to be true: You are probably anxious to get started and make a Flash movie.

Flash 8 is an application with multiple layers of complexity, so it's not something you can easily master overnight. In addition to the drawing and animation capabilities of Flash 8, the Flash scripting language, ActionScript, exists as an entirely different entity within the application. The Flash 8 Professional version of the application contains many advanced programming features, and for developers interested in programming, this would be their version of choice. ActionScript is a complex scripting language and it can take years for nonprogrammers to master. But don't be discouraged; the good news is that even a beginner can jump right into Flash and start making movies right away without any prior knowledge of ActionScript. A beginner can even incorporate a simple script into his or her movie while still knowing very little about ActionScript. So things are looking up already.

In this chapter, you will make a simple Flash animation. By doing so, you can take a look under the Flash 8 hood, kick the tires, and get a feel for how it drives before getting seriously engrossed in the application. You will experience the excitement of creating a Flash movie that has motion and a script attached. Creating your movie gives you a chance to experiment with the Flash 8 Timeline effects feature. In addition, you will assign a simple action to the timeline in Flash. The exercise will enable even a beginner with little or no experience to jump right in and start making movies.

In later chapters you'll learn more about creating text, using the drawing tools, creating animation, and working with Timeline effects as well as Flash Behaviors. Flash Behaviors allow you to add simple interactivity to your movie by choosing actions from a simple menu. Now you are about to experience the pure delight of making your first animation in Flash 8.

Make a Movie

As you are about to find out, making a simple movie in Flash 8 is an easy task even for a beginner. By the end of this lesson you will have made a movie with animated text. You could probably use an effect like this for an animated title in a Flash movie. Keep in mind that the features you will be using in this chapter are available in both Flash 8 Basic and Flash 8 Professional versions.

In this quick tour, you will get a glimpse of several different aspects of Flash. In doing so, you will get a feel for how the design process works in Flash.

Get Set Up

Before you make a movie in Flash, you need to launch the application and create a new file. When you launch Flash, you will see a Start page. The Start page allows you to select the type of document you want to create from a menu list. The Start page is covered in Chapter 2, but for the sake of getting started quickly, here you'll proceed directly to a new page.

1. In the middle column of the Start page, select Create New | Flash Document. A new page appears. In Flash, the white area on this page is called the *stage*. This is where you create your movie.

2. The background for the title you are about to create may be more compelling if it is given a color other than white. You can change the color of the movie background in the Properties Inspector. The Properties Inspector is a window located at the bottom of the workspace that allows you to set and change the characteristics of elements, also known as "assets," in Flash. To change the color of the background, first click the stage. Then, in the Properties Inspector, click the color swatch to the right of the word "Background." From the pop-up menu, select a background color or leave the background the default white. The Properties Inspector and color swatch are shown here:

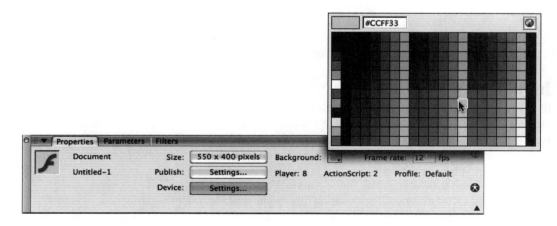

3. You should always save a Flash movie at the beginning of, and many times during, the creation of your project. Saving documents frequently will prevent you from pulling your hair out later if the application crashes and you lose your movie. To save your movie, select File | Save As from the menu. In both the Windows and Macintosh environments, the Save As dialog box is similar to those in most standard applications. Navigate to the folder where you want to save the file, give the file a name in the Save As input box, and click the Save button. The Save As dialog box is shown here.

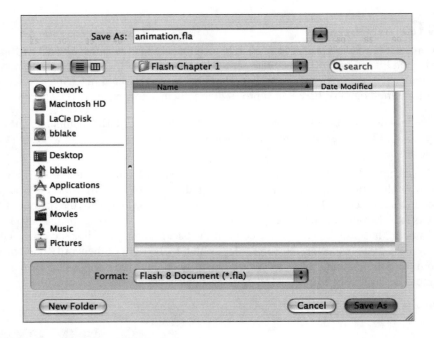

Next, you'll type some text onto the stage and format it.

Input Text

In this section you will create the text that will be animated in the next section. The completed movie will show an animated title in which a word spins around. To examine a completed version of this exercise, download the sample file for Chapter 1 for this book on the McGraw-Hill/ Osborne site (www.osborne.com) and click the "free code" link. The file is named animation.swf. Click the file to play the movie.

Here's a description of how the movie works. When it loads, the audience sees a spinning title that says "ANIMATION." The spinning title gradually fades out of sight.

To create the text in this movie, you'll need to use the Text tool in the Tools panel. This panel is a long rectangle with multiple icons. By default, it appears on the left side of your workspace.

The Tools panel is where all the tools you use to create graphics reside. The details of the Tools panel, also called the Toolbar, are discussed in Chapter 2. If you do not see the Tools panel, select Window | Tools from the menu.

1. In the Toolbar, select the Text tool. As in many other applications, it appears as a letter *A* in the Toolbar, as shown here:

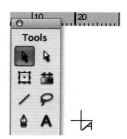

2. Before inputting the text on the stage, select the font, color, and size of the text you are about to create. To do so, go to the Properties Inspector, where you can set and modify the properties (characteristics) of the text you are about to create. From the Font pull-down menu, select Arial. To the right of the Font selection is the Font Size box. Type **40** in this box. Then click the Text Fill Color swatch to the right of the Font Size box and select a color from the pop-up menu to complement your background color selection. Make sure the font color you choose contrasts with the background color you originally chose. At the far right on the top row of buttons, select the Center Justify button. This button looks like a small paragraph whose text is centered. When you select this you can be sure that the text will be referenced from the center when you type it in. The appropriate settings for your text are shown here:

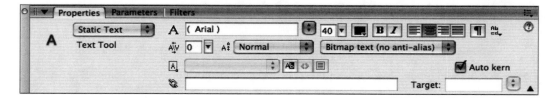

Tools and controls in the Toolbar and Properties Inspector conveniently display tooltips. When you position your pointer over a tool, its name appears. These tooltips help you get to know the various tools in Flash. Shortcut key information appears to the right of the tool name in the tooltip too, making it easy for you to memorize the shortcuts. Shortcut keys help you quickly access a tool by pressing a letter key. For example, by pressing the letter T you can access the Text tool.

3. Once the properties of the text are set, you can type in the text. Click in the middle of the stage and type the word **ANIMATION**. Once the word is typed out, click away from the text (anywhere in the Flash workspace) and then press v to access the Selection tool in the Toolbar. Use this tool, a black arrow, to select the text and position it on the stage. Position the arrow over the title until you see a crosshair appear in the bottom right of the arrow. The crosshair indicates that you have selected the text. Then click and move the text. The result should look similar to this illustration:

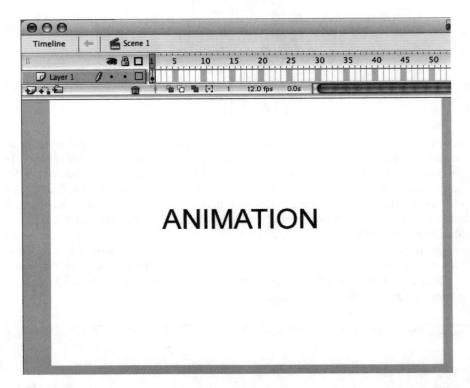

Now that the background is colored and text is created and in position, you can animate the text.

Animate Text

Basic animation in Flash is quite simple, as you are about to find out. Here you will use a Timeline effect to animate the text you just created. Specifically, you will make the text spin and move in time. In Chapter 10, Timeline effects are explored in more detail.

1. On the Toolbar, click the Selection tool (the black arrow) and then click the text on the stage. Select Insert | Timeline Effects | Transform/Transition | Transform from the menu. The Transform dialog box appears, as shown in the following illustration. Here you can adjust several of the characteristics of an object in time, such as the scale, spin rotation, and transparency.

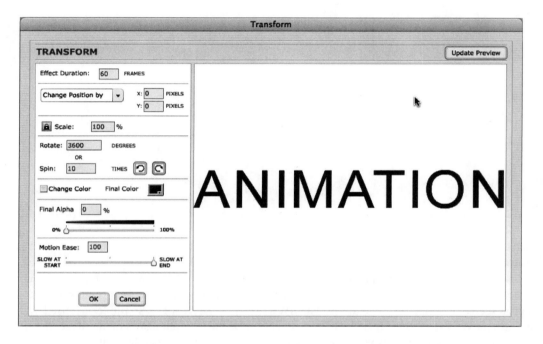

2. At the top of the dialog box, for Effect Duration, highlight the default number 30 and type in **60**. This will make the transformations last through 60 frames. The frames represent different states of an object in time or in various stages. Frames are represented in the timeline as little rectangles. With this setting, the text will animate for about five seconds.

3. In the Spin text input box, type **10**. This will make the text spin ten times by the time the animation reaches the last frame. Note that the Rotate number changes to 3600 when you do this.

4. Underneath that, for Final Alpha, type in a **0**. This will make the text fade out on the last frame.

5. For Motion Ease, type in **100**. This will make the spinning slow down on the last frame. Click the Update Preview button in the upper-right corner of the dialog box to get a glimpse of what the animation looks like, as shown in the following illustration.

To see what your animation looks like on the stage, click the OK button on the bottom left of the dialog box. Then, from the menu, select Control | Test Movie. An SWF file is generated and you can see your animation come to life. The SWF format is the native Flash file format used for Flash movie distribution. To some extent, you can preview your animation on the stage, but testing the movie always gives you a more accurate representation of what the audience will see when the movie is published. As expected, the word "ANIMATION" spins around and fades out over a period of five seconds. You have created your first animation in Flash.

 *Some people think SWF stands for "Shockwave Flash File." It actually means "Small Web Format," a nomenclature perfect for Flash movies, since Flash player files tend to be smaller than animations generated from other applications.*

If this were a real title, you obviously wouldn't want it to keep running over and over as it is doing in this example. The reason it's repeating itself is because the animation loops forever. To get it to stop when you want it to, you need to instruct the movie to stop when the animation reaches a certain point in the timeline. In the next section, you'll learn how to add a Stop action to make the movie stop playing when it reaches the last frame.

Add a Frame Action

By creating a little script, you can make the title stop on the last frame. Here you will add a Stop action to the last frame in the timeline.

The timeline is located at the top of the Flash workspace and is used in conjunction with the stage to create an animation. Notice that the transformation effect is indicated in the timeline, as shown in Figure 1-1. It is named "Transform" and it resides on a layer. Layers allow you to stack pictures or scripts on top of one another. There is also a gray bar that extends to the right and stops at the number 60, representing the frame number you selected in the Transform dialog box.

To get the animation to stop on frame 60 so it won't loop, you need to place a Stop action on the last frame. Before adding the action, you will create another layer for the action. If the Stop action is placed on its own layer, it will be easy to see in the timeline.

1. To create another layer in the timeline, click the Insert Layer button in the bottom-left corner of the timeline, shown next. Clicking this button will add another layer to the timeline on top of the Transform layer.

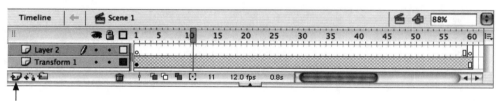

Insert Layer button

2. To create a Stop action on this new layer, first click frame 60 in the new layer and press F6 (or select Insert | Timeline | Keyframe). Doing so will make a keyframe, which appears as a white circle, as you can see in the previous illustration. A *keyframe* is a frame in an animation in which a change in content occurs. When the Stop action is added on this keyframe, the animation will stop.

If pressing F6 does not produce a keyframe, select Insert | Timeline | Keyframe. Your computer may not be configured to recognize function keys in Flash.

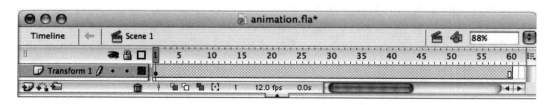

FIGURE 1-1   A Transform effect applied to the title text fills in frames in the timeline.

3. Next, display the Actions panel by selecting Window | Actions or pressing F9 in Windows or OPTION-F9 on the Mac. This will bring the panel forward even if it is already on the desktop. The Actions panel, shown here, is where you create scripts so you or your audience can control the movie.

Global Functions   Script Assist button

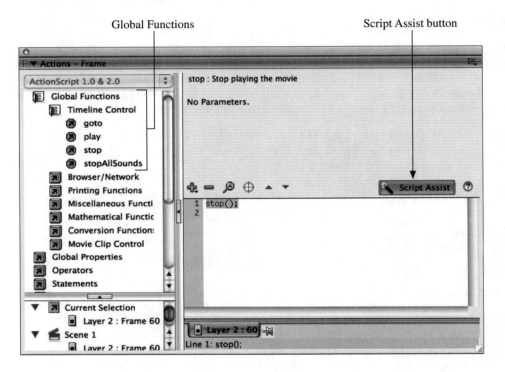

4. Click the Script Assist button (looks like a wand) in the upper-right column in the Actions panel, as shown in the illustration. This assists you in creating a script if you are a beginner at scripting in Flash. Underneath the Script Assist button is the *script pane*. This is the area where you build scripts for frames and objects. In the left column, click the Global Functions button to expand the contents.

5. Click the Timeline Control button to expand the contents and then double-click Stop. The word **stop();** now appears in the script pane.

6. As you can see in the following illustration, the letter *a* now appears on the last frame in the timeline, indicating that there is a script on frame 60. When the movie is played, it will stop when it gets to the last frame.

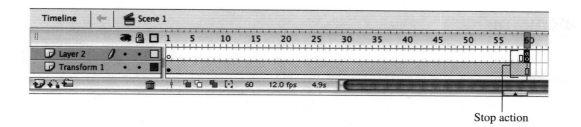

Stop action

Test Your Movie

The movie is now complete. It's time to check out the final results. To see the finished movie, select Control | Test Movie (CTRL-ENTER in Windows or CMD-RETURN on the Mac). As you will see, the text gradually appears out of nowhere because we adjusted the transparency setting (Alpha) to change in time. The text also spins, then stops after about five seconds. The following illustration shows a frame from the finished movie. It gives you an idea of the path the spin animation takes as it goes around.

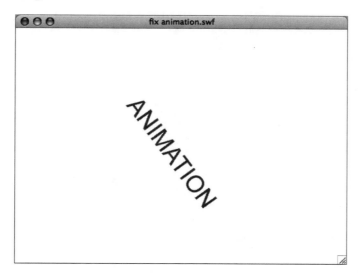

Congratulations! You have just created an animation in Flash. After you create an SWF version of your movie, you can put the movie up on the Web or distribute it on media such as CD or DVD.

Conclusion

There is much more to Flash than the tour you just took. Hopefully you have more questions than answers after having had a look around the workspace. The stage, the Properties Inspector, the timeline, and other windows will begin to look familiar after you make a few Flash movies.

In subsequent chapters, you will expand on your knowledge of the techniques learned here. The true journey begins in the next chapter, where some of the tools touched upon in the title exercise are explored in more detail. There you will learn all about the Flash stage, the tools in the Toolbar, the timeline, and the Properties Inspector, as well as other important windows and features in the Flash environment. Gradually you will become more comfortable with the Flash interface, and you'll be making movies in no time.

Chapter 2

Get to Know the Flash Workspace

How to. . .

- Create a new document
- Use templates
- Grasp the stage concept
- Control the way your movie looks
- Work with the timeline
- Understand the Tools panel
- Dissect the Properties Inspector
- Use panels
- Explore the Library
- Get help
- Use scenes

In the first chapter, you experimented with the Text tool and made an animation on the stage. In this chapter, you'll learn more about the specifics of the stage, the Toolbar, and the timeline, as well as other basic concepts. The basics reviewed in this chapter will provide you with a solid foundation that will springboard you to the next learning level in Flash.

Create a Document

Creating a document is an easy task. You create a document in Flash just as you would in most graphics-based applications. You'll get the most out of learning the Flash environment if you understand the different options available to you when you begin a new document.

Navigate the Start Page

When you launch the Flash 8 application, a three-column setup page appears, offering many different options. This page is known as the Start page. The Start page can be very helpful for beginners, as it provides you with several options, complete with a Flash tour, lessons, and help menus. The Start page on Flash 8 Basic and Flash 8 Professional will look similar, but the Professional version will have more developer-related options under the Create New column:

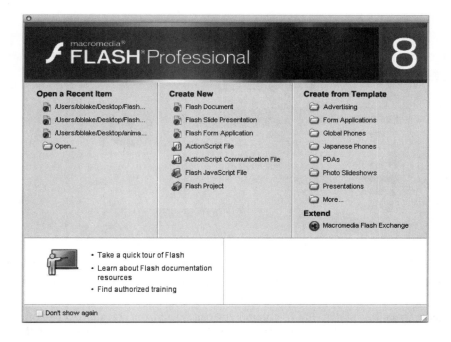

TIP *If you find the Start page annoying, check the Don't Show Again box in the bottom-left corner of the Start page. You can also select more start options in the Preferences menu. To do this, select Edit | Preferences | General and then select an On Launch option in the pop-up menu. On a Mac, select Flash (or Flash Professional) | Preferences | General and then select an On Launch option in the pop-up menu.*

Here you can choose your next move by selecting an item from one of three categories:

■ **Open a Recent Item**   This is used to open a Flash or Flash Player file that you recently worked on. Clicking the Open folder icon in this category displays the Open dialog box, shown next. Use the Open dialog box to navigate to the file you want to open. Highlight the file and click the Open button. This option can also be selected from the menu (File | Open).

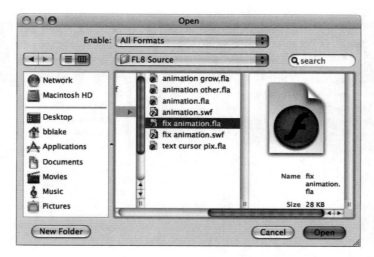

- **Create New** This option is used to begin a new document. It opens up a standard Flash page. This option can also be selected from the menu or with a keyboard shortcut (File | New or CTRL-N in Windows/CMD-N in Mac).

- **Create from Template** In this column you can select from an extensive list of document styles, sized to suit your project and set up with preset properties. In the next section, you will learn how to work with templates in Flash. Templates are particularly helpful to designers who may not be familiar with the specifications of a project.

NOTE

The Open and New dialog boxes on the Mac and Windows platforms have a slightly different appearance, although they perform the same function. Unless noted otherwise, illustrations in this book represent Mac dialog boxes.

You can also select Extend from the bottom right of the Start page. Listed under this option is Macromedia Flash Exchange. Clicking this link opens the Flash Exchange area of the Macromedia web site (http://www.macromedia.com/cfusion/exchange/). Here you can browse for ready-made assets like buttons, sounds, navigation menus, components, and various assets that developers share with other Flash users. Some are free and others cost a small amount.

Use Templates to Design Your Document

The list of template choices on the Start page demonstrates that Flash is used for many different applications. The list ranges in subject from banner ad templates for the Web to hand-held mobile device templates. Templates can be useful if you're designing for output you are unfamiliar with.

The presets for subject-specific templates relate to the output media. For example, if your final goal is to produce a standard quiz and you are new to Flash, selecting a Quiz template (under "More") provides you with a "fill-in-the-blanks" template.

Create a New Document from a Template

To select a new template from the Start page, click a folder in the Create From Template column. When you do so, the New From Template dialog box appears, as shown here.

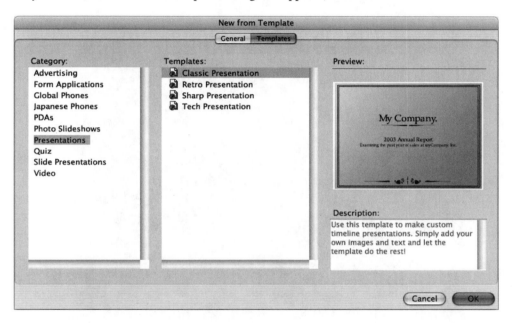

In this dialog box you can choose a specific template category and see a preview of the template if one is available. When you have decided on a template, click the OK button and the template will appear.

Templates contain information on the format you have selected. Some templates are more complex than others, as demonstrated in the presentation template in Figure 2-1. This template is complete with multiple layers and scripts on frames.

Create a Custom Template

If the Flash template selections don't work for your project, you can easily create your own template. Create a Flash document and select File | Save as Template from the menu. In the Save As Template dialog box (shown at the bottom of the next page), input a name. For Category, you can select from

FIGURE 2-1 Presentation templates contain many layers of preconfigured settings.

the pop-up list of Flash templates or create your own category. A description input box allows you to jot down notes relevant to the template style, such as dimensions, layers, colors, etc.

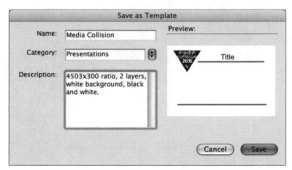

When you create a custom category, it will be added to the Flash template category list on the Start page. To delete a template, navigate to the Flash 8 templates folder on your computer. In Windows, the template folder is located in the Flash 8 folder (en | Configuration | Templates).

On the Mac, the template folder is located in the following path: Home | Library | Application Support | Macromedia | Flash 8 | en | Configuration | Templates. To delete a category or to delete templates in a category folder, drag the folder or template into the trash. Alternately, you can right-click and select Delete (in Windows) or CTRL-click and then select Move to Trash (on the Mac).

Working with templates allows beginners to jump into a project quickly. Templates can also hasten the workflow for more experienced designers.

Save a Flash Document

When you save a Flash document in its native FLA format, you can open the file at a later date to edit it, or you can share the file with another Flash author working on the project. You can also share the document across platforms if you include the Flash extension (.fla) as part of your naming convention.

To save an existing Flash document, choose File | Save. Select File | Save As to save a file with another name or to copy an existing file. Flash automatically assigns a name of Untitled in the Save As input field. In the Save As dialog box, shown next, navigate to the folder where you want to save the file, name it, and then click OK. Flash will save the file and all the assets used to create it to your hard drive for future use. *Assets* are different kinds of elements you use to build your Flash movie. They may consist of symbols, imported bitmaps, graphics, sounds, movie clips, buttons, and video.

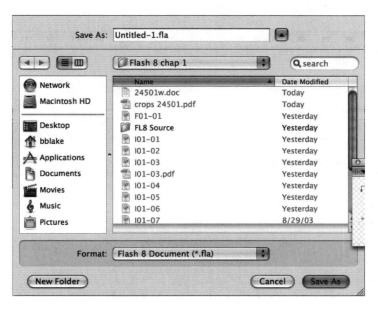

 *If your project is growing in size, you'll want to use the Save As command frequently as opposed to a plain old Save. This will help keep the file size smaller.*

Choose Movie Properties

Movies have characteristics just as the objects you create in Flash do. A movie has a size, a background color, and a frame rate. If you are not working with a template, it's important to set up the movie properly before you begin. Changing the movie properties in mid-creation can cause you to have to redo much of your creation. Here the various property selections are examined.

Modify the Movie Size

To modify the default size of your movie, enter the desired width and height values in the Document Properties dialog box (accessed from the Properties Inspector), as shown in the following illustration.

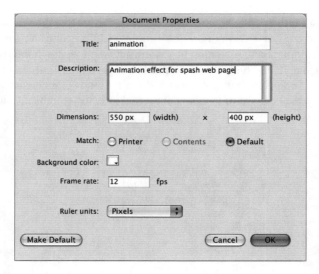

In addition, you can set a background color, frame rate for animation, and ruler unit of measurement. The Document Properties dialog box is accessed in one of five ways:

- Select Modify | Document from the menu.
- Press CTRL-J in Windows/CMD-J on the Mac.
- In the Properties Inspector at the bottom of the workspace, click the Size input box, as shown at right.

  Size: 550 x 400 pixels

- Right-click in Windows/CTRL-click on the Mac on either a blank part of the stage or the work area. Then from the pop-up menu, select Document Properties.
- Double-click the FPS setting at the bottom of the timeline as shown here.

To apply a new setting to a movie, input the new information and click OK. Flash will adjust the document accordingly.

You can also change the default size (550×400 pixels) of a new document. Change the default if you are working on a project that is based on a custom size. This will make your workflow a little more smoothly.

2

Grasp the Stage Concept

You had a glimpse of the stage in Chapter 1, so you have some familiarity with it. The stage is used to create, assemble, and edit graphics that eventually transform into your Flash movie. You can see the stage within the Flash workspace in Figure 2-2.

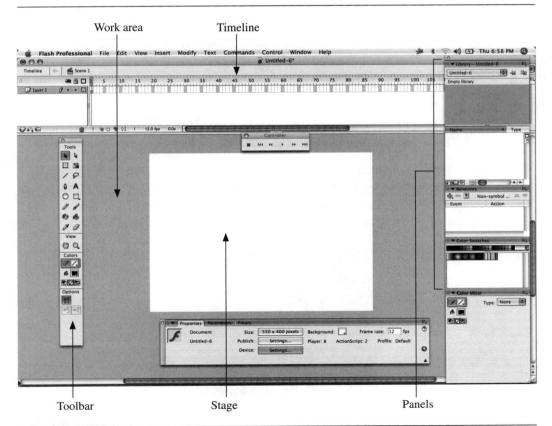

FIGURE 2-2   The stage and workspace in Flash

The stage defines the size of each frame in your finished Flash movie. In this sense, a frame on the stage would be the equivalent of a page if you were working in a typical graphics program. Just as in a drawing program, if you create or drag objects off the page (stage) onto the gray area, the objects won't appear in your movie when it's viewed. You can also deliberately position elements off the stage if you want an animated object to travel to and from the stage.

The other important element regarding the stage is that it also displays the current frame, or the frame that's playing at that moment. The current frame can have the same contents as the frame before it or it can change to display different objects. You, the individual who controls the contents of your movie, make all the decisions on how the movie plays out. Frames are made and controlled in the timeline, which we discuss later on in this chapter in the section "Work with the Timeline."

View Elements on the Stage

While working on a Flash document, you will often need to enlarge or reduce the view of an object on the stage. Flash offers many convenient features to change the view of the stage, as well as to navigate quickly to a specific area on the stage. Let's take a look at these tools.

Remember, you can also access a tool by using a shortcut key. Shortcut keys are listed in the Toolbar's tooltips. If you find tooltips annoying instead of helpful, turn them off in the General tab under Edit | Preferences.

Zoom In and Out

Zooming gives you the ability to enlarge or reduce the view of the Flash work area to make it easier to work in. The Zoom functions can be found in the View menu.

■ Selecting View | Zoom In magnifies elements on the stage, and selecting View | Zoom Out reduces elements. The Zoom function enlarges and reduces in increments of 100 percent.

■ Selecting View | Magnification presents a pop-up menu with various magnification settings ranging from 25 percent to 800 percent, as shown here.

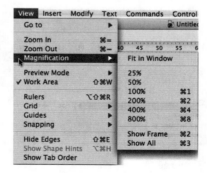

■ View | Magnification | Show Frame and View | Magnification | Show All provide you with two quick ways to view the entire frame as opposed to viewing an individual element on the stage.

2

Use the Zoom Control   You can also zoom in and out of the stage using the Zoom control located in the upper-right corner of the stage on the Edit bar, right above the timeline. This data also indicates the current zoom setting, as shown here:

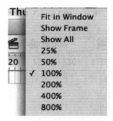

With the Zoom control, you can zoom in and out in on the stage in one of two ways:

- Select a preset zoom from the pop-up menu.
- Highlight the zoom number and type in a custom view.

The stage can be enlarged all the way up to 2000 percent and reduced all the way down to 8 percent. This zoom range is a little extreme, but if you wanted to, you could hone in on a minute detail using this tool.

Use the Zoom Tool   Although we're going to cover each element in the Toolbar in detail later on, it's important to mention the Zoom tool in the context of viewing a document in Flash. The Zoom tool, shown here, is in the View section of the Toolbar, to the right of the Hand tool.

The Zoom tool is a familiar sight to users of graphics applications, and it essentially works in Flash in the same way it does in most other programs.

To use the Zoom tool to enlarge an object, click the tool. When you do this, the cursor becomes a magnifying glass, and additional options related to the Zoom tool appear at the bottom of the Toolbar in the Options section, as shown next. The Options section of the Toolbar is contextual and changes depending on which tool you have selected.

On the left is the Enlarge Zoom icon with the plus sign (+), and on the right is the Reduce Zoom icon with a minus sign (–). These tools allow you to hone in on a specific object or area, as opposed to selecting Zoom from the menu.

To zoom in or out on an object or a portion of the stage, either click in the area you want to zoom in or out on or draw an invisible marquee around the area with the Zoom tool (see Figure 2-3).

You can use the marquee selection method with the Zoom tool if you want to quickly isolate a particular element on the stage. That way you don't have to scroll the page to target a particular area each time you try to enlarge the page.

TIP   *If you hold down ALT in Windows or OPT on the Mac while using the Enlarge Zoom tool, the tool turns into Reduce Zoom, and vice versa.*

FIGURE 2-3   Draw a rectangular marquee around an object with the Zoom tool to enlarge an area of the stage.

Scroll on the Stage

When the View tools are used to enlarge an area of the stage, you will often need to scroll to a different area of the stage to target a specific object or area. A quick way to navigate around a stage is to use the Hand tool. The Hand tool, shown here, is located in the View section of the Toolbar, right next to the Zoom icon.

When you click this tool in the Toolbar, your cursor becomes a hand icon. To use this hand to scroll around on the stage, click an area and drag. The Hand tool allows you to scroll very precisely and is perfect for honing in on a particular object. The keyboard shortcut to access the Hand tool quickly is H.

Another quick way of scrolling is to hold down the SPACEBAR, click, and drag around the stage. While the SPACEBAR is down, the Hand icon will replace the cursor. When you release the SPACEBAR, the cursor returns to its previous state.

Use the Grid

If you prefer to work on a stage with an organized structure, you can turn on the grid in the Flash workspace and align elements using this grid. Similar to most other elements in Flash, the grid has properties. You can make it visible or invisible, change spacing and color, and choose whether objects snap to grid points, among other things. If you choose View | Grid | Show Grid, Flash will display a grid, as shown in Figure 2-4.

2

FIGURE 2-4   A grid on the Flash stage

Use Grid Snapping

You can use the Flash grid in two ways: as a visual reference for manually aligning objects to grid intersections, and/or as a virtual reference in which Flash snaps objects to intersecting grid points. If you choose View | Snapping | Snap to Grid, Flash will snap an object to grid points as you move it across the stage.

When you employ Flash to align objects to grid points, the part of the object that aligns to the grid is the handle you clicked on the object to select it. Every object you create has a bounding box with a handle (an unfilled dot) in its center and a handle for each extremity of the bounding box. As you drag an object, the handle by which you are dragging the object becomes larger and darker when it nears a grid intersection point, as shown here:

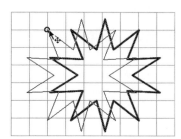 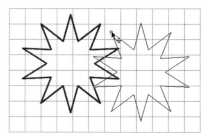

Edit the Grid

The default grid will display a light-gray line every 18 pixels along the document's width and length. You can modify the grid spacing and color to suit the document you are editing. Choose View | Grid | Edit Grid, and Flash will display the Grid dialog box shown here.

There are several grid properties you can change in the Grid dialog box, such as the color of the grid and the spacing of the grid lines. And grid-snapping accuracy can also be customized to suit your particular project.

Use Rulers

Flash has another useful tool that you can use to align objects in your movies: rulers. When you choose View | Rulers, Flash displays a vertical and a horizontal ruler, as shown in Figure 2-5. The rulers use the unit of measure you specified in the Document Properties dialog box. If you did not modify the Ruler Units option when you set up the movie, the rulers use pixels, the Flash default, as their unit of measure.

When you select an object on the stage and move it, Flash displays two small lines on each ruler that correspond to the object's width and height. As you move an object across the stage, these reference points follow, giving you a preview of the object's current position. You can use these reference points to accurately position an object on the stage. Rulers are also used to create guides for your document.

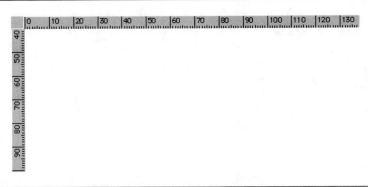

FIGURE 2-5   Rulers can be used to measure elements on the stage.

Use Guides

Another option you can use to align and position objects in your movies is the guides feature. *Guides* are visual references that you create and position where needed. You use guides to align elements in much the same way you use a grid. Unlike grids, however, guides can be positioned horizontally and vertically wherever you want them on the stage. Guides (and grids, by the way) will not be visible when the movie is published. To create guides for your document, you must first make the rulers visible by choosing View | Rulers. The guides are accessed through the rulers.

To create a vertical guide, click the vertical ruler and drag to the right. As you drag, a small vertical line appears (on the horizontal ruler), giving you a preview of the vertical guide's position. When the guide is in the desired position, release the mouse button, and Flash will create a lime-green vertical guide.

To create a horizontal guide, click the horizontal ruler and drag down. As you drag, a small horizontal line appears on the vertical ruler, indicating the current position of the guide. When the guide is in the desired position, release the mouse button. The following illustration shows vertical and horizontal guides added to a document.

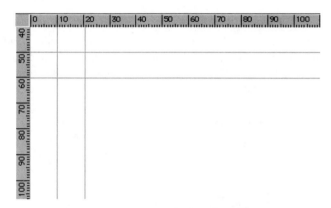

To toggle the visibility of guides, choose View | Guides | Show Guides. When you choose this command, Flash hides all visible guides from view. Select the command again and Flash will reveal the hidden guides.

Use the Snap to Guides Feature

After you create a series of guides, you can have Flash snap objects to the guides by choosing View | Snapping | Snap to Guides. After you choose this option, Flash will snap objects to guides as you drag the objects across the stage. The snapping takes place at the handle you chose when you selected the object. For example, if you select the object by its center, snapping will occur when the center of the object approaches a guide. If you select the object by one of its corners, snapping will occur when the corner approaches a guide. As mentioned previously, the object's handle (an unfilled dot) becomes darker and slightly larger when it approaches a guide that it can snap to.

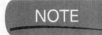

When you use the Snap To Guides feature, it's a good idea to disable snapping to the grid. If you have both options enabled at the same time, Flash will have so many targets to snap to that it will be difficult to ascertain when Flash is snapping an object to the grid or to a guide.

Move Guides

After you have created a guide, you can easily move it. As you near a vertical guide, a small arrow appears to the right of the cursor. Click the guide to select it, and then drag it to the desired position. Likewise, as you near a horizontal guide, a small downward-pointing arrow appears to the right of the cursor. Click the guide to select it and drag it to the desired position.

Lock Guides

When you have a series of guides positioned just the way you want them, you can lock them to prevent inadvertently selecting and moving a guide when you meant to select an object. To have Flash lock all guides used in your document, choose View | Guides | Lock Guides.

Edit Guides

You can edit guides after you create them. You can change the color of guides and modify the snapping accuracy Flash employs when you align objects to the guides. Choose View | Guides | Edit Guides and Flash will open the Guides dialog box, shown next. In this dialog box, you can change the color of a guide and the accuracy level for guide snapping.

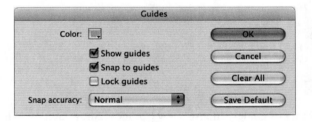

To get rid of all the guide settings, select View | Guides | Clear Guides. This will clear all settings and guides from the stage. Alternately, you can drag guides back toward the rulers to get them off the stage.

Snap Elements on the Stage

As discussed previously, the Snap To Grid and Snap To Guides features can help you align elements to grids or guidelines. In addition, there are three snapping options in Flash 8 that relate to the snapping of elements in relation to one another. For multiple objects that need to be aligned quickly, these snapping options can be useful:

- **Snap Align**   Snap Align makes aligning adjacent objects very easy. Turn on Snap Align by selecting View | Snapping | Snap Align. When this feature is turned on and you drag one object near another, horizontal and vertical dashed lines cross each other on the edge of the object nearest the other object, as shown in this illustration.

    The Snap Align lines change position in real time as you move the object. Use this feature if you prefer to align with the help of a visual cue. You can change the properties of the Snap Align feature by selecting View | Snapping | Edit Snap Align. In the Snap Align dialog box, you can customize the snap tolerance of objects. The default tolerance for this feature is 10 pixels.

- **Snap To Pixels**   This feature allows you to snap objects to their nearest pixel. To activate this feature, go to View | Snapping | Snap to Pixels.

- **Snap To Objects**   Snap To Objects allows you to snap the edge of one object to the edge of another. This feature can be activated in one of two ways: from the menu (View | Snapping | Snap to Objects) or from the magnet icon in the Options section of the Toolbar (shown here) when the Arrow tool is selected.

There are many other ways to control the alignment of objects on the stage and in relation to one another. These additional features will begin to unfold as you learn more about Flash.

Control the Way Your Movie Looks

The stage, of course, doesn't work alone. You'll use many props that work in conjunction with elements on the stage to dress up your Flash movie. We'll be going over each and every one of these elements so you can get the true feel of the Flash interface. The timeline is one of these important elements, and it works very closely with the stage to help you create your movie.

Work with the Timeline

As the name suggests, the timeline is where you work with the elements on your stage to change them over time. Objects in Flash can move, change size, rotate, and perform many other functions while time elapses. In Flash, you are in charge of how objects behave. This may seem like an abstract concept, but if you look at the way the timeline is built, it makes sense (see Figure 2-6).

Work with Layers

Layers are like transparent sheets of acetate, sitting on top of one another. Objects on the top layer can obscure objects on a lower layer. When you're working on a complex Flash document, layers can make it easier to separate and sort out all the elements you're using. You can also lock a layer, which freezes the objects on that layer in place, and you can turn off a layer's visibility. By turning off the visibility, you can make it easier to selectively see layers sitting beneath one another. It should be noted here that locking layers and making layers invisible does not affect

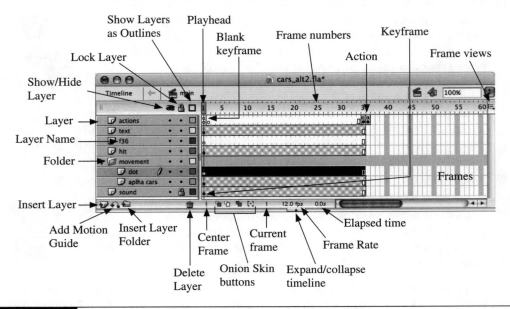

FIGURE 2-6 The timeline is a major component of the Flash interface.

your exported Flash Player file. These features are just bells and whistles that help streamline your production in Flash.

Layers in Flash can be stored in their own folders in the timeline. This allows you to conserve space by neatly organizing groups of related layers in their own folder. You create a layer folder by clicking the Insert Layer Folder icon on the bottom left of the timeline. You can create a layer by clicking the Insert Layer icon on the bottom left of the timeline. You will define, examine, and use layers extensively as you work with Flash. As we travel through this book, you'll get to know them intimately.

Work with Frames

Now that you've had an overview of layers, you are ready to look at how the other part of the timeline, the frames section, works. To the right of each layer is a series of

frame rectangles that appears in grid-like fashion, as you can see here. Each frame is numbered chronologically.

In these frame cells, you create the frames for your movie. Have you ever seen a filmstrip outside a camera? The film exists as a series of frames. However, when the movie is shown, the audience sees these single frames, one frame at a time, projected at a speed that simulates continuous action. So it is with Flash, but instead of residing on a celluloid filmstrip, Flash

Navigate the Edit Bar

The Edit bar is not technically part of the timeline, but it may appear as if it is to a beginner because of its close proximity. It sits right on top of the timeline, so now is a good time to address its purpose. The Edit bar contains tools to help you edit and navigate scenes and symbols and (in Windows) test your movie. The Edit bar is shown here:

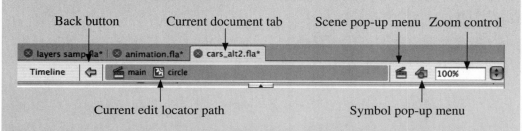

At the top of the Edit bar, you can toggle between Flash and SWF documents by clicking the tabs. Note that the name on the tab reflects the document you are choosing. This option is available only in the Windows interface.

frames exist in the timeline. You, as the director, can control the length of time layered objects are on the stage, pause time, or stop time altogether.

The actual frames you create can exist as keyframes, frames, or blank keyframes. A *keyframe* is represented with a black circle and is used for changing the contents of a frame. For example, if you wanted an object to appear blue on one frame and then yellow on the next, a keyframe would be required on both frame cells because the object changes from one color to another.

If an object on a keyframe remained the same and you wanted to extend the length of time this object appeared, you would create regular frames. Frames that have not been filled yet are depicted as white rectangles, and every fifth frame is shown in light gray to make it a little easier for you to keep track of the frames.

A blank keyframe is represented with a white circle. Blank keyframes are exactly that—blank. We will be examining keyframes in more depth in Chapter 9.

Understand the Tools Panel

We have already looked at the View options in the Tools panel (also known as the Toolbar), and many of the other Flash tools probably look familiar to you (see Figure 2-7).

The Toolbar is divided into four sections:

- ■ **Tools** This is where tools related to drawing and editing objects are stored.
- ■ **View** These tools give you options for viewing the stage.

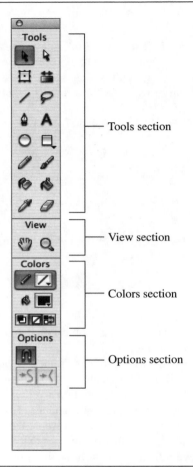

Tools section

View section

Colors section

Options section

FIGURE 2-7 The Toolbar contains tools for drawing, editing, viewing, and modifying graphics.

- ■ **Colors** In this segment of the Toolbar, you can select and edit colors of elements on the stage.
- ■ **Options** Additional options become available depending upon which tool is selected.

When you select a tool and position your mouse over the stage, the cursor changes its appearance, depending upon the tool you selected. For example, if you click the Zoom tool and position the cursor on the stage, the cursor becomes a magnifying glass. If you click the Circle or Rectangle tool and position the cursor on the stage, the cursor becomes crosshairs. As you gain more proficiency with Flash, you will become increasingly familiar with Flash's visual interface.

2

Flash 8
Professional

Use the Filters Panel

In Flash Professional there is also a Filters panel whose tab by default is docked with the Properties Inspector. Filters allow you to apply glows, drop shadows, and bevel effects to movie clips, buttons, and text, as shown here:

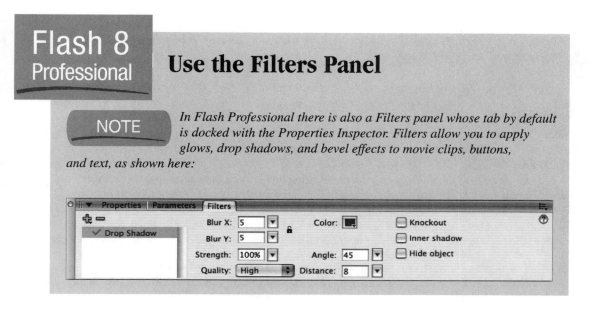

Dissect the Properties Inspector

The Properties Inspector displays current information about a selected element of your Flash document (see Figure 2-8). When an object is selected, the Properties Inspector displays information about the object in context and also allows you to edit certain properties of the element. There are additional sets of windows, called *panels*, that you can use for editing elements in the movie. Panels are covered in the next section.

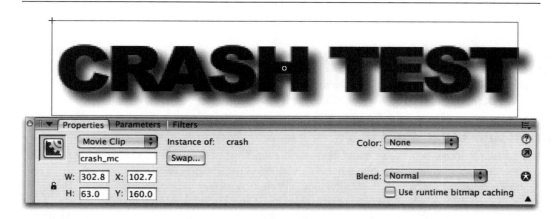

FIGURE 2-8   You can set, modify, and get information on objects in the Properties Inspector.

 *If the Properties Inspector disappears from view, you can open it by selecting Window |*
Properties from the menu.

Use Panels

In addition to the timeline and Properties Inspector, a myriad of other panels are available in Flash. Panels help you create and edit elements in your movie. In fact, the Properties Inspector is a panel, too.

You can customize the workspace with panels, displaying only the panels that are relevant to your current work session. You can arrange them any way that helps you be more productive. Over twenty panels are available, including the timeline, Toolbar, Library, and Properties Inspector. You could really clutter up your screen with all of these panels if you wanted to. Flash fortunately provides some assistance in helping you maintain a neat and well-organized work environment.

 *If you don't see a panel you need to use because it's been closed or isn't listed in the*
default panel layout, you can access it by going to the Window menu. Panels are located
in the Window menu and in the Window submenus under Other Panels.

Dock Panels

Panels can *dock* to other panels. "Docking" refers to anchoring one or more panels together to form one big window or panel. When a panel is not docked, it can float freely around the workspace and you can place it anywhere that's convenient for you.

When you launch Flash, you'll see the panel configuration from your last session. An example is shown in Figure 2-9. To tear off a docked panel, grab the little dots in the upper-left corner of the panel, known as the *grabber handle*, and drag the panel outside the docked set.

Rearrange Docked Panels

Sometimes you may not like the order of your docked panels. You can rearrange the order of the panels to suit your needs. To rearrange docked panels, tear off the panel that you want to move, click the grabber handle in the upper-left corner of the panel, and position the panel over the panel you want it to be docked with. You will see a black line indicating the location where the panel will dock. Once you get used to the technique, you'll discover that it's quite easy to customize docked panels.

Open and Close Panels

It's important to know how to open and close panels quickly, especially if you're working in a one-monitor environment. To open a panel, select Window | *Panel name*.

The Toolbars subset of selections offers a Controller panel (for playing animations on the stage) and the Edit bar, which sits above the stage and is used to track editing and display views. Additional panels including Accessibility, History (which records your actions), Scenes, and Web

FIGURE 2-9   Docked panels in Flash

Services are available in the Window | Other Panels subset of selections. Throughout the book, these panels will be explored in relation to other tasks performed in Flash.

You can close floating panels in Windows by clicking the close box in the upper-right corner of the panel. On the Mac, you can close a panel by clicking the circle icon in the upper-left corner of the panel. Both platforms are shown in the following illustration. You can also close all panels (excluding the timeline) by pressing F4.

Close box in Windows   Close box on Mac

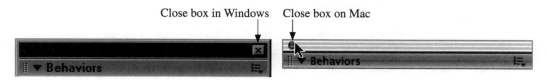

Once you get a feel for the panels, your workflow will become more productive. You also need to become familiar with the many options available in panels. As part of your learning journey, you should take the time to familiarize yourself with these options. It's important to spend some time experimenting, clicking, and displaying. A good dose of curiosity can help accelerate your learning experience.

Explore the Library

Another panel you'll be using a lot in Flash is the Library panel. The Library panel is where you store various elements you'll be using in your movie. These elements can be graphics, buttons, movie clips, imported pictures, sound, and video. When you want to call upon one of these elements to perform on your stage, you drag it onto the stage from the Library (see Figure 2-10).

To display the Library panel, select Window | Library or press CTRL-L in Windows/CMD-L on the Mac. Alternately, you can press F11.

When you become a more experienced Flash user, you'll discover that the most efficient way to work is to organize as many elements as possible into symbols. *Symbols* (graphic symbols, movie clips, and buttons) are elements you create that become stored in the Library.

Since symbols are a key component in understanding Flash, you'll be using the Library a lot. We will be examining the Library in detail in Chapter 8.

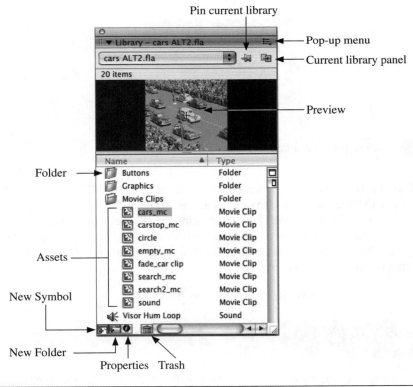

FIGURE 2-10 The Library panel

Get Help in Flash

Sometimes even experienced Flash users forget how to perform certain tasks. Beginners and seasoned Flash users alike often need to refer to the Flash Help system. The Help panel is thorough and provides several different browsing options, including a Search function and a list of common topics as shown in Figure 2-11. In addition, the Help panel also includes tutorials, a component reference, an ActionScript reference, features information, and a compilation of the Flash reference manual that you can navigate in a nonlinear fashion. You can even update the panel as new help information becomes available by clicking the Update button on the top right of the panel. To update the Help contents you must be connected to the Internet because the information is downloaded remotely.

Access a Tutorial

If you are new to Flash you may find some of the concepts confusing. You may also want to be walked step-by-step through a technique. There are tutorials right within the Flash program. To keep your screen neat and uncluttered, the tutorial selections are tucked neatly away in the Help panel. The following explains how to access them.

1. To review the list of tutorials available in Flash, first display the Help panel.

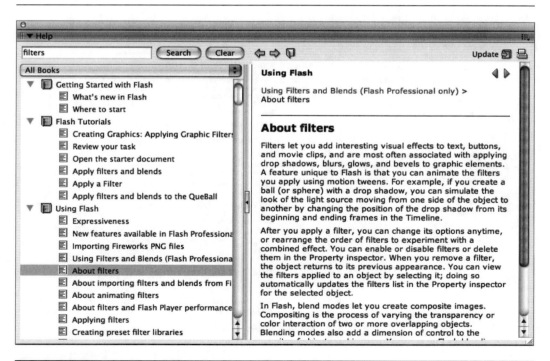

FIGURE 2-11 The Help panel in Flash includes a Search function and a list of common topics.

2. In the Topics pop-up menu (the default topic is All Books), select Tutorials & Samples. The tutorial topics appear in the column below the topic head, as shown here.

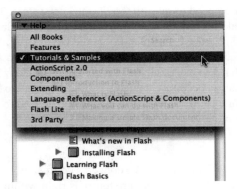

3. The tutorials are stored in folders. To view the contents of the folder, click the arrow to the left of the folder to expand its contents, as shown here.

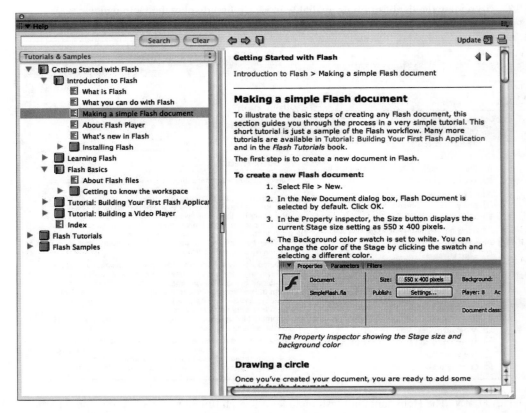

4. Click a topic and the tutorial will appear in the right column.

Use the Scene Panel

If your Flash movie is lengthy and contains a lot of animation, you can break your movie into scenes. A movie with scenes is like a three-act play; after the finale of one scene, another starts.

Use the Scene panel to create, delete, and arrange the order of scenes in your movie. To open the Scene panel, shown next, choose Window | Other Panels | Scene or press SHIFT-F2. The Scene panel is essentially a window that lists the scenes in your movie. The buttons at the bottom of the panel are used to duplicate, add, and delete scenes from your movie.

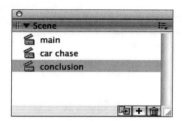

In this panel, you can manage scenes in the document. Management includes creating new scenes, duplicating existing scenes, changing the order of scenes, and deleting scenes you don't need. You perform these functions by using the icons at the bottom of the Scene panel. You also use this panel to navigate between scenes. When you become an experienced Flash user, you'll be better able to determine what kind of Flash movies best lend themselves to multiple scenes.

Set the Preferences

Like most graphics applications, Flash has preferences that can be set. Preferences offer you yet another way to customize your workspace so it works more efficiently for you. You can change the way you select elements or the way the drawing tools work, among other things.

To display the Preferences dialog box, select Edit | Preferences in Windows and Flash Professional | Preferences on the Mac. The Preferences dialog box consists of seven tabs: General, ActionScript, Auto Format, Clipboard, Drawing, Text, and Warnings, as shown in Figure 2-12. You can change dozens of settings in these tabs. For example, in the General tab, you can change the number of undo levels in Flash. The default number is 100. The Undo Levels setting indicates the number of times you can undo the last move to get back to a particular point in time. Preferences can be reset at any point in your Flash production to affect any task you perform after resetting it.

Although as you begin to work with Flash you may not have cause to change the Preferences dialog box in a document now, it would be well worth your time to browse through this window and at least become familiar with the settings. You never know when you might need to select one in the future.

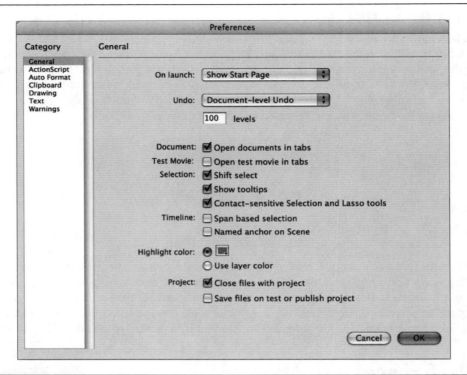

FIGURE 2-12   The Preferences dialog box is used for customizing settings.

Conclusion

In this chapter you gained a familiarity with the Flash workspace. This included learning how to start a new document as well as how to save one. Several windows important to the interface were explored, including the Toolbar, timeline, Library, and a myriad of small windows, known as *panels* in Flash. In addition, you learned how to set properties of a document which included characteristics of the Flash stage.

Flash is a rich and complex program, and there are many other features that are essential in your Flash journey. This chapter has provided you with a foundation on which to base your future studies. In the next chapter, you will use some of the tools discussed in this chapter.

Part II

Add Graphic Elements to Your Flash Movies

Chapter 3

Make Simple Graphics

How to...

- Use the Toolbar
- Make objects
- Apply fill and stroke colors
- Draw lines and curves
- Create basic shapes
- Sample and apply colors to objects

In Chapter 2, the Toolbar was explored as a major component of the Flash workspace. In this chapter, we return to the Toolbar, this time to learn to use the drawing tools.

Drawing is a big part of the Flash interface, since many of the elements you'll be animating and making interactive need to be drawn first. Flash sports a complete set of drawing tools, from a Brush to a Pen tool, with which you can make perfect curves. You'll find that the variety of tools in Flash should address most of your drawing needs.

Designers accustomed to the drawing tools in their favorite vector-based, or drawing, program will be happy to know that graphics from programs like Adobe Illustrator and Macromedia Freehand can be imported into Flash too. What's more, you can edit those drawings in Flash and then proceed to build your movie from there. Importing graphics from other applications is covered in Chapter 6.

For those who are accustomed to working in other drawing programs and are new to Flash, the drawing interface may seem a little strange. This is because some of the tools you'll discover, such as the Lasso tool and even the Eraser, are not commonly associated with drawing programs. You'll find that once you get used to the feel of drawing in Flash, it's not as strange as it looks. With that said, let's first learn the basics of using tools in the Toolbar.

Locate the Right Tool in the Toolbar

Drawing in Flash always begins with selecting a tool in the Toolbar (see Figure 3-1). This panel is home to all of the tools you use to create and modify objects you will use to make your Flash movie.

The Toolbar is made up of four sections:

- **Tools** Houses the tools you use to create, select, and modify objects.
- **View** Includes two tools that you use to zoom in or out on objects and pan your view of the stage.
- **Colors** Includes two color wells, one that modifies the object's stroke (outline) color and one that changes the fill color of the object.

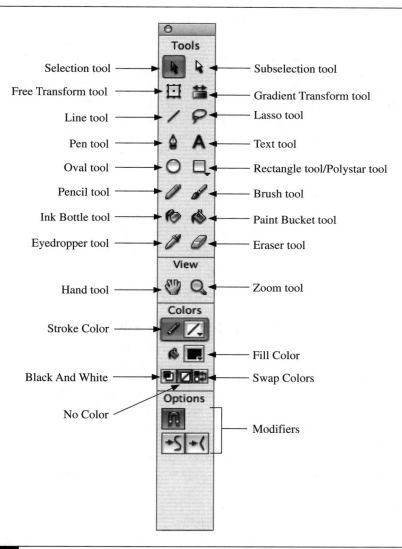

Selection tool

Free Transform tool

Line tool

Pen tool

Oval tool

Pencil tool

Ink Bottle tool

Eyedropper tool

Hand tool

Stroke Color

Black And White

No Color

Subselection tool

Gradient Transform tool

Lasso tool

Text tool

Rectangle tool/Polystar tool

Brush tool

Paint Bucket tool

Eraser tool

Zoom tool

Fill Color

Swap Colors

Modifiers

FIGURE 3-1   The drawing and transform tools in the Flash Toolbar

■ **Options**   Contains the modifiers for a selected tool. Many of the tools have multiple modifiers; some have none. For example, if you select the Oval tool, the Options section comes up blank. In contrast, if you select the Brush tool, you then can choose various options for the size and shape of the brush.

To select a tool from the Toolbar, simply click it. After you select a tool, Flash updates the Options section to display the tool's modifiers, if any.

Create Objects for Your Movies

It's quite easy to create a simple object in Flash. Once you travel beyond the simple rectangle or brushstroke, things appear to become a little more complicated. We suggest you begin with understanding simple drawing and then progressively build on your knowledge as you go along.

Basically, creating a simple object involves selecting a tool from the Toolbar, sometimes setting properties related to a particular object, and specifying the fill and/or stroke color for the object you are creating. You adjust the tool's modifiers to control the performance of the tool and modify the type of shape it creates. To draw the object, you simply position your cursor on the stage and draw. Let's take a look at the various shapes you can create.

Create Basic Shapes

Flash gives you three basic shapes to work with: a rectangle, an oval, and a polygon/star. Although these are certainly rather basic shapes, they can be manipulated and combined with other shapes to create some dynamic images depending on your level of creativity. After you create a basic shape, for example, you can modify it, move it, rotate it, skew it, or combine it with other shapes to create a new shape. In this chapter, you'll learn how to create simple objects. In Chapter 5, you'll learn how to change the shapes you make.

Create Shapes with the Oval, Rectangle, and Polystar Tools

You use the Oval tool to create circles and ellipses for your Flash movies. The Rectangle tool is used to create rectangles and squares. The Polystar tool is used to create polygons and star shapes, which explains the origin of its name.

The Polystar tool is located in a pop-up menu under the Rectangle tool, as shown in the illustration at right. To access this tool, click the little arrow at the bottom right of the Rectangle tool and then select the icon that looks like a polygon. The tool displayed will now be the Polystar tool. It's called the Polystar tool because you can make a polygon or a star with this tool, depending on how you set the properties. You'll learn more about this in the next section.

Shapes can be filled with color, referred to as a *fill* in Flash, and/or they can have an outline, commonly referred to as a *stroke*.

To draw a simple circle, rectangle, polygon, or star, simply click the appropriate icon in the Toolbar (see Figure 3-1), position your pointer on the stage, click and drag to draw the shape, and that's it. This is a pretty easy task, as you can see. Of course, the shape will be more interesting if you jazz it up a little by using some of the following techniques.

Set the Properties of a Shape

If you're making a stroke on an oval, rectangle, or polygon/star, you need to set the characteristics, or "properties," of the stroke. You can do this most easily in the Properties Inspector, shown next.

Did you know?

Choose from Two Drawing Models in Flash

There are two different types of drawing models you can choose from to create shapes in Flash: the *merge drawing* model and the *object drawing* model. The merge drawing model merges overlapping shapes into one object. The default model in Flash is merge drawing. The object drawing model, on the other hand, treats shapes as separate objects and allows you to overlap them with other shapes. Object drawing shapes are created and manipulated as they would be in a typical drawing program. To activate object drawing, select a drawing tool such as the Rectangle or Ellipse, then click the Object Drawing icon in the Options section of the Toolbar, as shown at right. Drawing models are discussed more in Chapter 5. When object drawing is turned on and you draw a shape, a blue frame will appear around the shape, as shown here.

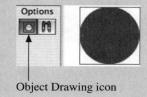

Object Drawing icon

As with all other objects, you can set the properties of an oval, rectangle, or polygon either before you begin to draw or after you've made the object.

Stroke Color   Strike Height   Stroke Style

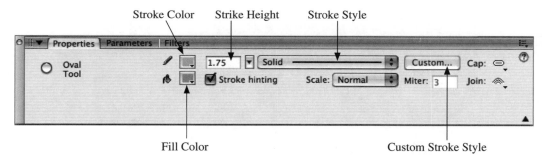

Fill Color   Custom Stroke Style

To set the stroke characteristics of a shape or the stroke of a line in the Properties Inspector, click the Stroke Style pop-up menu in the Properties Inspector. In this menu, you can select the style of the actual stroke. Styles available include solid, dashed, dotted, and textured.

The *height* of the stroke is its thickness. To set the height, click the pop-up Stroke Height menu and select a number. You can also type in a number from 0.1 through 10 pixels, which represent the minimum and maximum values of a stroke for a shape.

In the Properties Inspector you can also check Stroke Hinting. When stroke hinting is enabled, the line strokes will appear sharper in the Flash Player. Additionally, stroke properties also include caps and joins. The *cap* selections allow you to choose how the ends of a line are going to appear. *Join* refers to the corners of a stroked object, or the point where two strokes meet. Both cap and join options are available in a pop-up menu. On open-ended strokes with two or more sides, you can combine both cap and join options in any way that suits your project. Examples of the cap and join options on a single stroke and an object are shown next.

NOTE *Caps and joins only apply to solid strokes. You cannot use caps and joins on fills.*

NOTE *If you apply a Square cap to a line, the line becomes longer according to the line's height because it squares the ends of the line with the sum of the height. If you choose a Normal cap, on the other hand, the beginning and the end of the line remain exactly the way they were when you drew them.*

To further customize a stroke style for a shape, click the Custom button in the Properties Inspector. Then, in the Stroke Style dialog box (shown here), you can set the shape of the stroke, the thickness, the sharpness of the corners of the shape, and other properties.

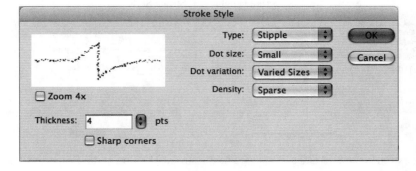

TIP *To draw a symmetrical shape, hold down SHIFT while dragging. Remember to release SHIFT before releasing the mouse button; otherwise, the tool will revert to its unconstrained shape mode.*

Create a Polygon or Star

Earlier in this chapter it was mentioned that the Polystar tool was used for making polygons as well as stars. Polygons are multisided shapes. Therefore, one of the properties of a polygon or a star is the number of sides to the shape.

3

When the Polystar tool is selected in the Toolbar, the Properties Inspector offers an additional Options button that allows you to set the type of polygon/star and the number of sides of the shape.

To create a star shape or set the properties of a polygon, click the Options button to access the Tool Settings dialog box for your shape. Here you can pick the style (polygon or star) as well as the number of sides. If you are creating a star, you can also type in the size of the points on the star. A high number makes the points on the star dull, and a low number makes the points on the star sharp. The star in the following illustration has a point size of 0.5 pixels.

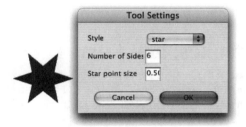

Set the Fill and Stroke Color of a Shape

To set a fill or stroke color for the shape you are about to create, use the Properties Inspector's Fill and/or Stroke Color palettes. Alternately, you can access the same palettes in the Colors section of the Toolbar. To assign a color, simply click the color swatch and, in the pop-up color palette, click a color, as shown in the next illustration. When you draw the shape, it appears with the color you selected.

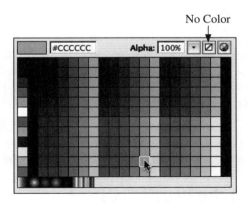

NOTE   *The current colors represented in the Fill and Stroke Color swatches become the current colors in the Toolbar. So, you can also select the current fill or stroke color from the Toolbar. In fact, all color panels within Flash will represent the currently selected colors. This includes the Color Mixer and the Color Swatches panels. The color panels are discussed in Chapter 5.*

If you do not want a stroke color or a fill color on the shape you are creating, click the No Color button as shown in the previous illustration. The No Color button appears as a white swatch with a red diagonal line through it. In the pop-up color palettes, it is located at the top right. The No Color icon is also located in the Toolbar, at the bottom of the Colors section.

Did you pick ugly fill and stroke colors, and you long to change to good old black and white? You can do so with the click of a button. Clicking the Black And White button in the Toolbar to the left of the No Color swatch will return the fill and stroke colors to black and white.

Draw Lines, Brushstrokes, and Curves

In addition to the tools covered in the last section, the Flash Toolbar provides you with one tool for drawing lines and three tools for drawing lines, curves, and brushstrokes.

The Line tool enables you to create the simplest geometric shape, the straight line. You use the Pencil tool to create lines, curves, or shapes. This tool has extensive modifiers that give you the ability to create anything from a freeform line to a recognizable geometric shape, such as a circle, rectangle, or triangle. You use the Brush tool to add calligraphic splashes of color to your movies, or you can use this tool to create a more fluid line or shape. To create a line, path, or shape with point-to-point control and precision, you can use the Pen tool. Next, we'll learn how to use each of these tools.

Draw with the Line Tool

The Line tool is used to create straight lines that go from point A to point B. To create a straight line, select the Line tool, adjust the line style, and select a stroke color and a stroke height in the Properties Inspector, as outlined previously.

Click and drag on the stage in any direction to create the line. Hold down SHIFT while dragging to constrain the line to 45-degree increments, as shown in this illustration. Keep in mind that a line has only a stroke color and no fill, so any color in the Fill swatch will be disregarded when you draw the line.

You can also use the Ink Bottle tool from the Toolbar to modify the color of a line, whether the line was created as a merge drawing or an object drawing. The ins and outs of this tool are discussed later in this chapter in the section "Use the Ink Bottle Tool."

Freeform Draw with the Pencil Tool

The Pencil tool has a freehand feel to it and works much like a real pencil. To draw a line or a shape with the Pencil tool, click the tool in the Toolbar and just start drawing. You can create a line with this tool as well as a closed shape. This illustration was created with the Pencil tool.

3

If you are drawing with a mouse and not a drawing tablet, it may feel as if you have little control over the Pencil tool. You can actually set the Pencil tool's modifiers to allow you a little more precision with the tool. *Modifiers* are additional settings available on some tools that allow you to further customize an object or the tool itself.

If you're used to working with Bézier curves in a drawing application and prefer the precision associated with them, the Pencil tool will feel like a very strange alternative. For those of you not accustomed to working with Bézier curves, you probably are wondering what they are. Bézier curves are curves drawn with mathematical precision and are used in graphics applications like Adobe Illustrator and Macromedia FreeHand. They allow users to draw perfectly smooth lines by defining a series of points and then clicking and dragging these points to define the length and the angle of the curves in between these points. The Pen tool works in a similar manner to these other graphics applications.

In the Properties Inspector, stroke hinting, caps, and joins can be set for lines drawn with the Pen tool just as they can be for any stroke object created with the Line, Rectangle, Polystar, and Oval tools.

Use a Pencil Modifier

There are three different Pencil modifiers that give you varying degrees of assistance while you are creating a freeform shape with this tool. These modifiers, shown here, are contextual and become available if the Pencil tool in the Toolbar is selected.

To select a Pencil modifier, click the Modifier icon in the Options section to display the Modifier pop-up menu. To select the desired modifier, click the appropriate button. You have three Pencil modes to choose from:

- **Straighten**   Choose this mode to create a line made up of straight-line segments and interconnecting paths.

- **Smooth**   Choose this mode when you want to draw smooth-flowing curved lines.

- **Ink**   Choose this mode when you want to create a freeform line with no assistance from Flash. You might prefer this mode if you are an accomplished artist working with a digital tablet or if your movie calls for an irregular line.

TIP

Shapes and lines can also be modified with the Selection tool. When a merged or drawing object is selected, the Options section of the Toolbar offers the Straighten, Smooth, and Ink modifiers as options. It also contains a Snap To Objects button, which, if you activate it, will force the snapping of objects to one another. To use the modifiers with the Selection tool, click an object you want to modify with the Selection tool and then click the modifier as many times as it takes to reshape the object or line.

Figure 3-2 shows sample lines created with the Pencil tool in each mode. As you can see, the images reflect the properties of each of the modifiers. To change a line with a modifier after you create it, click the line segment (or double-click the line segment to grab the entire line). Then click the appropriate mode. Each time you click, the modification to the line will be augmented.

Smooth

Ink

Straighten

FIGURE 3-2 Straight, smooth, and freeform lines can be created with the Pencil tool.

To quickly create a geometric shape with the Pencil tool, use the tool to sketch something resembling what you want and then click the Straighten mode until the shape transforms into what you want it to look like. Draw a shape resembling an oval, a rectangle, or a polygon, and Flash will transform your creation into its proper geometric shape.

Draw with the Pen Tool

The Pen tool in Flash works much as similar tools work in other drawing applications. So, if you're accustomed to the quirks of a Pen tool, you'll get a feel for the Flash Pen tool in no time. If you've never worked with a Pen tool, using the Flash Pen tool will probably seem a little frustrating at first. If you fall into this category, you will probably want to rely on the Pencil tool and its modifiers for more control over lines and curves.

You use the Pen tool to create lines, strokes, point-to-point paths, and Bézier curve paths. In other words, it's kind of like the Pencil tool in that the lines yield a similar result. It's different from the Pencil tool in that it requires more skill to draw precise objects.

With the Pen tool, objects are formed by clicking from point to point instead of just drawing as if the tool was a real pencil. In effect, it's like manipulating a string (the line) between two knitting needles (the points connecting the lines). Sound confusing? We'll try to clear it up for you in the next section. After that, the best thing to do is practice drawing with it. Learning how to draw with the Pen tool is a little like learning to ride a bike. With perseverance, you will get the feel for it.

Make Open and Closed Paths with the Pen Tool

An *open path* is a series of line segments that remain a line and don't close. In other words, the first point you create never meets the last point, as shown here.

In contrast, a *closed path* is a series of line segments where the first point meets the last point and they close to create a shape.

To create an open path with the Pen tool, select the tool and select a line style and stroke, as outlined earlier in this chapter. Click the spot on the stage where you want the line segment to begin, and Flash will create a single corner point. Click the next point, moving in the direction of the path you want to create, and click again and again until your path is complete.

To end the path, double-click the last point. Alternatively, you can CTRL-click in Windows/ OPT-click on the Mac anywhere on the stage to end the path. To exit the Pen tool and return to the Selection tool, click the Selection tool or press v to access it. If you don't end the path, the tool will keep drawing, which can be a little irritating, especially if your path looks perfect as is.

TIP   *To constrain a line segment to 45-degree increments, hold down SHIFT while clicking from point to point.*

To create a closed path, begin drawing the same as you would for an open path, but then click the first point you created. Flash will close the stroke and apply the currently selected color. Note that a little white circle appears at the bottom right of the Pen tool when you position your mouse over a point that can close the path into a shape, as shown here.

Make a Curved Path

Creating a curved path with the Pen tool involves the same technique as creating a straight path, with a slight variation. To create a curved path instead of a straight path, you click *and drag* the end point instead of just clicking. This will create a *curve point.* As you drag, Flash creates a pair of tangential handles that define the shape of the curve. As mentioned earlier, the handles are almost like knitting needles that help guide the curve, and the curve becomes the yarn between them. The tips of the knitting needles would be the equivalent of the points on the path. The end of the knitting needle is the handle you drag to manipulate the needles, or *curve handles,* as they are called. The difference between the Pen tool's curve handles and a knitting needle is that the Pen tool's handles point in the same direction as the curve, as shown in Figure 3-3. So, you drag a handle in the direction you want your curve to go. The other difference is that it would be pretty hard to knit a sweater in Flash.

To create a curve segment, select the Pen tool and then set the properties of the tool in the Properties Inspector.

On the stage, click a line segment and drag the pointer in the direction you want the curve to go, release the mouse, position your pointer where you want the next point to be, and repeat the process. The direction and the distance you drag on the end of the handle determine the slope and length of the handles. Continue this process until you have created the curved path you want.

Double-click the last point to end an open curved path. To close a curved path, click the end point on which you want to close the path. In other words, you end a curved path the same way you end a point-to-point straight path.

When the curve segment is the approximate shape you desire, release the pointer. You can now go back and adjust the curve if need be. You can modify each point along the path with the Subselection tool (the white arrow) to the right of the Selection tool, or you can add points to the path or delete unneeded points with the Pen tool.

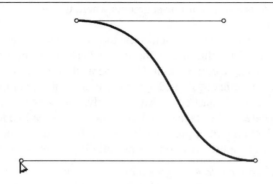

FIGURE 3-3   On a curved path, curve handles point in the direction of the curve itself.

When you draw with the Pen tool, you can combine curve points and corner points, as shown next.

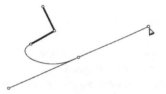

To combine straight, point-to-point paths with curved paths, simply use the rules outlined previously, only combine them. In the previous illustration, the path was created by making a three-point path that creates two nearly perpendicular straight lines. After the fourth point was clicked, the mouse was dragged to the upper right of the stage, thus creating a curve that slants to the left. Note also that the handle is dragged in the opposite direction of the curve, but the angle of the curve is the same as the angle of the handle.

Don't worry if you mess up your curve. Flash makes it easy to fix mistakes. In fact, paths are so easy to fix that you shouldn't ever expect them to look perfect when you first draw them. In the next section you'll learn how to quickly fix your path so it will look just right.

This book probably makes the process of drawing curves sound easy, but it's not. Don't be frustrated if drawing curves seems difficult at first. It takes a long time to get a feel for it, and some designers never do. Take heart, because you still have the Pencil and Line tools to fall back on.

Modify Paths

Once you have created a path with the Pen tool, you can easily modify it by manipulating the points that make up the path. You can add or delete points, convert corner points to curve points and vice versa, or move points to modify a path. By default, Flash displays selected corner points as hollow squares and selected curve points as hollow circles.

3

There are several tools you can use to change the way your path looks:

- To move a point along a path, select the Subselection tool (the white arrow to the right of the Selection tool) and position the pointer over the point you want to move. When the pointer displays a white rectangle at the bottom right, as shown next, click the point you want to move and drag it to a new position. When you release the mouse, Flash readjusts the shape of the path to reflect the point's new position.

- To nudge a point, again use the Subselection tool and position the pointer over the point you want to move until the pointer displays a white rectangle at the bottom right. Then click the point. Use the keyboard's arrow keys to nudge the point in the desired direction. To nudge more than one point, select the first point with the Subselection tool and add points to the selection by clicking them while holding down SHIFT. Alternatively, you can drag a marquee around the points you want to select with the Subselection tool. Use the arrow keys to nudge the selection of points to a new location.

NOTE   *If you position your Subselection tool pointer over a point and a black rectangle appears in the bottom-right corner of the white arrow, nudging or dragging will move the entire path. The white rectangle indicates that you have selected a point on a path, whereas the black rectangle indicates that you have selected the entire path.*

- To add a point to a path, click the path with the Pen tool. Then position your pointer over the path. As you approach the path, the Pen cursor appears with a plus sign (+), as shown in the illustration at right. Click to add a point to the path.

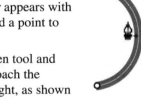

- To delete a corner point from a path, select the path with the Pen tool and move toward the corner point you want to delete. As you approach the point, the Pen cursor displays a minus (–) sign at the bottom right, as shown next. Click the point to delete it.

- To delete a curve point from a path, select the curve with the Pen tool and move toward the curve point you want to delete. As you approach the point, the Pen cursor displays a white arrow at the bottom right, as shown in the illustration at right. Double-click the point to delete it. (The first click converts the point to a corner point; the second click deletes it.) Alternatively, you can delete any point from a path by first selecting it with the Subselection tool and then pressing DELETE.

■ To convert a corner point to a curve point, select the point you want to convert with the Subselection tool and then drag while holding down ALT (Windows)/OPT (Mac). As you drag, Flash creates a pair of tangential handles that define the shape of the curve point. When you release the mouse button, Flash redraws the path.

To practice using the Pen tool, try tracing over freeform images you have created with the Pencil tool.

Adjust Pen Tool Preferences

You can configure the Pen tool to change the appearance of the Pen tool cursor, display line segments as you draw, or change the appearance of selected points to suit your working style.

You modify the Pen tool's performance by choosing Edit | Preferences in Windows or Flash 8 | Preferences on the Mac, and then clicking Drawing under Category, as shown here.

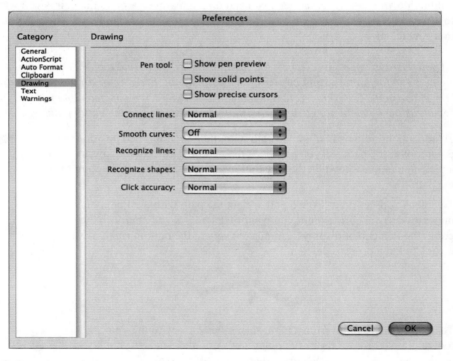

In the Pen tool section, you can select from the following options:

■ **Show Pen Preview** When you select this option, Flash creates a preview of each line segment as you move the cursor across the stage, before you create the end point of the segment.

■ **Show Solid Points**   This option causes Flash to display selected points as hollow points and unselected points as solid points.

■ **Show Precise Cursors**   With this option selected, Flash displays the Pen tool as crosshairs. Use this option when you need to align path points to precise locations along the grid.

Note that there are other selections you can make regarding lines in the Drawing Preferences (Connect Lines, Smooth Curves, Recognize Lines, Recognize Shapes, and Click Accuracy). These modifiers determine the accuracy of lines shapes and curves as you draw. The default setting for these modifiers is Normal. Unless you have a special drawing need, it is best to keep these settings at Normal.

Paint with the Brush Tool

You use the Brush tool when you want to add splashes of color that appear as if they came from a paintbrush. You can also use it to draw much like the Pencil tool. The difference is that with the Brush tool you can select various shapes and sizes of brushes to achieve a painterly kind of effect.

To make a basic brush stroke, click the Brush tool, position your pointer on the stage, and start painting. Like the other drawing tools, you can turn on Object Drawing for the brush tool. When you do this, the brush stroke you created becomes an object that can be manipulated and can stack on top of or behind other objects on the same layer. If Object Drawing is turned off, the brush stroke is a merged drawing.

You'll most likely want to control the way your brush strokes look. In this section we'll review the various properties available for brush strokes. The illustration shown at right was created with the Brush tool.

Although line segments drawn with the Line tool are done in the stroke color, objects created with the Brush tool are drawn in the fill color.

The Brush tool has modifiers that let you vary the shape of the brush tip, as well as the width of the brush. There's even a modifier you can use to vary the width of the brush stroke when drawing with most pressure-sensitive tablets. However, you will see this icon only if you have a pressure-sensitive tablet installed on your system. The modifiers for the Brush tool are shown here.

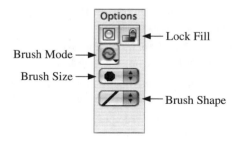

The Brush modifiers in the Options section of the Toolbar (seen when the Brush tool is selected) include the following settings:

- **Lock Fill** This tool is located to the right of the Brush Mode button. Use this tool if you've chosen a gradient fill as your color and you want the color to blend once across all the brush objects on the stage. If Lock Fill is not used, each shape will contain a separate gradient blend.

- **Brush Size** Use this modifier to choose one of ten brush sizes that can be selected from a pop-up menu.

- **Brush Shape** This modifier is used to select one of nine different brush shapes. The shapes available include circles, ovals, rectangles, squares, and a variety of calligraphic shapes.

- **Brush Mode** This feature allows you to further hone in on the style of brushstroke by selecting a paint modifier. Paint modifiers define how the brush paints the selected area. Paint modifiers can be chosen from the Brush Mode pop-up menu. Brush modes are discussed in the next section.

TIP *To create a brush stroke that varies in width with your computer's pressure-sensitive tablet, click the Pressure Sensitive button. Then click the triangle to the right of the Brush Size window and choose a brush size from the drop-down menu. If you are not using a tablet, you will not see this option.*

Check Out the Brush Modes

At the top of the Options section is the Brush Mode modifier. Brush modes allow you to control how the paint interacts when it comes into contact with another shape. Since Flash acts like a paint program if shapes are not drawing objects, grouped, or symbols, the Brush modes (shown here) allow you to control how color is applied. (Grouping elements is covered in Chapter 5 and symbols are covered in Chapter 8.)

To select a Brush mode, select the Brush tool, click the Brush Mode button in the Toolbar's Options panel, and choose one of the following paint modifiers:

- **Paint Normal** This selection causes the brush to apply paint over existing lines and fills on the selected layer.

- **Paint Fills** If this option is chosen, the brush will apply paint to all filled shapes and blank areas on the stage, leaving lines unaffected.

- **Paint Behind** The brush will apply paint behind existing lines and fills, and color to blank areas of the stage, when this option is selected.

- **Paint Selection** This selection causes the brush to apply paint within a selected filled shape while leaving lines and blank areas of the stage unaffected.

- **Paint Inside** In this mode the brush will apply paint within the filled shape where you begin the brush stroke, without affecting surrounding lines, surrounding fills, and blank areas of the stage. If you like painting within the lines, choose this mode.

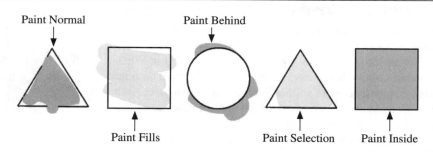

Paint Normal   Paint Behind

Paint Fills   Paint Selection   Paint Inside

FIGURE 3-4   Brush modes let you choose how paint is applied with the Brush tool.

Figure 3-4 shows how you can modify where brush strokes are applied with the different Brush modes.

Select Graphic Elements

The Selection tool has a revered position in the upper-left corner of the Toolbar for good reason. It is one of the most versatile tools you have at your disposal. You use the Selection tool to select, move, and sometimes even to edit objects.

Depending on whether the object you are creating is a merged or drawing object, the way you select the object will differ. With merged drawing shapes, a stroke and a fill on a shape are interpreted as two separate objects that can be selected and edited independently. Remember earlier in this chapter, when it was mentioned that the way you draw in Flash is different from the way you draw in other drawing programs? The ability to draw, select, and edit in two different drawing models is what sets Flash apart from vector-based drawing applications. In fact, most drawing applications work like the object drawing model. For example, if you draw a rectangle in another drawing application, the fill and stroke move as a single entity. This is not the case in Flash. The fill and stroke must be selected separately. In Chapter 5, we will cover this process in detail; but for now, we'll just cover the basics.

Select an Object's Fill

To select an object's fill, click the Selection tool, position your cursor over the filled section of the object, and click. On a merged drawing shape, the fill will highlight with a screen when selected, as shown here.

On an object drawing, the entire object will be selected with a blue frame surrounding the boundaries.

Notice that when the fill is selected on a merged drawing shape, a screen appears over the selected area. You can now edit the fill independent of the object's stroke. To select the entire object (fill and stroke) of a merged object, double-click it.

Select an Object's Stroke

You also can select a merged drawing's stroke with the Selection tool. To select a merged object's stroke, click the Selection tool and move your cursor over the object's stroke. Click the stroke to select it. When a merged drawing's stroke is selected, it appears as a screened highlight just like when a merged drawing's fill is selected, as shown here. After the stroke is selected, you can modify it with menu commands or other tools. On an object drawing, the stroke is selected in the same way as a merged drawing. The difference is that on the object drawing a visual cue (screen) will not highlight the stroke.

To move a merged drawing on the stage, click it with the Selection tool. Your cursor becomes an angled arrow with a four-headed arrow just below it (as shown in the previous illustration). Once this cursor appears, you can move the object anywhere on the stage.

Reshape Objects with the Selection Tool

You can use the Selection tool to reshape any object you create with the drawing tools whether it be an object drawing or merged drawing. When you move the Selection tool toward an object without clicking it, the cursor pointer changes, alerting you to the type of shaping you can do. In the following illustration, the Selection tool is indicating that it can be used to pull the nearest line segment into a curve (left) or to move the corner point (right).

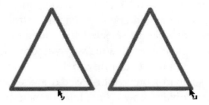

To alter a curved segment, click the Selection tool and move your cursor toward the segment of the object you want to modify. When a curved-line icon appears below the cursor, click and then drag the segment to modify it, as shown at right.

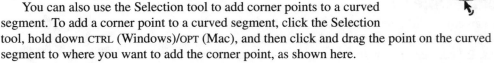

You can also use the Selection tool to add corner points to a curved segment. To add a corner point to a curved segment, click the Selection tool, hold down CTRL (Windows)/OPT (Mac), and then click and drag the point on the curved segment to where you want to add the corner point, as shown here.

Create a Selection of Objects

If you're changing the same properties on similar objects, it's often easier to select the objects simultaneously and then apply the change to the selection all at once. This process can often save you a lot of time and minimize mistakes. For example, if you created a series of circles and you need to move them all at once, or if you wanted to change them all to the same color, it would be easier to perform this task just once. To select several elements on the stage at once, you can use the multifunctional Selection tool or the Lasso tool.

Create a Selection with the Selection Tool

When you use the Selection tool to create a selection of objects, there are two ways you can go about it. The default method of selecting several objects with the Selection tool is to click one object, and then, while holding down SHIFT, click other objects you want to add to the selection. To deselect an object from the selection, click that object again to deselect it.

The other way you use the Selection tool to select objects is by creating a marquee selection. To create a marquee selection, click the Selection tool and then click and drag the tool down and across the stage. As you drag the tool, Flash creates a rectangular bounding box that gives you a preview of the marquee selection area, as shown here.

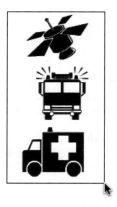

Release the mouse button, and Flash creates the selection. Merged drawings will appear highlighted with a screen, and object drawings will have a blue selection frame surrounding all of the selected objects within the parameters of the marquee.

Create a Selection with the Lasso Tool

The Lasso tool is located in the Tools portion of the Toolbar and looks like a cowboy's lasso. You use the Lasso tool in its default mode to create a freeform selection of objects, or in Polygon mode to create a point-to-point selection of objects.

Select in Freeform Mode   To create a freeform selection, select the Lasso tool, click anywhere on the stage, and drag around the objects you want to select. As you drag the tool, Flash creates a line that gives you a preview of the selection area, as shown next. When you have surrounded (lassoed) the objects you want to select, release the mouse button.

Select in Polygon Mode   When you use the Lasso tool in Polygon mode, you create the selection area by making a point-to-point bounding box to define the boundary of the selection area. To create a point-to-point selection, select the Lasso tool. In the Options section of the Toolbar, click the Polygon Modifier button, as shown here.

Polygon Modifier button

Click anywhere on the stage to define the first point of the selection; click to create the second point, and Flash creates a straight line between the two points. Continue adding points until you have defined a selection area that encompasses all the items you want to select. Double-click to complete the selection, and Flash highlights the items you have selected.

TIP   *You can select a piece of a merged drawing shape with the Lasso tool or by creating a marquee selection on a portion of the merged drawing.*

Sample Fill and Stroke Colors

There are a few tools in the Toolbar that can help you set or modify the fill or stroke properties of a merged drawing shape. These tools are the Ink Bottle tool, the Eyedropper tool, and the Paint Bucket tool. In many ways, they replicate functions in the menu, the Properties Inspector, and the Options area of the Toolbar.

Use the Ink Bottle Tool

You use the Ink Bottle tool to apply a stroke to an object that doesn't have one or to modify an existing stroke in your movie. It's easy to spot in the Toolbar, as it looks similar to the old-fashioned ink bottles used to fill fountain pens.

To apply or modify a stroke on an object, click the Ink Bottle button in the Toolbar. In the Properties Inspector, you'll see the properties you can modify, which include stroke color, height, and style. Select the new properties and then click anywhere on the shape; it will take on the new properties you set. Here you can see the Ink Bottle tool being used to change the properties of a circle's stroke.

You can also modify the properties of a stroke by clicking the stroke and modifying it from the Properties Inspector.

Use the Paint Bucket Tool

The Paint Bucket button is in the Toolbar, to the right of the Ink Bottle button. You use the Paint Bucket tool to apply solid fill colors, or color blends known as *gradients*, to objects in Flash. The polar opposite of the Ink Bottle tool, the Paint Bucket tool can be used to fill an existing shape with no fill or to modify an existing fill. Generally, you would use it to apply a fill to an object that doesn't currently have one.

To apply a fill with the Paint Bucket tool, select the tool. Then, in the Colors section of the Toolbar, select a solid fill color or gradient from the palette. Position the Paint Bucket over the area of the shape you wish to fill and click, as shown next.

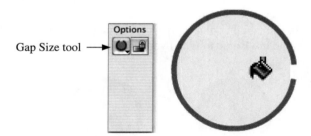

Gap Size tool

Like the Brush tool, the Paint Bucket tool has modifiers. The modifiers for the Paint Bucket tool differ in that they provide you with selection alternatives for filling strokes with various kinds of gaps in them. If the object you are filling was created with the Pencil or Pen tool and there are small gaps in the shape (if the shape is not totally closed), click the Gap Size tool in the

Options settings (as shown in the previous illustration) and choose one of the options from the drop-down menu.

The Gap Size options are as follows:

- **Don't Close Gaps**   This is the default setting. Flash will only apply the fill to objects with no gaps.
- **Close Small Gaps**   This setting tells Flash to apply the fill to an outline with small gaps.
- **Close Medium Gaps**   This setting tells Flash to apply the fill to an outline that has medium-sized gaps.
- **Close Large Gaps**   This setting informs Flash that you want the fill applied to an outline with large gaps.

Once you have all the Paint Bucket properties set, click an object on the stage to apply the fill. The object then takes on the new fill color you selected.

You can also modify the color of a fill by clicking the fill and selecting a new fill color from the Toolbar or Properties Inspector.

Use the Eyedropper Tool

The Eyedropper tool appears as an eyedropper in the Toolbar, to the left of the Eraser tool. You use the Eyedropper tool to sample fill and stroke colors and apply the sampled color to other objects in your movie. You can also use the tool to sample a bitmap fill, a technique that is covered in Chapter 6.

To sample an object's stroke or fill, click the Eyedropper tool and move it onto a shape or a line. If a Pencil icon appears under the Eyedropper tool, you are sampling a stroke color. If a brush appears under the Eyedropper tool, you are sampling a fill color. Note that the pencil and the brush that appear in the bottom right of the Eyedropper tool are extremely small and therefore a little hard to see. Both are shown in the next illustration. Click the stroke or fill to sample it. When you click a shape to sample a fill, the Eyedropper tool becomes the Paint Bucket tool and you can proceed to fill another object. When you click a stroke to sample a stroke, the Eyedropper tool becomes the Ink Bottle tool and you can then change the stroke on an object.

Use the Eraser Tool

The Eraser tool is located in the Toolbar to the right of the Eyedropper tool. Its icon is unmistakable because it looks just like the pink erasers you used in grammar school.

When you select the Eraser tool, three modifiers appear in the Options section of the Toolbar: the Eraser Mode, Faucet, and Eraser Shapes, as shown next. These modifiers allow you to control exactly what is erased and how. Use the Eraser tool to erase editable lines, fills, or a combination thereof.

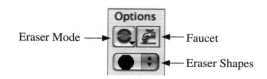

Eraser Mode

The Eraser Mode tools allow you to customize the manner in which you erase an object or a part of an object. To erase an object using the Eraser tool, select the tool first. In the Options section of the Toolbar, click Eraser Mode as shown in the previous illustration and, in the pop-up menu, select one of the following options:

- ■ **Erase Normal**   This selection causes strokes and fills on a layer to be erased as you drag the tool across them.
- ■ **Erase Fills**   This option causes only fills to be erased; strokes are not affected.
- ■ **Erase Lines**   This causes only strokes to be erased; fills are not affected.
- ■ **Erase Selected Fills**   This selection causes a fill from a selected shape to be erased without altering its stroke.
- ■ **Erase Inside**   This option causes an object's fill to be erased from the point where you begin the eraser stroke, without altering surrounding fills or strokes.

Once you've chosen a modifier, click the Eraser Shapes modifier and choose a shape from the pop-up menu shown here.

Finally, drag the tool on the stage over the object you want to erase. Note that the behavior and look of the eraser is based on your previous settings.

> **TIP**   *To erase everything on the stage quickly, double-click the Eraser tool in the Toolbar.*

Erase Fills

The Eraser tool's Faucet modifier makes it easy for you to soak up all of an object's fill or stroke. To completely erase a stroke or fill on an editable object, select the Eraser tool; then click the Faucet modifier. Click an object's stroke to erase a stroke; click its center to remove a fill.

Conclusion

You've learned a lot about the tools in the Toolbar in this chapter. From time to time throughout the book, you'll return to the Toolbar, learning more about the exciting things you can do with just tools and modifiers. You'll get to know the Toolbar quite well as you continue on your learning journey.

In the next chapter, we will concentrate on learning all about creating text in Flash. For this task, you'll use another tool in the Toolbar: the Text tool. The subject of text in Flash is so broad that it needs a chapter of its own.

Chapter 4

Design with Text

How to...

- Create and edit text
- Change the look of your text
- Change the direction of text
- Spell check
- Find and replace text
- Create input text fields
- Create dynamic text fields
- Load rich text into a dynamic text field

You can create three different types of text in Flash 8: static, input, and dynamic. *Static text* is basic text and *input text* is text that allows your audience to type in text for applications such as forms or games. *Dynamic text* is display text that can be updated dynamically. All three types of text are covered in this chapter.

Once you create text in Flash, it doesn't just have to sit and look pretty on the stage. There are many exciting effects you can achieve with text and properties you can assign. For example, you can make breathtaking motion graphics, with text zooming across the screen and fading out. You can create scrolling text boxes, too. The many uses of the text object are limited only by your imagination, and once you become more experienced in Flash, you will discover the infinite possibilities of designing with text.

The other important point about Flash text is that it is vector based. Fonts, therefore, are not only scalable but also look crisp and clean in a Flash movie.

As easy as making text in Flash may sound, there are still many things you need to know about Flash text. In this chapter we cover the basics of creating text. Throughout the book you will continue to build on your knowledge of text in Flash. So let's get going and start designing with text.

Create Basic Text

Basic text—or static text, as it is known in Flash—is easy to create; the interface is so simple it's almost self-explanatory. You create text using the Text tool in the Toolbar. Text in Flash resides within a rectangular block, so you can manipulate the rectangle to control the width of the text block. As is the case with any object you make in Flash, you can assign properties to text. The properties associated with text include size, color, character spacing, and paragraph formatting.

The following list outlines the process for creating basic text in Flash:

1. Go to the Toolbar and select the Text tool, shown here.

2. Set the attributes of the text you are about to type in the Properties Inspector. Here is where you set the color, size, and alignment of the text, among other things. Additional text attributes are covered later in this chapter.

3. Drag the tool onto the stage to the point where you want the text positioned and click. Notice that the cursor transforms into a text-input icon (crosshairs with the letter *A* in the bottom right), as shown here.

4. Start typing and you'll see text appear in a text block with a circle in the upper-right corner. The circle is the handle that allows you to change the width of the text block. A circle handle icon in the top right of the box indicates that you've created an *extended-width* text block, as shown here.

As you type, the text box expands in width to accommodate the text you're typing. If you need to type more than one line, you must press ENTER (Windows)/RETURN (Mac) to go to the next line, just as in a word-processing program; otherwise, the line you are typing will go on indefinitely. This kind of behavior is indicative of an extended-width text block. As you can see, this kind of text lends itself to small, one-line text blocks.

To modify text, select the Text tool from the Toolbar and highlight the text you want to modify. With the text area highlighted, start typing over the old text. The new text will automatically appear where the old text was located.

An extended-width text block is limiting if you need to input a paragraph or more of text. When this is the case, you can use a fixed-width text block, which you'll learn about next.

Manipulate a Fixed-width Text Block

Unlike an extended-width text block, a *fixed-width* text block constrains the text you type to the parameters of the text box. The constraining function of the fixed-width text block is similar to the left and right margins in a word-processing program. It creates its own soft return that conforms to the width of the block. Both the extended- and the fixed-width text blocks have no vertical limit. The height of the block can be whatever you want.

To make a text block with a fixed width, click the Text tool in the Toolbar, set the text properties, and position the pointer where you want the text to appear on the stage, just as you would for an extended-width text block. But instead of just clicking, as you do for an extended-width text block, click and drag the text block to the desired width. This will create a fixed-width text block. The handle on a fixed-width text block appears as a square in the upper-right corner, as shown here.

Change the Width of a Text Box

So you created an extended-width text block and you meant to make it a fixed-width? Or perhaps you made a fixed-width text block and you need to change the width. Fortunately, it's easy to change the width of a text block.

To modify the width of a text box, select the Text tool. Click and drag your pointer (which transforms into a double-headed arrow) over the handle in the upper-right corner to expand or reduce the width, as shown here.

Modifying the width of a text block does not distort the actual text within the box. It just rewraps the text within the block, much like what happens when you change margins in a word-processing program.

Convert an Extended-width Text Block

You can change a fixed-width text block to an extended-width text block. To do this, double-click the square handle in the upper-right corner. The square icon transforms into a circle and snaps the text box back to the last character in the block, indicating that the block is now an extended-width text block.

Control the Look of Text

All objects in Flash, including text objects, have properties that can be set and changed. And as with any other object, there are numerous ways you can change the look of your text in Flash. The easiest way to control the look of text is to use the Properties Inspector, which enables you to set or change the font, size, and paragraph attributes, among other things, of new or existing text (see Figure 4-1).

In the bottom right of the Properties Inspector, there is an arrow that expands and contracts the contents of the bottom half of the Properties Inspector, as shown in the figure. The settings in the top portion of the Properties Inspector are general character attributes and character style settings. On the bottom half, the settings include text block location and position information, a URL link box, and other settings related to dynamic and input text, which are discussed later in this chapter in the section "Understand Input and Dynamic Text Fields."

Some of the text options in the Properties Inspector will be dimmed if static text is selected as a text type because these options are not applicable to static text. Likewise, other selections are dimmed for both input and dynamic text fields.

Set the Text Attributes in the Properties Inspector

You used the Properties Inspector to set attributes on simple graphics in the last chapter, so no doubt you're becoming familiar with its functionality. If you recall, the Properties Inspector is contextual, reflecting attributes of the currently selected object, which in this case is text. So, quite naturally, when you select text the properties relate to that class of object and include such options as size, font, and color.

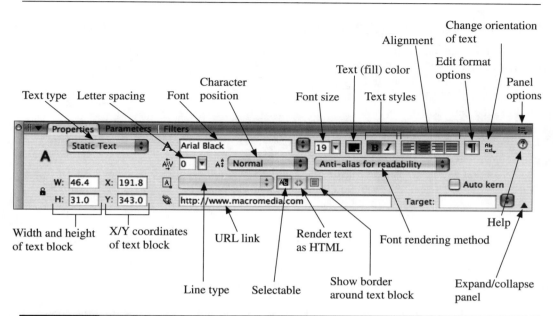

Text type   Letter spacing   Font   Character position   Font size   Text styles   Alignment   Change orientation of text   Edit format options   Text (fill) color   Panel options

Width and height of text block   X/Y coordinates of text block   URL link   Render text as HTML   Font rendering method   Help

Line type   Selectable   Show border around text block   Expand/collapse panel

FIGURE 4-1   Use the Properties Inspector to set or change the attributes of text.

To set the appearance of text *before* you input text, select the Text tool and then select a font, color, size, style, alignment, spacing, and so on, in the Properties Inspector. Next, position your pointer on the stage, click and drag to create a fixed-width text block (if you're typing in more than a word or two), and begin typing. The type will reflect the selections you made in the Properties Inspector. It's that simple to set the characteristics of text.

To change the appearance of existing text, select it with the Text tool or the Selection tool and choose the new attributes in the Properties Inspector the same way you would for new text. The selected text will change accordingly.

Now let's look more closely at specific text attributes you can set or change in the Properties Inspector. Some attributes are obvious and don't need much explanation. For example, to set a font, you simply click the Font pop-up list and select a font. To change an existing font, select the text block or the individual characters you want to change and select a font from the Properties Inspector in the same way.

The following sections provide a rundown of the various settings in the Properties Inspector for creating and modifying regular text. As mentioned earlier, to create text, first set the properties for the text and then type it in. To modify existing text, always select the text first and then modify the properties.

Selecting Text with the Text Tool Versus the Selection Tool

It stands to reason that before you modify the properties of text you need to select the text first. You can always select the text you are about to modify with the Text tool. One easy way to edit text without clicking on the Text tool first is to double-click the text with the Selection tool. When you do this, a text cursor appears in the block and the Text tool becomes the current tool.

You can also modify most text properties by selecting the text with the Selection tool. In fact, the only properties you can't modify this way are attributes that involve the changing of characters themselves, such as text input or character spacing.

When you get up to speed in Flash, you'll probably find it easier to select text with the Selection tool because it's the tool you'll be using most often.

Set Basic Text Attributes

To set the *size* of text, select a text size from the pop-up Font Size list or type a number in the Font Size box. Text is measured in points.

To set the *fill color* of text, click the Text Fill Color button and select a color from the pop-up palette, shown here.

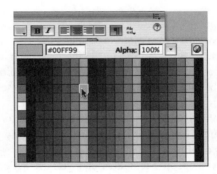

To choose a *bold* text style, click the B button in the Properties Inspector. To select an *italic* style, click the I. To make the style both bold and italic, click both buttons.

To change the *alignment* of text or a paragraph of text, click one of the four alignment options: left, centered, right, or justified.

TIP *Font properties can also be accessed from the Text menu. Additionally, you can set the text's fill color from the Fill color palette in the Toolbar as well as the Color Mixer and Color Swatches palettes. If these palettes are hidden you can access them in the Window menu.*

Set the Letter Spacing

Letter spacing is the space between characters. You can widen the space between characters to make a word appear "airy," or you can contract the space to make it appear tight or congested. To adjust the letter spacing for a block of text, first select the text with the Selection or Text tool, then click the arrow to the right of the Letter spacing box and use the pop-up slider to select a number.

Dragging downward on the slider displays negative spacing, or less space between characters. Dragging upward on the slider displays positive numbers, giving you more space between characters. A setting of 0 is the default spacing. You can also type in a custom number in the Letter Spacing box. A word selected with the Text tool and given a letter spacing of 7 pixels is shown here:

You can change letter spacing on any selected text. For example, if an entire word is selected and you adjust the letter spacing, the change will apply to the entire word. If you select three letters in a sentence and change the letter spacing, only those letters would be spaced at your new setting.

Kerning is adjusting the space between specific characters. Clicking the Auto Kern box in the Properties Inspector allows Flash to determine what the most visually appealing space is between problematic pairs of characters. For example, the "il" letter pair may require different kerning (depending on the font selected) than the "wi" letter pair. If text is monospaced and not kerned, it ends up looking like it has too much or too little space between characters. Clicking Auto Kern addresses the special problems between character pairs.

You can also change the character spacing for a highlighted block of text or between two characters by selecting the text (or the two characters) and pressing CTRL-ALT-LEFT/RIGHT ARROW in Windows or OPT-CMD-LEFT/RIGHT ARROW on a Macintosh. To kern in larger increments, hold down SHIFT when you press these keys. This is an important technique, since the Auto Kern setting in the Properties Inspector doesn't always do a perfect job. You'll often need to use this method to manually adjust kerning.

Assign a Character Position

Character position refers to the position of text vertically in relation to the baseline of the text. The default position (on the baseline) is Normal, superscript positions are above the baseline, and subscript positions are below the baseline, as shown here.

To change the position of text in relation to the baseline, click the pop-up list and select any of the settings. Changing character position is useful for footnotes, scientific equations, trademarks, or any design in which you need the text to have an irregular baseline.

Assign Paragraph Attributes

Once you've created your text and set the appearance, you may need to finish it off by setting paragraph formatting attributes if you have a text block with two or more lines of text. If your text is in paragraph format, you need to make additional design decisions about such things as indents, margins, and line spacing. By clicking the Edit Format Options button in the Properties Inspector, you can change these attributes.

When you click this button, the Format Options dialog box appears. Here you can adjust various paragraph attributes, such as indents, line spacing, and margins. To change any of the formatting in this box, select the text you want to change and click the slider to the right of the input box. The new value will appear in the input box. As with the other input boxes in the Properties Inspector, you can manually type a number in, too.

To see the adjustments you're making in real time, position the Format Options dialog box next to the selected text. When you adjust the settings, you will be able to preview them, as shown in Figure 4-2. Once you've decided upon an appropriate setting, click the OK button.

Set the Font Rendering Method

In Flash 8 the new rendering settings improve the appearance of text in both the Flash application and the Flash 8 Player. "Rendering" refers to the representation of text or the way it is drawn in Flash. You can adjust the appearance of your type by selecting one of the five styles in the Font Rendering Method pop-up menu in the Properties Inspector, as shown next.

When you click on Edit format options in the Properties Inspector, the Format Options dialog box appears.

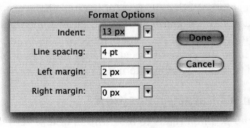

FIGURE 4-2   You can preview formatting in real time if you position the Format Options dialog box next to the selected text.

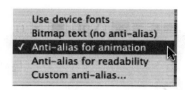

_Serif device font
Bitmap text (no antialias)
Antialiased for animation
Antialiased for readability

4

You apply a rendering option by selecting a text block and picking one of the five styles from the pop-up menu. When applied to a block of text, these rendering options can produce dramatically different results, as shown at right.

> **NOTE**   *If the sans, serif, or typewriter fonts (device fonts) are selected in the Font list, the text rendering options will not be available.*

Text rendering options are important because the text you will be creating in Flash may be used for many different types of projects. For example, your text may be used in a moving animation, or it may be used for a text-intensive quiz. Type with fast movement on a screen requires a different kind of rendering then does static type that needs to be carefully read, and this is where rendering options come into play. The following provides a description of each of these rendering options and explains which option is appropriate for different uses.

- **Use Device Fonts**   Use this option if you want to produce a smaller file size resulting in a faster display. This option also reduces file size because it makes use of the fonts already installed on the viewer's computer. Device fonts are explained in the next section.

- **Bitmap Text (no anti-alias)**   Experiment with this option if you find that smaller-size fonts (size 8 and under) in your Flash movie appear too blurry to read. Bitmap text has sharp edges as opposed to the fuzzy edges created by anti-aliased-type options that sometimes make smaller font sizes harder to read. You can also use this option to deliberately create a font that appears jaggy and computerized. This option does result in a larger file size because font descriptions are embedded in the SWF (Flash Player) file.

- **Anti-alias for Animation**   Use this option for text in motion. It will produce text that blends well with the background of the animation resulting in a smooth play. This option results in a larger file size because font descriptions are embedded in the SWF file.

- **Anti-alias for Readability**   Use this option for exceptionally readable text. This option results in a file size larger than any other rendering option because font descriptions and additional font information are embedded in the SWF file.

- **Custom Anti-alias**   Use this option if you need readable text but you want to tweak the settings. The default Custom setting is based on the "Anti-alias for readability" settings. From here, you can manipulate the settings to complement obscure fonts or special characters. This option results in a large file size similar to the Anti-alias for Readability option since it also embeds font descriptions and additional information. When you select Custom Anti-alias, a dialog box appears, as shown next. Here you can customize the thickness and sharpness dynamically.

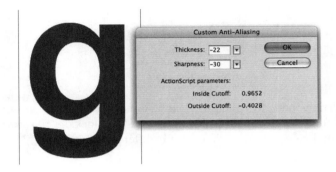

Aliased text is bitmapped text. It appears as if the edges are jagged. Text that is *anti-aliased*, on the other hand, appears smooth because the edges of the text subtly blend in with the pixels of the background. Theoretically, small anti-aliased text may appear blurry because of this blending of pixels. In some cases, aliased text may appear crisper than anti-aliased text. Since different designs can produce different outcomes, experiment with these settings to find the correct balance of readability and quality for your project.

 *Sans serif fonts such as Verdana, Arial, and Helvetica are more readable at smaller sizes than serif fonts such as Times Roman or Garamond.*

Use Device Fonts

Device fonts are fonts not embedded in the Flash Player file (SWF) you publish. If you design your Flash movie with device fonts, when an SWF file is played on a viewer's computer, the default serif font and sans serif font in that computer's system will appear in place of the device fonts. To use device fonts, check the Use Device Fonts in the Font Rendering Method pop-up menu in the Properties Inspector, as discussed in the previous section.

A sans serif font will default to a font that looks like Arial, Helvetica, or Verdana. A serif font will default to a font that looks like Times Roman. A typewriter font will default to a font that looks like Courier. You can also assign device fonts from the Font list in the Properties Inspector. The device fonts are listed as sans, serif, and typewriter.

Since device fonts are not embedded in the SWF file, a movie with a lot of text that uses them should, in theory, be smaller in size. One of your goals in building a successful Flash movie is to keep the file size as small as possible without sacrificing quality.

Identify a URL in the Properties Inspector

URL stands for *uniform resource locater*, which in plain English is a web address. The address can be an HTML file or a Flash Player file (SWF). The URL address will determine where your file will be located. You can set a link to a remote URL, a local URL, or an SWF file. To assign a URL to a text block, first select the text with the Text tool. Then in the Properties Inspector URL Link input box, type in the full URL. For example, if you want users to link to the Macromedia web site when they click a text block that says "click here for Flash plug-in," you can easily do so. In the URL Link box for this text block, you would type in the following:

```
http://www.macromedia.com
```

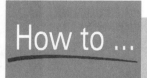 **Substitute a Missing Font**

On occasion when you open a Flash file, you may get a Missing Fonts alert. This may happen if your file is opened on another computer or if the file in question was created by someone else and their system has different fonts from yours. To remedy the missing font problem without having to go back and search for and replace each font, click Choose Substitute, as shown here.

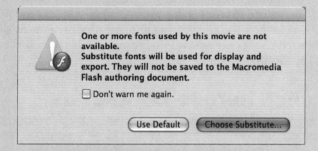

When you see the Font Mapping dialog box, select a substitute font from the pop-up menu in the bottom right, as shown next. To dismiss the Missing Fonts alert, click Use Default. Flash will then use the default font in your computer.

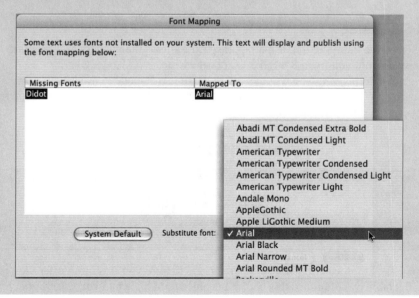

When the user clicks on this text on the Web, his or her browser will go to the Macromedia web page. Note that a dashed line appears under the text block with the URL link.

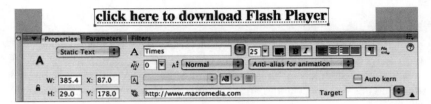

To create a link to an e-mail address, type **mailto:** in the URL Link box and then the e-mail address. For example, if you wanted to create a link to your e-mail address, you would type something like the following in the URL Link box: **mailto:ssmith@nsc.edu**, as shown in the following illustration. When the user clicks the text in the movie, a blank, addressed page will open in his or her e-mail application.

Make Text Selectable

Clicking the Selectable button in the Properties Inspector allows the viewers of your Flash movie to select text. By default, text in an SWF file is not selectable.

You may be wondering why you would want to make text selectable. Making it selectable allows viewers to copy text from your SWF file and paste it somewhere else, as shown here, much as users can in an HTML document.

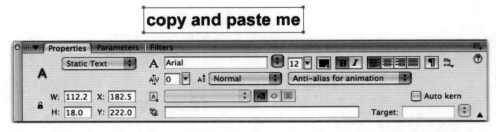

If your SWF file is information-heavy, this may be a feature you'll want to offer viewers. Input text is selectable by default, so this button becomes dimmed when you select input text.

Change the Orientation of Text

In the Properties Inspector, you can set the orientation and the rotation of text. The *orientation* of text refers to the direction the text reads. By default, text in Flash appears the way you usually read: horizontally, left to right. You can also set text to read vertically, as shown in Figure 4-3.

The Vertical, Left To Right setting creates text that reads from left to right, as text reads in English and many other languages. Text with a setting of Vertical, Right To Left reads in the opposite direction, as is the case in many Asian languages. If you find yourself working on a project that requires text always to be formatted to read right to left, you can globally change the text orientation of the document by accessing the Text Category in the Preferences dialog box.

4

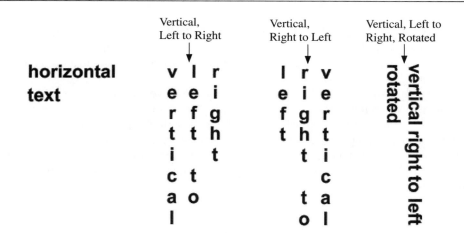

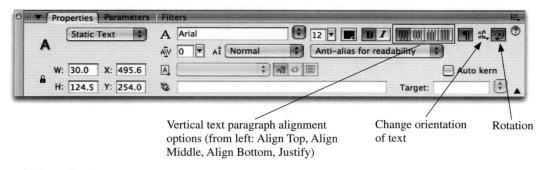

Vertical text paragraph alignment options (from left: Align Top, Align Middle, Align Bottom, Justify)

Change orientation of text

Rotation

FIGURE 4-3   The Change Orientation of Text button has three different settings.

You can find this dialog box by navigating to the Edit menu in Windows and the Flash 8 menu on the Mac.

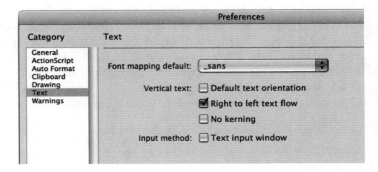

To set text to read vertically, click the Change Orientation Of Text button. Then, in the pop-up list, select either Vertical, Left To Right or Vertical, Right To Left. The resulting text will be vertically typed. Note that you will learn another way of changing the rotation of text in Chapter 5 when you practice using the Transformation tool.

When the orientation of your text is set to Vertical, you also have the option to rotate it. The combination of these two settings makes your text appear as it does on the right in Figure 4-3.

When text has a vertical orientation, the paragraph alignment tools appear sideways as opposed to horizontal. Aligning vertical text would be disorienting if you were using the traditional horizontal alignment icons. For example, as you can see in this illustration, the Align Right button will align a vertical paragraph to the bottom of a text block as opposed to the right, as it would in a horizontal text block.

 *Device fonts, selectable text, vertical orientation, and rotation of text are settings that are available only for static horizontal text.*

The Show Border and Render Text As HTML selections are discussed later in this chapter.

Set Text Attributes in the Menu

Even though many Flash designers prefer working with the Properties Inspector, there are those who like the old, tried-and-true menu interface. If you're a menu kind of person, you'll be happy to know that you can also change text properties from the menus.

The Text menu offers font, size, alignment, style, and kerning selections. Just as in the Properties Inspector, you can set these properties after selecting the Text tool and before inputting the text, or you can modify existing selected text. The settings work essentially the same way. The only differences are the manner in which you select them and the availability of a couple of additional useful tools that appear only on the menu.

To set a font attribute from the menu, click the Text tool and go to the Text menu. Click the category that contains the action you want to perform, and then click the right arrow to display the flyout menu for that category. When you select an attribute, the attribute will be set. This illustration shows the attributes that can be set from the Style flyout menu.

It's just as easy to set a property from the menu as it is to set it from the Properties Inspector. Flash gives you dual options on many settings, so you can work in the environment that's most comfortable for you.

Check the Spelling of Text

In Flash you can check to see if you have made any typos in a document. Similar to the spell-check function in a word-processing program, you can check to see whether you made spelling mistakes in your text. This is particularly useful if you are inputting lengthy paragraphs of text or if your document has many layers, scenes, and/or symbols.

Before you can check spelling, you must set your preferences in the Spelling Setup dialog box.

Customize the Spelling Setup

The Spelling Setup dialog box allows you to customize the spell checker's performance throughout your movie. To display the Spelling Setup dialog box, select Text | Spelling Setup from the menu.

The Spelling Setup dialog box, shown here, is divided into four sections.

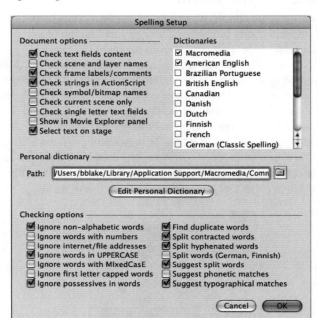

These sections offer various options:

■ **Document Options**   The nine options in this section are document-specific settings. Most of them deal with checking the spelling in scenes, layers, frame labels, and symbols. At a minimum, make sure that Check Text Fields Content is checked so that you can check text in text blocks.

■ **Dictionaries**   The Dictionaries option allows you to select the number of built-in dictionaries you'd like the check-spelling feature to reference. Click the boxes to activate dictionaries.

■ **Personal Dictionary**   The Personal Dictionary section allows you to collect and save words you use frequently that are not in the built-in dictionary. To create a personal dictionary, click the Browse For Personal Dictionary file icon to the right of the Path input box. It's the file-folder shaped icon on the right in the previous illustration.

   1. In the Open dialog box, browse to the folder in which you want to store your dictionary and then click OK. The path of your dictionary file appears. Note that, at the end of the path, the dictionary file is named "my dictionary.tlx."

   2. To add or edit entries to your personal dictionary, click the Edit Personal Dictionary button. To add entries in the Edit Personal Dictionary dialog box, click in the box and start typing, as shown next. To edit entries, click to highlight the word in this dialog box and type over it.

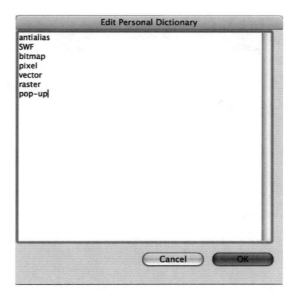

- ■ **Checking Options**   The Checking Options section at the bottom of the Spelling Setup dialog box allows you to decide how certain letters and words (such as URLs, numbers, hyphenated words, etc.) should be displayed. To select an option, click the check box to the left of the option.

Once all the settings have been selected in the Spelling Setup dialog box, click OK and then proceed to spell check.

Use the Check Spelling Feature

To check the spelling, select Text | Check Spelling from the menu after you have set up the features in the Spelling Setup dialog box. In the Check Spelling dialog box, shown in Figure 4-4, you will see that words not found in the dictionary are highlighted. A change is suggested, based on the dictionaries loaded. You can concur with the suggestion and click the Change button, or you can select another spelling from the Suggestions list. You can also type your own change in the Change To input box.

From this dialog box you can also add a word to your personal dictionary by clicking the Add To Personal button. Click the Setup button to return to the Spelling Setup dialog box.

Click the Change (or Change All) button to accept a spelling change or click the Ignore (or Ignore All) button to leave the spelling as is. The spell checker will then navigate to the next suspect word. To delete a word, click the Delete button. A message box will alert you when the spell check is complete.

NOTE   *When you perform a spell check, an alert dialog box may appear that says, "Based on your settings, there is nothing to be checked in this document." If this occurs, go back to the Spelling Setup dialog box and try checking more document and checking options to widen the criteria for your spell check.*

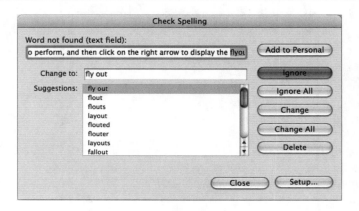

FIGURE 4-4 Use the Check Spelling dialog box to correct spelling errors.

TIP

If you create a large Flash movie and decide later you need to change a type of font or a recurring word, you can use the Find And Replace feature in Flash to do this. To use the Find And Replace feature, select Edit | Find and Replace from the menu or press CTRL-F in Windows and CMD-F on the Mac. In this dialog box you can find/replace text, fonts, and text color. Simply check the criteria in the Find And Replace dialog box, then click the Find button. To replace text, type the new text in the Replace With: input field, then press the Replace button. The editing occurs dynamically.

Understand Input and Dynamic Text Fields

Input and dynamic text fields are created in much the same way that static text fields are created. They use most of the same attributes that apply to static text, such as font, font size, color, and alignment, but there are a few settings that are exclusive to a particular text type.

You cannot change the orientation of input or dynamic text to vertical, nor can you kern or adjust the spacing between characters. You also cannot assign a URL to input text. All of these "cannots" exist because the text is being typed in by the user or is being displayed on the fly. Naturally, you don't have as much control over the way this kind of text will appear for a large and diverse audience.

Input text is displayed in a text input field on your audience's screen. You can use input text for many purposes such as gathering information from viewers of your movie or for computer games that involve audience input. Text fields are powerful because they can pass information from one file to another.

Dynamic text is created in a dynamic text field. You use dynamic text fields for information that updates quickly and often, such as weather reports and current events. You can also load rich text into dynamic text fields. *Rich text formatting*, or RTF, preserves the text attributes and hyperlinks that were set in the text-editing program in which the document was generated. Later in this chapter you'll learn how to work with rich text formatting and dynamic text fields.

Create Input and Dynamic Text Fields

You create input and dynamic text fields by using nearly the same techniques in the Properties Inspector, although there are a couple of options exclusive to each type of text field.

To create input and dynamic text, first click the Text tool in the Toolbar. Then, in the Properties Inspector, navigate through the following selections:

1. In the Text Type drop-down list (shown here), click either Input Text or Dynamic Text.

> NOTE   *Make certain that the Expand/Collapse Information Area arrow in the bottom right of the Properties Inspector is pointing up, meaning that the Properties Inspector is currently expanded. There are settings in the expanded area germane to both input and dynamic text.*

2. For Line Type, select from the following choices:

- **Single Line**   Select this to restrict the user from typing more than one line of text in a field.

- **Multiline**   Click this setting to allow users to type in two or more lines of text.

- **Multiline No Wrap**   Select this setting to prevent the user from seeing text input beyond the width of the text field unless he or she presses ENTER/RETURN.

- **Password**   Select the Password setting if you want the user to enter an encrypted password before continuing to navigate in the movie.

3. The Line Type list is shown here.

4. Select from the following settings related to the type of text field you are creating. The settings are available for both input and dynamic text types unless otherwise noted.

- **Selectable (dynamic text only)**   Clicking this setting enables the user to select, type, and edit text in a field. This option is only available for dynamic text. Static text isn't interactive and input text is used for user input in a text field.

- **Render Text As HTML**   Click this selection if your text was created with rich text formatting and you want to retain this formatting.

- **Show Border Around Text**   Select this setting if you want your text field to be displayed with a border instead of invisible boundaries.

■ **URL Link (dynamic and static text only)**   Here you can enter a URL link for text in the text field the same way you would create a hyperlink in HTML. You can set a link to a remote URL, a local URL, or an SWF file. When you create a link to an SWF file, the SWF file will open in a browser.

■ **Target (dynamic and static text only)**   If you create a URL link, you can also decide how you want it to appear in the browser. Generally, you would want to specify a target if the SWF file was opening within a URL with framesets and you wanted to have some control over how it appears.

■ **Embed**   For input and dynamic text, you can selectively choose to embed all, some, or no characters in the text field. When you embed a character, the font outline information for that character becomes attached to the text field. Embedding characters does increase the size of the file. Generally, you would embed a character in situations where you need to display unusual text like special symbols (mathematical, Greek, etc.) that may not be available on the user's computer. To embed a character, select the character and then click the Embed button in the bottom right of the Properties Inspector. In the Character Embedding dialog box shown here, select the desired setting. This setting will be determined by factors surrounding your movie, such as desired file size versus the importance of a font in the overall design of the movie.

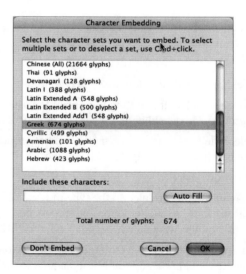

■ **Instance Name**   Input and dynamic text fields can have instance names. You assign an instance name to an object (such as a movie clip or a text object) so that you can refer to the object in a script. The instance name is typed in the box below the Text Type pop-up list in the Properties Inspector, as shown in the next illustration.

■ **Variable Name**   Assigning a variable name to a text field enables the contents of the field to change. The variable name is typed in the Var box on the right side of the Properties Inspector, as shown next.

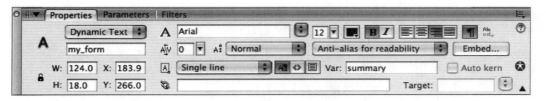

5. Create the text field by clicking and dragging your pointer on the stage in the place where you want the text field to appear. Note that both input and dynamic text field blocks have a square handle in the bottom right, as shown in Figure 4-5.

Now that you know how to make input and dynamic text fields, you need to understand how to use them. Next, you'll perform a couple of simple tasks so you can experience firsthand what makes them different from static text.

Create a Simple Input Text Field with a Variable

The following exercise will give you a bare-bones understanding of how input text works with variables. In this example, you will create two input text fields and assign the same variable name to both of them. In the finished sample, shown here, you'll see that when the user types text into an input field, it will appear as input in the other input field.

Name Colleen

Hello Colleen

You'll also create a couple of static text blocks to instruct the user what to type in the input text field. Static text is often used to instruct the user about how the interface works.

One example of a variable in action is on the Web. When a site prompts you for information about yourself such as your name, and then throughout the site, your name seems to be remembered, a variable is used to make this happen. It may sound confusing, but after you review the following steps you will have a better idea of how a variable works in the scenario that was just painted. You will see how a text variable in Flash can recall something as simple as a name.

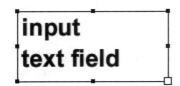 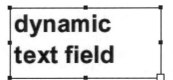

FIGURE 4-5   Both input and dynamic text fields have square handles.

Understand Variables in Text Fields

Input text and dynamic text can work with a script action called a *variable*, which is assigned to the text field. By now you know that an easy way to assign a variable to a text field is to do so in the Properties Inspector.

Variables are called such because they can change, or vary, depending on the directions in the designer's script. A variable acts as a container, and the information it contains can change. Variables can also be assigned to other objects, such as the MovieClip, Button, Sound, Date, and TextField objects, to name a few.

A variable is assigned a value. The value can be either textual or numeric. If you prompt your viewer to fill out a form in which you want him or her to indicate his or her age, the *variable* may be a text box named *age*, but the *value* of the variable is whatever number the user types in the text field. Variables are discussed further in Chapter 15.

Sounds complicated, doesn't it? Actually, it will all eventually fall into place. For now, you just need to know that if you assign a variable name to an input or dynamic text field, you'll be able to perform some fancy tricks.

First, you'll create the static text blocks that explain what the user needs to type in the input text fields.

1. Select the Text tool from the Toolbar and in the Properties Inspector Text Type pop-up list, select Static Text. Also, select a font type of Arial or Verdana, a font size of 24 points, a black fill color, and a right alignment.

2. Click somewhere in the left side of the stage and type in **Name**. Press ENTER/RETURN two times and type **Hello**.

3. Now, you'll set the attributes for the input text fields that reside to the right of the static text. For Text Type in the Properties Inspector, select Input Text. Click the Show Border button so that the text field will have a border around it in the movie. This indicates to the user where they should type the text. For Line Type, select Single Line in the pop-up list. In the Var (variable) text box, type **name**. This becomes the variable name for the input field. Change the alignment for this field to left because you'll want the text the user types in to appear after the instruction. Leave the other attributes in the Properties Inspector unchanged.

4. Now, you will make the input text field into which the user will type his or her name. Click and drag the cursor to the right of the "Name" static text block to make a single-line text input field. Make sure that the width of the text field is large enough to accommodate a viewer's first name. If it's not, simply select the Text tool again, click in the text field, position your pointer on the handle in the bottom right, and drag the square handle to expand the width. Don't worry about aligning the text boxes vertically. You can do that later.

5. Next, you need to make an input text field to the right of the word "Hello." Instead of starting from scratch and making another input text field, duplicate the previous input text field. The easiest way to do this is to press ALT-SHIFT (Windows)/OPT-SHIFT (Mac) and then click the input text field with the Selection tool. A plus (+) sign appears at the bottom right of your pointer, indicating that you are about to duplicate an object. Drag the duplicate input text field down until it's approximately aligned with the word "Hello" from the static text block, as shown here.

Name ⬚

Hello ⬚

6. If you want the Hello response to look more natural when a person's name appears next to it, get rid of the border around the accompanying input text field. To do this, click the input text field to the right of the word "Hello", and in the Properties Inspector, click the Show Border Around Text icon to turn the border off.

7. Now both text fields are identical (except for the border around the input text box), with the same variable name. You can verify this by clicking the new text field and checking the settings in the Properties Inspector. See Figure 4-6 to get an idea of how the stage and Properties Inspector should appear.

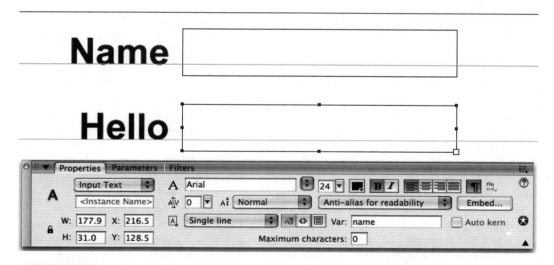

FIGURE 4-6   The Properties Inspector shows that the second input text field also has the variable name, "name".

The bottom of the input text field will not align with the baseline of the static text. To make sure that what the user types in is aligned with the baseline of the static text instructions, you can drag guidelines from the rulers (View | Rulers) and align them with the static text. You may need to type some temporary text in the input text fields on the stage to help you align the text baselines. If you do, make sure you delete the dummy text before testing the movie again. Notice how the guides are set up in Figure 4-6.

8. You're finished and ready to test the movie. To test it, press CTRL-ENTER (Windows)/ SHIFT-CMD (Mac). Alternately, you can select Control | Test Movie from the menu. In Test Movie mode, type a name in the input text field. Note that the same name appears in the text field to the right of the "Hello" greeting. This variable will remain the same until instructed to change.

9. To save the movie, select File | Save As from the menu. In the Save As dialog box, navigate to the folder in which you want to save this file and click the Save button.

10. To quickly publish the movie as an SWF file, select File | Export | Export Movie from the menu. Navigate to the folder in which you want to save the movie, type in a file name, and click the Save button.

This is a simple exercise that doesn't even begin to touch upon the power of variables. It does, however, introduce you to an important concept in Flash ActionScript: the variable.

Work with Dynamic Text Fields

A dynamic text field is different from a static text field in that it is used to display text that changes on the fly.

Like input text fields, dynamic text fields work with variables. Variables in a dynamic text field can be loaded within Flash 8 or externally, from a separate document. The document has to conform to certain rules, as you are about to find out.

To better understand how a dynamic text field works, you will perform a simple exercise using a dynamic text field and a separate text file you will create. In the finished exercise, when the movie loads, a text file named "text.txt" with variable text named *sample* will load into a dynamic text field with a variable name of *sample*. You will also learn how to apply a script to the movie to instruct Flash 8 how to handle the loading of the variable text from an outside file into the dynamic text field in your movie.

Since you'll need to generate a text file that will load into the dynamic text field, you'll need to launch a word-processing program. Although you can use any word-processing program, it's easiest to stick with the simple text editors your operating system shipped with.

In Windows, launch Notepad or MS Word. If you are working on a Mac, use any word-processing program that allows you to save text in a Text Only format (.txt). You should also launch Flash 8 to get ready to do this exercise. First, you create the dynamic text field in Flash 8 and then use the text editor to type the variable text. Put the text editor aside now and launch Flash 8. Later, you will type text in this editor.

1. Create a new file in Flash and save the file. It's important that you save this file in the same folder that you will be saving the text file you'll be creating in the next section, so keep this in mind. Both files need to be in the same folder in order for the exercise to work properly. This is also true if you want to test this file by uploading it to a server. Both files must reside in the same folder in order for them to work when someone calls the Flash movie up in their browser.

2. Select the Text tool. In the Properties Inspector, for Text Type, select Dynamic Text. For Font, pick Verdana or Arial; for Font Size, select 12; for Alignment, select Left. On the bottom half of the Properties Inspector, for Line Type, select Multiline.

3. Click in the stage and draw a dynamic text block about the size of the one in the following illustration.

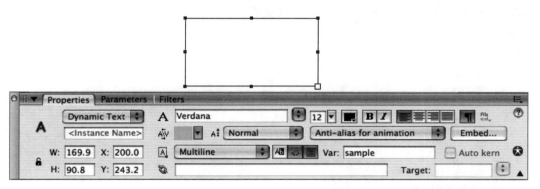

4. Click the dynamic text field and in the Var (variable) box in the Properties Inspector, type **sample**, as shown in the previous illustration. The variable name in the text you create in the text editor will have a variable name of *sample*, too. You now have a formatted dynamic text field in Flash with a variable name of *sample*. Now, you need to create the script that tells your Flash file to load the external variable named *sample* into the dynamic text field named *sample*. You will write the script in the Actions panel.

Scripts are written in the Actions panel, which has two different modes of scripting; one for beginners and the default mode for the advanced user. The beginner mode is called "Script Assist." When this feature is activated, the script window prompts you in the construction of the script. This exercise provides you with a brief introduction to the Scrip Assist feature in Flash 8. The Actions panel and ActionScript are discussed further in Chapter 15.

5. Display the Actions panel by selecting Window | Development Panels | Actions or pressing F9 in Windows and OPTION-F9 on the Mac.

6. Click Frame 1 of the timeline and, in the first column of the Actions panel, click Global Functions to expand the contents of this folder. Click Browser/Network to expand this folder, and then double-click LoadVariables. In the top of the right column, click in the URL field and type the following exactly as you see it:

```
text.txt
```

7. In the middle of the right column, the script you just created should read like this:

```
loadVariablesNum("text.txt", 0);
```

The Actions panel will look like this:

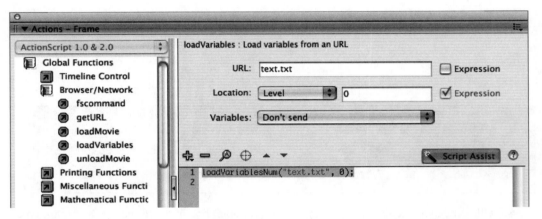

8. Hide the Actions panel and test the movie by selecting Control | Test Movie from the menu or ALT-ENTER in Windows or CMD-RETURN on the Mac.

Ordinarily you would create a separate layer for a script on a frame in the timeline because it makes your scripts easier to keep track of. For the sake of simplicity, in this exercise the script resides on the same layer as the object.

Let's examine in plain language what the above script is saying. It's telling the timeline that when the Flash movie loads in a browser it will load the variable text named *sample* from the text file named *text.txt* (which you will create in the next section) into the dynamic text field also with a variable name of *sample*. Remember, earlier you named the dynamic text field *sample* in the Properties Inspector. As mentioned earlier, the text in the file you will create in the next section will have a variable name of *sample* also. As a result, this text will load in the text field variable named *sample*.

Let's also look at the structure of the line of script. The loadVariablesNum function in the Flash ActionScript panel reads text from an external source such as a text file or an SWF file. The parentheses contain the parameters for this function. In this case, the parameters are the URL ("text.txt"). Note that there are quotations around text.txt because the variable is reading the text only as the value. You did not put the parentheses around the text as this is the default treatment of URLs in the Script Assist mode.

Quotation marks are used for strings in ActionScript. *Strings* consist of information that has no value other than the plain text itself. The 0 represents the level on which the variable is loading, 0 being the top level.

Levels in Flash allow you to perform complex scripting tasks as you can address objects on other timelines as well as externally located movies. Sound confusing? Don't worry about that now because ActionScript is a completely different facet of Flash. Because of its extensive scope, ActionScript is not fully addressed in this book. It's important to understand, however, that one of the reasons Flash is such a powerful program is that it allows users to address objects located in different places within the movie as well as externally located movies.

These instructions are fairly easy, as you can see. To make this exercise completely functional, you just need to create the text in a text editor with a variable name of *sample*, which you will do in the next step.

9. In the text editor you launched earlier, create a file and save the file as text.txt in the same folder in which the Flash file is saved. This is important; otherwise, when the SWF file loads, it won't be able to find the external text to load into the *sample* dynamic text field. It is equally important to name the text file exactly the same name as in the script you wrote in Flash: text.txt. Otherwise, when the user loads the movie, he or she will only see a blank box.

10. In the word-processing program, type out the following text exactly as you see it, including the spacing:

```
sample=Current Weather Conditions: Cloudy with a chance of
showers later on this afternoon.
```

11. The word "sample=" gives the text that follows it the same variable name as the dynamic text field in Flash. As a result, this text becomes the value of the variable named *sample*. The equal sign (as in sample=) is used to bridge the variable name with the variable, which in this case is a blurb on weather conditions.

In the following illustration, this text was created and saved in MS Word as a text-only document.

12. Make sure the Flash file has been saved since you last worked on it. Keep these files because you will use them again in the next section.

The exercise is done, and you can test it to see if it works. To check the movie out, press CTRL-ENTER (Windows)/CMD-RETURN (Mac). As expected, the text you typed in the word-processing program that is stored in the same folder as the Flash file now dynamically appears in the text field.

Experiment with Rich Text Formatting   In the previous exercise, the text that loaded into the dynamic text field appeared as plain vanilla with not much style. Sure, you can assign a color, alignment, and font type in the Properties Inspector, but you're not guaranteed that the viewer will see your text exactly as specified.

Another variation on the previous exercise is to create your text file using rich text formatting. Rich text formatting contains tags that can be read by the SWF file. For example, if you wanted to intermittently vary the headline color, style, or font size of the text file loading into the field from an external source, you could do so using tags.

HTML standard formatting tags can be used for the formatting of the text file. If you're not familiar with HTML tags, you can check out the site www.html-tags.info, which provides you with a free reference on HTML tags.

Keep in mind that not all HTML tags are supported in rich text format. Only the very basic tags such as <FONT COLOR>, <FONT FACE>, <FONT SIZE>, <B> (bold), <I> (italic), and <P> (paragraph) are supported. In addition, just like in HTML formatting, tags appear in brackets and must be closed with a back slash. For example, the closing tag for a bold tag is </B>. Nevertheless, text with varied color and font attributes can be a little more interesting than just plain old text.

Returning to the exercise from the last section, here you will expand on the text file you typed out previously. If you recall, you created a Flash file with a dynamic text field and gave it a variable name of *sample*. Then you created a plain text file that began with "sample=". The text after the equal sign represented the value of the variable named *sample*, which loads into the dynamic text field when the viewer opens the SWF file.

In this section you will add tags to the existing text file and then test the movie again. The text that loads will be styled as per the changes you make to the text file.

Open the text file you created from the previous section. Edit the text by adding the following tags exactly as they appear here:

```
sample=<B><FONT COLOR="#CC0000">Current Weather
Conditions:</FONT></B><BR><FONT COLOR="000000">Cloudy with a
chance of <I>showers</I> later on this afternoon.
```

Save the text file (with the same name as before, text.txt) and return to the Flash file that has the dynamic text field. The first thing you must do is click the Render Text As HTML button in the Properties Inspector (shown at right). Flash will then be able to read the HTML tags you set in the text file.

Test the movie again (Control | Test Movie or CTRL-ENTER in Windows/CMD-RETURN on the Mac). The resulting SWF file should look like the illustration at right.

Note that the words "Current Weather Conditions" appear as bold, red text. The <B> tag represents bold text and the "#CC0000" in the <FONT COLOR = "#CC0000"> code represents a hexadecimal red color. *Hexadecimal* colors are chosen according to a system used for the Web in which colors are identified by an alphanumeric numbering system. For a reference chart that lists all hexadecimal colors, check out www.htmlhelpcentral.com/hexcolors.html.

Flash 8
Professional

Apply Filters to Text in Flash Professional

Flash 8 Professional allows you to assign filters to text. Filters are ready-made effects that include Drop Shadow, Blur, Bevel, Gradient Glow, Gradient Bevel, and Adjust Color. Once you apply a filter to text, you can adjust the properties of the filter in the Filters tab in the Properties Inspector. The following is a word with a Gradient Bevel Glow applied on the outer area of the object.

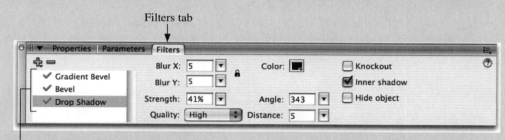

You can apply multiple filters to a text block or selected text within the text block. If you use a specific filter setting often, you can save it as a preset from the Preset selection in the Add Filter pop-up menu. To apply a filter to text, select the text and then click the Filters tab in the Properties Inspector. Click the plus (+) icon and select one of the filters, as shown next.

Filters tab

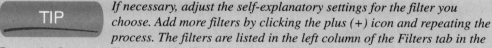

Multiple filters added to a text block

> **TIP**   *If necessary, adjust the self-explanatory settings for the filter you choose. Add more filters by clicking the plus (+) icon and repeating the process. The filters are listed in the left column of the Filters tab in the Properties Inspector. You can reshuffle the order of filters by clicking a filter in the list and moving it up or down. Changing the stacking order of filters will change the effect on the selected text. To remove a filter, click the filter in the list and then click the minus (–) icon.*

To export this text file as an SWF file, select File | Export | Export Movie from the menu. In the Export Movie dialog box, for File Name, type in a name for your exported file and navigate to the location where you want the file saved. When you're done, click the Save button, and there you have your finished file.

NOTE

If you plan on putting this file on the Web, you must upload the SWF file along with the text file that loads into the dynamic text field. In addition, both files must reside in the same folder (just as they must when you build the movie) in order to function properly.

You can see how easy it is to update a dynamic text field by just going in and revising the variable text that loads into it. This exercise is very basic, but you can take this concept and use it as a recipe to build other dynamic text fields.

Conclusion

You learned a lot about text in Flash. Specifically, the three types of text that can be made in Flash were covered: static, input, and dynamic text. The spell checker was examined, as were variables and the process of loading rich text into a dynamic text field.

In the next chapter, the focus is on the numerous ways you can modify and transform text and graphics once you create them. You've learned a few techniques for modifying graphics and text, but there's still a lot more to learn about modifying in Flash.

Chapter 5

Manipulate Graphics and Text

How to...

- Change the look of merged drawing objects
- Control graphics
- Group merged drawing objects
- Edit merged and object drawing objects
- Control the stacking order of object drawing objects
- Apply transformations to objects
- Arrange objects on the stage
- Keep track of elements
- Apply colors and gradients to graphics and text
- Use the Fill Transform and the Lock Fill tools

Creating basic objects and text is easy in Flash, as you have learned in Chapters 1 and 2. Beyond knowing how to make these elements, your movie will require many modifications before it's cooked to perfection. Because of this, you need to know all about the tricks available to you for manipulating and changing graphics and text in Flash.

There are many different ways you can modify the compelling images you create in Flash. The tools used to modify graphics and text can be accessed in several different ways, such as via the Toolbar, the Properties Inspector, and the oh-so-simple shortcut keys. The way you access the transformation tools is largely a matter of personal preference.

In the next section you will learn a little bit more about manipulating different drawing models. Once you become accustomed to working with them, you will feel confident working with these drawing models.

Control Graphics in Flash

As discussed in the previous chapter, merged drawing objects in Flash behave a little differently than drawing objects. If you are creating shapes in the merged drawing mode, it may seem to the beginner as if you don't have much control over the shapes you are creating. This section examines the anatomy of both the merged and drawing object modes. There are circumstances when one model may suit you better than the other. You need to be aware of the various strengths and weaknesses of these models in order to make that determination.

Understand Merged Objects

The default drawing mode in Flash is the merged drawing. A merged drawing shape can be identified by the distinct screen pattern that appears when it is selected with the Selection tool.

Let's consider the interaction of two or more merged drawing shapes on a single layer. When two merged drawing shapes of the same color are overlapped, Flash combines them into a single shape, as shown here. This kind of behavior between objects is more typical of a paint program than a drawing program. In a paint program, overlapping shapes drawn on the same layer would connect in the same manner. This explains why these kinds of drawings are referred to as "merged."

When two shapes of differing colors are overlapped on the same layer, then deselected and selected again, you will find this results in the creation of multiple shapes in the first shape drawn (bottom shape) that are delineated by adjacent colors. Similar to a paint program, the different color shapes are now identified as separate objects.

Two overlapping merged drawing shapes

Bottom shape breaks into multiple separate shapes

What's more, if you move one of these new shapes, you will find that the top shape will cut a piece out of the bottom shape. For example, if you place a gray circle halfway over a black circle, deselect by clicking somewhere in the stage (not an object), and then click the black circle and move it to the right, it cuts a hole out of the black circle so it resembles a crescent moon, as shown here.

You can use the merged drawing behavior to your advantage for certain effects—for example, if you want to create an animation and have one shape morph into another, as discussed in Chapter 11. For other projects you will find merged drawing behavior more annoying than useful. You can also group a merged drawing, which essentially transforms the shape into an object drawing, where the objects can then be stacked on top of one another and behave as if created in a drawing (vector) program. The only reason you may want to group merged drawings is if you created complex shapes and you then decided to make them behave like drawing objects instead. However, if you do this, keep in mind that grouped objects are not as easy to edit as merged or drawing objects. In order to make a simple edit like change the fill or stroke of a grouped object, you have to enter a special editing mode. Editing grouped objects is explained in the next section.

Once you group merged drawing objects, you can easily move them around, stack them on top of one another on the same layer, and transform them. You can also group drawing objects and symbols. Drawing objects are explained later in this chapter and symbols are covered in Chapter 13. Now that you understand merged drawing, you'll examine the "how-tos" of grouping any kind of objects, whether they are merged, drawing, buttons, or movie clips.

 *Symbols in Flash are objects that have been created on their own timeline. These include graphic symbols, buttons, and movie clips. Copies of symbols, also known as* instances, *can be used multiple times in the same movie without increasing the file size. Buttons can be interactive and scripts can be applied to movie clips. Symbols are very powerful elements in Flash and, as mentioned earlier, they are discussed in detail in Chapter 13.*

Group Shapes in Flash

Grouping elements in Flash is one way to move them around the stage, stack objects on top of one another, and perform additional modifications in a single-layer environment. When you group elements in Flash, you can manipulate them as one entity. Drawing and desktop publishing programs offer the ability to group objects, so if you are accustomed to working in a program such as this, grouping objects will be a familiar task.

It is quite easy to group merged and drawing object shapes into a single object in Flash. To make a group out of a single editable shape, first click the shape that makes up your graphic. Then select Modify | Group or press CTRL-G in Windows/CMD-G on the Mac to group it.

To select more than one shape for the group, SHIFT-click each object to select all of them, then select Modify | Group as outlined previously.

Alternately, you can select multiple shapes on the stage by clicking and dragging a marquee selection in the shape of a rectangle around the items, then selecting Modify | Group as outlined previously (see Figure 5-1). The marquee selection displays a guide box as you drag your pointer so you can see the shapes included in the selection. This technique can also be used to group movie clips and buttons.

Grouping Objects Versus Movie Clips

Although the ability to group merged and drawing objects seems a convenient feature for more complicated graphic compositions, using movie clips also allows you to contain multiple objects in a "group" of sorts. When you become a more experienced Flash user, you will find that, for many reasons, movie clips are more useful for grouping objects than using the Group command. For example, movie clips are reusable "assets" in Flash. *Assets* are the elements you use to build your movie. Additionally, movie clips are compact and help create smaller file sizes. Complex movie clips are easier to edit than grouped objects, and they can be interactive. There are many more reasons why movie clips are preferable over grouped objects, all of which are discussed in Chapter 13. But you will undoubtedly need to group objects sometime while working in Flash, and learning to group objects serves as a good springboard for understanding more advanced object control in Flash.

FIGURE 5-1   A marquee selection around several merged drawing objects

5

To select several shapes with a marquee:

1. Click the Selection tool.

2. Think of the objects you are about to select as being contained within a rectangle. With this in mind, position the pointer in one of the rectangle's corners.

3. Click and drag a marquee rectangle to define the boundaries of the selection.

4. When you release the mouse, the objects are selected, as indicated by the screen over the objects. This illustration of a globe shows a selected group of multiple objects.

To deselect one or more objects within the selection, hold down SHIFT and click the object(s). To add an object to the selection, with SHIFT pressed, click another object. Likewise, you can also selectively SHIFT-click objects that are not in close proximity to one another to select them.

Once you've made your selection, you can then group these objects using the same method you did for a single object (Modify | Group or CTRL-G in Windows/CMD-G on the Mac).

After the graphic is grouped, a blue frame, representing a bounding box, appears around the object, as shown in this illustration. Note the bounding box around a grouped merged drawing object appears identical to the blue bounding box around a drawing object.

Now the graphic is a separate entity that can be stacked above or below other grouped objects on the same layer, as shown here.

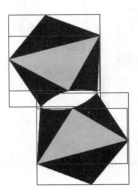

 *To tell the difference between grouped objects and a single drawing object, select the object and look in the Properties Inspector. There, it will indicate the type of object you are selecting.*

Ungroup Objects

To ungroup an object or objects, click the grouped object(s) and go to the menu. Select Modify | Ungroup or press CTRL-SHIFT-G in Windows/CMD-SHIFT-G on the Mac. Once the graphic is ungrouped, it will return to its original state.

Nest Objects

A *nest* brings to mind a bunch of baby birds chirping for their mother in the comfort of their home. Nested groups don't exactly contain baby birds, but they are safely contained within one another. A *nested group* is a group contained within another group, the groups existing on different levels in Flash.

To make a nested group, select one or more groups of objects and make another group out of them. Your groups can be arranged in any hierarchy you like, and you can nest as many groups as you want, but you should plan and organize the groups in a logical manner.

What is the value of nesting groups? If your graphic is complex and contains a lot of pieces, it's easier to edit the pieces later if they are contained in groups. What's more, if objects require similar adjustments, it's easier to perform these modifications on a group instead of individually. Remember, however, that when you become more experienced using Flash, you will discover that you can also nest objects inside one another by making objects into movie clips. Movie clips are little movies within your movie. You can have as many nested inside of one another as you like. Movie clips can also include merged and object drawings. There may also be occasions when you need to nest group objects within your movie clips. As such, nested groups are an important concept to understand in Flash.

Edit Grouped Objects

If you try to click a grouped object to change the color of the individual shapes inside of it, it won't work. A group has to be in an editable state before you can change its color.

Your grouped object is like a department store that contains various levels. Nested groups contain even more levels than a single group. One of these levels is known as the *root level*, which includes the main timeline. Another is the level for the editing mode for the current group.

You can get to the various levels by "taking the elevator" to the correct level. Your grouped object doesn't have the convenience of an elevator, of course, but you can travel from level to level to edit your object with a click of your mouse in the right place.

You can enter the editing mode for a single grouped object in one of two ways:

- ■ Double-click the object.
- ■ Select the object and choose Edit | Edit Selected from the menu.

You are now at the group editing mode level. The stage looks a little different in this mode. The status bar above the timeline indicates the mode you are in with a graphic icon and the name "Group" to the right of the Scene icon, as shown in this illustration. For nested objects, the status bar also indicates the position of the level you are on within the hierarchy of the group. In the illustration, the Group icon is one below Scene 1 as indicated in its descending order to the right of Scene 1.

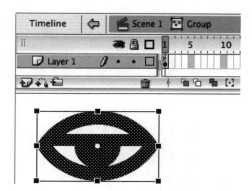

When your graphic is in editing mode, you can apply additional modifications such as changing the shape of the editable object. When you're done editing, you can exit editing mode in one of four ways:

- ■ Click the scene name in the status bar to return to the root (main) level.
- ■ Click the left (back) arrow at the top of the window (next to the status bar) to return one level at a time back to the root (main) level.
- ■ Select Edit | Edit All from the menu. This returns the object to its grouped state.
- ■ Double-click the editing stage.

Once you return to the root level, you can see that the object is again grouped and the changes you made in editing mode have been applied.

Edit Nested Groups

You can also edit groups nested within one another using the method just discussed. When you enter the editing mode of a nested group, you must continue to double-click the object to navigate to groups nested deeply.

The hierarchy of your nesting is indicated in the status bar. Each time a level within the group is uncovered, another Group icon appears next to the previous one, as shown in Figure 5-2. In this figure, the group being edited is nested three levels from the main, or root, level (Scene 1). Note also that as you navigate through the levels, the graphics on the stage become dimmed, except for the graphics on the current level.

To navigate back to another group within the nest, click the arrow in the status bar or click the group level you want to navigate to. To return to the main (root) level, click the Scene 1 icon to the left of the status bar.

You can ungroup a nested group by applying the Ungroup command (Modify | Ungroup, or CTRL-SHIFT-G in Windows/CMD-SHIFT-G on the Mac) to each group in the level hierarchy.

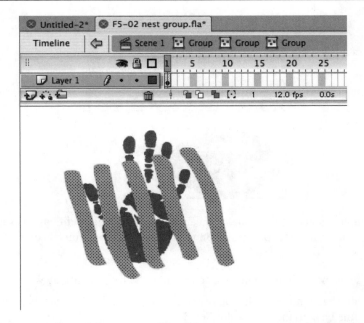

FIGURE 5-2   Nested groups on the stage assume a level hierarchy, as indicated in the status bar.

Break Apart Graphics and Text

Breaking objects apart separates the objects into editable objects or merged drawing objects. For example, if you wanted to modify the color of a merged drawing object in a grouped graphic, you could break it apart to do so. So, in this sense, the Break Apart command would be used in the same way you would use the Ungroup command, which would also break the grouped object down into an editable graphic. The Break Apart command works with merged and object drawings, movie clips, buttons, graphic symbols, and even imported bitmaps. Because you can ungroup graphics easily to make them editable, the Break Apart command is generally used only for text and bitmaps.

You can break apart text and objects by clicking the object and selecting Modify | Break Apart or CTRL-B in Windows/CMD-B on the Mac. In this illustration, the Break Apart command is being selected from the Modify menu.

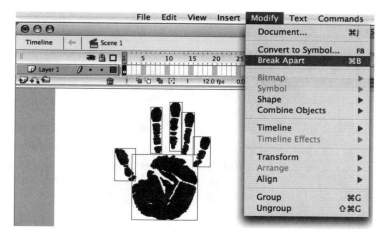

With text and with nested grouped objects, you'll need to select the Break Apart command as many times as it takes to make the entire object editable. For example, if an object is nested in a group, the first time you use the Break Apart command, it ungroups the object from the nest; the next time you use the Break Apart command, it breaks it apart.

As mentioned previously, imported bitmap pictures can be broken apart, too. Flash provides some fun tools to manipulate a broken-apart bitmap. These will be covered in Chapter 6, where importing bitmaps is discussed in detail.

Change the Stacking Order of Objects

As mentioned earlier, drawing objects, grouped objects, and symbols can be selected individually and stacked on top of one another on a single layer, just as in all drawing/vector-based programs.

If drawing objects, grouped objects, and symbols (movie clips, buttons, or graphic symbols, which are discussed in Chapters 8 and 13) are capable of having a stacking order, the next question is, Which object gets the top position? The answer is actually quite logical. The stacking order is determined by the last element that was created on the Flash stage. The first element created takes the position behind subsequent elements. If you were to create a grouped rectangle as an element on the stage, then create another drawing object, grouped object, or symbol on the stage and position the second element on top of the first, the first element would be hidden by the second element. This is the natural stacking order of grouped elements in Flash. Figure 5-3 shows two drawing objects, stacked one of top of the other and vice versa.

You can easily change the stacking order of drawing objects, grouped objects, or symbols in a single-layer Flash document. To change the stacking order of one object in relation to another, select one of the objects. In the menu, select Modify | Arrange | Send to Back or press CTRL-SHIFT-DOWN ARROW (Windows)/CMD-SHIFT-DOWN ARROW (Mac). This brings a graphic element all the way to the back in the stacking order on the layer.

Selecting Modify | Arrange | Bring to Front or pressing CTRL-SHIFT-UP ARROW (Windows)/OPTION-SHIFT-UP ARROW (Mac) places the selected graphic element at the top of the stacking order, as shown here.

NOTE   *When you draw a merged drawing shape without grouping it and it overlaps an object drawing, symbol, or grouped object, the merged drawing shape will always assume the bottom place on the stacking level until it is made into a symbol or grouped.*

To move the stacking position of your object drawing, symbol, or grouped object up or down one level, instead of all the way to the back or all the way to the front, select Modify | Arrange | Bring Forward (CTRL-UP ARROW in Windows/CMD-UP ARROW on the Mac) or select Modify |

FIGURE 5-3   A single-layer drawing with drawing objects stacked on top of one another

Arrange | Send Backward (CTRL-DOWN ARROW in Windows/CMD-DOWN ARROW on the Mac). This works well if a single-layer design requires multiple stacking, as is often the case with designs of medium to difficult complexity.

When an experienced Flash designer tackles a complex movie with a lot of graphic elements, he or she will often create all the ancillary parts of the drawing as symbols (movie clips, buttons, and graphic symbols). This makes all the pieces more modular and easy to organize. Symbols, like groups, stack easily and are simple to edit. Chapters 8 and 13 cover symbols in more detail.

Transform Graphics and Text

There are many ways to transform graphics in Flash. You can scale and rotate them to change their size and angle. You also can skew a graphic if you want to distort its perspective, or flip it for a mirror effect. For the most part, text can be transformed in the same way that graphics can. Both merged and drawing objects can be transformed as well as grouped graphics and symbols.

There are three different ways you can perform basic transformations in Flash. You can use the menu, the Transform panel, or the Free Transform tool in the Toolbar. The Free Transform tool is a very intuitive tool, as you will see next.

Change Objects with the Free Transform Tool

The Free Transform tool, shown at right, is located in the Toolbar, directly under the Pencil tool. This tool enables you to scale, rotate, and skew objects. First, we'll take a look at how to scale with this tool.

Use the Free Transform Tool to Scale an Object

The Scale command is used to reduce or increase the size of an object. To scale an object, do the following:

1. Click the Free Transform tool in the Toolbar, then select the object to be scaled. Eight transform handles surround the object.

2. The Options section of the Toolbar offers modifiers for the Free Transform tool. Click the Scale icon, as shown here.

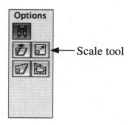
Scale tool

3. To scale the width and the height of the object, position your pointer over one of the handles in the four corners of the bounding box. The pointer turns into a diagonal double-headed arrow. This is the Scale icon.

4. Click and drag inward to reduce the width and height. Drag outward to increase the width and height of the object. A preview outline appears around the object to help you determine the size, as shown here.

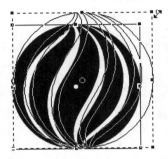

5. When you are done, click off the object or select another tool.

To constrain the width and height of the object in proportion to one another, hold down SHIFT while dragging the handle.

To scale only the width of an object with the Free Transform tool, repeat the previous steps but position your pointer over the middle-left or the middle-right handle. Note that the handle

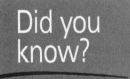

Transform Without the Aid of Modifiers

You can also scale an object with the Free Transform tool without selecting the Scale modifier in the Options section of the Toolbar. In fact, you can scale, rotate, and skew by positioning your pointer either on, or in the vicinity of, a transform handle. To transform an object without choosing any of the modifiers, click the Free Transform tool and then select the object. Position your pointer on any of the handles. When the proper pointer icon for a particular modifier appears (double-headed arrows for scaling, a circular arrow for rotation, and double-headed half arrowheads for skewing), click and drag accordingly. You already know all about the scaling tool. In the next two sections that follow, you'll learn about how to rotate and skew an object.

For beginners, it's easier to select the modifier associated with the transformation you want to perform in the Options section prior to applying the transformation. When you select a modifier, only that transform tool will be available when you click and drag the handle. For example, if you choose the Scale modifier, the Free Transform tool will only scale. If you're not familiar with the pointer icons associated with a particular transformation, it's easier to select a modifier first.

will turn into a horizontal double-headed arrow. Click and drag the handle to the desired width, as shown here.

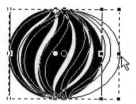

To scale only the height of an object with the Free Transform tool, repeat the previous steps, but position your pointer over the middle-top or middle-bottom handle on the object. The handle will turn into a vertical double-headed arrow. Click and drag the handle up or down to increase or decrease the height of the object.

To remove any transformation, select Modify | Transform | Remove Transform or press CTRL-SHIFT-Z (Windows)/SHIFT-CMD-Z (Mac).

Rotate with the Free Transform Tool

You can also rotate with the Free Transform tool. To do so, follow these steps:

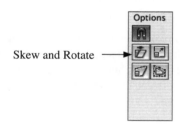

Skew and Rotate

1. Click the Free Transform tool and then select the object to be rotated.

2. In the Options section of the Toolbar, click the Rotate And Skew modifier icon.

3. Position the pointer on one of the four corner handles on the object. An elliptical arrow icon appears, as shown here.

4. Click and drag the icon to rotate the object. When you are done, click off the object or select another tool.

5

To constrain the rotation of an object to 45-degree increments, hold down SHIFT while dragging one of the corner handles.

If you are a menu lover, you can also access the Free Transform tools from the menu under Modify | Transform. In the top section of the menu, you can select Free Transform, Distort, Envelope, Scale, and Rotate And Skew. Selecting any one of these options will activate the Free Transform tool and the modifier associated with it.

Skew with the Free Transform Tool

When you skew an object, it becomes slanted along a single axis. Skewing can give a 3-D look to a 2-D object, as shown here.

To skew a grouped or editable object with the Free Transform tool:

1. Select the Free Transform tool in the Toolbar and then click the object.
2. In the Options section of the Toolbar, click the Rotate And Skew tool.
3. Position your pointer over any of the middle handles surrounding the object. The pointer turns into a double line with arrowheads on opposite sides. If you choose a bottom- or top-middle handle, the double line is horizontal, indicating that dragging this line will skew the object horizontally. If you choose a left- or right-middle handle, the object will skew vertically, as shown here.

4. Click and drag the selected handle to perform the skew. When you are done, click off the object or select another tool.

How to ... Create a Drop Shadow Effect with Depth

You can use the skew modifier to create many interesting effects that are limited only by your imagination. In this mini-exercise, you'll learn how to give a word a "quasi-3-D" drop shadow effect using the skew modifier. First, you need to create a word. Here are the steps you can take to create such an effect:

1. Select the Text tool and in the Properties Inspector, select the Arial Black font, with a size of 60 points and a color of black. Arial Black is a good font for type effects, since it is thick and bold and is devoid of serif flourishes.

2. Type a short word on the stage. This word will become the drop shadow for the duplicate word.

3. Click the Selection tool and then click the word. Now you'll duplicate the word. The duplicate becomes the main word, and the original will be the drop shadow. **word word**
To duplicate, press and hold CTRL (Windows)/OPT (Mac) and then click the word and drag it to the right of the first word, as shown here.

The duplicate word assumes the top stacking order when these words are put on top of one another. Next, you'll change the color of the first (drop shadow) word so that you'll be able to distinguish it from the top word.

1. Double-click the word to the left (the original) and change the color to a light gray.

2. Now, you will skew the gray word so that it looks like a drop shadow. To skew the word, you need to decide approximately where the light source that creates the drop shadow is located. For this exercise, you'll assume that the light source is shining from the top front of the object. Click the Free Transform tool and in the Options section of the Toolbar, click the Rotate And Skew tool. Click the gray word and select the top-middle handle. Drag the handle to the left so the result looks like the following illustration.

3. Drag the drop shadow so it sits exactly underneath the top word, as shown here. To make the effect appear a little more realistic, you can skew both words a little so it appears as if the top word is positioned at an angle. You'll do this next.

4. Select both words and then click the Free Transform tool. In the Options section, click the Rotate And Skew tool once again. Click the right-middle transform handle of your selection and drag it upward about a half an inch. The word and the drop shadow now appear to possess a little bit of depth because they reside on a slight angle, as shown here.

5. To give the drop shadow a softer, more realistic look, you can blur the edges of the shadow with the Soften Fill Edges command. Before you apply the Soften Fill Edges command to the drop shadow, you must make the word editable. Once it is, you can no longer edit the text. You can make text editable by breaking it apart, which you'll do next.

6. Click the drop shadow word with the Selection tool and then press CTRL-B (Windows)/CMD-B (Mac) two times to make the drop shadow editable.

7. With the drop shadow still selected, choose Modify | Shape | Soften Fill Edges. In the Soften Fill Edges dialog box, shown here, you can customize the way the soft edges will look.

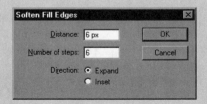

8. Type in **6** for both Distance and Number Of Steps. For Direction, select Expand to expand the soft fill beyond its current borders. Click OK. The result is a soft drop shadow that appears to be cast by the top word, as shown in this illustration.

You may want to go back and experiment with different settings in the Soften Fill Edges dialog box. You can undo your previous steps by pressing CTRL-Z (Windows)/CMD-Z (Mac). If you go back one too many steps, press CTRL-Y (Windows)/CMD-Y (Mac) to undo your last undo. Another option is to use the History panel to return to previous states and go forward from there. The History panel is discussed later in this chapter in the section "Track Your Steps with the History Panel."

Flash 8
Professional

Drop Shadow Filter in Flash 8 Professional

As discussed in the last chapter, drop shadows are one of the filters that can be applied to movie clips and button symbols as well as text. Filters are effects such as drop shadows, blurs, and bevels that can be applied to text, movie clips, and button symbols at the click of a button. The drop shadow filter becomes available in the Filters tab in the Properties Inspector when you select text, movie clips, or button symbols on the stage. The properties you can adjust on a drop shadow are limited to color, opacity, angle, quality, blur, inner shadow, and distance from the selected object. To customize a drop shadow, you can either add multiple filters to the object (Glow, Bevel, Gradient Glow, Gradient Bevel) on top of the drop shadow filter, or you can make your own drop shadow using a technique similar to that explained in "Create a Drop Shadow Effect with Depth" earlier in this chapter.

Distort Using the Free Transform Tool

You may have noticed that when editable objects are selected with the Free Transform tool, additional modifiers become available in the Options section of the Toolbar.

One of the additional options is the Distort modifier. This modifier allows you to pull the corner transform handles to distort an editable shape. You can use this to give a 2-D object a sense of depth, or you can use it to create fresh, new shapes out of old, run-of-the-mill geometric staples. Here's how to distort an editable object:

1. Click the Free Transform tool and select the editable shape.

2. In the Options section of the Toolbar, select the Distort modifier, as shown here.

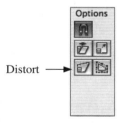

3. Position your pointer over one of the corner transform handles surrounding the object. The pointer turns into a white selection arrow. Click and drag the handle to distort the shape, as shown here.

4. To distort more corners or edit distortions, repeat the process of dragging the handles. As you can see in the illustration at right, you can suggest a sense of depth for a flat object by using this tool.

You can also distort an object by selecting the command in the menu, Modify | Transform | Distort.

Use the Free Transform Tool's Envelope Modifier

The Envelope modifier, shown here, is another option available for transforming editable objects when the Free Transform tool is selected.

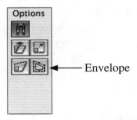

The Envelope modifier places numerous points with curve handles in between line segments. The points and curves can be moved and dragged to create cool warp, wave, bloat, and arch effects, as in this illustration.

To use the Envelope modifier on an editable object, do the following:

1. Click the Free Transform tool and then click the object.

2. In the Options section, click the Envelope tool. Note the numerous points that now surround the object.

3. Click and drag any of the points to create the effects mentioned previously. When you do this, handles appear on the points, as you can see in this illustration. The handles can be manipulated as Bézier curve handles.

You can also activate the Envelope modifier from the menu by selecting Modify | Transform | Envelope.

Use the Transform Panel to Transform Objects

The Transform panel is another tool that can be used to scale, rotate, and skew editable objects, grouped objects, and symbols. The Transform panel works differently than the Free Transform tool does. When you scale, rotate, or skew with the Transform panel, you type numeric values into the panel. Also, the Distort and Envelope modifiers are not available. The Free Transform tool is used more for freeform transformations (as the name implies) and doesn't lend itself to precise percentages.

To access the Transform panel, select Window | Design Panels | Transform or press CTRL-T (Windows)/CMD-T (Mac).

To scale an object in this panel, select an object and type in a new width and height. Note that the default width and height is 100 percent, as shown in Figure 5-4. To constrain the width and height of the object, click the Constrain box. Constraining adjusts the scale percentage of the width and height to be the same amount.

To rotate or to skew horizontally or vertically on an object, type in the amount you want to rotate or skew in degrees.

To apply your transformation, press ENTER (Windows)/RETURN (Mac). Pressing the Reset button resets the object back to its original settings. The Copy and Apply Transformation button makes a copy of the transformed object on top of the original.

Use the Properties Inspector to Transform the Size of an Object

Although you can't scale an object using numeric percentages from the Properties Inspector, you can change the width and height of an object. This method works wonderfully when you want to size an object to exact proportions.

To use the Properties Inspector in this way, select the object. Then, in the Properties Inspector, type in a new width and height. The graphic now assumes the new dimensions you typed in. The scaling area of the Properties Inspector is shown here.

W: 41.0
H: 41.0

To constrain the scaling so that the width changes in proportion to the height or vice versa, click the Lock icon. The Lock icon now appears to be "locked." To turn off the constraint, click the Lock icon again. The Lock icon will appear unlocked, and the lines that connect the height and width boxes disappear.

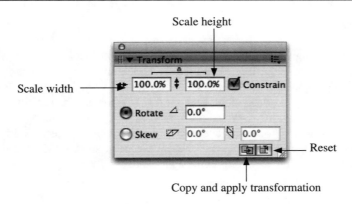

Scale height

Scale width

Reset

Copy and apply transformation

FIGURE 5-4   The Transform panel is used to transform numeric values.

Transform Objects from the Menu

There are four transformations listed in the Modify | Transform menu that are not available anywhere else in Flash. As such, they are worthy of mention. These include a couple of rotation transformations and a very cool command that enables you to flip an object.

The two rotation-related options exclusive to the menu are Rotate 90° CW (CTRL-SHIFT-9 in Windows/CMD-SHIFT-9 on the Mac), which rotates the object 90 degrees clockwise; and Rotate 90° CCW (CTRL-SHIFT-7 in Windows/CMD-SHIFT-7 on the Mac), which rotates the object 90 degrees counterclockwise.

Before Rotate 90 degrees CW applied ———>  <—— After

You use these tools by clicking the object to be rotated and selecting the desired transformation from the menu.

You can undo a rotation by clicking the object and choosing Modify | Transform | Remove Transform (CTRL-SHIFT-Z in Windows/CMD-SHIFT-Z on the Mac). This command completely removes the transformation and returns the object back to its original state before any transformations were applied. Alternately, the Edit | Undo command (CTRL-Z in Windows/CMD-Z on the Mac) undoes your last move. Selecting Edit | Undo multiple times will undo each step, one by one, up to 99 steps.

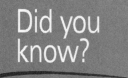

Lock and Unlock Objects

On a single-layer drawing with many components and multiple stacking orders, you may want to lock an object into place so you don't accidentally move or change it while modifying other objects around it. This can be done with any grouped elements or symbols.

To lock a grouped object or a symbol, select it from the menu. Then select Modify | Arrange | Lock or press CTRL-ALT-L (Windows)/CMD-OPTION-L (Mac). The object will be visible but you will be unable to manipulate it. To unlock the object, select Modify | Arrange | Unlock All or press CTRL-ALT-SHIFT-L (Windows)/CMD-OPTION-SHIFT-L (Mac). This unlocks all the elements on the stage that were previously locked.

You also can flip a graphic horizontally or vertically to create a mirror effect. The flip transformation options can be found in the menu under Modify | Transform | Flip Horizontal or Flip Vertical.

You can use the flip commands to create a mirror replication of an image. In this illustration, the hand was duplicated. To flip the object, Flip Horizontal was applied.

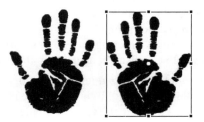

Arrange Objects on the Stage

When you're creating a Flash movie with many objects on the stage, arranging the objects precisely becomes an important issue. If your stage layout demands balance and it's cluttered with many objects, you can use several Flash options to help you make your layout appear more orderly.

You can align and distribute objects in relation to one another and the stage using the Align panel, as shown in Figure 5-5. You display the Align panel by selecting Window | Design Panels | Align.

In addition to standard alignment features in the panel, the size, height, and width of two or more objects can be matched. You also can space objects evenly on a horizontal plane and/or a vertical plane.

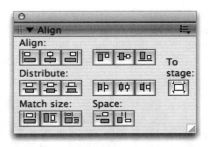

FIGURE 5-5   Use the Align panel to align two or more objects.

Aligned and distributed objects can be aligned and distributed to the actual stage if you click the To Stage button. Within this panel, every possible scenario for alignment of two or more objects exists. The alignment options in the panel are represented as icons that are easy to interpret. The following are the elements of the Align panel:

- **Align**   From left to right, the six options are Left Edge, Horizontal Center, Right Edge, Top Edge, Vertical Center, and Bottom Edge. The Align options align two or more selected objects (grouped objects or symbols) according to the alignment icon you selected. Aligning objects arranges them up on a central baseline. The position of the object in relation to the baseline is visually depicted in the panel.

- **Distribute**   From left to right, the six options are Top Edge, Vertical Center, Bottom Edge, Left Edge, Horizontal Center, and Right Edge. The Distribute options space evenly two or more selected objects (grouped objects or symbols).

- **Match Size**   From left to right, the three options are Match Width, Match Height, and Match Width and Height. The Match Size options match the dimensions of two or more selected objects (grouped graphics or symbols). These options will make the height (or width) of all selected objects match the height of the tallest object (or the width of the widest object).

- **Space**   From left to right, the two options are Space Evenly Vertically and Space Evenly Horizontally. The Space options space evenly, either horizontally or vertically, two or more selected objects (grouped graphics or symbols).

- **To Stage**   This button enables you to use the alignment features in conjunction with the stage as a whole. When this icon is selected, objects can be aligned in relation to the stage, as well as to one another.

To use the options in the Align panel, first select the objects and then click the appropriate icon(s) in the panel.

Figure 5-6 illustrates six individually grouped objects with two different alignment features applied. Align Vertical Center was selected from among the Align options. For Distribute, Distribute Horizontal Center was selected.

In Figure 5-7, the same selected objects now have the Match Height and Width option in the Match Size section applied to them. Note that the heights and widths of all selected objects are now identical.

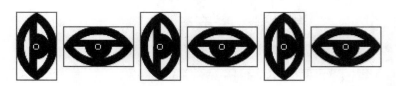

FIGURE 5-6   Objects aligned and distributed evenly

FIGURE 5-7   The height of the tallest object and the width of the widest are matched to all objects.

5

You can use the Align panel instead of the Snap To Grid and Snap To Guides features to align several selected objects. Personal preference will dictate which method will be more effective for your project.

Keep Track of Objects

Flash movies can become very large and complex. This, coupled with the fact that your movie architecture may contain many levels of nested groups and symbols, means that you sometimes need assistance navigating through the movie structure. Fortunately, Flash comes equipped with many tools to assist you in getting information about elements and finding them, too.

In Chapter 2 you explored the Properties Inspector, which provides information on selected elements and allows you to edit them. Another helpful tool for getting information about elements is the Info panel. The Info panel is a floating panel that displays information about objects currently selected. You can also dock the Info panel to other panels in the work area.

The Movie Explorer is sometimes useful for getting information about your movie, among other things. It provides you with a synopsis of the structure of your Flash movie, giving you a detailed overview of all the movie's components, including frames, symbols, levels of symbols, and so forth. The Info panel provides information on currently selected objects, whereas the Movie Explorer window gives you the blueprints of the bigger picture.

Use the Info Panel

Use the Info panel by clicking an object and selecting Window | Info or pressing CTRL-I in Windows/CMD-I on the Mac. This illustration shows the Info panel for the selected graphic.

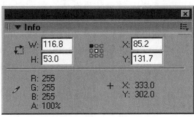

The Info panel displays the width, height, x and y coordinates, RGB values, and Alpha percentage of the selected object. Just as in the Properties Inspector, you can find out the exact location (x and y coordinates) of a selected object on stage.

The reference point icon in the middle of the top half of this panel allows you to reference the xy coordinates from either the upper-left corner or the center of an object. You can also modify the properties of a selected object right in the Info panel. To do this, type the new data in the appropriate box. For example, if you want to change the width and height of a selected object, just type a new value in both the width box and the height box.

The RGB setting indicates the proportions of RGB colors of a selected, editable graphic. Because there can be multiple colors in a selected object, the RGB values and the Alpha percentage reflect the colors and transparency of the graphic over which the pointer is currently positioned.

The Alpha percentage indicates the level of transparency that's applied to the graphic. A setting of 100 percent is an opaque color and 0 percent is the absence of color (transparent). RGB and Alpha data are available only on editable objects.

Get Movie Information from the Movie Explorer

The Movie Explorer panel gives you a complete description of the components that make up your movie, including objects, symbols, layers, frames, actions, sounds on different timelines, and more (see Figure 5-8).

When your movies become complex with multiple layers, frames, movie clips, scenes, and actions, the Movie Explorer keeps a running track of the components of the movie as you build it. Sometimes, you may know there is an object or a script hidden somewhere in the movie and you just can't find it. That's when you want to turn to the Movie Explorer.

It also can help you find and modify elements in the movie. This is particularly important when multiple users are building the same movie. On large Flash productions, teams of people often work on different chunks of the same movie at different stages. One person can track the work of another with the aid of the Movie Explorer. It's even difficult to dissect components of your own movie when it becomes very involved. The Movie Explorer can sometimes help bring the project back into focus for you.

Display the Movie Explorer by selecting Window | Movie Explorer or pressing ALT-F3 (Windows)/OPTION-F3 (Mac). The window displays a collapsible hierarchy of all elements and events that are part of the current movie. Each time you change the movie, the Movie Explorer window is updated to include new additions.

Elements are arranged in a folderlike hierarchy with scenes, layers, symbol definitions, and other titles acting as containers to organize elements in the movie. Plus and minus signs reside next to each container, enabling you to expand and collapse the container's contents. A plus sign indicates that the container has elements in it, whereas a minus sign indicates an empty container.

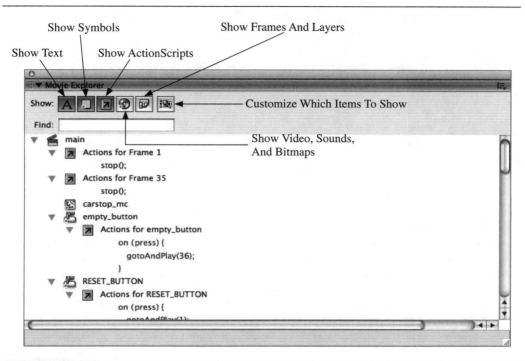

FIGURE 5-8   The Movie Explorer maps out the structure of the movie.

On the top of the Movie Explorer, you can choose to view only specified elements in the movie hierarchy. The icons are, from left to right:

- Show Text
- Show Symbols
- Show ActionScripts
- Show Video, Sounds, And Bitmaps
- Show Frames And Layers
- Customize Which Items To Show

The last selection, Customize Which Items To Show, enables you to customize your display to include only those elements that you are interested in monitoring. When you choose this selection, the following dialog box appears:

Movie Explorer Settings

Show

- ☑ Text   ☑ ActionScript   ☐ Layers
- ☑ Buttons   ☐ Bitmaps   ☐ Frames
- ☑ Movie clips ☑ Graphics
- ☐ Video   ☐ Sounds

Context

- ☑ Movie elements   ☐ Symbol definitions

OK

Cancel

If you know the name of an element, you can find text, ActionScripts, video, sounds, bitmaps, frames, and layers by entering the name of the item in the Find field of the Movie Explorer box. The Movie Explorer will go to that item in the Movie Explorer list.

You can also edit elements of your movie right from the Movie Explorer by double-clicking the entry in the Movie Explorer. For example, if you need to edit text on any level in your movie, you can do so directly in the Movie Explorer window. Click the Show Text icon in the Movie Explorer (see Figure 5-8, earlier in this chapter) and all the lines of text in the movie will appear in the Explorer panel. To edit text in the movie from the Movie Explorer panel, simply highlight the text in the panel, type in the revision, and it will be reflected in the movie.

When you become more experienced and your movies get more complex, try out the Movie Explorer.

Track Your Steps with the History Panel

The History panel allows you to undo and redo steps on open Flash documents. It contains additional features beyond the standard Undo and Redo commands. In this panel you can undo

Number of Undo and Redo Steps

The Undo and Redo commands share some characteristics with the History panel. For example, the Undo command and the History panel both have a default number of undo and redo steps, which is set to 100. You can modify this in the Preferences window (Edit | Preferences | General in Windows/Flash 2004 | Preferences | General on the Mac) and change this number to as many as 9,999 steps.

You should be aware, however, that a higher number of undos causes a greater potential for slower system performance. Therefore, it's advisable to keep the default setting.

or redo chunks of steps as opposed to just one at a time. You can also create commands, clear, replay, and copy and paste steps all in this little panel.

Access the History panel (see Figure 5-9) by selecting Window | Other Panels | History from the menu or by pressing CTRL-F10 (Windows)/OPTION-F10 (Mac).

You can access the panel before, during, or after a session in Flash. Once you close the file and open it again, the history of that session will be gone unless you save the steps as a command. Then you can apply them at another time.

Manipulate Steps in the History Panel

The History panel is very simple to use once you get a feel for it. The following lists the basic operations of the panel:

- ■ **Undo**   To undo steps, drag the History slider upward to the step you want to return to. The undone steps become dimmed. Each step becomes undone in real time as you drag the slider. To undo several steps at once, click the History slider arrow up to the step you want to undo.

- ■ **Redo**   To redo steps, drag the History slider downward to the step you want to redo. The steps up to and including that step then become active again. Each step becomes redone in real time as you drag the slider. To redo several steps at once, click the History slider arrow on the step you want to return to.

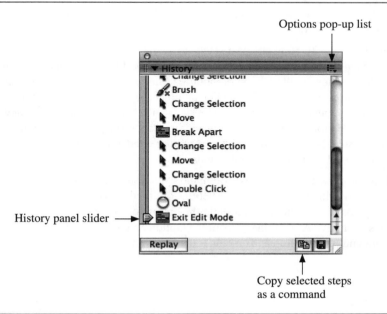

Options pop-up list

History panel slider

Copy selected steps
as a command

FIGURE 5-9   The History panel contains powerful tools that help you undo and redo steps.

■ **Replay**   To replay a single step, click an object, click the step, and then press the Replay button. Replaying a step duplicates a step on the same object or another selected object. For example, if you wanted to repeat a rotation you applied to one object on several new objects in the same movie, you could select these multiple objects (SHIFT-click), as shown here, and then click the rotate step in the History panel and press the Replay button to rotate all selected objects simultaneously. This could be a real timesaver if you need to apply the same edits to multiple objects.

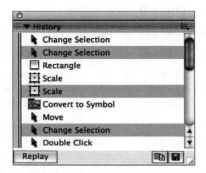

Similarly, you can replay multiple nonadjacent steps on selected objects. To do this, select the object or objects, then click and drag the steps within the steps column, as shown here. Then press the Replay button. To replay noncontiguous steps, select the objects, CTRL-click (Windows)/CMD-click (Mac) the steps you want to replay, and then press the Replay button.

■ **Copy and Paste**   To copy and paste steps to a new Flash document, select the step or steps you want to copy using the selection methods outlined previously, and click the Copy Selected Steps to the Clipboard button. (Alternately, you can select Copy Steps from the Options pop-up list.) Then click an object in the new Flash document and select Edit | Paste in Center from the menu. The steps will then be applied to the new object. In the History panel of the new document, multiple pasted steps will be listed as "Paste." Note that commands containing a red X (as shown here) cannot be copied, pasted, or made into commands.

■ **Create a Command**   To create a command from a step sequence, select the step or multiple steps using the selection instructions outlined previously. Then click the Save Selected Steps As A Command button in the bottom of the History panel. Alternately, you can select Save As Command from the Options pop-up list. The steps are now listed as a command in the Commands menu at the top of the Flash window, as shown next.

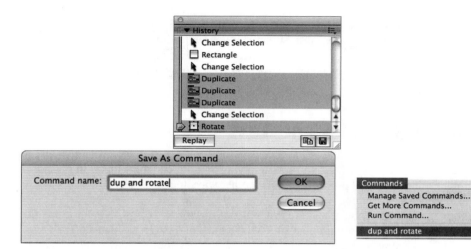

To apply a command to another document, select an object and then select the new command in the Commands menu.

To delete a command from the menu, select Commands | Manage Saved Commands. In the Manage Saved Commands dialog box (shown here), click the Delete button. To rename a command, click the Rename button.

■ **Clear the History** To clear the history from the panel, click the Options pop-up menu (or right-click in Windows/CTRL-click on the Mac) and select Clear History.

TIP

When using the History panel to undo steps that involve large files such as imported sounds, videos, or bitmaps, you'll need to save your document with the Save And Compact command. Even if you undo the import of a large image, video, or sound from your Flash movie, the file size remains bloated as if it were still there, because the History function preserves it to enable you to redo the steps. If you save and close the file and then reopen it, although the previous History is gone from the panel, the file size will still be large, as if the large file were still part of the document. Using the Save And Compact command will remove all elements that were deleted, thus compacting the file size.

The History panel can be a terrific tool for performing repetitive tasks. And as is true of many of the tools in Flash, its purpose is to streamline your workflow.

Color is also an important property that you often need to edit in your Flash movies. Next, you'll examine the important things you need to know about applying color to graphic elements in Flash.

Apply Color to Graphics and Text

In Chapter 3, we used the Stroke and Fill swatches in the Toolbar and in the Properties Inspector to apply color to a selected object. As you saw, applying color to editable objects in Flash is a pretty simple, straightforward process. There are other ways to apply color to objects too, and those are explored in this section.

In addition to using the Toolbar and the Properties Inspector to work with color properties, you can also set and adjust color with the Color Mixer and Color Swatches panels. The Color Swatches panel looks almost exactly like the pop-up swatch list you're accustomed to seeing in the Toolbar and the Properties Inspector. In fact, fills and stroke color are applied to editable and grouped objects the same way they are applied from the other two sources.

Color is applied to an editable or grouped object the same way with the Color Mixer, but in this panel you mix your own custom colors. You can also make custom gradient colors.

These two color panels also have settings not available in the Toolbar or Properties Inspector. Here, you'll examine these additional features.

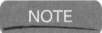 *Stroke color cannot be applied to a text object. To apply a stroke to text, you must break it apart and make it into an editable object. To break the text apart, click the text with the Selection tool and select Modify | Break Apart or press* CTRL-B *(Windows)/* CMD-B *(Mac).*

Use the Color Swatches Panel to Select Color

The color display of the Color Swatches panel is just like that of the Fill and Stroke Color pop-up palettes. The difference is that this panel can remain on the stage at times when the pop-up interface of the fill and stroke palettes can't, making it easier for you to compare colors.

The top of the Color Swatches panel lists the default Flash color swatches. The bottom strip is reserved for gradient colors and colors custom mixed in the Color Mixer panel. New gradients that you create also are stored in this panel.

The Options pop-up menu in the upper right of the panel, shown next, enables you to further customize the Color Swatches panel settings.

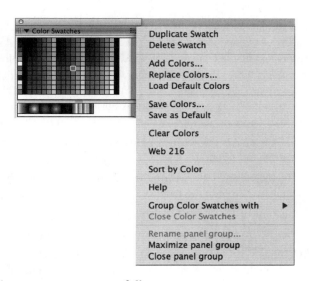

The options in the pop-up menu are as follows:

■ **Duplicate Swatch and Delete Swatch**   To duplicate or delete a swatch, click a swatch you want to modify and select Duplicate Swatch or Delete Swatch in the pop-up menu. If you duplicate a swatch, it will appear in the bottom of the swatch window. Deleting a swatch removes it from the swatch color table of this file.

■ **Add Colors and Replace Colors**   Add or replace colors in the palette by selecting one of these options in the pop-up menu. The Import Color Swatch dialog box appears. You can add color sets from other Flash files, color tables created in other programs (such as Photoshop, Fireworks, and Director), and colors from GIF files. You can also replace the colors in the palette with color sets from these sources.

NOTE   *The difference between Add Colors and Replace Colors is that Add Colors loads the new color set and retains the old set. Replace Colors loads the new color set and deletes the old color set. When you mix custom RGB colors and gradients, they are saved only in the Flash movie you are working on, not in the Flash application Preference file. When an application's Preference file is changed, the change is retained on the application level and doesn't change until the Preference file is altered or trashed.*

■ **Load Default Colors**   To reload the original Flash default colors, click this option. The default color table as well as other color tables are located in the Flash application folder | First Run | Color Sets. Use this feature if you've loaded another color table and you want to revert back to the original.

- **Save Colors** Colors can be saved in the Flash Color Set format or as a color table. Save colors by selecting Save Colors. A Save dialog box will appear. In the dialog box, type in a name for the colors and then navigate to a place where you want the color palette to be saved. For Format, select either Flash Color Set or Color Table from the pop-up list. A color table file is saved with an .act extension. Files with this extension can be imported into other programs such as Photoshop or Fireworks. A Flash Color Set file is saved with a .clr extension. These color sets can be imported and exported into Flash movies.

- **Save As Default** This makes the selected color palette the new default for that movie and replaces the current default color set.

- **Clear Colors** This deletes all colors from the current selection, leaving only one black and one white swatch available in the palette.

- **Web 216** Use this option if you want to display the web-safe palette.

- **Sort By Color** Select this option to sort current colors by hues ranging from light to dark.

- **Group Color Swatches With** This option offers a pop-menu that allows you to group the Color Swatches panel with any other panel. For example, if you wanted the Color Swatches panel to be grouped with Color Swatches, you could choose this from the pop-up menu.

Use the Color Mixer Panel to Set Color

The Color Mixer panel offers a multitude of ways to set colors. Display the Color Mixer panel by selecting Window | Color Mixer.

The Color Mixer panel allows you to mix RGB fill color, stroke color, and gradient color. In this panel you can also set the alpha percentage and save colors as swatches in the Color Swatches panel (see Figure 5-10).

To use the Color Mixer to set a solid fill or stroke color for an existing object, first select either the fill or the stroke of the object. Then select Solid from the Type pop-up menu, which you access by clicking the down arrow in the lower-right corner of the current fill or stroke color. Select a color from the pop-up swatches, using the eyedropper to navigate through the colors. The following illustration shows a fill color being chosen from a collapsed Color Mixer panel.

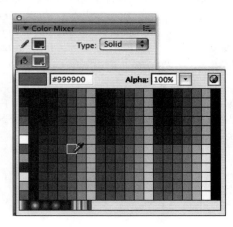

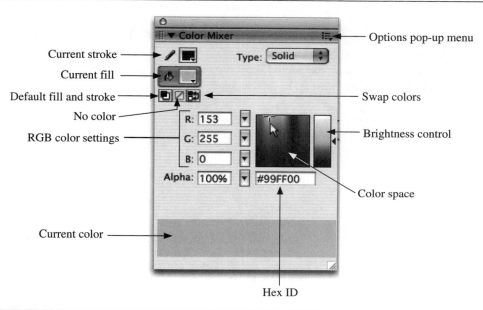

Current stroke

Current fill

Default fill and stroke

No color

RGB color settings

Options pop-up menu

Swap colors

Brightness control

Color space

Current color

Hex ID

FIGURE 5-10   Create new colors using the Color Mixer panel.

To set a custom fill or stroke color, click the fill or stroke icon and then click and drag in the color space with the crosshairs pointer until the current fill or stroke color is acceptable to you. The color you mix in the color space becomes the current fill or stroke color.

The *alpha* setting is the transparency index of a color. An alpha setting of 100 percent produces a solid color, and an alpha setting of 0 percent makes the color invisible. Alpha values in between produce varying degrees of transparency. To apply an alpha percentage to a color, type a percentage number in the Alpha value field or use the pop-up Alpha slider by clicking and dragging the arrow and selecting a percentage.

When two objects are overlapping one another and the top object has an alpha percentage of less than 100 applied, you can see the bottom object through the top object, as shown in the illustration at right.

In the Color Mixer panel, there is a Default Fill And Stroke button under the Current Fill (paint bucket) icon. This is the same Default Stroke And Fill button that exists in the Toolbar. Click this to return the stroke to white and the fill to black.

Next to the Default Fill And Stroke button is the No Color button. Select the No Color button if you want a fill without a stroke, or vice versa.

To select No Color as a fill or stroke option on an object you are about to draw, select a drawing tool first, then select the Fill or Stroke swatch. Click the No Color button to select

No Color. You can use the No Color button from the Color Mixer or from the Color options at the bottom of the Toolbar.

To change an existing color on an editable object to no color, click the fill or stroke of the editable object and press the DELETE key.

Next to the No Color button is the Swap Colors button. You can swap the fill color with the stroke color, and vice versa, by clicking this button.

Use the Color Mixer Options Pop-up Menu

You can change the Color Mixer to reflect different color models by clicking the pop-up menu at the top right of the panel, as shown here.

The following additional options are available on this menu:

- **RGB** Select RGB mode if you want to create an RGB color.
- **HSB** Select HSB to make a color using the hue value, saturation, and brightness method.
- **Add Swatch** To add a custom color swatch that you mixed to the Color Swatches panel, select either the stroke or the fill color in the Color Mixer. Then, in the pop-up menu, select Add Swatch. The custom color will appear in the bottom of all the swatch color windows.

Create a Gradient Color in the Color Mixer

In Flash, gradients are created with the Color Mixer. Gradient color changes from one hue, saturation, alpha, color, or tint to another. There are many different effects you can create using gradient color. You can start with a solid color and fade out to no color, or you can have several colors in a gradient that gradually transform into one another. There can be up to sixteen colors in a gradient, and you can apply one to the fill or stroke of an object.

There are two types of gradients that can be created in the Color Mixer:

- **Linear** This option gradates color in a straight horizontal or vertical direction. You use linear fills for rectangular shapes or objects where you want the fill to appear in a straight line.
- **Radial** This choice gradates color from a center point outward, in a circle. You can use radial fills for ellipses or any object where you want the gradation to appear to be radiating.

If you click the Fill Color pop-up palette in the Color Mixer panel, you'll notice that there are several ready-made default gradient colors at the bottom of the swatch list. There's not much of a choice in gradients, so it's good to know how to mix your own. The following steps outline the process of creating a gradient fill color:

1. From the pop-up Fill Style menu in the Color Mixer, select a gradient type of either Linear or Radial. In this example, a linear gradient is created and applied to an editable object.

2. When you select a gradient type from the Fill or Swatch Style pop-up menu, a gradient definition bar appears in the Color Mixer, as shown next. This horizontal bar provides a preview of the current gradient blend.

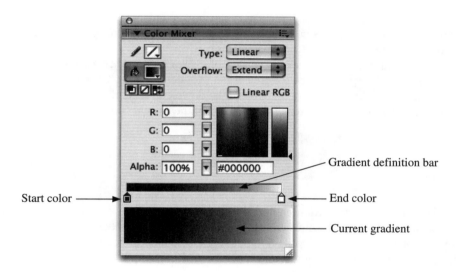

3. The Start Color and End Color arrows under the gradient definition bar mark the entrance and exit of a color. If you drag the arrows to the left or right on the bar, the balance of the gradient mix changes.

4. To change the color on the Start Color arrow, select the arrow and then click and drag in the color space. Alternately, you can click the fill color or stroke color and from the pop-up menu, select a color. Your gradient color on the Start Color arrow changes in the gradient bar. Repeat the process to change the End Color arrow's color. Drag the arrows if you need to readjust the gradient color balance.

5. To apply an alpha percentage to a gradient color arrow, click the arrow and then click the Alpha slider. Drag the Alpha slider to the opacity percentage you desire. The Current Color swatch gives you a preview of the opacity. As you can see here, a grid appears in the Current Color swatch to help you preview the level of opacity.

6. To control the way a gradient appears past the edge of the object you are applying it to, select from one of the three settings in the Overflow pop-up menu, as shown next. Choose from the displayed settings, which are Extend (to extend the gradient scheme you made), Reflect (to mirror the gradient), and Repeat (to repeat the gradient).

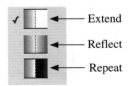

- Extend
- Reflect
- Repeat

Create a Custom Color for the Gradient   You can create custom colors from the color space by clicking and dragging the crosshairs in the space. The current custom color is reflected in the Fill or Stroke Color swatch icons and the Current gradient bar.

The Brightness Control slider to the right of the color space (shown here) can be used in conjunction with the color space to create a greater range of color values. Create more color values by dragging the slider arrow. Dragging the slider down creates darker shades of the current color; dragging the slider up creates lighter tints of the current color.

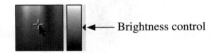

- Brightness control

Add More Colors to the Gradient Definition Bar   To *add* another gradient color arrow in order to create a multicolor gradient, click anywhere on the bottom of the gradient definition bar. You will know that your pointer is positioned correctly under the gradient definition bar when you see a plus (+) sign under the arrow, as shown here.

To assign a new color to the new arrow after it has been created, select a color from the Color Proxy pop-up palette or select a custom color in the color space. You can create as many new gradient color arrows as needed.

To *delete* a color from the gradient bar, click that color's arrow and drag it outside the Color Mixer.

Add a Gradient Color to an Object

Once your gradient has been created, the Fill Color swatches in both the Toolbar and the Properties Inspector display the new gradient. The next object you create will fill with this color.

To change the gradient on a merged or drawing object, display the Color Mixer panel and click the object. You can then drag the gradient color arrows left or right to rebalance the distribution of the colors. Alternately, you can click a gradient color arrow and select another color from the Fill Color swatch, Stroke Color swatch, or the color space to change the color.

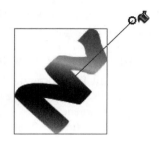

The default linear gradient blends from left to right. To change the angle of a gradient and the blend on an editable object, select the Paint Bucket tool from the Toolbar, position the Paint Bucket over the object, and then click and drag in the desired direction, as shown here.

NOTE *Make sure that the Lock Fill icon in the Options section of the Toolbar is not highlighted. Otherwise, the gradient will not blend correctly. In a later section you will use the Lock Fill icon to control the blending of a single gradient over several objects.*

Experiment with clicking and dragging in different directions and different locations on the object. Clicking different angles and places on the object will yield different results.

NOTE *Gradients can't be applied to text unless the text is broken apart.*

Save a Gradient Color

Gradients can be used on the currently selected object(s) or added to the current movie's Color Swatches palette. If you like a gradient you have created, you can store it in the gradient swatch area of the Color Swatches palette, just as you can store custom solid colors in the palette.

To store a gradient color or a solid color, click the Options pop-up menu in the upper-right corner of the Color Mixer and select Add Swatch. The swatch will now appear in the bottom of all the Fill Color Swatch menus (including the Color Swatches panel) as a color option. Custom solid colors are stored in a row above the gradient colors to make it easier for you to spot the difference.

Custom gradient

You can customize the way linear and radial gradients display, too, which we will discuss in the next section.

Modify Gradients with the Gradient Transform and Lock Fill Tools

To change the angle of a gradient on an object quickly, you can use the Paint Bucket method, as discussed previously. But for more control over the process, you need to use other techniques.

Once you've assigned a gradient color to an object, there are other ways to adjust the angle of the gradient on an object. You can also apply a gradient across several selected objects and change the way the gradient appears. The Gradient Transform and Lock Fill tools can be used to achieve some interesting gradient color effects.

Use the Gradient Transform Tool

The Gradient Transform tool (shown at right) is located on the Toolbar. This is a fun tool to use because you can create some dramatic effects by manipulating the size and the angle of a gradient color.

To adjust a linear fill on an object, follow these steps:

1. Click the Gradient Transform tool in the Toolbar. Then click an editable object that has a gradient whose direction you want to change. If you choose an object with a linear fill, two vertical lines indicating the direction of the linear fill will appear on either side of the object, as shown here. A center point designates the center of the gradient fill, and a ring handle (rotation) appears on the top of the line to the right. In the center of the right line, a width adjustment icon appears.

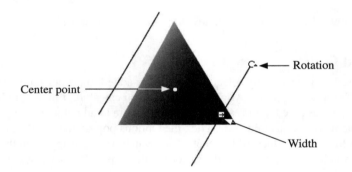

2. To reduce or enlarge the gradient width, click and drag the width adjustment icon handle. This can dramatically change the look of the gradient as it shortens or elongates it. The two black horizontal lines indicate the direction the gradient is angled. Rotate the angle of the gradient by clicking the top-right ring handle and dragging clockwise or counterclockwise to change the angle of the color.

3. Change the center point of the gradient by clicking and dragging it.

Transform a Radial Fill   Transforming a fill on a radial gradient is done slightly differently than transforming a linear gradient fill. Because the color radiates in a circle, it requires a different kind of adjustment.

To transform a radial gradient on an object, follow these steps:

1. Select the Gradient Transform tool. Click an editable object with a radial fill. An ellipse appears around the circumference of the object. Like a linear gradient, there is a center point in the middle of the radial gradient. Additionally, there is a focal point icon that allows you to change the light source's direction by dragging it, and there are handles to change the width, size, and rotation of the radial gradient, as shown here.

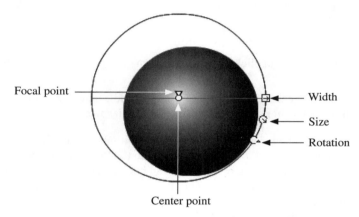

2. Adjust these handles by clicking and dragging. Just like the behavior of the Gradient Transform tool on a linear gradient, the Width, Size, and Rotation icons perform the same functions on a radial gradient.

Use the Lock Fill Tool

Use the Lock Fill tool to adjust your color in a continuous gradation across several objects. Figure 5-11 demonstrates how the Lock Fill tool can be used. In this figure, the text is broken apart and a gradation with a locked fill has been applied separately to each character in the word. Instead of the gradation treating each character as a separate object with a separate gradation for each character, the characters are treated as one object with one gradation applied.

This technique displays a kind of masking effect on two or more selected objects. It creates the illusion of a gradient in the background being masked by the objects you've created.

a locked fill

FIGURE 5-11   A locked fill creates a continuous gradient over several objects.

The Lock Fill tool becomes available in the Options section of the Toolbar when you choose the Paint Bucket or the Brush tool. Fills can be locked on bitmap fills also. Bitmap fills are discussed in Chapter 6.

To create a locked fill, let's go over the steps that were used to create the illustration in Figure 5-11:

1. Create some text on the stage.

2. Click the text and break it apart using Modify | Break Apart or CTRL-B in Windows/CMD-B on the Mac. Select the text.

3. Create and/or select a gradient fill color from the Fill Color Swatches palette.

4. Select the Paint Bucket and click the Lock Fill icon (shown here) in the Options section of the Toolbar.

5. Click each one of the characters, starting from the middle and going outward, and the gradient will be locked in position, as if the text graphics were one object.

You can also span the gradient fill over several objects with the Lock Fill button *unlocked*. First select the objects and click the Paint Bucket tool. With the Lock Fill button in the Options section of the Toolbar unlocked, select a gradient fill and click and drag the Paint Bucket tool over the span of objects. Depending upon how you drag and what the direction of the angle is, the gradient will appear differently.

Use the Brush Tool with Locked Fills

The Brush tool can also be used to create locked fills. To lock a fill within a series of brush strokes, select a gradient fill color. Then select the Brush tool and click the Lock Fill button in the Options section of the Toolbar.

When you use the Brush tool to draw a series of separate brush strokes, the gradient color will span the series of brushstrokes. You can create some interesting effects using this technique, as you can see here.

Modify Fills with the Shape Menu

Flash comes equipped with a few ways to creatively manipulate fills. These can be found in the Modify | Shape menu. This menu offers three modifiers for shapes:

- **Convert Lines To Fills**   Use this to convert what was previously a line into an object made from a fill. To apply this to an editable object, select the object first and then select Modify | Shape | Convert Lines to Fills.

- **Expand Fill**   Use this setting to expand or contract a fill. To do so, first click an editable object and then select Modify | Shape | Expand Fill from the menu. In the Expand Fill dialog box, indicate the amount you want to expand or contract the fill in the Distance box. Click Expand to make the fill larger or click Inset to contract the size of the fill.

■ **Soften Fill Edges**   This option works well for creating the blurry-edge effect usually associated with bitmap graphics. You can blur the edges of a fill by clicking an editable object that has a fill. Then select Modify | Shape | Soften Fill Edges. In the dialog box that appears, indicate the distance you want the fill to expand or reduce.

Here's an example of a circle with an expanded soft fill. The effect was created with a Distance value of 15 pixels and 15 steps. Keep in mind that a large number of steps will create a softer edge, but it will bloat the file size. The default number of steps is 4.

Set the direction of the soft edge by clicking Expand to make it larger or Inset to make the blur effect go inward. You can achieve some spectacular effects by experimenting with the Soften Fill Edges settings.

Conclusion

This chapter covered a lot of ground on graphics and text in Flash. Emphasis in this chapter was on learning new ways to set and manipulate these elements. In addition, many key concepts were covered, such as object grouping, stacking order, alignment, the use of the transform tools, the creation of gradients, and the modification of fills.

In the next chapter, you learn how to import pictures from other sources into your Flash movies. These include line drawings and bitmap images. Importing images from external sources opens up many new creative options in Flash.

Chapter 6

Add Images to Your Flash Movies

How to...

- Understand vector and raster graphics
- Import images into Flash
- Import from Fireworks, FreeHand, and Illustrator
- Import file sequences
- Modify and edit bitmaps
- Trace bitmaps
- Break apart bitmaps
- Paint with a bitmap

By now, you know that Flash is packed with an impressive array of drawing tools. But what about using graphics and other elements you created from other programs? Flash can import images in other formats from many different sources. You can import both vector and raster file images (also known as *bitmap* images) into Flash movies. In addition, you can import video and sound into Flash. Importing video and sound is covered in Chapter 7.

Before examining the process of importing images into Flash, you'll examine the differences between vector- and raster-based graphics as they relate to the images you'll be importing.

Understand Vector Graphics

Vector graphics are defined with mathematical precision. An object created in a vector-based program is described with a series of lines and curves that move from point to point to create a shape.

Unlike bitmaps, vector graphics maintain their quality at any scale, as shown in Figure 6-1, where the image has been enlarged from 100 to 300 percent.

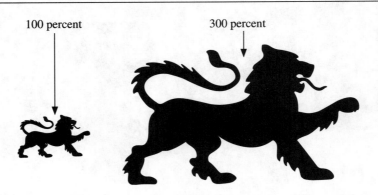

100 percent   300 percent

FIGURE 6-1   A vector illustration maintains quality when it's scaled up 300 percent.

The Pen tool's drawing features of Flash are vector-based (except when they are editable), as are drawing programs such as Macromedia FreeHand and Adobe Illustrator. Use vector graphics for logos, technical drawings, crisp text, or any art where precision is important.

Understand Bitmap Images

Unlike vector illustrations, which are sleek at any scale, bitmap (raster) images are created from pixels arranged in a grid format. Each pixel is assigned an RGB color value, and the juxtaposition of pixels creates the illusion of an object. Bitmaps are commonly associated with photographic pictures, images with gradient color, or images with a lot of color variation.

Zoom in on a bitmapped image in its native program, or even in Flash, to see how the pixels are arranged in a gridlike order. The more you zoom in on the image, the more the pixels appear as a group of squares. Zoom in a lot, and the image no longer resembles the original art. Rather, it looks more like an abstract painting made out of squares on a grid. Zooming in on a bitmap provides a good idea of how a bitmap is made. Programs such as Adobe Photoshop are raster-based applications.

Bitmaps are very different from vector art. When you modify a bitmap, you change the properties of each pixel within the selected area. If you reduce or enlarge a selected bitmap, the pixels reduce or enlarge within the scheme of the pixel grid.

Enlarging a bitmap object can cause a *pixilated* effect (see Figure 6-2) and seriously downgrade the quality of the original image. Unlike vectors, bitmaps have resolution issues, too. *Resolution* is a mathematical calculation relating to the way images display their final output, which could be in various forms of print or multimedia (on the Web, in a video, or in slides). The higher the resolution of the image, the clearer the image will display or output.

At higher resolutions, pixels become more densely populated and, as a result, display a better quality of picture. The image size increases, too. This might not be a problem if the final output is for print. If the bitmap is being put up on the Web, however, bigger files mean longer download times.

Raster-based programs such as Photoshop enable you to smooth out the edges of pixels to eliminate some of the jagged edges that occur on bitmaps with a lot of flat color. This is

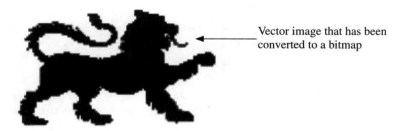

Vector image that has been converted to a bitmap

FIGURE 6-2   Raster (bitmap) images become pixilated when enlarged.

a technique known as *anti-aliasing*. Anti-aliasing creates extra pixels around an object that provide a more gradual transition of color from object to background.

To make anti-aliased text in Flash, select the Text tool in the Toolbar, then click one of the three anti-alias selections from the Font Rendering Method pop-up menu. These include Anti-alias for Animation, Anti-alias for Readability, or Custom Anti-alias. From the Font Rendering Method pop-up menu, you can also choose Bitmap for Aliased Text. The functions of these settings are discussed in Chapter 4.

If you plan to import vector images and bitmaps into Flash, you need to familiarize yourself with file export formats for web media to ensure a smooth transition into Flash.

Import Graphics into Your Flash Movie

When you create graphics in other programs for use in Flash, they must be saved in a file format that Flash recognizes. Flash imports many different file formats from vector, raster animation, and 3-D programs, to name a few.

To import a file onto the Flash stage, select File | Import | Import to Stage or press CTRL-R in Windows/CMD-R on the Mac. From the Import dialog box, shown here, you can navigate to the file you want to import. The Files of Type (Windows)/Show (Mac) pop-up list allows you to choose from over 29 file formats. Selecting All Formats will display files in all formats recognizable to Flash, as shown in the illustration. When you have selected the desired file, click Open (Windows)/Import (Mac).

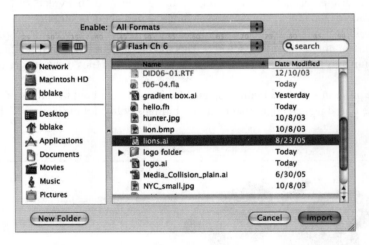

To make your search for a file easier in the Import dialog box, for Files of Type (Windows)/Show (Mac), select a specific file format from the pop-up list. This will narrow your search for the file.

Some file formats offer an additional settings dialog box that allows you to customize the import. These settings are discussed in the next section. Once all the settings have been selected, the file appears on the stage as well as in the Library. You took a brief tour of the Library in Chapter 2, so you probably recall that this is where imported pictures, sounds, videos, and symbols are stored.

Sometimes importing a file can be annoying because it may fall on top of a merged drawing object or in an undesirable area. In this case, Flash offers an alternative command that lets you store the file directly in the Library. This way you can control when an instance is placed onstage.

To import a file directly into the Library, select File | Import | Import to Library. Navigate to and select the file in the Import dialog box, as outlined previously, and click Open (Windows)/ Import (Mac).

Although it's easy to import art into Flash, there are some rules and issues you should familiarize yourself with to ensure that your import works to your advantage. In the next four sections, various methods of importing graphics from popular applications are examined, as are the file formats you can import from.

Import from Fireworks

Fireworks is Macromedia's image manipulation and editing program. Fireworks is like a hybrid program because you can create and edit in a bitmap mode, as well as draw vector objects and generate vector-based text. The native file format for Fireworks is PNG, and since it shares the same lineage with Flash, there are multiple export options available in Flash for this format.

To import a Fireworks PNG file into Flash, select File | Import | Import to Stage. In the Import dialog box, navigate to the Fireworks PNG file and then click Open (Windows)/Import (Mac). In the Fireworks PNG Import Settings dialog box (see Figure 6-3), you can customize your import. Here you can select various import options relating to layers, rasterizing, and text.

FIGURE 6-3   The Import Settings dialog box in Flash for a Fireworks PNG file

If the Fireworks file you are importing consists of multiple layers, you can retain the layers if you import the file as a movie clip in the File Structure settings. *Movie clips* are movie objects that have their own layers and timelines. Movie clips are discussed more in Chapter 13.

In the Objects settings, if Keep All Paths Editable is checked, vector art created in Fireworks can be edited in Flash. In the Text settings, you can also keep text editable.

You also can copy and paste a graphic from a Fireworks file into Flash by clicking the object and selecting Edit | Copy from the Fireworks menu (CTRL-C in Windows/CMD-C on the Mac). Select Edit | Paste (CTRL-V in Windows/CMD-V on the Mac) from the Flash menu to paste the graphic on the Flash stage. This copies the object into Flash as a bitmap or vector (depending on the origin of the image you selected) with an opaque background. Alternately, you can drag and drop an image from Fireworks into Flash. Keep in mind that when you use the copy-and-paste or drag-and-drop method, the object imports as a flattened, single-layer image.

Import from FreeHand

Files created in Macromedia FreeHand 7.0 through MX import seamlessly into Flash. Although FreeHand files can be imported in many different formats into Flash, most often you'll import files from FreeHand in an FH format (.fh). FH is the native file format for FreeHand. This format offers more options than other methods for retaining the integrity of FreeHand art in Flash. When you select an FH format for import, the FreeHand Import dialog box appears, as shown here.

You can customize your import by selecting the settings in this dialog box. The settings are described here:

■ **Mapping/Pages** This section allows you to determine the way FreeHand pages translate onto the Flash stage. You can map a FreeHand page to a scene or a keyframe in Flash. Mapping to scenes places all pages in the FreeHand document in a separate scene, and mapping to keyframes places every page in the FreeHand document in a separate keyframe.

- **Mapping/Layers**   This section allows you to determine the way FreeHand layers translate into Flash. You can map a FreeHand layer to a Flash layer or choose Keyframes to map FreeHand layers into individual keyframes. You can also select Flatten as an option if you want the FreeHand document to be one frame, one layer.
- **Pages**   The options in this section allow you to specify a particular page or pages for import from FreeHand to Flash. (In FreeHand, you can create multiple pages.)
- **Include Invisible Layers**   This selection imports invisible layers along with your FreeHand layers that contain objects. Use this feature for FreeHand files that have invisible layers that you need to view in Flash to complete a picture.
- **Include Background Layers**   This option, when selected, retains the background layer from FreeHand.
- **Maintain Text Blocks**   This selection keeps the width of text blocks intact from one program to the other. The text is then editable in Flash.

You can copy and paste graphics from FreeHand to Flash (or drag and drop from Freehand to Flash) by selecting the object and choosing Edit | Copy from the Fireworks menu (CTRL-C in Windows/CMD-C on the Mac) and then selecting Edit | Paste from the Flash menu (CTRL-V in Windows/CMD-V on the Mac). This copies the objects into Flash as editable vector objects. This method of import works quite well for quick, simple things and can be a timesaver if you don't need to save your FreeHand art or retain layers. You can display both programs, create art in FreeHand, copy it, and paste it into Flash, albeit without all the customized options. Objects on multiple layers will appear stacked on one layer.

If you're going to import a gradient into Flash that was created in FreeHand and saved in an FH format, it's best to try to stick with eight colors or fewer when you create it. Otherwise, Flash has to create clipping paths to simulate the gradation. Clipping paths could mean trouble because the file size can increase dramatically. Blends saved in the FH format that import into Flash also are interpreted as separate paths, which also increases the file size.

Feel free to use as many colors in a gradient as you want if you plan on exporting the FreeHand gradient to an SWF format, for import into Flash. Gradients will be converted to Flash gradients and will look the same as if they were created in Flash. Exporting from FreeHand to an SWF format will ensure the most reliable gradient results.

TIP   *Symbols created in FreeHand import as symbols into Flash.*

Import from Illustrator

Adobe Illustrator is a vector-based application like FreeHand, and Flash does a wonderful job of importing and exporting files from Illustrator 10 and under.

Illustrator file formats import nicely into Flash. Illustrator files saved in the AI format (Illustrator's native format) can be imported into Flash if they are saved in versions 6 and under or in version 10. You can also import Illustrator files saved in PDF, EPS, and SWF formats.

The same features that apply to FreeHand files when imported in the SWF format apply to Illustrator files. Gradients aren't supported in versions of Illustrator before version 5. Gradients saved in the SWF format import beautifully into Flash. Bitmaps are supported in version 6 and later. You also can copy and paste between Illustrator and Flash.

 *You can import and export solid and gradient color palettes between Flash and Fireworks and between Photoshop and Fireworks.*

To import an Adobe Illustrator (.ai) file, select File | Import | Import to Stage or Import to Library from the menu. The Import Options dialog box appears, as shown here.

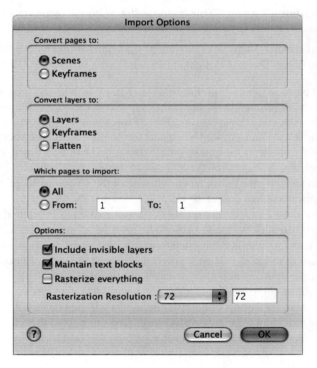

Select from the following:

- **Convert Pages To** The options in this section allow you to check either Scenes or Keyframes. Selecting Scenes converts each page from Illustrator to a scene in Flash. Selecting Keyframes converts each page to a keyframe.
- **Convert Layers To** In this section, you can check Layers, Keyframes, or Flatten. Selecting Layers converts all Illustrator layers to Flash layers. Selecting Keyframes converts layers from Illustrator to keyframes in Flash. Selecting Flatten converts all layers in Illustrator to a single scene in Flash.

■ **Options**   Other options in this dialog box are Include Invisible Layers, Maintain Text Blocks (select for editable text), and Rasterize Everything, which flattens all Illustrator art into a bitmap.

When art is imported from Illustrator, the elements used to make the objects are grouped together and the stacking order is maintained in Flash. The objects can be ungrouped in Flash.

Import from Other File Formats

Files generated in Adobe Photoshop, ImageReady, Acrobat PDF, and other popular graphics programs can be imported into Flash using any of the appropriate extensions listed in Table 6-1. This table lists several of the most common file formats that import into Flash.

When you import a file from any of the formats listed in Table 6-1, select File | Import | Import to Stage or Import to Library. Navigate to the folder where the file is located, and click Open (Windows)/Import (Mac). A dialog box relevant to the file format will appear. Select the appropriate choices and then click OK.

The Import Options dialog boxes for EPS and PDF file formats are identical to the dialog box for Adobe Illustrator.

Import and Export File Sequences

You also can import file sequences generated from other programs such as Bryce, Poser, Strata 3D, Lightwave, Maya, Carrarra, Adobe Premiere, After Effects, FinalCut Pro, QuickTime Pro, AutoCAD, and many more. A *file sequence* is a series of files that, if viewed together on individual keyframes, can give the illusion of a flipbook or a frame-by-frame animation. Flash recognizes a group of files as sequential if the files have the same names but end in sequential numbers.

To import sequential files, select File | Import | Import to Stage or Import to Library. Navigate to the folder containing the files you want to import. Click the first file in the numerical file sequence. On a PC, click the Open button. On a Mac, click the Add button and then the Import button. This alert appears:

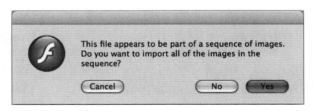

Click the Yes button to complete the import.

In Figure 6-4, sequential images were exported in a PNG format into Adobe After Effects, a motion graphics and special effects application. They appear in the Flash timeline as individual keyframes. Importing to keyframes creates a frame-by-frame animation in Flash. *Frame-by-frame* animation is an animation that changes properties on every keyframe. The specifics of frame-by-frame animation are discussed in Chapter 9.

File Type	Extension	Windows	Macintosh
Adobe Illustrator	.ai	Yes	Yes
AutoCAD DXF	.dxf	Yes	Yes
Bitmap	.bmp	Yes	No
Digital Video	.dv	Yes	Yes
Enhanced Windows Metafile	.emf	Yes	No
FreeHand 7-10	.fh	Yes	Yes
GIF	.gif	Yes	Yes
JPEG	.jpg	Yes	Yes
PICT	.pct, pict	No	Yes
PDF*	.pdf	Yes	Yes
PNG	.png	Yes	Yes
Flash Player	.swf	Yes	Yes
Illustrator 6-10	.ai	Yes	Yes
Windows Metafile	.wmf	Yes	No
WAV Audio	.wav	Yes	No
AIFF Audio	.aif	No	Yes
PostScript*	.eps, .pdf	Yes	Yes
WAV Audio*	.wav	Yes	Yes
AIFF Audio*	.aif	Yes	Yes
Silicon Graphics*	.sai	Yes	Yes
TGA*	.tgf	Yes	Yes
PICT*	.pct	Yes	Yes
QuickTime Image*	.qtif	Yes	Yes
QuickTime Movie*	.mov	Yes	Yes
Digital Video*	.dv	Yes	Yes
Flash Video	.flv	Yes	Yes (Flash Video*)
MPEG*	.mgp, .mpeg, .mpeg2, mp3	Yes	Yes
Audio Video Interleaved	.avi	Yes	Yes

* For QuickTime 4.0 or over

TABLE 6-1   File Types That Flash Can Import

FIGURE 6-4 A sequential file format created in After Effects and imported into Flash

You also can export a multikeyframe file sequence made in Flash to another program. Do this by selecting File | Export | Export Movie. The Export Movie dialog box appears, as shown here.

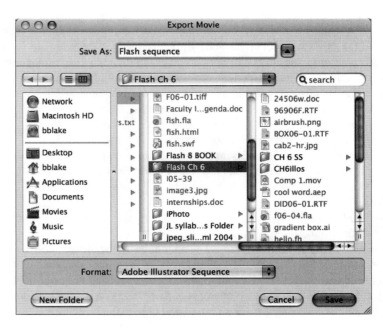

In Windows, type in a filename and select a file type in the Save As Type pop-up menu. You can export a file sequence to the following formats:

- PICT (Mac) or BMP (Windows) Sequence
- EPS 3.0 Sequence
- AI (Adobe Illustrator) Sequence
- DXF Sequence
- JPEG Sequence
- GIF Sequence
- PNG Sequence

Once you export a file sequence from Flash, you can then import your sequence into another application, such as Premiere, AfterEffects, or FinalCut Pro, to enhance a video, or Fireworks to make a GIF animation. This method works well for projects with multiple pieces. It makes it easy to use parts of a Flash animation in other support materials for print and web applications.

Import SWF Animation from Other Applications

The SWF file format has become so universal that many other applications besides vector applications offer it as an export option. Because the SWF format generates such beautiful, low-bandwidth images on the Web, it's no wonder more and more software developers are embracing this technology.

Not all applications that support the SWF format enable you to import the SWF file into Flash and have full functionality with layers and symbols. However, there are at least a couple of applications worth mentioning because they address a special niche in the developer market.

As was mentioned in the previous sections, you can import SWF files from the Macromedia software programs FreeHand and Fireworks as well as Adobe Illustrator, AfterEffects, Photoshop, and Apple's Motion. Additionally, CorelDraw allows you to do the same.

Toon Boom Studio is a 2-D, vector-based application for cartoon animation. It includes features important to cartoon animation developers such as lip synching, smoothing of animations, and perspective tools. Toon Boom animation can be exported to the SWF format. You can also import your cartoon animations into Flash using the Toon Boom Studio Importer plug-in for Flash MX. Once the animation is brought into Flash, you can add interactivity to your cartoon animations.

You can download a free evaluation copy of Toon Boom, as well as the full application for purchase, at www.toonboom.com.

Swift 3D by Electric Rain is a vector-based, 3-D animation application that offers an easy-to-use set of tools that enable you to extrude, rotate, and lathe vector objects, among other things. If you're accustomed to working in a 3-D environment, the tools will be very easy to work with. Since Flash does not offer any 3-D drawing of any sort, Swift 3D is one of the best programs to use for this purpose because it is vector based. You can export in sequential file format into Flash but there would be little reason to do so as you can export directly from Flash. This is a full-bodied, 3-D program and it is relatively inexpensive considering all the bells and whistles it ships with.

Did you know?

Export Graphics from Flash

6

In addition to bringing images into Flash, you can also export Flash images to other programs.

To export a single frame image, select File | Export Image (Windows)/File | Export | Export Image (Mac). If your timeline consists of multiple frames, choose the frame you want to export. It will export all contents of the selected frame.

The wording in the Export Image dialog box is slightly different in Windows than on the Mac. In Windows, navigate to the folder where you want the image saved. Then type in a name for the file in the File Name line. For Save as Type, click the pop-up list and choose from one of the following format options:

- **Flash Player 8 and Below (.swf)** This is the native format for Flash. An Export to Flash Player dialog box appears, and additional selections become available.

- **Enhanced Metafile (.emf) and Windows Metafile (.wmf)** These formats are exclusive to Windows.

- **EPS 3.0 (.eps)** A common format for vector images, EPS stands for encapsulated PostScript.

- **Adobe Illustrator 10 or Under (.ai)** This is the native file format for Adobe Illustrator. AI files export as editable vectors.

- **AutoCAD DXF (.dxf)** This is a format used in AutoCAD 2-D and 3-D.

- **Bitmap (.bmp)/Pict (.pct)** Bitmaps are used for Windows applications and are similar to PICT files on the Mac. An Export Bitmap (Windows)/Export Pict (Mac) dialog box appears with additional settings for resolution and color depth.

- **JPEG Image (.jpg)** JPEG stands for Joint Photographic Experts Group. This format creates 24-bit continuous-tone art if the system is capable of viewing 24-bit color. JPEG format doesn't support Alpha channels, and it is lossy compression (which creates image deterioration). Alpha channels are a feature in photo- and video-editing applications that provide an area where you can store masks.

- **GIF Image (.gif)** GIF stands for Graphics Interchange File. This format supports indexed color (a 256-color palette) and produces a medium- to low-quality exported image.

- **PNG Image (.png)** PNG stands for Portable Network Graphic format. This native file format for Fireworks supports 8-bit color, 24-bit color, and Alpha channels.

If you are working on a Mac, the Export Image dialog box looks a little different than it does in Windows. For Save As, type in a filename. For Format, choose from the format selections just listed. For Where, navigate to the folder where you want to store the file.

On the product web site, www.swift3d.com, you can preview a diverse group of 3-D examples that can be exported in SWF format (see Figure 6-5).

In any of these programs, you can export a file to SWF format or you can import it directly into Flash as an SWF file. From Flash, you can add interactivity. For example, if you wanted a user-controlled, 3-D object such as a car or a robot, you could easily generate the 3-D animation in Swift 3D and then import it into Flash to add the finishing touches.

Wildfx from Wildform (www.wildform.com) generates animated special-effects text and video that exports in an SWF format. The interface is simple plug-and-play; you type the text and select the effect from hundreds of choices. There is also a Pro version that allows you to encode video, as well as create type and then export to Flash.

There are many other applications that export to SWF format, such as Swish and Corel R.A.V.E. However, the applications previously mentioned are the most interesting in terms of producing special-graphics animation beyond the capabilities of basic Flash. Also, these programs are more niche-specific.

FIGURE 6-5   Swift 3D by Electric Rain exports 3-D images in the SWF file format.

Use Bitmapped Images in Flash

Bitmapped images are commonly associated with paint or photo-editing programs. They can be images produced in these programs, or they can be photographic images scanned or shot with a digital camera. Because you may sometimes need to use bitmap images in your production, this section explores Flash's guidelines on importing and manipulating bitmaps.

You import a bitmap into Flash the same way you do a vector image, as was outlined in the previous section: Select File | Import | Import to Stage or Import to Library, choose the file(s) you want to import, and click Open (Windows)/Import (Mac). The Import dialog box will appear, as shown next.

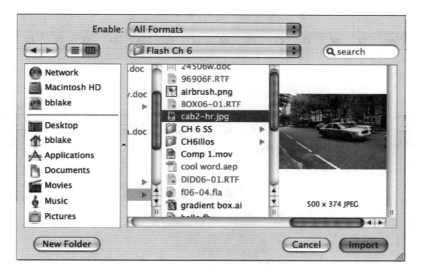

NOTE   *The bitmap formats you can import into Flash are listed in Table 6-1, earlier in this chapter.*

Set or Modify the Properties of a Bitmap

Just like any other graphic element, bitmap images have properties you can change. Although the properties are limited, there are still some interesting effects you can achieve with bitmaps if you're a creative designer.

When you import a bitmap into Flash, it is stored in the Library, even if you selected the Import to Stage option. If the bitmap is deleted on the stage, the original bitmap still remains in the Library until it is deleted from the Library. You can generate as many instances of this bitmap as you want by clicking the bitmap's icon in the Library and dragging it to the stage. The next illustration shows a bitmap that has been stored and selected in the Library. The thumbnail of the selection enables you to preview your selection. The Library is discussed in detail in Chapter 8.

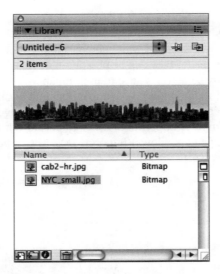

Bitmaps can be transformed with the transformation tools just like any other object can. You can scale, rotate, skew, and flip a bitmap horizontally and/or vertically (see Chapter 5). In this illustration, the bitmap is selected with the Free Transform tool and skew and rotate effects are being applied.

Use the Bitmap Properties Dialog Box

The Bitmap Properties dialog box allows you to adjust the compression settings on your bitmap to ensure the best balance of size and image quality in your final movie.

To display the Bitmap Properties dialog box for a specific bitmap, do the following:

1. Display the Library (Window | Library or CTRL-L in Windows/CMD-L on the Mac).

2. Right-click (Windows)/CTRL-click (Mac) the bitmap in the Library to display the Options pop-up menu. (You can also access this menu by clicking the pop-up menu arrow in the upper-right corner of the Library.)

3. Select Properties from the menu, as shown next.

In the Bitmap Properties dialog box, there are several options to choose from, as shown in Figure 6-6. The top part of the box provides you with information about the file: when it was created, its size, and a thumbnail preview of the image.

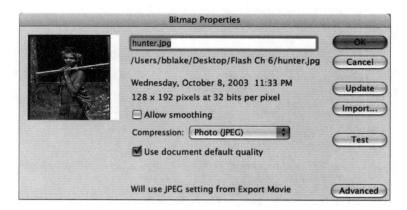

The Bitmap Properties dialog box

The following options are also available:

- **Allow Smoothing**   Select Allow Smoothing for an anti-alias effect. This will smooth rough edges in a bitmap.

- **Compression**   In the Compression pop-up list, select from one of two compression schemes (see the "Photo (JPEG) Versus Lossless (GIF/PNG) Compression" sidebar for more information).

- **Use Document Default Quality**   Checking this box enables you to keep the previous quality setting. If the box is unchecked, you can enter a new value of quality between 1 and 100 in the Quality box that appears. You cannot change the image quality of a JPEG image in the Publish Settings dialog box—this dialog box allows you to pick from many custom settings for several different export formats and is discussed in Chapter 18. If you need to modify the quality setting, it must be done in the native program or here in the Bitmap Properties dialog box.

- **Update, Import, and Test**   These buttons enable you to update the file throughout the movie, import it to an alternative file format, and view the results of your new quality setting. When you click the Test button, the size and quality statistics appear at the bottom of the dialog box.

Swap One Bitmap Image with Another

A bitmap that's placed on the stage can be swapped with another bitmap in the Library. Use the technique described here to save time if you have many instances of a bitmap throughout the movie and/or on multiple levels in Flash. With the click of a button, one image can be swapped with another in all instances of the image.

To swap one bitmap with another, right-click (Windows)/ CTRL-click (Mac) one instance of the bitmap on the stage. In the pop-up menu, select Swap Bitmap. In the Swap Bitmap dialog box (shown here), click the new image and then click OK. All instances of the bitmap are now swapped with another bitmap.

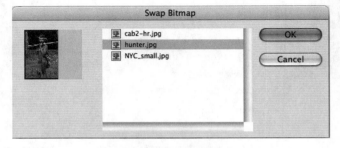

Next, you will learn how to edit bitmaps in Flash. Flash has a limited but unique set of editing tools reserved exclusively for bitmaps.

6

Photo (JPEG) Versus Lossless (GIF/PNG) Compression

How do you know what compression scheme is best for your image? That depends on the nature of your original. If color and image detail are important, as would be the case in a photograph, JPEG is the best choice.

It's also important to know that JPEG format offers "lossy" compression. This means that each time you resave a JPEG file the quality will be diminished slightly. Ideally, you only save once to a JPEG format to maintain optimal quality.

If your bitmap in the Library was already imported into JPEG, make sure you check Use Imported JPEG Data in the Bitmap Properties dialog box associated with the JPEG file to ensure that the file does not compress again. To access the Bitmap Properties dialog box, select the image in the Library and then from the Options pop-menu, select Properties. If, however, your bitmap was imported into Flash from a lossless file format such as PCT, BMP, or PNG, you can compress with JPEG in Flash and adjust the JPEG quality settings by deselecting the Use Document Default Quality box. Additional custom settings will then become available to you that will allow you to compress in the JPEG format when the file is published to an SWF file.

Use lossless compression for bitmaps that contain large areas of flat color such as type or nonphotographic bitmap illustrations.

Edit Bitmaps

There are a few ways to edit bitmaps in Flash. You can launch an external editing program from within Flash, you can select pixels in a bitmap, you can trace with a bitmap, and you can paint with a bitmap image. You can have lots of fun with the bitmap-editing features in Flash.

Edit in Another Program

If you need to modify a bitmap in its native program, you can launch the program from within Flash. To do this, select the bitmap in the Library. From the Options menu, click Edit With (or right-click in Windows/CTRL-click on the Mac to display the context menu). In the Select External Editor dialog box, navigate your hard drive to find the application the bitmap was created in, as shown here.

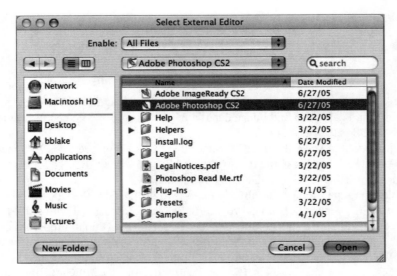

When you select the application, it will appear in the File Name box. Once you locate the program, click OK. The file opens in the program it was created in. Make your changes and resave the document. When you return to Flash, the edited version will now be in the Library. If you have an instance of this bitmap on the stage, the change will be reflected in that also.

You can also launch the editing program on a selected bitmap instance by clicking the Edit button in the Properties Inspector. Editing a bitmap instance in its native application will globally change all instances.

Trace a Bitmap

When you trace a bitmap, Flash paints over it and renders it as editable art—your bitmap is gone. You also can create some cool effects using this technique. Additionally, choosing the correct settings can substantially reduce your movie file size. If tracing is not done in the right way, though, it can increase the size of the file beyond belief.

Sometimes tracing a bitmap adds a great look to an image, and sometimes it can look like an unrecognizable blob. Because the results of tracing can be unpredictable, you need to experiment with the settings to get just the right effect.

To trace over a bitmap, select a bitmap on the stage. Choose Modify | Bitmap | Trace Bitmap. The Trace Bitmap dialog box appears, as shown in Figure 6-7. You can customize tracing options in this dialog box to achieve a variety of results.

From the top, your options in the Trace Bitmap dialog box are as follows:

- **Color Threshold** Increasing the threshold decreases the number of colors used to trace the image. The default is 100, but you can choose between 1 and 500.

- **Minimum Area** This sets the number of neighboring pixels surrounding a dominant color. A low number gives you more areas of color because fewer pixels are surrounding a color. The default setting is 8 pixels. You can enter a value between 1 and 1000 pixels.

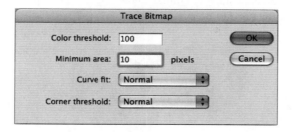

FIGURE 6-7   Use the Trace Bitmap dialog box to automatically trace over a bitmap.

- **Curve Fit**   These options determine the smoothness of an outline. From the pop-up menu, select from the following:
  - **Normal**   This is the default setting.
  - **Pixels, Very Tight, Tight, Smooth, and Very Smooth**   The Pixels setting has many points for detail, and Very Smooth has the fewest points between curves.
- **Corner Threshold**   From the pop-up menu, select from the following options to determine the way edges will look:
  - **Normal**   This is the default setting.
  - **Many Corners**   This setting gives the resulting trace more detail.
  - **Few Corners**   This setting gives the resulting trace less detail.

CAUTION   *In some cases, these settings might cause the file size to become too large. Check the resulting file size before settling on the image.*

Flash recommends the following settings for a decent-looking trace:

- A Color Threshold setting of 10
- A Minimum Area setting of 1 pixel
- Curve Fit set to Pixels
- Corner Threshold set to Many Corners

A trace can look as good as the original only if you can find the correct settings. Remember that if the quality of the bitmap you are tracing is substandard, the trace will be too. Also, certain bitmaps with a lot of detail or dark colors don't lend themselves to being traced.

The following illustration is traced from a bitmap picture of a pair of dice. The left tracing was selected after being traced. As you can see, the tracing becomes editable when selected.

The tracing is very clean and appears very similar to the original bitmap. This tracing uses the recommended settings for tracing a bitmap.

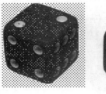

Try experimenting with multiple settings in the Trace Bitmap dialog box. You can also achieve a painterly, or *posterized*, effect by adjusting the settings. This illustration was traced with a Color Threshold of 100, a Minimum Area of 60 pixels, and a Curve Fit and Corner Threshold of Normal.

Just like other objects in Flash, bitmaps can be broken apart and edited. In the next section, you'll examine the process of performing this task.

Break Apart a Bitmap

Breaking apart a bitmap is another way to achieve some creative effects in Flash. When you break apart a bitmap, the selected picture becomes broken up into an editable object. You can modify these objects by filling them with color and applying transformations such as scaling, rotation, and skewing. You also can make the bitmap the current color in any Fill Color swatch icon. With this option, you can actually fill or paint with an object using the broken-apart bitmap as the fill color.

To paint with a bitmap image, do the following:

1. Select the bitmap on the stage and choose Modify | Break Apart or CTRL-B (Windows)/CMD-B (Mac). Depending on how the bitmap is constructed, you may need to repeat the process of breaking apart. You will know a bitmap is broken apart when you see a screen appear over the object, as shown here.

2. Select the Eyedropper tool in the Toolbar and click the bitmap to sample it. The bitmap's content will reflect the Fill Color option. You can now fill objects with this bitmap image. In the following illustration, a star object is filled with the hat bitmap that became a fill color.

You can also paint images using the bitmap as the fill color. In the next illustration, the same hat bitmap is used to create a painterly effect.

To paint with a bitmap, make certain the current fill color is the bitmap you want to paint with by sampling the editable bitmap with the Eyedropper tool. Then click the Brush tool, set the properties of the tool, and start painting. Use this technique to create masklike effects with the Brush or to fill objects with bitmap background effects (shown here) such as clouds or a landscape.

6

Modify a Broken-apart Bitmap

When a bitmap is broken apart, it becomes editable in the same way merged objects do in Flash. For example, when you select the broken-apart bitmap, it highlights with a screen over it just like a merged drawing. You can manipulate the edges of the bitmap, and broken-apart bitmaps merge when they overlap, just like a merged object.

Once the bitmap is editable, parts of the image can be selected. Once selected, bitmaps can be transformed or their color can be changed. Many creative effects can be achieved by breaking bitmaps apart.

To break apart a bitmap and modify the fill colors:

1. Select a bitmap on the stage and choose Modify | Break Apart as often as necessary to make the object editable.

2. In the Toolbar, select the Lasso tool. The Options portion of the Toolbar now displays the Magic Wand tool, the Magic Wand Properties button, and the Polygon Mode tool, as shown here.

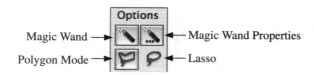

The Magic Wand tool enables you to select an area of similar color within a bitmap that has been broken apart. In this illustration, red pixels of similar value on the top of the dice were selected with the Magic Wand tool.

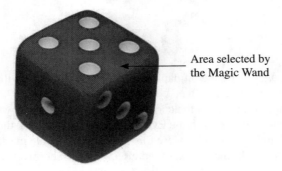

Area selected by
the Magic Wand

You can customize the properties of the Magic Wand tool by clicking the Magic Wand Properties button. This displays the Magic Wand Settings dialog box, shown here.

In this dialog box, you can set Threshold and Smoothing:

- **Threshold** This option can be set between 1 and 200 pixels. The Threshold number determines how close the colors have to be in hue to be included in the selection. A low setting indicates a more exact selection, picking only colors similar to the few pixels you have selected. A higher number gives you a broader and more diverse selection of pixels.

- **Smoothing** The Smoothing options are Pixels, Rough, Normal, and Smooth. The Pixels option gives you a pretty rough-edged selection. Smooth evens out the pixels on the edge of your selection. The selections of Rough and Normal fall somewhere in between these two extremes.

TIP *Pictures with contrasting colors or broad areas of color are easier to select from with the Magic Wand tool.*

To use the Magic Wand tool, first set the properties of the wand (if needed). Then click the Magic Wand icon and click the broken-apart bitmap. The area of color you selected with the Magic Wand tool is now editable with the Paint Bucket or any of the transformation tools. With the object selected, click the Paint Bucket to color it. You can apply a fill or gradient as you would to any editable or merged object in Flash.

To transform the object, click the part of the object you want to transform using the Magic Wand tool, and then select it with the Arrow tool.

Use the Free Transform tool in the Toolbar to scale, rotate, or skew, as outlined in Chapter 5. Since the object is editable once you break it apart, you can also make a selection by drawing an invisible marquee around a portion of the object. Once you've made a selection, it can be transformed, as shown here.

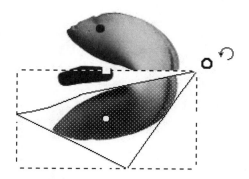

You can also make a selection with the Polygon Lasso tool. This tool allows you to make a freeform selection on an area in an editable bitmap or graphic. Use this tool by following these steps to select a piece of a broken-apart bitmap:

1. With the editable bitmap selected, click the Lasso tool. In the Options section of the Toolbar, the Polygon mode will be highlighted as this is the default mode for the Lasso tool.

2. Position your pointer over the object or area you wish to select. Click and drag over the area to make a freeform selection.

3. To make a polygon selection, click the Polygon tool in the Options section of the Toolbar.

4. Click and drag the pointer as many times as necessary to create a point-to-point polygon.

5. To end your selection, double-click the last point.

Your selection will now appear as an editable merged drawing object. Any modification you can make to a regular merged drawing object can be made to this element, too.

Conclusion

This chapter covered the many aspects of using bitmaps in Flash. Importing from programs such as Fireworks, FreeHand, and Illustrator was explored. You also learned in this chapter that there are other specialty vector-based programs (such as those that produce 3-D, cartooning, and titling images) that output to the Flash SWF format. Art created in these applications can be easily integrated into Flash. Finally, the process of modifying bitmaps was examined. You learned that you can create some pretty amazing effects by tracing and by painting with a bitmap as your fill color.

In the next chapter, you'll learn the basics of importing multimedia into Flash. Specifically, you'll import video and sounds, and you'll learn all about the settings available in Flash for these media types.

Chapter 7

Work with Video and Sound

How to...

- Import video
- Use the Video Import wizard
- Export video
- Link QuickTime video
- Import and assign sounds
- Modify sound
- Compress sound

The inclusion of video and sound in a Flash movie can make for a very exciting viewer experience. This is especially true on the Web. In the early days, when the Web was a newborn, using video and sound was unthinkable because of long download times and file size limitations. Flash helped relieve some of the limitations of the Web, especially with sound and video, and video and sound have remained powerful design tools in Flash.

The video capabilities in Flash 8 Basic are limited but certainly sufficient for the designer who needs to add a simple video clip to a Flash movie. If you need to integrate sophisticated video capabilities into your interactive animations, you need to use Flash 8 Professional. The professional version contains advanced encoding, blending, video components, embedded cue points—features that assist you in delivering professional-quality video output. Additionally, the video in Flash 8 Professional in your Flash movie can be stored on a remote server and loaded into a viewer's SWF file, reducing the size and load time for the viewer. There are other video-related features in Flash 8 Professional, some of which are discussed throughout this chapter. The Professional features are so extensive that they are beyond the scope of this book. This chapter covers the video features available in Flash Basic. However, if you happen to be using Flash 8 Professional, the topics reviewed in this chapter are available in this version, too.

Video is imported via a Video Import wizard that allows you to adjust settings, including trimming and codec tweaking, on clips prior to import. A *codec* is a hardware or software component (short for "compressor-decompressor" or "code-decode") that reduces the size of your video file, image, or audio by compressing it. When the file is played back, it is decompressed. The term *encoding* refers to the hardware or software codec in the process of compressing the data according to the rules of the particular codec you have selected to do the job. Selecting the right codec for your job is an important consideration, because when you are producing video for the Web or for a DVD, you need the file to be small in size and good to excellent in quality.

Flash uses Sorenson Spark and On2VP6 as codecs, which you'll learn more about in the next section. Flash 8 Professional also offers a much higher level of encoding than Flash Basic and produces near-perfect-quality Flash video. This chapter focuses on the video features of Flash 8 Basic in addition to covering some of the Flash 8 Professional features along the way.

Sound files can be imported into Flash, too. The volume and balance of sound can be adjusted right in Flash. Sounds can be applied to the timeline, buttons, and movie clips. Sound, like video, is assigned a codec either in Flash or imported with one. You'll also learn about audio encoding in Flash and additional settings and properties that can be customized.

In this chapter, you'll learn the basics of importing and exporting video and sound into Flash. In Parts III and IV, you will expand on this knowledge by learning to put these skills to work to create interactive video and sound in your Flash movies.

Import Video into Flash 8

Flash 8 allows you to import *embedded* video. When video is embedded in a Flash file, it becomes part of your movie. You can also link a QuickTime video to your Flash movie, but the final output can only be exported (or *published* as it is also called in Flash) to a QuickTime movie. These two features for handling video are also available in Flash 8 Professional. However, video capabilities in the Professional version of Flash are far more extensive than in the Basic version, as is discussed in the "Import Video into Flash 8 Professional" sidebar later on in this chapter. Linked video in Flash 8 Professional is discussed later on in this chapter.

No matter what kind of video you are importing, and regardless of the destination of your final output, there are many decisions that need to be made in the importing process. Flash provides a Video Import wizard to help you make decisions and adjust video settings. Among other things, settings in the Video Import wizard allow you to choose what kind of size and quality will best suit your Flash movie, depending on the bandwidth of your target audience's computers. The wizard makes importing video very easy for beginners and more advanced users alike.

Let's first take a look at importing embedded video via the Video Import wizard.

Video Import File Formats

If your video clips are destined for Flash, you need to know which format to use when preparing them for export in your video-editing program. Some of the options vary depending on which platform and video-editing application you're working with.

You can import into Flash video clips in many popular formats. On the Mac, if you have QuickTime 7 or later installed on your computer, you can import files in the following formats:

- QuickTime (.mov)
- Digital Video (.dv, .dvi)
- MPEG Movie (.mpg, .mpeg)
- Video For Windows (.avi)
- Flash Video (.flv)

If you have QuickTime 7 or later (Mac or Windows) or DirectX 9 or later (Windows only) installed on your system, you can import video clips in all of the formats above, including Windows Media (.asf, .wmv).

Files compressed in MPEG formats and imported into Flash will not give you optimal quality, and if embedded, will have little to no editing capabilities within Flash.

Import Embedded Video with the Video Import Wizard

As mentioned in the beginning of this chapter, Flash uses the Sorenson Spark and On2VP6 codecs as import standards for video. Without encoding video, embedded video in Flash would be way too big to deliver via the Web. Videos with a duration of more than a few seconds would take so long to load on a modem or DSL line that your web audience would grow impatient and probably begin to surf elsewhere on the Web, unless of course the surfer is a close friend or relative. The size could also crash a computer and use up all the available space on a server.

> **TIP**   *If you use the On2VP6 codec in Flash Basic or Flash Professional, your audience must have Flash 8 Player installed in their browser in order to view your content correctly. If you are unsure of your user configuration, you need to use the Sorenson Spark codec and target Flash Player 7 users in the Publish Settings dialog box, which is discussed in Chapter 18. The On2VP6 codec is the default setting in both Flash 8 Basic and Professional. If you are planning on using the On2VP6 codec for your Flash movie, you can direct your audience to the Macromedia site to download the free player at www .macromedia.com/downloads. It only takes a minute for your audience to do so.*

Compression always requires a trade-off between file size and output quality. With the Sorenson Spark and On2VP6 codecs, you can balance these settings to customize the movie for your particular output goal. For example, if your Flash movie with embedded video is bound for the Web and you're delivering to a low-bandwidth audience, the quality of the video will take a backseat to file size. These adjustments can be made in the Video Import wizard dialog box.

No matter which codec you use, frame size/rate you have, or length you select for your video, there are ways you can ensure your embedded video looks good and works as efficiently as it possibly can. If you are outputting the Flash movie with video to the Web, embedded video should never last longer than ten seconds, especially if there is an accompanying video track. Importing longer video clips results in synchronization problems where the video track plays faster than other assets, such as the audio tracks and other animations occurring simultaneously.

Additionally, you must always make certain the frame rate of your video is exactly the same as the frame rate in Flash. *Frame rate* refers to the number of frames in an animation that play in a second to give the illusion of continuous movement. The DV NTSC video frame rate is close to 30 fps (frames per second). PAL video, the standard in Europe and Japan, is 25 fps. The default Flash frame rate is 12 fps, so either you need to boost the frame rate in Flash or reduce the frame rate in your video-editing program before exporting to video. Consistency in the frame rate settings will result in more stable video playback on the Web.

> **TIP**   *If you need practice video clips for this chapter, you can download some (including the clip used in the following steps) from the McGraw-Hill/Osborne site (www.osborne .com). Follow the links for free code and then look for the title of this book.*

> **NOTE**   *Some features pictured in the following windows may not be available in the Flash 8 Basic or Professional program.*

The following steps demonstrate how to embed a simple video clip into Flash. To import an embedded video that does not require additional editing in Flash:

1. Select File | Import Video. In the Import Video dialog box's Select Video pane, answer the question "Where is your video file?" by checking On Your Computer, and then select the Choose button. Navigate to the video you want to import. Double-click the file or select Open (Windows)/Import (Mac). Then press the Next button at the bottom of the Import Video dialog box:

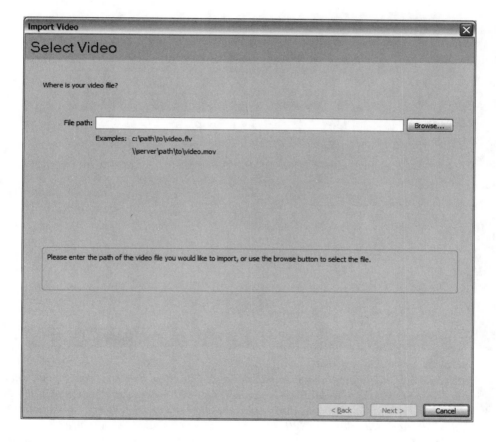

NOTE *In step 1, you can alternately select File | Import to Stage (or File | Import to Library) and then navigate to the video file in the Import File dialog box. Once you select the video file, the Video Import wizard dialog box appears just as it does if you had chosen File | Import Video. Import to Stage is the equivalent of Import to Video; this stores the video clip in the Library and creates an instance on the stage. Import to Library stores the video in the Library.*

2. In the Deployment pane, click Embed Video In SWF And Play In Timeline, as shown next. Then click the Next button to proceed to the Embedding pane.

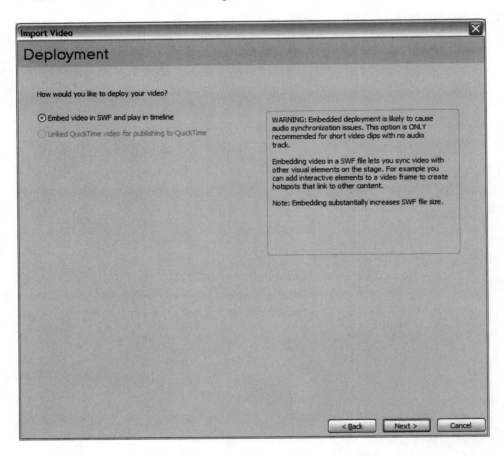

NOTE

Take note of the warning that appears in the right column of the Deployment pane when you select Embed Video In SWF And Play In Timeline. It warns you about potential audio synchronization problems during playback. What's more, it alerts you that an embedded video will bloat the SWF file size. It is recommended that you use very small video clips with no sound for optimal video playback quality. If your Flash video projects require more flexibility and large file sizes, then you ought to invest in the Professional version.

3. The wizard asks the question, "How would you like to embed the video?" For Symbol Type, select Movie Clip from the pop-up menu. The other options are Embedded Video or Graphic. Movie Clip is always a good selection because it can save a step for you later if you want to address the movie clip with a script.

4. Make sure Place Instance On Stage is checked if you want an instance of the movie clip to appear. If your symbol is a movie clip, deselect this option. In this exercise, you want to drag the movie clip instance to the stage from the Library; otherwise, a copy of the video appears on the stage and you have to delete it.

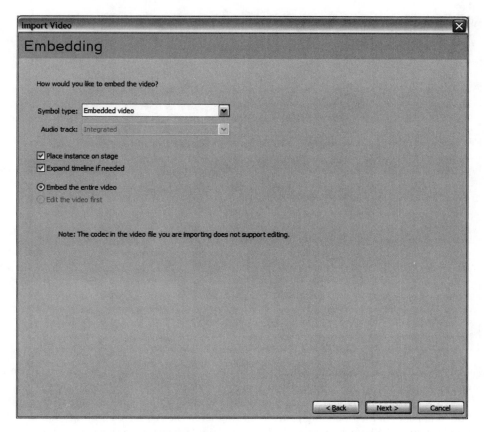

5. Expand Timeline If Needed is selected by default. This expands the video on the timeline if the frames are shorter than the duration of the frames in the video. You can also edit the video in this pane, which is discussed in the next section. Click the Next button to proceed to the Encoding pane.

6. In the Encoding pane, under Please Select A Flash Video Encoding Profile, select the encoding profile that best suits your delivery method, as shown here. The settings include the Flash 8—High Quality (700kbps), Medium Quality (400kbps), and Low Quality (150kbps).

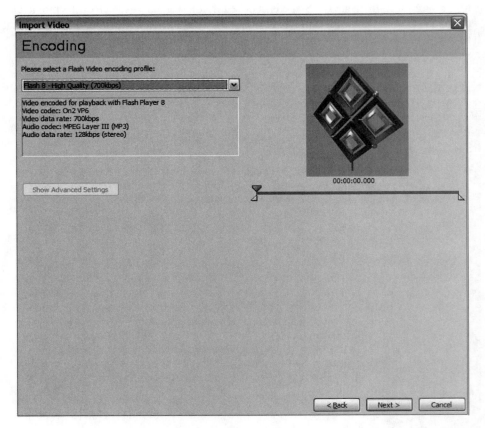

7. You can also select a Flash 7 profile from the Encoding Profiles pop-up menu. The Flash 7 encoding profiles are as follows: High Quality (700kbps), Medium Quality (400kbps), and Low Quality (150kbps). When you select a Flash 7 profile, an Advanced Settings button appears in the Encoding pane, as shown here. The Advanced Settings button toggles between Show Advanced Settings and Hide Advanced Settings as it alternately shows and hides the Advanced Settings portion of the Video Import wizard window.

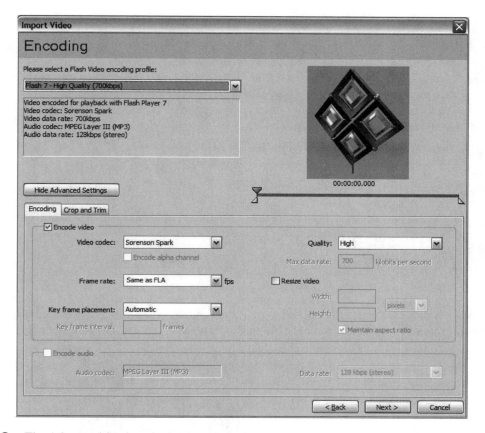

8. The Advanced Settings include an Encoding tab and a Crop And Trim tab. Select the Encoding tab to further customize your Flash 7 video codec (Sorenson Spark in this example). Here, you can also change the frame rate of the video for import into Flash (the default frame rate is 12 fps), change the size of the video, and/or change the keyframe placement. Use the default settings for most projects and they will result in excellent quality output. When you become more experienced working with Flash video and you need to customize your work, Flash 8 Professional provides many more custom settings than does Flash 8 Basic.

TIP

Want to find out which Flash Player version your audience is most likely to be using? Go to http://www.macromedia.com/software/player_census/flashplayer/ to get the latest statistics and profiles for a variety of criteria to help you better target your audience. Unfortunately, these statistics only include web surfers who live in the USA. Since all web sites can be globally accessed, the survey is lacking statistics of a much wider scope. Still, it will give you some idea of the distribution of the Flash Player in the US, which is currently used by 96.7 percent of all Internet-enabled PCs (as of June 2005).

Change the Keyframe Placement

When video is encoded, keyframes are placed on frames at even intervals. For example, if the frame rate of your video is 30 fps, the default keyframe placement in Flash is every two seconds, or every 60 frames. For a five-second video, there would be keyframe placements every ten frames. *Keyframes* store complete data on a frame and discard repetitive data on the in-between frames. When redundant data is not needed, the file size becomes smaller. Conversely, the closer the keyframe placement, the larger the final file size will be. If a video has limited movement, such as a person sitting and talking behind a static background, then you might be able to successfully reduce the size of your video and maintain superior quality by widening the keyframe placement. If your video has a lot of movement and you are not satisfied with the quality of your Flash video using the default keyframe placement, you might need to increase the amount of keyframes. Increasing the keyframe placement number also increases the size of the video because less compression is taking place.

To preview the video clip in the Encoding pane, click and drag the arrow above the thumbnail preview (playback head) over the scrubber bar, as shown here.

Playback head for scrubbing
through thumbnail video

00:00:01.412

9. After selecting your encoding setting, press the Continue button to proceed to the Finish Video Import pane. Here you can review your import settings. If you need to edit the settings you previously selected, select the Go Back button.

10. Select the Finish button. A Flash Video Encoding Progress dialog box will appear, showing you the progress of the encoding, as illustrated next.

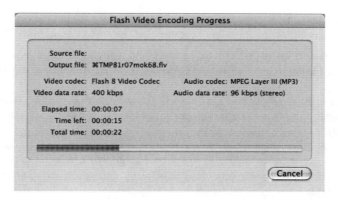

Depending on the symbol type you selected in the Embedding pane and whether you opted for the video to appear on the stage or in the Library, your video will reflect the settings you assigned in the Video Import wizard. If you chose a symbol type of Movie Clip as suggested in the above steps, the video clip and the movie clip with an instance of the nested video both appear in the Library, as shown next.

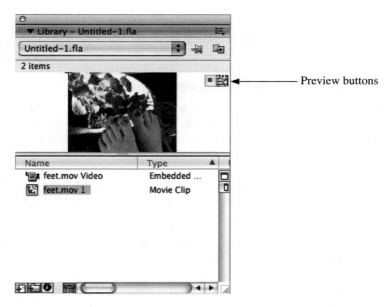

Note that the embedded video shows up in the Library with a Type as Embedded Video. If you select the movie clip in the Library, a thumbnail preview of the video that is nested in the movie clip appears. You can preview the video by clicking the control buttons in the upper-left corner of the thumbnail preview, as shown in the previous illustration.

11. Drag an instance of the movie clip to the stage and test your Flash movie by selecting Control | Test Movie or CTRL-ENTER in Windows and CMD-RETURN on the Mac.

TIP

When you test the movie, if you get an error message that says, "This movie uses features that are not supported in Flash Player Version X," check your Publish settings (File | Publish Settings) to change the player version you are targeting. In the Publish Settings dialog box, select Flash. In the Flash pane, check the Player version. Versions range from Flash Player 1 to Flash Player 8. The On2VP6 codec will only work with Flash Player 8 and above, and the Sorenson Spark codec only works with Flash Player 7 and above. There may be custom settings you chose for your movie that don't work in various versions of Flash players. Fortunately, Flash alerts you if there is going to be a Player conflict. Since the alert does not tell you which version is supported, troubleshoot in the Publish Settings dialog box by selecting a version number in the range you expect your target audience will be using, and then test the movie again until you no longer see the error message. For example, if you feel confident that your target audience will at least have Flash Player 6, which is still loaded on many systems, then specify version 6 for your player.

As you noticed in the Embedding pane of the Video Import wizard, you can also crop and trim your video in Flash. Next, you will examine the process of editing an embedded video.

Edit Embedded Video in the Video Import Wizard

Have you trimmed your clip in the wrong place and don't want to return to your editing application? Flash allows you to trim and crop video clips from within the Video Import wizard. It's a simple process that can save you the time of having to go back, trim, render, and import again. This feature is available for embedded video only in Flash 8 Basic and Flash 8 Professional.

To crop and trim video in the Video Import wizard, repeat steps 1 and 2 as outlined in the previous section, "Import Embedded Video with the Video Import Wizard." In the Import Video Embedding pane, do the following:

1. The wizard asks the question, "How would you like to embed the video?" For Symbol Type, select either Movie Clip or Embedded Video or Graphic, depending on the nature of your project, as outlined in the previous section.

2. Select Place Instance On Stage to add an instance of the video on the stage.

3. Select Edit The Video First, as shown in the next illustration. This allows you to crop and/or trim the video clip before importing it into Flash and before proceeding to the Encoding pane.

Import Video

Embedding

How would you like to embed the video?

Symbol type: Movie clip

Audio track: Integrated

☑ Place instance on stage
☑ Expand timeline if needed

○ Embed the entire video
◉ Edit the video first

⚠ Note: No supported audio track in this file was detected.

(Go Back) (Continue) (Cancel)

4. In the Split Video pane, scrub through the thumbnail preview by dragging the playback head over the scrubber bar. Decide how you would like to trim the video. Trimming the video gets rid of unwanted footage and allows you to tweak the footage directly in Flash. You can also use the playback controls under the thumbnail preview to play the clip instead of scrubbing. These controls consist of Stop, Start, Rewind, and Fast Forward buttons, allowing you to preview the clip quickly or in regular time, as shown in Figure 7-1.

NOTE   *Trimming video in Flash does not destroy the original video file, which is kept intact. If you make a mistake in trimming, delete the video and re-import it.*

5. To trim the video and create a new clip, move the In and Out points at the bottom of the thumbnail preview to the left and right until the video starts and stops at the point where you want it, as shown here. You can also use the playback controls to move the playback head to the point you want. Use the elapsed time counter at the bottom of the preview to determine the length of the clip.

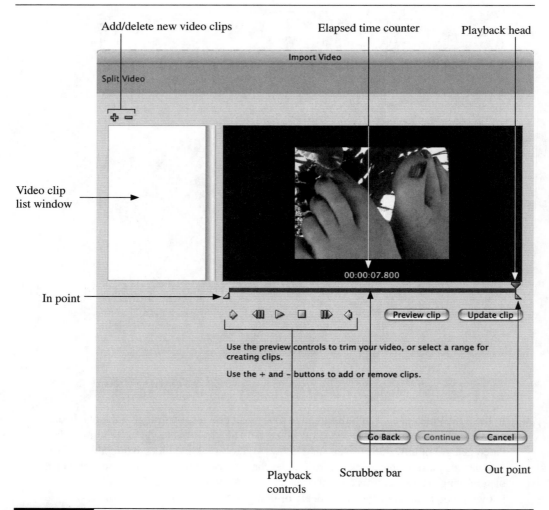

FIGURE 7-1   The Split Video pane in the Video Import wizard

6. To create multiple clips from the original, select the Add button (+) at the top of the Clip List box. This adds clips to the box, as shown here. To delete a clip from the list, select the Remove button (–).

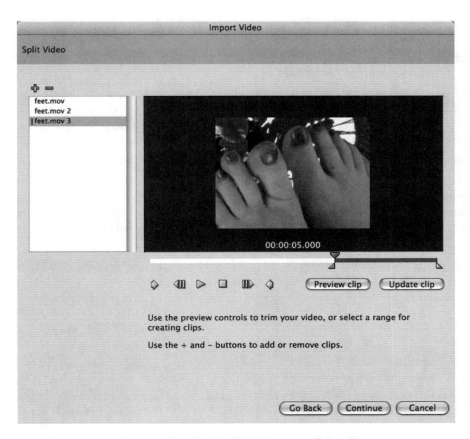

7. To edit the name of a new clip, double-click the name of the clip in the Clip List box and type in the new name, as shown at right.

8. To reorder a clip in the list, click the clip and then click the Move Clip Up or Move Clip Down arrow above the Video Clip List window.

9. Select the Continue button to proceed to the Encoding pane.

10. In the Encoding pane, under Please Select A Flash Video Encoding Profile, select the encoding profile that best suits your delivery method, as shown in the following illustration. The settings include Flash 8—High Quality (700kbps), Medium Quality (400kbps), and Low Quality (150kbps).

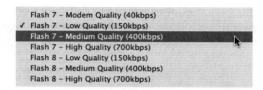

11. If you want to customize your codec, click the Show Advanced Settings button if the Advanced Settings are not visible.

12. Select the Encoding tab to tweak the encoding settings. The Crop And Trim tab allows you to crop the size of the clip as well as change the In and Out points of a single clip. Note that if you have previously edited the video in the Split Video pane you will not be able to crop and trim here. Cropping and trimming are discussed in the next section.

13. Select the Continue button to proceed to the Finish Video Import pane.

14. The Finish Video Import pane summarizes the selections you made in the wizard. If you want to change the settings, press the Go Back button at the bottom of the window, as shown here. If the settings are correct, then press the Finish button. The video will appear either on the stage, in the Library, or both, depending on the choices you made in the wizard.

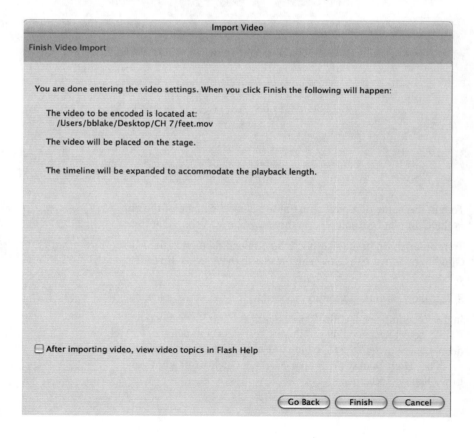

NOTE   *Trimming a clip does not alter the original clip. The In and Out points you set are applicable only to the clip in the file's Library. You can import trimmed clips from one Library to another by dragging them into the Libraries of other files.*

You can also use the Crop and Trim settings in the Advanced Settings tab to make simple edits to the video you are about to import. The interface for performing these tasks is different from the interface for splitting video. Next, you will learn how to perform these edits on a clip in Flash.

NOTE   *You can crop and trim only embedded video in Flash 8.*

Crop and Trim a Video Clip

When you crop a video clip in Flash, it masks out part of the clip so you can see only the area you designated as cropped. This is a convenient tool if you do not want to return to the native video-editing program to do this.

Trimming a video in Flash is similar to splitting the video, as discussed in the previous section. You may wonder why you would want to use the Crop and Trim settings in the Video Import wizard when you are able to split a video in Flash into several pieces. If you don't intend to split your video clip up into several separate scenes, it's easier just to trim using the Crop And Trim tab in the Advanced Settings pane.

To crop a video clip in Flash using the Video Import wizard:

1. Follow steps 1 and 2 in the previous section.

2. In the Embedding pane, leave the default settings selected and press the Continue button to proceed to the Encoding pane.

3. In the Encoding pane, select a Flash Video encoding profile from the pop-up menu, as discussed in the previous section.

4. Click the Show Advanced Settings button.

5. Click the Crop And Trim tab.

6. To crop the video clip, type in a number in the four input boxes, as shown next. These numbers represent where the top, left, right, and bottom margins of the clip reside. Alternately, you can crop the video by clicking and dragging the arrows (to the right of the crop input boxes) up and down. This allows you to dynamically preview the crop in the thumbnail preview, as shown in the following illustration. At the bottom of the crop area in this pane, the current cropped video size appears.

Crop preview
(dashed line frame)

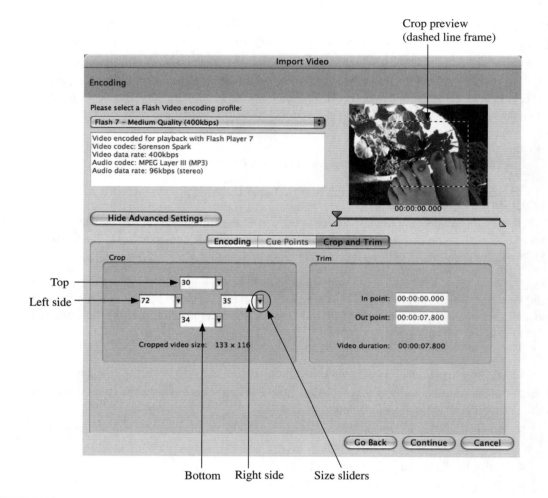

Top

Left side

Bottom   Right side   Size sliders

TIP   *Flash 7 and Flash 8 Player encoded files can be cropped and trimmed.*

To trim a video clip in the Advanced Settings pane:

1. Follow steps 1–5 as outlined above to access the Crop And Trim tab.

2. Use the playback head to decide what part of the video you want to trim.

3. Select the In point and drag it to the video clip's new starting point. Select the Out point and drag it to the video's new ending point. The scrubber bar will appear, as shown next. Note that the time codes for the In point and the Out point are indicated in the Trim box. Additionally, the new duration of the video clip appears at the bottom of this box.

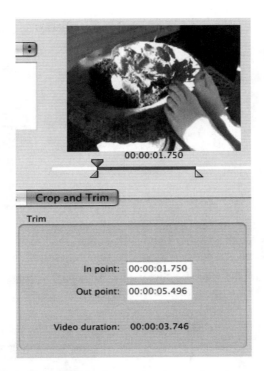

Once you edit video in Flash, there is always the chance that the source video may change later on. In Flash you can update video in case this happens. In the next section, the process of replacing video is covered.

Update and Replace Embedded Video Files

Often, you may need to return to the source video and edit it. If you have already built most of your Flash movie and it includes interactivity relating to the video, this could cause a real problem. Fortunately, you can edit a source video and then update it in Flash, keeping it in its original position in your Flash movie.

To update a video that has been changed in its source application:

1. Select the video in the Library and from the pop-up menu, select Properties. Alternately, you can right-click (Windows)/CTRL-click (Mac) the video clip. Even easier, double-click the video icon in the Library (not the movie clip icon for the embedded video clip). The Video Properties dialog box for this video clip appears, offering several option buttons and also reconfirming statistics relating to the clip selection (path, file size, etc.), as shown next.

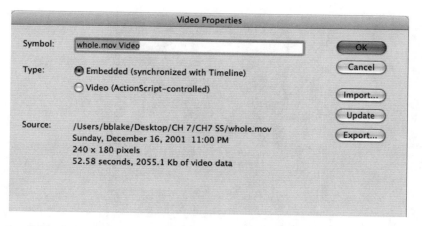

2. In the dialog box, select the Update button. This opens the Encoding pane in the Import Video dialog box. Here you can edit the codec you originally chose.

3. You can crop and trim the video by clicking the Advanced Settings button and then selecting the Crop And Trim tab, as shown here.

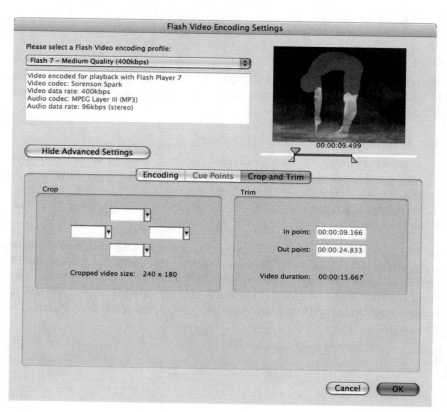

Once you have edited the video, click OK. The video will encode again. Your edits to this video clip will be noted in the thumbnail preview of the video clip that displays when you select the video clip in the Library.

TIP *If you imported the video clip as a movie clip, the video clip will be updated in the movie clip, too.*

You can also replace a video encoded in the FLV (Flash video file) format in the Video Properties dialog box. To replace the video clip and the movie clip in which the video clip is nested:

1. Select a video clip in the Library and double-click the icon. The Video Properties dialog box appears.

2. Click the Import button.

3. In the Open dialog box, navigate to the new movie and click the Open button. Note that the File of Type (Windows)/Enable (Mac) input box indicates the video needs to be a Macromedia Flash Video (FLV), as shown here.

7

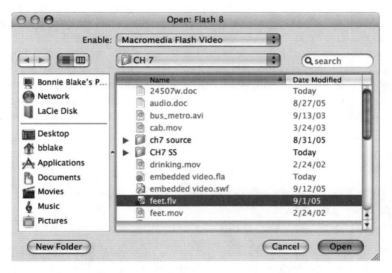

As mentioned at the beginning of this book, you can also import a QuickTime movie into Flash as a linked movie. This capability is not new to Flash as it has been a feature since version 5. Back then it was the only way in which you could incorporate video in your Flash movie. Times have changed since version 5. Video compression for the Web has become more efficient, a larger percentage of your target audience is using broadband connections, and video is becoming more prevalent on the Web and especially in Flash. In the next section, you will learn how to link QuickTime video to your Flash files and weigh the pros and cons of doing so.

Import Video into Flash 8 Professional

Flash 8 Professional allows you to embed video into your Flash movie as well as import an external, or "linked," video. Importing embedded video in Flash 8 Professional involves the same process as it does in Flash 8 Basic. Importing linked video allows you to place video that is located on a remote or local server into a Flash movie. When you do this, Flash creates a path between the Flash movie and the video file because you assign a URL to the video clip. In the Select Video pane of the Video Import wizard in Flash 8 Professional, you can link a video by indicating a remote path for a Flash movie residing on a web server, Flash Video Streaming Service, or Flash Communications Server.

Import Linked Video into Flash

As you are about to find out, linked video in Flash behaves differently than embedded video on your Flash stage. With linked video, you create a pointer in Flash to an external video file much in the same way you would in an HTML document. You can play the video and scrub the timeline on the Flash stage, but you can't test the movie in the Flash Player. The movie can only be seen once it's been exported (also known as *published*), and it must be exported as a QuickTime video. In essence, your movie is no longer Flash-based as the audience now needs the QuickTime Player to view the file. You may wonder why anyone would want to link a QuickTime video to a Flash file and then export in QuickTime. There may be little application for this but it's still a tool that may

Using QuickTime Pro

QuickTime is not a native video file in Windows as it is in Apple. Most often, video files are saved in an AVI file format, the Windows equivalent of QuickTime. If you need to convert an AVI file to QuickTime, you can use a utility like QuickTime Pro from Apple. QuickTime Pro can be downloaded from the Apple web site (www.apple.com/quicktime). QuickTime Pro allows you to export your movies in many different formats. It also has some video-editing capabilities and even a few effects that can be added to video. As of this writing, QuickTime version 7.02 is shipping and the Pro version costs $29.99. For that price, this utility has a lot of impressive capabilities.

be utilized for custom purposes. For example, let's say you wanted to add an effect to a video that you could only achieve with Flash and the final output was being burned to DVD as a video file. You may in this case choose to do some of the work in Flash.

QuickTime versions 4 through 5 can contain Flash tracks. This means that the QuickTime file you export from Flash can retain some Flash scripting. For example, if you want your movie to include buttons to control the main timeline, this interactivity will be retained when you export the movie to QuickTime format. If you open a QuickTime movie in Apple QuickTime Pro and it was done in Flash, you can actually view the Flash track, as shown in Figure 7-2.

To import linked video into Flash:

1. Select File | Import | Video/Import to Stage/Library, navigate to the video file you want to import, and click Open (Windows)/Import to Library (Mac).

2. In the Import Video dialog box's Select Video pane, select the file path of your video and then click the Continue button.

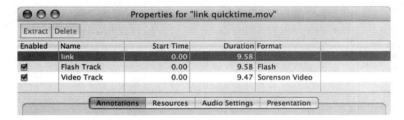

FIGURE 7-2   You can view the Flash track in a QuickTime movie in QuickTime Pro.

3. In the Deployment pane, answer the "How would you like to deploy your video?" question by clicking Linked QuickTime Video For Publishing To QuickTime. Press the Finish button to complete the import, as shown here. Since you cannot edit linked QuickTime video in Flash, your selections in the Video Import wizard are limited.

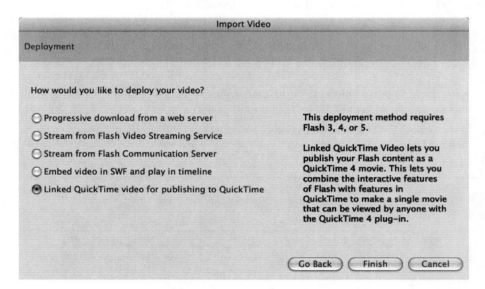

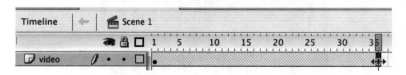

NOTE *The Deployment pane portrayed here is from Flash 8 Professional and has more options listed than in Flash 8 Basic. However, the Linked QuickTime Video For Publishing To QuickTime button is available in both versions.*

When the video is finished importing, an instance appears on the stage and frames fill the length of the timeline. Scrub the playback head across the timeline to see a video preview. If the length of the frames in the timeline is not in sync with the length of the imported video, you can shorten or lengthen the duration of the frames. To do so, navigate the timeline's playback head to the tail, or end, of the video's last frame. In Windows, press CTRL and drag the last frame to the left (CMD and drag on the Mac) to shorten and to the right to lengthen, as shown next.

Additionally, the Library identifies the type of video as Linked Video (shown next).

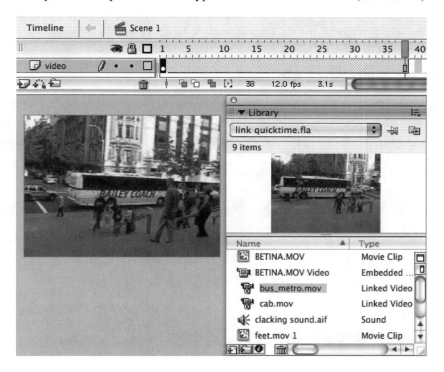

 NOTE   *Compression settings cannot be set for linked video in Flash. The video plays at the settings that were assigned when it was exported from the video-editing application.*

Did you know?

Read the Deployment Pane

In the Deployment pane in the Video Import wizard, take note of the information regarding deploying the QuickTime movie format in Flash. The note reads, "This deployment method requires Flash 3, 4, or 5." These versions of Flash refer to the Flash Player version. It goes on to explain that although QuickTime files published in Flash export as QuickTime 4 files, an audience using QuickTime 4 and over can view your movie.

Export Linked Video to QuickTime

As mentioned at the beginning of this section, when your movie that contains linked video is completed, you need to export it in QuickTime format. Chapter 18 gets into the specific details on exporting (publishing) to QuickTime format. In this section, a simple export to QuickTime is examined.

To export a Flash movie with linked video:

1. Select File | Export | Export Movie (CTRL-ALT-SHIFT-S in Windows/OPTION-CMD-SHIFT-S on the Mac).

2. In the Export Movie dialog box, type a name for the file in the File Name (Windows) or Save As (Mac) text box, as shown here. In Windows, for Save As Type, select QuickTime (.mov) and then click the Save button.

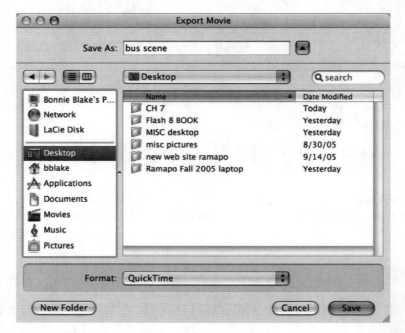

3. In the Export QuickTime dialog box, shown next, check the Match Movie option to match the dimensions of the exported movie to the original. Deselect this option if you want to type in custom dimensions. For streaming QuickTime sound (sound that plays as it loads), check Use QuickTime Compression and then click the Settings button. In the Sound Settings dialog box, you can indicate a compressor, rate, and size, and whether you want mono or stereo. When you are done, click OK. (For more information on sound in Flash, refer to the section on importing sound in the last section of this chapter.)

Export QuickTime

	Width	Height	
Dimensions:	300	x 300	☑ Match movie

OK
Cancel

Alpha: Auto

Layer: Auto

Streaming sound: ☐ Use QuickTime compression

Settings...

Controller: Standard

Playback: ☐ Loop
☐ Paused at start
☐ Play every frame
(Will disable sound if enabled)

File: ☑ Flatten (Make self-contained)

4. In the Export QuickTime dialog box, you also have options for adding a controller to provide playback controls in the QuickTime viewer. In addition, there are playback options you can choose from. When the movie loads into a user's browser, you can set it to play continuously by checking Loop. If you want the movie to pause at the start of the movie and have the user control the playback, check Paused At Start. To ensure every frame is played and not skipped over, check Play Every Frame. Check Flatten if you want to make the movie self-contained, not linked to any external files. When you have finished setting your options, click OK and the file will export.

Next, you'll explore how to export to a Flash video file.

Flash 8 Professional

Benefits of Flash 8 Professional

Flash video files generate excellent quality video. Flash 8 Professional ships with the Flash Video Encoder application. The Encoder application allows you to edit video, batch-process video files, and embed cue points on your timeline. *Cue points* are markers placed on selected parts of the timeline. A script in your Flash movie can trigger an action on any of these cue points, allowing you to create a real multimedia experience. Flash 8 Professional also installs .flv plug-ins into your video-editing applications such as FinalCut Pro, Adobe Premiere, Adobe After Effects, and QuickTime Pro, in addition to several more applications. This plug-in allows you to encode your video project directly into an FLV format, resulting in crisp, beautiful video that can immediately be imported into Flash. Because of the many additional video-related features in Flash 8 Professional, if you plan on working extensively with video in Flash, it is wise to update to the Professional version.

Export Flash Video Files

The Flash video file format, also known as *FLV* (.flv), was designed to be used in Flash movies containing video that is used for streaming, remoting, and videoconferencing applications, as well as sharing data from the Flash Communications Server. Flash video files are compressed using Sorenson Spark. If you are a Flash 8 Basic user, it is unlikely you will be exporting video as a Flash video file; however, you may find yourself working with a hosting service that uses the Flash Streaming Server or the Flash Communications Server; or, if you have clients, they may ask for a video file in this format.

In Flash 8 Basic and Flash 8 Professional, you can export a selected video to a Flash video file format (FLV) from the Video Properties dialog box. FLV files can also be imported into Flash, and FLV files in an external location can be played and controlled from a remote location. Flash remoting is beyond the scope of this book, but the process of exporting in this format is quickly outlined here.

To export an embedded video to FLV format:

1. Double-click the video icon in the Library. Alternately, you can right-click (Windows)/ CTRL-click (Mac) the video in the Library and select Properties from the pop-up menu. Click the Export button.

2. In the Export FLV dialog box, shown here, navigate to the folder where you would like to save the video, type in a name, and click the Save button.

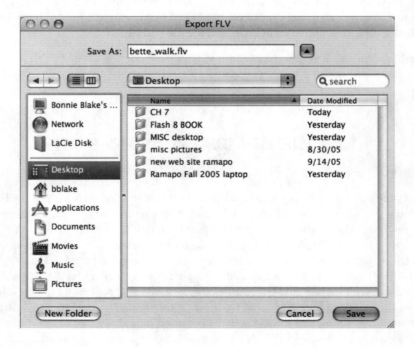

To import a file in the FLV format into Flash, simply use the steps as outlined earlier for importing embedded video.

In addition to video, sound is an important aspect of any multimedia project in Flash. Just like video, sound must be imported into Flash. There are very few ways, if any, to edit sound in Flash. As such, you want to make sure the sound you import into Flash is well planned in advance. Next, you will explore the various ways in which you can liven up your Flash movie by adding sound.

Import and Assign Sounds

Sound is an essential component in Flash. Often, you'll want to incorporate sound effects, sound tracks, or loops in your Flash creation. The ability to import and adjust digital sound in Flash is another feature that categorizes Flash as a full-featured, multimedia-authoring program. In this section, you'll learn how to import sound into Flash. In later chapters, you will expand on this knowledge by adding sounds to symbols and controlling the playback of sound in Flash.

To modify and mix sound to import into Flash, you need to use a sound-editing program independent of Flash. In such a program, you can change the tempo, insert and delete audio tracks, delete part of a sound, remix it, and make many other changes so the sound will complement your Flash movie when you import it. Once your sound is imported into Flash, you can fade the sound in or out.

First, you will look at the process involved in importing sound in Flash. There are sound files available on the McGraw-Hill/Osborne web site (www.osborne.com) in the Chapter 7 folder for this book if you want to experiment with sound in Flash.

Import a Sound File

When a sound file is imported into Flash, just like a picture or video file, it must be compressed and saved in a format that's recognizable to Flash. The following sound file formats can be imported into Flash:

- **AIFF (.aif)**   This format is the standard Mac sound format. Windows with QuickTime 4 can read AIFF files.

- **WAV (.wav)**   This format is the standard sound format for Windows. Macs with QuickTime 4 can read WAV files.

- **MP3 (.mp3)**   MP3 format is becoming an increasingly popular file format because of its impressive compression capabilities. It can reduce the size of an audio file considerably and still retain good sound quality. It is both Mac- and Windows-compatible.

You can import the following additional file formats into Flash if you have QuickTime 4 or later installed on your system:

- Sound Designer II (Mac)
- Sound Only QuickTime Movies (Windows and Mac)

- Sun AU (Mac)
- System 7 Sounds (Mac)

Importing a sound into a Flash file is as easy as importing a graphic. To do so, follow these basic instructions:

1. From the main menu, choose File | Import | Import to Library. In the Import dialog box, navigate to the sound file you want to import and click it. Click Open in Windows or click Import on the Mac.

NOTE *Even if you select Import to Stage, the sound file will appear only in the Library of the movie you are importing to.*

2. To preview the sound you imported, choose Window | Library. Sound is depicted with a loudspeaker icon in the Library. A preview thumbnail of the sound wave is shown in the top of the Library panel, as shown in Figure 7-3. The graphic preview of the sound wave gives you an idea where in the sound the amplitude peaks and wanes.

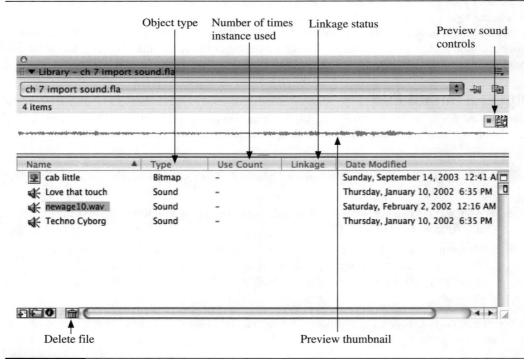

FIGURE 7-3 You can preview a graphic image of a sound in the Library.

If you are using WAV or AIFF sound files, it is recommended that you save them at a bit rate of 16 bits, 22 kHz mono, before importing them into Flash. Mono sound is half the size of stereo.

Sample the sound by clicking the control arrow in the top right of the sound wave. Stop the sound by clicking the square Stop button.

Assign Sounds to Your Flash Movies

You've probably noticed that Flash technology on the Web is chock-full of sounds these days. With the new MP3 compression standard and streaming capabilities, sound is easier to use and to hear on the Web than ever before. Getting sound from its original source into your movie is pretty easy to do.

You can do some interesting things with sound in Flash. You can determine how the sound will load into the movie when it's played by choosing a sync type. There are also tools with which you can edit the balance and the volume of the sound and set time in and out points.

Once you import your sounds, they become stored in the Library. To make a sound work, you need to place it on a timeline in your movie. You can add sounds to layers, buttons, and movie clips, and you can play sounds residing in other files. First, you'll learn to add sound to a layer in the main timeline.

Add Sound to the Timeline

Putting a sound on a timeline is simple. Generally, it's a good idea to place a sound on its own layer. That way, the sound is visible (it displays as a waveform), which makes it easier to manipulate.

Multiple sounds can be added at different points in the timeline and to multiple layers. To add sound to a layer, do the following:

1. Import a sound following the steps outlined previously.

2. Create a new layer in the timeline by clicking the Insert New Layer icon in the bottom left of the timeline, as shown here. This layer will be the sound layer, on which sounds will be placed.

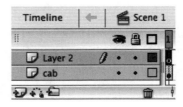

3. Name the layer by double-clicking the layer name and typing in a new name. In the next illustration, the layer is named "sound." It's a good practice to name all of your layers. In Chapter 9, you'll learn how to organize layers according to their purpose and name.

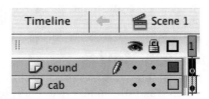

4. Click the new sound layer. Click a sound in the Library and drag it anywhere on the stage. You will see the sound wave appear in the first keyframe of the layer, as shown next.

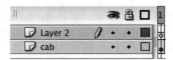

5. To hear the results of your imported sound, test the movie by selecting Control | Test Movie or CTRL-ENTER (Windows)/CMD-RETURN (Mac).

If you want to see the entire waveform of the sound in the timeline to get a graphical representation of where it will end, add frames to the sound layer. Do this by clicking the first sound frame in the timeline and then inserting as many frames as it takes to display the whole waveform (press F5 or select Insert | Timeline | Frame). As you insert frames, you will see the visual of the entire waveform appear, as shown next.

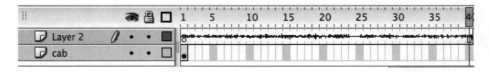

If you create too many frames on the timeline and need to delete some, click any of the frames in this layer and press SHIFT-F5 (or choose Edit | Timeline | Remove Frames) as many times as you need to delete frames.

Modify Sound

When you test the movie, the sound loops only once. With the Properties Inspector, you can modify the properties of the selected sound to have it play as many times as you like and synchronize sound to the frames in a movie.

First, you'll look at effect settings, which allow you to adjust the pan (balance) and amplitude (volume).

Adjust Effects

There are several preset effects that can be applied to a sound. In addition, custom effects can also be created. To add an effect, do the following:

1. Click the sound wave on the layer in the timeline, and then look at the Properties Inspector (shown next). The Properties Inspector enables you to do some minimal editing on the selected sound. It's convenient to be able to do this, especially if you don't have access to an audio-editing program.

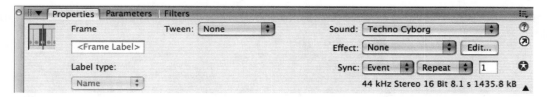

2. In the Effect pop-up list, shown here, you can set the balance and volume of the sound.

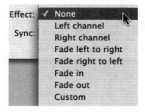

3. The following settings are available in this list:

- **None**   This is the default setting. It applies no effects, and it also removes any previously applied effects.

- **Left Channel and Right Channel**   Use one of these options to play in one of the selected channels.

- **Fade Left To Right and Fade Right To Left**   Use one of these options to fade a sound from one channel to another.

- **Fade In and Fade Out**   Select one of these options to gradually fade in or out the loudness of a sound.

- **Custom**   This option displays the Edit Envelope dialog box where you can customize your effect. This dialog box is discussed next.

Use the Edit Envelope Dialog Box The Edit Envelope dialog box becomes available when you select Custom from the Effect pop-up menu. This dialog box enables you to further customize preset effects. In fact, if you select an effect such as Fade Right To Left or Fade Left To Right, and then click the Edit button, the Edit Envelope dialog box will graphically display the results of that effect.

You can easily alter the sound envelope on a predefined effect by clicking the Edit button to the right of the Effect list. When you're finished adjusting the sound, you will have created a new effect (see Figure 7-4). If you're a beginner, it's probably easier to start with a predefined effect and then tweak it by selecting the Edit button in the Properties Inspector.

The Edit Envelope dialog box displays the selected effect in the top left of the box. This is your starting ground for modifying the volume and balance of a sound. The sound waves are displayed one on top of another, the top wave representing the left channel and the bottom wave representing the right channel.

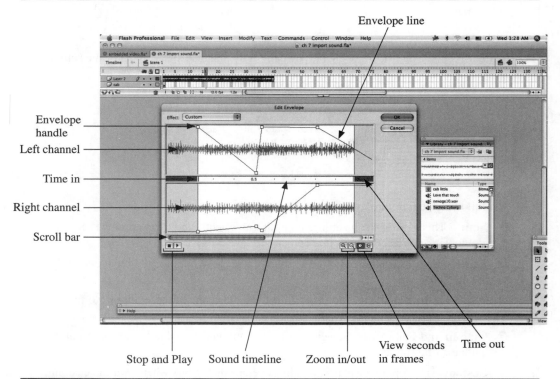

FIGURE 7-4 You customize sound volume and balance in the Edit Envelope dialog box.

The envelope handles are the little squares attached to the envelope lines. Click and drag these square handles to change the amplitude (volume) of the sound. Add handles to the envelope by clicking anywhere on the envelope line, as shown here.

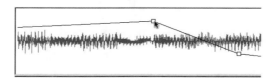

Notice that when you add a handle, a mirror handle appears in the bottom channel. When you drag a handle up or down, this action is not mirrored in the other channel. However, horizontal dragging of the handle is reflected on both channels.

In between the left and right channels is the sound timeline, on which reside the Time In and Time Out controls. These appear as little gray bars at the beginning and end of the sound timeline. If the sound is long, you may need to scroll horizontally using the scroll bar at the bottom of the right channel to navigate to the end of the sound.

The Time In and Time Out controls enable you to determine where sound starts and stops. Use the Time controls to trim the sound's beginning and end. To use the Time In and Time Out controls, click and drag the bar to the new point in the sound timeline where you want the sound to begin or end, as shown here.

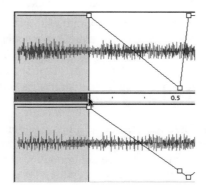

This illustration shows the sound timeline in fractions of seconds. To toggle between displaying frames and seconds on the sound timeline, you can use the Frames and Seconds buttons in the bottom-right corner of the window.

In the bottom right of the Edit Envelope dialog box, you can also select the Zoom In and Zoom Out buttons to magnify the sound waves for pinpoint precision when you are setting the options in this dialog box.

The bottom of the dialog box offers a scroll bar so that if the magnified sound wave exceeds the size of the box, you can scroll left and right. The bottom left of the box offers sound controls that allow you to test the state of the current sound. Use these to experiment with envelope settings and test them.

Once the sound is adjusted, it can be synchronized to your Flash movie. Let's take a look at how this is done.

7

Sync Sound   The Sync option in the Properties Inspector has a pop-up list, shown here, that enables you to synchronize your sound with your movie.

This is an important feature because if your movie is dependent on sounds playing in conjunction with graphics, you want to make sure the sound doesn't skip or appear to play at the wrong time. The options in this pop-up menu are as follows:

- **Event**   Event sound is synchronized to an event, such as a user's press of a button. The sound continues to play regardless of when a movie stops. Unlike streaming sound, event sound needs to download in its entirety before it begins to play.

- **Start**   This option is identical to event sound. The only difference is if an instance of a sound with a Start event is playing and another instance of this same sound is loaded into the movie, the first instance of that sound needs to stop playing before the next instance starts.

- **Stop**   Select Stop if you don't want the sound to play when the movie loads. Stop is the option to use if you want the sound to play on an event such as a mouse click.

- **Stream**   This option makes sound keep up with the animation in the movie, so the sound doesn't fall out of sync with the animation. The number of frames determines the length of a streaming sound. MP3 sounds synchronized for streaming must be recompressed in the Sound Properties dialog box (discussed later in this chapter). Streaming sound begins playing as soon as enough frames are loaded, then continues to play as the remaining frames load.

To the right of the Sync selections, you can set the looping options as shown next. These options indicate how many times a sound will repeat a play action. If you want the sound to continue playing until the audience exits the file, select Loop. If you want the sound to play for a specified amount of time, select Repeat and type in a number.

Compress Sound

Just like video files, sound files tend to be large. If your Flash movie is bound for the Web, your sounds need to be as compact as possible. As with video, you need to identify the perfect balance between quality and size. Generally, you will be compressing your sound as part of your preparation for the export of the movie.

Sometimes, after sound is compressed, it doesn't sound the way you expected it to. It may sound tinny, or like a poor-quality broadcast from an old AM radio station. In the Sound Properties dialog box, you can set compression and test your settings to make sure the sound is maintaining its integrity.

To edit the compression on a sound in the Library, double-click the Sound icon in the Library or right-click in Windows/CTRL-click on the Mac to display a pop-up context menu. From this menu, select Properties.

In the Sound Properties dialog box, you can compress your sound or recompress it in another format. For example, if you've imported a WAV file and want to recompress it in an MP3 format to reduce file size, this is where it's done. You also can change a sound and test the quality of several different compression ratios.

Figure 7-5 shows the Sound Properties dialog box as it looks when it is displayed for a sound named "touch," which is a WAV file. The name of the sound file appears at the top of the dialog box. Under the name, the file path, date, and settings are displayed.

7

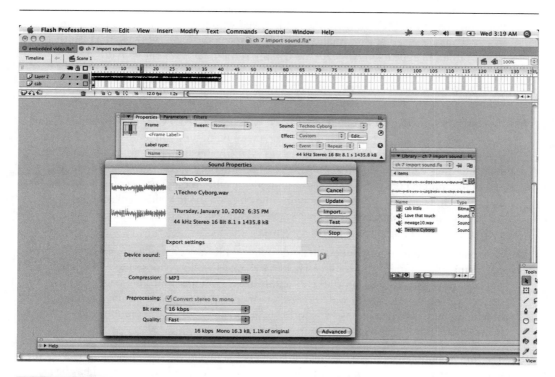

FIGURE 7-5   The Sound Properties dialog box allows you to compress, test, and update a sound.

In the Compression box, you can experiment with different compression formats and ratios. To set a compression scheme, click the pop-up list and select from it. Generally, the MP3 setting will balance size and quality well in Flash.

> **TIP**
>
> *You also can set export settings for sound in the Publish Settings dialog box, which is discussed in Chapter 18. If you don't select export settings in the Sound Properties dialog box, you can assign export settings to sounds in the Publish Settings box. You also can chose to ignore the export settings in the Sound Properties dialog box. The Override Sound Settings check box in the Publish Settings dialog box lets you retain two sets of files to be used for different purposes, with different audio export settings.*

The Compression pop-up menu offers the following compression formats: MP3, ADPCM, and Raw. When you select from one of these three compression formats, additional menu selections become available relating to the format you selected:

- If you select MP3 as your compression, you can also set the bit rate and quality of the sound file from pop-up menus. The bit rates range from 8kbps (kilobytes per second) on the low end of the sound spectrum to 160kbps on the high end. From the Quality menu, you can select Fast, Medium, or Best. A file saved with the Fast quality setting is smaller in size than one saved at Best quality. When you select different bit rates, the resulting file information appears underneath the Quality setting. Experiment with different settings by clicking the Test button in this dialog box. Notice the difference in sound quality, for example, between a file with a bit rate of 8kbps and a file with a bit rate of 48kbps.

- If you select Adaptive Differential Pulse-Code Modulation (ADPCM) as your compression, you can select a sample rate from the pop-up menu that gives you a range from 5 KHz to 44 KHz. You also can select the number of ADPCM bits in a pop-up menu. Mono or stereo settings can be checked also. ADPCM is commonly used in voice technologies and digital phone networks. ADPCM compresses well (although not as well as MP3) and, as such, is a viable choice for keeping file sizes on the low side. This compression format was the default setting on older versions of Flash and is useful for short sounds, such as those you might use on button events.

- Raw enables you to export uncompressed sound. With Raw compression selected, you can change the sample rate from 5 KHz to 44 KHz, as well as choose mono or stereo settings. Raw audio offers big file sizes and lossless compression. This wouldn't be an option you would choose for web movies, but there might be some special circumstance in which you would need to use this format. As a general rule for beginning and intermediate Flash users, just ignore it.

Use the Import button to replace the currently selected sound with a new one. This is a useful technique if you need to globally update instances of sound. Select Update if a sound has been changed in another program. Click Update, and the sound will automatically be updated.

Conclusion

The ability to import video and sound into Flash is certainly one of the program's most exciting features. The basics of video and sound were both covered in this chapter. You learned to import embedded video as well as linked video into Flash. You also learned how to play video and sound, set compression on both types of files, and test the compression to see if your settings optimize the quality.

NOTE   *Chapter 13 covers sound on buttons and movie clips.*

In the next chapter, you will learn how to create symbols in Flash. You will also learn how to use and navigate symbols in the Library. As you will discover, symbols are a powerful component in Flash because they pave the way for more complex capabilities such as animation and interactivity.

7

Chapter 8

Create and Store Symbols in the Library

How to...

- Create graphic symbols, buttons, and movie clips
- Convert a graphic into a symbol
- Edit symbols
- Nest symbols
- Place and edit instances
- Change the behavior of an instance
- Transform an instance
- Break apart an instance
- Modify an instance
- Swap symbols
- Navigate the Library

Symbols are an important feature of Flash. They are powerful because they lay the groundwork for interactivity. When you learn how and when to make symbols, you'll be on your way to understanding advanced Flash concepts.

Like video, sound, and bitmaps, symbols are stored in the Library. The symbol in the Library acts almost like a master symbol, or the master plan for the symbol. When you want to use a symbol, you simply drag it from the Library and drop it onto the stage. Each time you do so, you create an instance. An *instance* is like a copy of the original. The difference between a copy and an instance is that an instance doesn't increase the file size as a copy does. In fact, you can use as many instances throughout the movie as you want without increasing file size. You can even share symbols between Libraries.

There are three kinds of symbols: graphic symbols, buttons, and movie clips. Each symbol has its own unique purpose. The most basic type of symbol is the *graphic symbol*. Generally, graphic symbols serve only as building blocks for more sophisticated symbols such as movie clips and buttons. When you import a vector graphic in FH, AI, or EPS format, it arrives in Flash as a graphic symbol already.

Buttons, on the other hand, are used for viewer interaction. A visitor on your web site may click a button to advance to another frame or to drag an object. Buttons can contain graphic symbols and movie clips. They can contain sound and animation, too.

A particularly powerful symbol is the movie clip. A *movie clip* is a movie that runs on its own timeline. In Chapter 13, you will learn more advanced techniques for working with movie clips.

There are a few differences among the three symbols' behavior. For example, a graphic symbol can be animated, but not on its own timeline, and sounds and interactivity won't work with a graphic symbol. It's not likely you would ever animate a graphic symbol on the main timeline because movie clips provide a much smarter and more streamlined workflow for creating animated objects. In fact, the ability to animate a graphic symbol on the main timeline is an old throwback from much older versions of Flash that provided animation tools that are primitive compared to Flash 8. Another difference in the behavior of these three symbols is that the timeline for a button is different than the timeline for the other two types of symbols. In this chapter, you'll learn the similarities and differences among the symbols, and you'll get a grounding in the basics of working with symbols and keeping track of them in the Library.

Create Symbols

In Chapters 2–7, you learned to create and edit shapes, merged drawing objects, object drawings, bitmaps, vectors, and video. All of these objects can be converted into a symbol. As you will discover in this chapter, working with symbols gives you a lot more flexibility in terms of object and time management, file size, and interactivity. In this section you learn how to make a basic symbol.

A symbol can be created from an element already on stage or from scratch on the symbol editing stage. You can even make a symbol from a symbol, and when you become more experienced in Flash, you will find yourself doing this often. Sound complicated? Once you get the hang of creating and organizing symbols, it's a breeze. First, you'll look at how to take an existing object and turn it into a symbol.

Convert a Graphic Element into a Symbol

Converting an existing object of any type into a symbol is easy. Use this technique if you have an existing object on the stage and, as an afterthought, want to convert it into a symbol:

1. Select an object on the stage. If you want to select more than one object to make your symbol, hold down SHIFT and click each element, or drag a selection marquee around the objects you want to convert. The elements can be merged, drawing objects, grouped, bitmaps, vectors, or video, or any of these in combination.

2. Once the object or objects are selected, select Insert | Convert to Symbol in the menu or press F8.

3. In the Convert To Symbol dialog box (shown here), type in a name. In this illustration, the graphic symbol is given the name "swish."

4. For Type, click one of the three selections: Movie Clip, Button, or Graphic. The Type setting determines the way a symbol will behave. The Registration option refers to the point of reference on the object. The default reference for symbols is always the top-left corner. This can be changed by clicking one of the nine registration handles in the Registration thumbnail in this dialog box.

5. Note that in the bottom-right corner of this dialog box there is an Advanced button. Clicking this button will expand the dialog box with additional linkage selections. The linkage selections enable you to assign an identifying name to the symbol in the movie's Library. A symbol with a linkage identifier can be shared with other movies.

6. When you are done, click OK.

The graphic symbol now appears in the Library window. If the Library is not visible, select Window | Library or press CTRL-L (Windows)/CMD-L (Mac). As you can see in the following illustration, the Library provides a thumbnail preview of the new symbol when the symbol is selected, and the icon under Name also represents the symbol type.

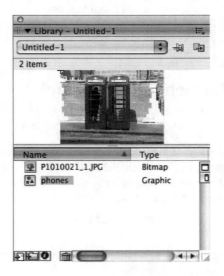

You can also access the Convert To Symbol dialog box by dragging an object from the stage to the Library.

Create a New Symbol

Creating a symbol from scratch is just as easy as converting a graphic to a symbol. You create a new symbol by entering Symbol Editing mode. The Symbol Editing mode for each symbol type has its own special stage and timeline. Most everything you can do to an object on the main timeline can be done in Symbol Editing mode, too. In this sense, creating a symbol is much like

Use the Advanced Features
When Creating a Symbol

Perhaps you noticed in the Convert To Symbol dialog box an Advanced button. If you were curious you selected it and you noticed it expands the dialog box and gives you more selections regarding linkage. Linkage names and URLs allow you to "link" symbols to Libraries in other Flash files whether the file exists locally on your server or remotely. In the "Navigate the Library Window" later in this chapter, linkage is discussed in detail as this is also an option that can be accessed from the Library options.

making a regular object. You can have multiple layers, groups of any kind of objects, imported bitmaps, and vector art—basically anything you want, and you can add other symbols, too.

You create a new symbol from scratch by selecting Insert | New Symbol or pressing CTRL-F8 in Windows/CMD-F8 on the Mac. The Create New Symbol dialog box appears, as shown here.

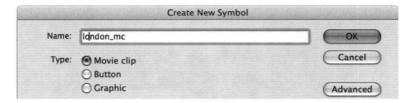

In this box, assign a name to the symbol, select the appropriate behavior, and click OK. This will bring you to Symbol Editing mode, in which symbols are created and modified. Let's further examine this mode and how to work in it.

Use Symbol Editing Mode to Create a Graphic or Movie Clip

The Symbol Editing stage and timeline for a graphic symbol or a movie clip look just like the stage and timeline at the main, or *root*, level, also sometimes referred to in scripting as _level0. (The stage for a button symbol looks a bit different and is discussed later in this section.) The only differences between this stage and the stage in the main timeline is the existence of alignment crosshairs in the center of the editing stage, and in the upper-left corner of the stage you will notice a symbol icon with the name you just assigned, as shown next. Here, the symbol is a movie clip named london_mc.

To make a simple graphic symbol or movie clip on the editing stage, do the following:

1. Press CTRL-F8 in Windows and CMD-F8 on the Mac to create a new symbol.

2. In the symbol editing stage, create an object with the drawing tools or text tools, or import graphics, bitmaps, video, or sound from an external application. Position the graphic using the crosshairs on the editing stage as your guide. Generally, it's best to position the crosshairs so they reside in the upper-left corner of the object you are creating, as shown here. This represents the default alignment for a symbol.

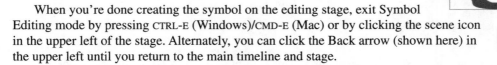

When you're done creating the symbol on the editing stage, exit Symbol Editing mode by pressing CTRL-E (Windows)/CMD-E (Mac) or by clicking the scene icon in the upper left of the stage. Alternately, you can click the Back arrow (shown here) in the upper left until you return to the main timeline and stage.

Use Symbol Editing Mode to Create a Button

The editing stage and timeline for a button symbol look different than other stages and timelines. Sure, there are layers, crosshairs, and frames, but the frames are altogether different. As you can see here, there are four frames named Up, Over, Down, and Hit. The function of these frames will be made clear in the steps that follow.

To create a button, do the following:

1. Select Insert | New Symbol (CTRL-F8 in Windows and CMD-F8 on the Mac). In the Create New Symbol dialog box, type in a name for the new symbol and select Button for Behavior.

2. On the button editing stage, draw or place an object on the stage and use the crosshairs to align it, preferably with the crosshair at the top left of the button. Just like other symbols, the object you use can be any kind of merged or drawing object, grouped, graphic symbol, or movie clip. In the following illustration, a star shape was created as a graphic symbol and placed on the Up frame in the timeline. That frame now contains a black circle, as you can see in the illustration. The black circle on the Up frame shows that the frame is a keyframe. You could exit the editing mode at this point and still have a button, but here you'll go on to add some interactivity so that something happens when the user positions the mouse pointer over the button and when he or she clicks the button.

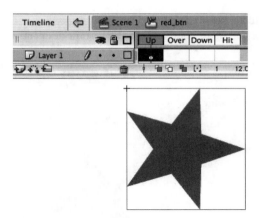

3. Press F6 to create a keyframe on the Over frame. Repeat this process by clicking on the Down frame and then on the Hit frames, which will create a duplicate object on each frame. In this illustration, note that all four frames now are keyframes. Duplicating the object in the Over and Down states by adding a keyframe makes it easy to modify the object slightly on the different frames.

4. Click the keyframe labeled Over. Over represents the state of the button when the user positions his or her mouse pointer over the button. Change the properties of the object on this frame to make it appear different when the user places the mouse pointer over the button. You can change the color of this object, move it, scale it, rotate it, or transform it, just as you can any other object in Flash. Or you can replace it with a different picture altogether. In the following illustration, the rotation of the button in the Over state was changed with the Free Transform tool in the Toolbar.

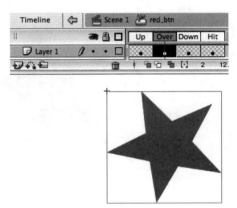

8

5. Click the Down state and again change the object's properties. In the following illustration, the star has been rotated in another angle and the color adjusted.

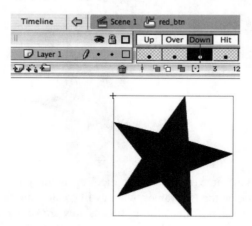

6. The only state that remains is the Hit state. On this frame you assign the active, clickable area of the button. Any graphic placed here will not show up. First, you'll create a layer for the clickable area to reside on. That way it won't get tangled up with button graphics on other layers. Create a new layer in the Button timeline by clicking the Insert Layer icon at the bottom left of the timeline.

7. Click the Hit frame in the new layer and press F6 to create a keyframe, as shown in the illustration.

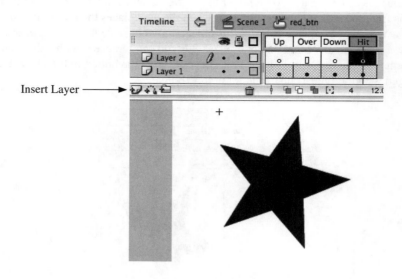

8. Now click the Rectangle tool in the Toolbar. Draw a rectangle around the object to indicate its boundaries. The rectangle can be larger than the object if you want to extend the clickable area, and it can be any color or alpha level. If you want to see the graphic, you can move the rectangle layer under the button layer by dragging it underneath, as shown next.

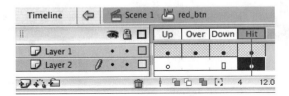

NOTE

It's a good idea to build buttons from other symbols. As you will find out later in this chapter, you can easily edit symbols that are nested in other symbols right from the Library.

To see a preview of what the button looks like in its various states (except the Hit state) drag or scrub the playback head (also known as *playhead*) over the three frame states. The result for the star example is shown in Figure 8-1. Depending on how much you modified the object in

Understand Button States

The Up, Over, Down, and Hit frames represent different states of a button. When the movie loads, the button will appear in the Up state. If a user drags the mouse pointer over a button, the graphic on the Over state will appear. Dragging the mouse pointer over the object becomes the event. If the user clicks the button, the Down state appears. The Hit state defines the area on the button that is active when a user interacts with it. You do not have to place an object on all states to make the button work. In fact, you can make a blank button by addressing only the Hit state. Why would you want to create a blank button? One reason would be if you needed an area or a movie clip to be clickable but you didn't need a graphic on the button.

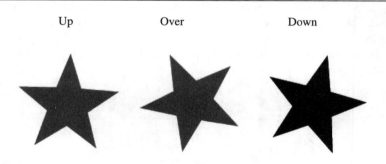

Up   Over   Down

| FIGURE 8-1 | The Up, Over, and Down states of a button |

these frames, the button will appear as an animated movie. In fact, a button *is* a movie, on its own unique timeline. Instead of playing all the frames continuously, the button stops at each frame until the user makes the next move.

To test the interactivity of the button, exit the editing mode (press CTRL-E in Windows/CMD-E on the Mac). Click the Selection tool, open the Library (CTRL-L in Windows/CMD-L on the Mac), and drag an instance of the button object to the stage. Select Control | Enable Simple Buttons from the menu (CTRL-ALT-B in Windows/CMD-OPT-B on the Mac) and position your pointer over the button. This will give you an idea of how the button will behave when the user interacts with it.

Of course, you can always use the old, tried-and-true Test Movie method (CTRL-ENTER in Windows/CMD-RETURN on the Mac) to check out the button's behavior. Testing the movie brings you out of the stage environment and shows you what the button will look like to the user. The method you use to preview buttons is simply a matter of personal preference.

NOTE   *Once you have enabled buttons, you can no longer directly select a button object by clicking it. To move the object while button behaviors are enabled, draw an invisible marquee around the button with the Selection tool. To move a button selected in this manner, use the arrow tools to move it up, down, left, or right.*

Edit a Symbol

Symbols can be edited very efficiently in Flash, since they exist as compact, self-contained objects. In this section, you'll explore the process of going back into a symbol to alter elements within it. Altering a symbol changes every instance of the symbol globally. If you want to edit only one instance of a symbol, the technique is completely different. To learn how to modify one instance of a symbol, see "Work with Instances on the Flash Stage" later in this chapter. Here you will learn how to edit a symbol so that the changes take effect globally.

When you need to make changes to a symbol, you must work in Symbol Editing mode. As just mentioned, changes made in the editing mode become global. For example, if you change the color of a movie clip in the editing mode, all instances of that movie clip will change.

There are a few ways to return a symbol to Symbol Editing mode. You can double-click an instance on the stage or a symbol in the Library. Additionally, you can select an instance on the stage or a symbol in the Library and press CTRL-E (Windows)/CMD-E (Mac). Personal preference dictates which method you use.

When you modify a symbol by double-clicking an instance on the stage, other elements surrounding it become dimmed, as shown next. This makes it easy for you to see your edit in relation to other elements. This method of editing a symbol is helpful if you want to preview the symbol in relation to other elements on the stage.

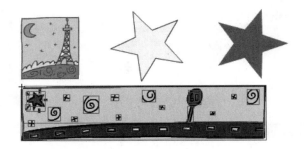

When you modify a symbol from the Library, you will see only the object being modified on its own stage and timeline. Both methods will globally change all instances of this particular symbol.

Exit Symbol Editing mode by clicking the Scene name in the upper-left corner of the stage, selecting Edit | Edit Movie, or pressing CTRL-E in Windows/ CMD-E on the Mac.

Nest a Symbol Within a Symbol

Symbols can be built in a number of ways. You learned earlier in this chapter that they can be created with editable objects and groups of objects. You also can place symbols within symbols, which sometimes is referred to as *nesting*. Graphic symbols, movie clips, and buttons are often nested in more complex buttons or movie clips. If you are adding interactivity to your Flash movie, you can address movie clips that are nested within other movie clips by indicating their location or "path" in the script associated with them.

If the symbol is a complex one, it's often most efficient to build it from other symbols. With this method, you create the component parts first, then put them together into the whole symbol. When you go to edit the symbol, you only need to edit the component. In this section, you'll learn how to put symbols inside other symbols to build a better, more efficient "mousetrap."

For example, let's suppose you were designing an animated cartoon of a person's face as a movie clip. An efficient way to plan this cartoon would be to create the different components of the face as graphic symbols or movie clips first—the eyes, nose, mouth, face, and eyebrows. Then you could assemble them on the movie clip editing stage, as shown in Figure 8-2.

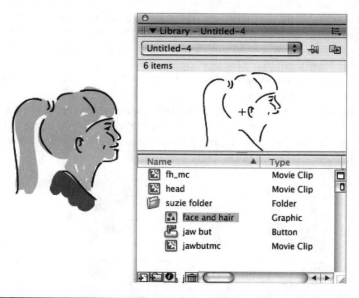

FIGURE 8-2   This movie clip was created by assembling buttons, graphic symbols, and movie clips.

Although the main symbol is a complex movie clip, it's easy to go back to each nested symbol and edit it on its own timeline. Just as with nested groups, you can get to the editing mode of a symbol by double-clicking the symbol until you reach the level you want to edit. Navigate back to the root level by clicking the icons in the upper-left corner of the stage, as shown here.

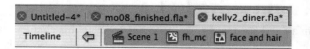

Work with Instances on the Flash Stage

As mentioned before, one of the benefits of using symbols is the ability to generate multiple copies of the original symbol stored in the Library. These copies are known as *instances*. Instances don't increase the file size beyond the original symbol, no matter how many copies you use in your movie.

To view the master symbols available in your movie, display the Library by selecting Window | Library or by pressing CTRL-L in Windows/CMD-L on the Mac. To make an instance from a symbol, click a symbol in the Library and drag it onto the stage. You can also click the thumbnail preview and drag that to the stage, as shown next.

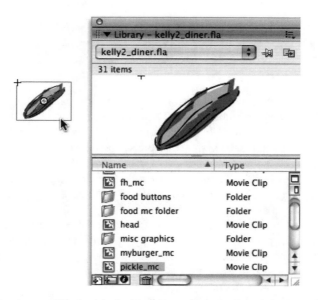

Instances can also be modified with the Free Transform tool or the Properties Inspector. Doing so makes the instance look different from the original symbol. Next, you'll learn how to transform an instance with the Free Transform tool.

Use the Free Transform Tool to Transform an Instance

As with any other object in Flash, you can apply the transformation tools from the Toolbar and the Modify | Transform menu to transform an instance. Figure 8-3 shows an instance being scaled with the Free Transform tool. You can use any of the transformation tools on a symbol.

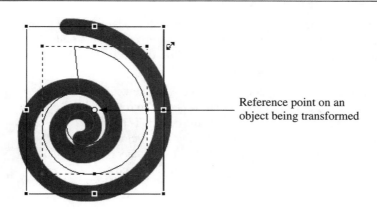

Reference point on an object being transformed

FIGURE 8-3 You can transform the size of an instance using the Free Transform tool.

Manage and Identify Symbols

When creating a symbol, it's important to name the symbol in a manner that helps you keep track of it in the Library. In addition to applying a name to a symbol, movie clips and buttons can also have instance names. Instance names, which also help keep tract of multiple iterations of the same symbol, can be assigned to the selected instances in the Properties Inspector. Although not necessary for movies comprised of simple animation, if you plan on making your Flash movies interactive in the future by assigning scripts, it's good to get into the habit of assigning instance names to movie clips and buttons. The name can be anything you like, but again, if you plan on adding scripts to your movie, you should name the movie clips and buttons using the proper syntax. You can use upper/lowercase and spaces in the naming convention, but using underlines in place of a space (_) and consistent use of upper/lowercase (as in "blackCar_mc") is the preferred naming convention. For naming movie clip instances, use "_mc" at the end of the name (as in car_mc), and for naming button instances, use *"btn" at the end of the name (as in car*btn). Using interactivity by assigning scripts to movie clips and buttons is discussed in Chapters 15 and 16.

To transform an instance:

1. Select the Free Transform tool from the Toolbar and then click the instance.

2. To scale the object, click the Scale tool in the Options section of the Toolbar. Click and drag one of the nine handles in the corners of the object. Then drag the handle in the direction you want the object scaled. As you drag, you will see a preview outline of the new scale.

3. To constrain the scale on an instance, hold down SHIFT and click one of the transform handles in any of the four corners. Drag outwards to enlarge the scale of the object and inwards to reduce the size of the object. Constraining scales the width and height proportionately in the same increment.

4. To rotate or skew the object, click the Rotate And Skew icon in the Options section of the Toolbar, as shown here. To rotate an instance, click one of the four handles in the corner. The pointer turns into an arched arrow. Click and drag the object clockwise or counterclockwise to rotate. To skew the object, click any of the four handles on the middle edges of the object. Click and drag until the object is sufficiently skewed.

Break Apart a Graphic

Let's say you created a symbol and then wanted one of the instances to return to a merged or drawing object state. You can do this by breaking the instance apart, which will break the link from the instance to the symbol. As you know, when a symbol is revised, all instances update, too. An instance that has been broken apart no longer has any association with the symbol. It becomes an independent graphic.

Why would you want to break apart an instance? Well, sometimes you may want to reuse an element used to build one symbol on another symbol, without redrawing it. You could break the object apart, extract the part you need, and create a new symbol from the new illustration without affecting any other elements of the movie. This method provides a way to reuse pieces and saves a lot of time in the process.

You can break apart any type of symbol. When you break apart symbols that contain multiple layers, animation, sound, and interactivity, you lose everything but the static object. Objects grouped and nested within the symbol remain intact when the symbol is broken apart.

8

Individual instances can also be modified in other ways without globally changing the properties of the master symbol. Next, you will learn how to change color properties on an instance.

Use the Properties Inspector to Modify an Instance

Editing an instance of a symbol is a little different than editing a regular graphic or a grouped graphic because the method of doing so is tied to the fact that it's a copy of a symbol. Because of this, the properties you can change on a single instance are limited.

The most intuitive way to modify an instance is to use the Properties Inspector. Since the Properties Inspector works in context with your selection, when you select an instance of a symbol, the properties you can change for that symbol appear in the Properties Inspector. Let's take a look at how this feature works.

If you try to change the color on an instance by selecting it and then selecting a new fill color from one of the color palettes, nothing will happen. When you want to modify the tint (color), alpha (transparency) level, or brightness of an instance, you use the Properties Inspector to do so. You apply color to an instance by selecting the object and then setting the adjustment in the Properties Inspector, as shown in Figure 8-4.

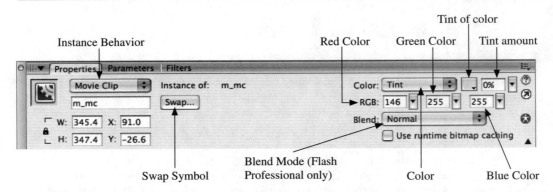

Instance Behavior · Swap Symbol · Blend Mode (Flash Professional only) · Red Color · Green Color · Tint of color · Tint amount · Color · Blue Color

FIGURE 8-4 Use the Properties Inspector to modify color and transparency on an instance.

To change the color of an instance:

1. Select the instance. Then, in the Properties Inspector, click the Color pop-up list and select Tint, as shown here.

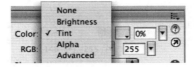

2. Click the Tint color swatch and from the pop-up swatch list, pick a new color. Clicking and dragging the Red, Green, and Blue sliders in the Properties Inspector can alter the tint of the color. The amount of tint applied to the instance can be changed by using the Tint Amount slider to the right of the color swatch, as shown here.

In addition to being able to change the tint of an instance, you can also change the brightness and transparency/opacity (alpha). Do this by selecting the symbol and in the Properties Inspector, select the setting in the pop-up menu. You can also assign several color-related properties to an instance by using advanced settings. Let's take a closer look at these additional color-related properties available in the Color pop-up menu:

- **Brightness** Select Brightness to make the instance lighter or darker in increments that range from 100% for pure white to 100% for black. Use the vertical slider to select a percentage.

- **Alpha** Set an Alpha value to modify the opacity of an instance. Use the vertical slider to select a percentage, or type a percentage in the box. A 0% setting on an instance makes the object transparent, and a 100% setting is total opacity. The slider looks similar to the Brightness slider.

■ **Advanced**   The Advanced setting enables you to blend tint and alpha color together on a selected instance. To apply advanced effects, first select Advanced from the Color pop-up list and then click the Settings button. In the Advanced Effect dialog box, shown next, you can adjust RGB color and Alpha with the sliders associated with each box. You can alter the intensity of an RGB color by multiplying it by the current color, as indicated by the multiplication (×) symbol between entry boxes. The intensified value appears in the boxes to the right. The numbers in the right boxes can also be set with sliders or typed in. Experiment with the sliders to create custom color effects.

You can achieve some compelling effects by using the Properties Inspector to apply color effects to instances. For example, you can change the tint or alpha of an instance to create an object whose color or transparency changes over a period of time in an animation. This technique is discussed in conjunction with motion tweening in Chapter 11.

Change the Behavior of an Instance

The *behavior* of a symbol refers to a symbol's type and how it functions. A button is used for objects that need to be clicked by the viewer. A movie clip is used if you need to create a movie on its own timeline.

The behavior of a selected instance can actually be changed. For example, if you wanted a movie clip instance to behave like a button or vice versa, this can easily be done. To change the behavior of an instance, click the instance and then select an option from the pop-up behaviors list in the upper-left corner of the Properties Inspector, as shown here.

You may wonder why you would want to assign a different behavior to an instance. There may be a time when you need an isolated instance to behave differently. If you make the change in the Properties Inspector, you won't have to go back and build a separate symbol from scratch and assign a different behavior. The drawback is that the new behavior won't have all the functionality you may require for a button or movie clip. But if you need a quick script relating to a static button or movie clip, this provides an instant change in behavior.

For example, let's say you created a movie clip symbol of a circle. You want to apply a script to one instance to make it transparent when it loads into the viewer's browser. But on one frame in the timeline, you want it to act as a button. You want the viewer to be able to click it to advance to the next frame. It's the same symbol but the instances have now changed behaviors. Scripting buttons and symbols is covered in Chapter 15.

Swap Instances

With all three types of behavior, you can swap one instance with another. The Swap feature acts like a kind of global "find and replace" for instances. Swapping can be a convenient way of exchanging one symbol for another on a large-scale project.

Swap an instance by clicking the instance you want to replace and then clicking the Swap button in the Properties Inspector. This displays the Swap Symbol dialog box, which provides a running list of the current symbols you can swap with, as shown next. Note that when you swap a symbol, you are swapping an instance of the symbol.

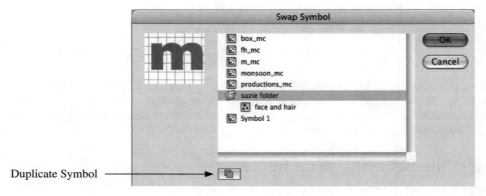

Duplicate Symbol

To replace the selected symbol, navigate to the new symbol in this dialog box and click OK.

You can also duplicate a symbol from the Swap Symbol dialog box by clicking the Duplicate Symbol button in the bottom left of the dialog box. This displays the Duplicate Symbol dialog box, shown next. In this box, you can rename the copy of your new, duplicate symbol. The new symbol appears in the Library.

Using this technique to duplicate symbols can be a timesaver. You can use a copy of one symbol to create another symbol that has similar characteristics. Once you have a copy, you can go back in and edit this symbol. If the symbol is really complex, you don't have to rebuild it from scratch.

Flash 8
Professional

Use a Blend Mode

Flash Professional offers an additional property that can be applied to movie clip instances: *blend modes*. Blend modes allow you to blend, or composite, overlapping images together by changing the color and/or transparency of the top image. The top image must always be a movie clip and the blend is always applied to this image. The interaction of the overlapping images produces a unique effect when the overlap occurs. The top image can be either on the same layer or on a separate layer than the bottom image. Blend modes are accessed in the Properties Inspector, shown here, and they become available when you select a movie clip instance on stage.

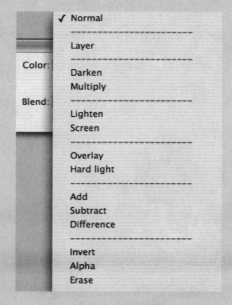

Blend modes create different effects depending on which ones you apply. They include the following selections:

- **Normal, Layer**   These two effects will not produce a visible blend and are used for more advanced precompositing functions.

- **Darken**   This effect is particularly useful for overlapping text and images. It will react to underlying colors that are lighter than the color created by the overlap of images.

- **Multiply**   This effect produces dramatic shadows as the overlapping images produce a dark blend.
- **Lighten**   Like the Darken blend, the Lighten blend is good for overlapping text and images. It will react to underlying colors that are darker than the color created by the overlap of images.
- **Screen**   This effect is good for producing highlights as it creates a "bleaching" effect in the resulting blend.
- **Overlay**   This effect is successful at producing a shaded blend as multiplies colors, creating a more saturated and often darker blend.
- **Hard Light**   This effect is excellent for producing a spotlight effect on the underlying object or a shade effect. It either multiples or screens the resulting blend, depending on the colors in the objects.
- **Difference**   Use this effect to create high-contrast colors that stand out. In the blend, the colors with the brightest value are subtracted. The resulting blend can have the same look as a color negative, as shown next.

- **Invert**   This inverts the colors in the bottom image.
- **Alpha**   This effect would be used for masking out parts of an instance as it overlays another image. In order to work, the movie clip with the Alpha blend must be placed on the timeline of the movie clip instance with a Layer blend.
- **Erase**   The Erase blend must also be used with the Layer blend, but it produces the opposite effect of the Alpha blend.

Navigate the Library Window

As you become more experienced with Flash, you'll realize the importance of organization and structure in a movie. A complex movie can have hundreds of elements, including several movie clips all running on their own separate timelines. Most often, you'll be creating and gathering all the assets of the movie before you begin. A well-organized Library will help you easily find what you're looking for when you build your movie. Flash offers many tools to help you customize and organize your Library just the way you want it.

As you'll recall, the Library window serves as a container for symbols, imported sound, bitmaps, vector drawings, and videos. Display the Library by selecting Window | Library from the menu or by pressing CTRL-L in Windows/CMD-L on the Mac.

When you click a Library entry, a thumbnail preview appears in a window at the top of the Library, as shown in Figure 8-5. The scroll-down Library window lists the name and kind of element, the number of times an instance has been used, links, and the last time it was modified. You can expand and contract the window horizontally using the Wide and Narrow view buttons in the upper-right corner of the list window. You can reverse the viewing order of elements by clicking the Sort button.

Flash provides four tools that help you manage the Library. These tools are located in the bottom-left corner of the window and are described here:

- **New Symbol**   The first button on the left creates a new symbol. When you click this button, the Create New Symbol dialog box appears. This is where you select the behavior of the symbol before moving on to Symbol Editing mode. Use this as an optional way of creating a new symbol, as opposed to using the Insert | New Symbol menu selection.

- **New Folder**   Click this button to create a folder within the Library. Name the folder by selecting the name and typing over it. You navigate the Library window as you do a standard window on the Mac and in Windows. You can create folders to further subdivide assets, as shown here. To add an element in the Library to a new folder, drag the element onto the new folder's icon. To expand and contract a folder's contents, click the folder.

- **Properties**   Click a symbol and select the Properties button to modify the properties of a symbol. This displays the Symbol Properties dialog box. This dialog box allows you to change the behavior of a symbol by clicking another behavior type (Movie Clip, Button, Graphic). Click the Edit button to quickly enter Symbol Editing mode for

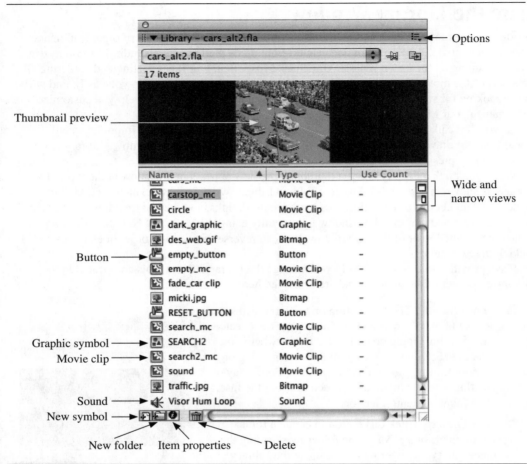

Options

Thumbnail preview

Wide and
narrow views

Button

Graphic symbol
Movie clip

Sound
New symbol

New folder   Item properties   Delete

FIGURE 8-5   The Library window is where all your movie assets are stored.

this symbol. Note that if you change the behavior of an existing symbol, when you press the Edit button, the look of the timeline reflects the new behavior. For example, if you changed the behavior of a graphic symbol to a button, the timeline would appear as a button timeline with the Up, Over, Down, and Hit states, instead of the standard timeline interface.

■ **Delete**   Click an element in the Library and select the Trash Can button to delete it from the Library. Items can also be dragged onto the Trash Can icon to be deleted.

To use a symbol instance in your movie, click the layer on which you want the asset to appear. If the instance is to reside on a particular frame, click that frame and then select the symbol in the Library and drag it to the stage to create an instance.

The Options menu in the upper-right corner of the Library window offers even more options to help you organize and manage your Library assets, as you can see here:

```
New Symbol...
New Folder
New Font...
New Video...
Rename
Move to New Folder...
Duplicate...
Delete
Edit
Edit with...
Properties...
Linkage...
Component Definition...

Select Unused Items
Update...
Play

Expand Folder
Collapse Folder

Expand All Folders
Collapse All Folders

Shared Library Properties...

Keep Use Counts Updated
Update Use Counts Now

Help

Group Library with          ▶
Close Library

Rename panel group...
Maximize panel group
Close panel group
```

The Library options are as follows:

- **New Symbol**   Select this to display the Create New Symbol dialog box. This dialog box also can be accessed from the New Symbol button in the bottom left of the window.

- **New Folder**   Select this to create a new folder in the library. Clicking the New Folder button in the bottom left of the window also can create a new folder.

- **New Font**   This displays the Font Symbol Properties dialog box. Use this dialog box to create a font symbol for fonts to be shared across multiple sites. Font symbols are stored in shared Libraries.

- **New Video**   This selection creates a new video object. Any methods or transformations that can be applied to a video object are available to the selected symbol.

- **Rename**   Select this option to rename a symbol.

- **Move To New Folder** This selection creates a new folder for selected items in the Library and then moves the new items into the new Library. To use this, select an item or multiple items in the Library (SHIFT-click). Then select Move To New Folder from the pop-up list. In the New Folder dialog box, give the new folder a name and click OK. The selected elements are then stored in the new folder.

- **Duplicate** This option displays the Duplicate Symbol dialog box and enables you to duplicate and rename an element.

- **Delete** This deletes an element from the Library. The Delete function also can be accessed from the Trash Can icon (Delete button) in the bottom left of the window.

- **Edit** This option takes you to the Symbol Editing mode of a selected symbol.

- **Edit With** This selection displays an Open dialog box that enables you to edit a bitmap in the program it was created in.

- **Properties** This option displays the Properties window associated with a selected object in the Library.

  - If a symbol is selected in the Library, the Symbol Properties dialog box will appear.

  - If a bitmap is selected in the Library, the Bitmap Properties dialog box appears. The Bitmap Properties dialog box allows you to update a revised bitmap from this location, import a replacement bitmap into the object, and choose a compression type. Compression can be in GIF, PNG, or JPEG formats. Check the Allow Smoothing box for anti-aliasing of the bitmap. In other words, if you want the edges of your bitmap to appear less jagged, check this option.

  - If a sound is selected in the Library, the Sound Properties dialog box appears. In this dialog box, you can import a replacement sound, update the current sound, test the sound to hear it, change the export settings, and set the compression rate. Compression options include Default, ADPCM, MP3, Speech, and Raw, all of which are discussed in Chapter 7.

  - The New Font selection displays the Font Symbols Properties dialog box. This is used to create a Font object that can be shared among multiple Libraries. Font objects are used in advanced ActionScript to display fonts in movies that are powered by a script. Further discussion of this feature is beyond the scope of this book.

  - If a video clip is selected, the Video Properties dialog box appears. Video in Flash can be either embedded as part of the movie or referenced from an external path. You can import QuickTime movies into Flash. In this dialog box, you can import, export, or update the video. Importing video is discussed in Chapter 7.

- **Linkage** This displays the Linkage Properties dialog box. Use this dialog box to assign linkage properties to a selected symbol. Linkage properties enable you to share a Library asset from a source movie with other movies and load assets from other Libraries into your source movie. The ability to assign linkage names is a very powerful feature in Flash. It provides another way to keep your file sizes smaller by sharing Library items. Further discussion of this feature is beyond the scope of this book.

- **Component Definition**   If you click a component in the Library, you can choose this option. This displays the Component Definitions dialog box. Here you can change the various parameters of your component. Chapter 17 discusses components in more detail.

- **Select Unused Items**   This highlights and identifies elements not yet used in your movie.

- **Update**   Use this feature to update any imported graphics that have been revised in an outside program.

- **Play**   This selection plays any interactive or animated element in Flash, such as sounds, buttons, and movie clips. Use this to test an interactive or animated element. You also can test an interactive or animated element by clicking the Play triangle in the upper-right corner of the Preview window in the Library. The Play button will only appear if you have selected a video, animated button, or animated movie clip in the Library.

- **Expand and Collapse Folders**   These options open and close selected Library folders. You also can double-click a folder in the Library to expand or collapse it.

- **Expand and Collapse All Folders**   These open or close all folders in the Library.

- **Shared Library Properties**   This displays the Shared Library Properties dialog box, where you can indicate a URL you want to share a library with.

- **Keep Use Counts Updated and Update Use Counts Now**   These selections update the number of times an instance from the Library has been used in the movie. The total is indicated in the Use Count column in the Library window.

- **Group Library With**   This option opens up a pop-up menu that allows you to group the Library panel with any other available panel in Flash.

8

Use the Common Libraries

The common libraries are separate from the Library that you store symbols in. Common libraries contain a small assortment of ready-made buttons and reusable scripts. You can access a common library by selecting Window | Common Libraries. In the pop-up menu, you can select from buttons, classes, and learning interactions libraries.

Although you have some ready-made samples in the common libraries, the real power of this tool is the fact that you can create your own common library and add such things as sounds, buttons, and movie clips you might commonly use. Common libraries are accessible in any Flash movie once they are created and installed.

To place an element in a common library, create and save a Flash file with the objects you want to make common in the Library. Name the file as you intend to name the Library. Then drag the file into the External Libraries folder, located in the Flash 8 | En | First Run folder. Once you have done this, quit the application. When you restart Flash, the new file will appear in the Common Libraries list.

You'll use the Library window frequently when creating multimedia movies. Because it contains a multitude of ways to display, manage, and customize your Library, it's a big help when it comes to organizing your project.

Conclusion

A lot of symbol basics were covered in this chapter. You learned how to create graphic symbols, buttons, and movie clips. The process of editing, modifying, and transforming symbols was also discussed. The properties of instances were covered, as was navigating the Library.

In the next chapter, you will learn the basics of frame-by-frame animation. Animation is an exciting component of Flash, and adding motion to graphics and symbols is the next step in your learning journey.

Part III

Put Your Flash Movie in Motion

Chapter 9

Learn the Basics of Flash Animation

How to...

- Understand animation
- Animate on different layers
- Create keyframes and frames
- Modify keyframes and frames
- Move, duplicate, copy, and paste framesets
- Create frame-by-frame animations
- Change the frame rate
- Test your animation
- Set Onion Skins

Animation has always been a major feature of the Flash authoring environment, and in Flash you can create beautiful, complex, and stunning animations. Years ago, animation was created traditionally on standalone animation stands. Animators were highly skilled technicians who had both the technical expertise and the artistic know-how to conceptualize and create linear animation by hand. The last decade brought professional animation and video-editing capabilities to the computer desktop, an achievement that was unimaginable in previous years. With computers getting faster by the moment, animation is no longer the mystery it used to be. Animation tools in Flash are right at your fingertips, and animations are relatively easy to create.

Create Multiple Layers in the Timeline

Before learning how to animate, you need to understand how layers work in Flash. As you learned earlier in this book, layers are like transparent sheets of acetate that sit on top of one another. When the acetate is empty, the viewer of your Flash movie sees nothing. But when an object is placed on the acetate, the object becomes visible.

Layers in Flash stack on top of one another, which means that an object on a higher layer will obscure an object on a lower layer. Take this a step further and you will discover that layers enable you to have one or more objects moving behind and/or in front of another simultaneously. Layers give a kind of stacking order to animation.

NOTE   *Although layers are used on the timelines of all symbols, their use in movie clips is especially powerful. A movie clip is a movie that runs independently on its own timeline. Flash is so compact that you can have movie clips with their own self-contained layers and frames running on different layers in the main timeline. This allows for endless creative possibilities where motion graphics are concerned.*

The following list provides a few basic instructions for working with layers:

■ To create a new layer in the timeline, click the Insert Layer button at the bottom of the timeline, as shown here.

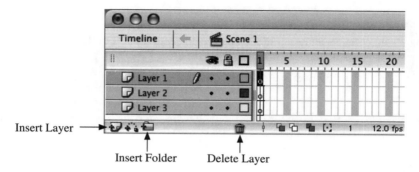

Insert Layer

Insert Folder   Delete Layer

As you can see, layers default consecutively to the names Layer 1, Layer 2, and so on. To name or rename a layer, select the layer name and type the new name. In this illustration, the second layer was given a new name of "name."

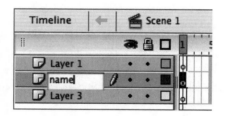

■ Change the stacking order of a layer by dragging it up or down in the layer stack.

■ Delete a layer by selecting the layer and clicking the Delete Layer icon (trash can) at the bottom of the timeline.

To help you keep all the layers in your movie organized, you can create folders for layers. Layer folders enable you to sort and store layers in a folder to which you can apply a custom name. This is particularly useful when you have more layers than can be displayed in the timeline and you have to scroll up and down to view the layers. Layer folders allow you to expand and collapse their contents, making it easier for you to navigate vertically through layers.
You can create and manipulate layer folders by doing the following:

■ Create a layer folder by clicking the Insert Folder button at the bottom of the timeline.

■ Add to the contents of a layer folder by dragging and dropping layers into it. The files in the folder become indented when the folder is expanded, as shown next.

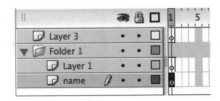

■ Expand and collapse a layer folder using the arrow to the left of the layer icon.

■ Name or rename a layer folder the same way you name a layer, by double-clicking the layer name and typing over the old name.

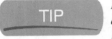

Layers and layer folders can also be named in the Layer Properties dialog box of a selected layer. To access this dialog box, double-click the layer or layer folder icon. In this dialog box, type in a new name.

Did you know?

The Origins of Animation

Remember the old animated Disney movies? Armies of artists were recruited to create hand-drawn, individually rendered frames. Artists would create keyframes where major shifts in movement occurred within the animation, and then sculpt the rest of the secondary frames around them. The in-between frames were the interpolation of movement between one keyframe and another. This is where the term *tween* comes from, referring to the frames "in between" the keyframes of the animation.

With this old technique, a substantial number of frames needed to be hand-rendered to create the illusion of fluid movement. Thirty seconds of animation might require up to 700 frames. As you can imagine, this required a large staff and a lot of time. Tricks were devised to make hand-drawn animation a little more streamlined. Animators painted their animation on cells, the transparent celluloid sheets used to render each frame. Because cells were transparent, parts of the cell animation that didn't change over a span of frames could be reused by placing them over or under new cells, thus creating a layer effect. This way, the artist didn't have to duplicate drawings in other cells.

You've probably noticed in old animations where a character may be running against a backdrop of some sort, like mountains or a field. If you've ever examined the animation closely, you would notice that the background loops and repeats itself at some point. It's the same moving backdrop (or layer, as it would be called in Flash) being repeated to create the illusion that the character is moving across the landscape.

Computer animation today is more streamlined than the hand-drawn animation of yesterday, but many of the basic rules still apply. Computer animation artists strive for consistency in their animation, and they still economize on visual elements just like in the old days of animation, when the cell technique was used.

Layers are one of the main ingredients in basic animation. Beginners often make the mistake of doing most of their animation on a single layer. Just like in traditional animation, it's easier to delete a cell—or in this case, a layer—than it is to trash a file because it wasn't planned out properly. The other problem you could run into in a one-layer animation is objects erasing one another or connecting when you didn't intend them to. Making use of multiple layers for objects and backdrops is a wise design decision.

The contents of layers are frames, and frames create the structure for the animation. Next, you will look at how to make frames on layers.

Insert Frames to Animate

If layers were a cart, frames would be the wheels that make the cart move. Frames reside on layers in the timeline, and this is where your animation comes alive.

There are two major types of frames used in animation: keyframes and frames. *Keyframes* contain objects that change in your animation. A keyframe is indicated by a black circle in the frame placeholder box on the timeline. Frames, on the other hand, extend the length of time a keyframe plays (see Figure 9-1). Frames between keyframes are depicted as dark gray boxes in the timeline. When several frames are butted up against one another, they are called a *frameset*.

There are also blank keyframes, which are used to display no content on a frame. For example, if you wanted an object to appear and disappear in a frame sequence, you might use a blank keyframe in place of frames where you want the object to disappear.

The timeline contains a structural framework of white, rectangular placeholders (protoframes) for frames to reside in once you create them.

You can identify a frame's position in the timeline by referring to the frame numbers at the top of the timeline. Every fifth placeholder is marked with a frame number indicated at the top of the timeline. In addition, every fifth placeholder rectangle contains a light gray fill. The numbers and color delineation in the placeholders make the task of navigating through the timeline much easier. Otherwise, you would have to negotiate through endless rows of small white rectangles, which would surely bring on a migraine.

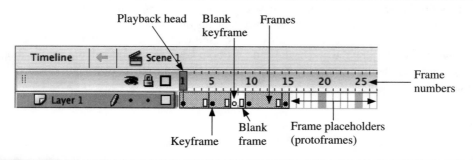

FIGURE 9-1   A timeline with frames and keyframes

Now that you are familiar with the timeline structure, you'll examine the mechanics of putting keyframes onto it.

Add Keyframes to the Timeline

When you begin a new document in Flash, the first frame in the timeline contains a white circle, which signifies an empty keyframe. When you draw on the stage, the blank keyframe turns into a black circle. The black circle signifies a keyframe with content because you just populated the empty keyframe.

If you intend to animate the object you just placed on the first keyframe and you want it to change in motion, you'll need to make more keyframes so the movie will change over time.

To create keyframes, do the following:

1. Begin a new Flash movie and draw an object or drag a symbol from the Library onto the stage. In this illustration, a movie clip instance of a cat was used.

2. Click the frame placeholder next to the new keyframe (frame 2) and select Insert | Timeline | Keyframe or press F6. A new black circle appears indicating that you've just created a keyframe. In addition, the stage contents on frame 2 are identical to what appears on the first keyframe. To prove to yourself that they are identical, scrub the timeline by dragging the playback head over both keyframes. You will not yet see motion because both keyframes are identical. Next, you'll flip the object over on the second keyframe.

3. Click the second keyframe and select the object on the stage. Flip the object horizontally by selecting Modify | Transform | Flip Horizontal. In the illustration here, the cat now appears as a mirror image on the second keyframe.

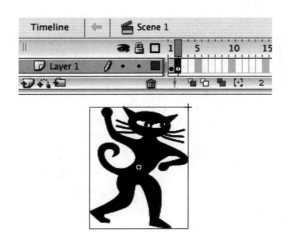

4. Manually play back the animation by scrubbing the playback head over the two frames. You'll notice that the image appears to move (because you flipped it on frame 2), creating an animated effect.

To test the motion of the movie, press CTRL-ENTER (Windows)/CMD-RETURN (Mac). Note that the two keyframes pulsate in an endless loop, speeding by so fast you can hardly see the motion. When frame 2 is finished playing, it returns to frame 1 over and over.

This may be appropriate for some animations where you rely on speed as part of the effect, but what if you wanted the animation to play a little more slowly? You can do this by adding more frames, which is discussed next. But another way you can slow down the motion is to change the frame rate in the timeline.

By default, the timeline displays 12 frames every second. This time may vary depending on the speed of your viewer's computer or the size of the objects on the frames, but this data provides you with an average speed to work with.

To change the default frame rate, double-click the frame rate at the bottom of the timeline to display the Document Properties dialog box, as shown next.

9

Document Properties

Title: |cat_dance|

Description: [   ]

Dimensions: [550 px] (width) x [400 px] (height)

Match: ○ Printer   ○ Contents   ● Default

Background color: [▾]

Frame rate: [2   ] fps ————————————————— Frame rate

Ruler units: [Pixels ▾]

(Make Default)   (Cancel) (OK)

In the Frame Rate input box, type a number less than 12 if you want to slow down the play of the timeline. Conversely, you can type in a number greater than 12 to speed it up. In the previous illustration, the frame rate was reduced to 2 frames per second.

Now, when the movie is tested, the cat in the previous illustration shifts his body left to right in a more realistic movement, since the frames have been slowed down.

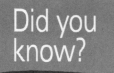

Change the Frame Rate

The default frame rate for Flash animation is 12 fps (frames per second), about half of a film's frame rate. You can adjust the frame rate in Flash if you want to slow the movie down or speed it up. Type in a higher number to speed up the frames and a lower number to slow the frames down. The frame rate you set is global throughout the movie.

Speeding up the frame rate should be done with caution if your file is being published to the Web. Users with slower system configurations may not be able to experience the motion at a very fast frame rate. If you do intend to change the frame rate setting for a movie to be published on the Web, it's not a bad idea to test the movie on a wide range of configurations and browsers after it's put up, to eliminate the prospect of undesirable results.

This was a pretty easy animation, as there were only two frames that looped endlessly. But what if you want to create an animation in which the contents of more than two frames change over time? You'll need to create multiple keyframes to accommodate the different contents. Creating multiple keyframes and frames on multiple layers is tedious work, so it helps to know how to insert and remove frames and keyframes expeditiously. Let's review some shortcuts for inserting, removing, and selecting frames and keyframes:

- To insert a frame, press F5; to insert a keyframe, press F6.

- To select a frame or a keyframe, click it.

- To select a span of frames between keyframes, double-click a frame in the frame sequence.To select all frames in a timeline, select Edit | Timeline | Select All Frames or press CTRL-ALT-A (Windows)/OPT-CMD-A (Mac).

- To move an individual keyframe to another place in the timeline, select the keyframe and drag it to its new location.

- To move a set of keyframes, hold down SHIFT while clicking each keyframe. This creates a movable frameset. Drag the selected set to its new location on the timeline. You also can move an individual keyframe or a frameset to a new layer by selecting it and dragging it onto the desired layer. To select the frameset, double-click it.

- To move a contiguous group of frames, press SHIFT while clicking the first and last frame of the group. Drag the selected frameset to its new location on the timeline. To select a noncontiguous group of frames, press CTRL (Windows)/CMD (Mac) and click the individual frames, as shown here.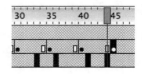

- To copy and paste frames onto another layer or onto the same layer in a different frameset, select a frameset using one of the methods outlined previously. Then select Edit | Timeline | Copy Frames (CTRL-ALT-C in Windows/OPT-CMD-C on the Mac). Click the starting frame in the new location. Select Edit | Timeline | Paste Frames (CTRL-ALT-V in Windows/OPT-CMD-V on the Mac). A copy of the frames will now reside in the new frames. Frames also can be cut from their location by selecting Edit | Timeline | Cut (CTRL-ALT-X in Windows)/OPT-CMD-X on the Mac). Selecting Cut or Copy places a copy in the clipboard, so multiple copies of the frameset can be pasted in the timeline if desired.

- To shorten or lengthen a frameset, press CTRL (Windows)/CMD (Mac) and position the pointer over the last keyframe. The pointer turns into a double-headed arrow, as shown here. Drag the end of the frameset to the new length.

- To turn a selected sequence of frames into keyframes, select Modify | Timeline | Convert to Keyframes.

9

- To add a blank keyframe, select Modify | Timeline | Insert Blank Keyframe (F7).

- To turn a selected sequence of frames into blank frames, select Modify | Timeline | Convert to Blank Keyframes.

- To duplicate a keyframe, use ALT (Windows) or OPT-click (Mac) and drag a keyframe. To clear a frameset, select the frames and press BACKSPACE (Windows)/DELETE (Mac). Clearing a frameset removes the frames as well as the contents on the stage associated with these frames.

- To clear individual frames from a frameset, select the frame and then select Edit | Timeline | Clear Frames (ALT-BACKSPACE in Windows/OPT-DELETE on the Mac). Clearing individual frames removes the frames as well as the contents on the stage associated with these frames.

- To convert a keyframe to a frame, right-click (Windows)/CTRL-click (Mac) the keyframe and in the context menu, select Clear Keyframe.

- To delete a keyframe, click a keyframe to select it. From the menu, select Modify | Timeline | Clear Keyframe (SHIFT-F6). If the keyframe is between several frames, this will remove the keyframe and connect the previous frames with the remaining frames, making the animation continuous.

- To delete frames, select the frames and then select Edit | Timeline | Remove Frames (SHIFT-F5).

The properties of frames can also be displayed by right-clicking (Windows)/CTRL-clicking (Mac) the frames to display the pop-up context menu, as shown here.

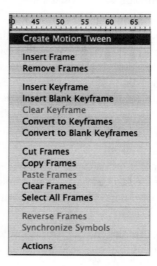

The options available in this pop-up menu are the same as those in the Insert and Edit menus. If you prefer using menus to shortcut keys, you may find the context menu quicker to navigate than the standard menus for frames, since many timeline-related frame commands are nested in submenus.

Make a Frame-by-frame Animation

If the same object is to change on every keyframe, you might ask, what kinds of things can you change? The possibilities are many in Flash.

Properties that can be edited in an animation include the object's position, scale, and color. You can make an object partially transparent, flip it horizontally or vertically, rotate it, and even skew it. You can even apply multiple property changes to a single object.

Figure 9-2 depicts four frames in a multilayer, frame-by-frame animation of a clock ticking. A *frame-by-frame* animation changes its contents on keyframes. You may be wondering what other types of animation you can create in Flash. You can also create tweening animations. A *tweening* animation smoothes out the changes in between two keyframes with different content so the frames display in a flowing manner, not choppy as they would otherwise be with a frame-by-frame animation. Tweening is discussed in Chapters 11 and 12. Also, don't forget about the timeline effects you can apply to movie clips (Insert | Timeline Effects), which were mentioned briefly in Chapter 1. These are discussed in detail in Chapter 10.

9

Frame 1

Frame 3

Frame 7

Frame 11

FIGURE 9-2   Four keyframe states of a clock depicted in storyboard form demonstrate a typical frame-by-frame, multilayer animation.

Manipulating Layers

The importance of layers becomes obvious when you are creating a frame-by-frame animation with many pieces. If you have more than one object on a layer and you want to animate only one of the objects, each time you select a keyframe, all objects on the layer automatically become selected. You must deselect all other objects to animate the one object. This is easy if you're animating only a few frames. If there are a lot of frames, it becomes confusing and inaccurate to have to deselect all items on each frame to alter the properties of one object. Consequently, making use of layers to draw different parts of your animation becomes very important to avert a potentially disastrous animation.

Getting back to the ticking clock, on each keyframe, the hand moves clockwise to the next point on the clock. The clock face, hands, and numbers are all on separate layers. Although it would be more efficient to create it as a movie clip, let's make this animated clock as a frame-by-frame animation by doing the following:

1. Create and name layers for the tick marks (triangles), the little hand, and the big hand in a new file, as shown in this illustration.

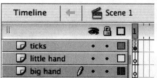

2. On the ticks layer, draw twelve tick marks in a circle, as they would reside on the face of a clock. You can create the ticks in Flash with the drawing tools. When you are done drawing, select all the tick marks and convert them to a symbol by pressing F8. In the Convert To Symbol dialog box, choose Graphic for Behavior, type in a symbol name, and then press OK.

3. Display the rulers (View | Ruler) and drag horizontal and vertical guides from the rulers so that they cross in the middle of the ticks, as shown here.

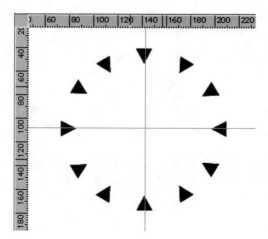

4. Click the big hand layer and draw an object that resembles the big hand of a clock. You can use the Line tool to do this or, if you're feeling confident about the tools, create something a little fancier, as was depicted previously in Figure 9-2. Position the big hand so it's pointing to the bottom tick mark at 6:00. Convert it into a graphic symbol by pressing F8 and name it. It should resemble this illustration.

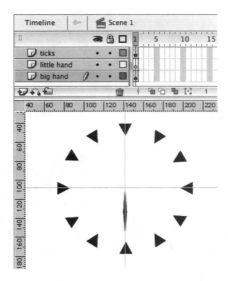

5. Click the little hand layer and repeat the process in step 4 to draw a little hand. Align the little hand so it's pointing at the 12:00 tick, as shown here. Convert this object to a graphic symbol (F8) and name it.

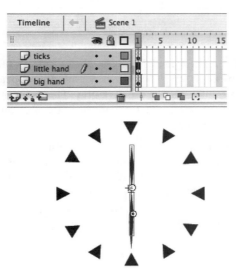

9

6. The little hand needs to rotate from its bottom center to give the illusion of ticking around the clock. Click the Free Transform tool and then click the little hand. You'll see the eight transform handles appear around the object. Click the white circle in the middle of the little hand and drag to reposition it on the bottom center of the object, as shown next. Now you will be able to rotate the little hand from the base of the object.

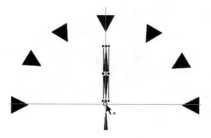

7. Before you rotate the little hand, extend the frame length of the ticks and big hand layers in the timeline. They need to be extended to match the number of frames that will populate the little hand layer, which will be 60 frames. If you don't do this, the ticks and the big hand will disappear from sight as you are animating the little hand on its layer. To add frames on the ticks and big hand layers, start by clicking frame 60 in the ticks layer and pressing F5. Doing so will create additional frames on this layer. Repeat this process on the big hand layer, and your timeline will now look like the one in the following illustration.

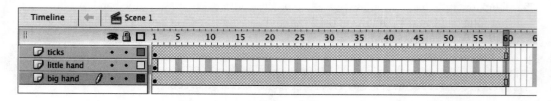

8. Now you will animate the little hand. To do so, click frame 5 of the little hand layer and press F6 to create a new keyframe. The little hand will now appear on frame 5. Note that the frames in between frames 1 and 5 are dark gray. This color indicates the presence of frames. The contents of the frames are the same as in the previous keyframe; in other words, the contents don't change.

9. Rotate the little hand to the next tick mark (1:00) on frame 5 by clicking frame 5 on the little hand layer, selecting the Free Transform tool, and then clicking the little hand to display the transform handles. In the Options portion of the Toolbar, click the Rotate and Skew icon. Position the pointer over the top of the little hand and drag the little hand so the tip points to the next tick (1:00), as shown next. An outline shows you where the rotation will occur when you click.

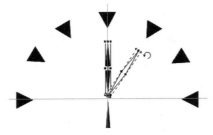

10. Repeat steps 8 and 9 to create a new keyframe on every fifth frame until you arrive at the 11:00 position. This will occur on frame 55. To even out the timeline, click frame 60 in the little hand layer and press F5. This will add regular frames from frames 56 to 60. This way, when the animation loops back to frame 1, there won't be a sudden jerky transition between the last frame and the first frame of the timeline. The finished timeline should resemble the one in the next illustration.

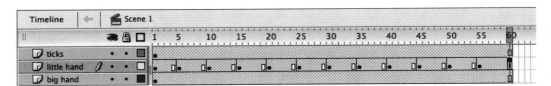

11. Play the movie on the Flash stage by scrubbing the playback head over the frames or using the Controller buttons (Window | Toolbars | Controller). Test the movie to experience the animation by pressing CTRL-ENTER (Windows)/CMD-RETURN (Mac). (Doing so creates an SWF file in the folder where your Flash file resides.) As you will see when you test the movie, the little hand ticks rhythmically around the clock at a nice, even pace. To slow the ticking down, add more frames in between keyframes by clicking in the gray blocks of frames (framesets) in the timeline and pressing F5. Each time F5 is pressed, another frame is added to the frameset.

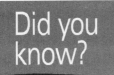

Preview in Browser

You can preview what your movie will look like in a browser right in the Flash environment. To do this, select File | Publish Preview | HTML. This will generate a temporary HTML file with your Flash SWF file embedded in it. This is a wonderful feature because the margins of your movie may look quite different when the movie is embedded in an HTML document. Flash automatically generates an HTML page and an SWF file, names them, and embeds the SWF file in the HTML page. Both files are automatically saved in the folder that holds the Flash movie you're previewing.

Set Onion Skins

When you create a frame-by-frame animation—or any animation, for that matter—sometimes it's hard to determine where you want to move the next keyframe in relation to the previous frames. Because you can only see one frame at a time while you're composing the animation, it's impossible to see where the animation originates from to determine where it's headed.

Tweaking an animation by randomly altering objects and playing them back could take hours. The Onion Skins feature resolves this problem in Flash. Onion Skins give you a glimpse of the path of existing frames in your animation. It allows you to see a preview of as many frames in your timeline as you want.

Onion Skins display a selected portion of the animation as translucent ghost images of the original. The term "Onion Skin" comes from the concept of onion-skin paper, a thin, see-through paper artists use to trace over images. How do you move an object from one end of the stage to another in a frame-by-frame animation if the next keyframe keeps jumping back to the original position of the object in the first keyframe? Onion Skins can help you see the entire path of the animation.

The Onion Skin marker appears as a translucent, rounded-corner rectangle over the frame numbers in the timeline, as shown here.

The Onion Skin marker enables you to customize the span of frames you want previewed. Adjust the marker by clicking and dragging the round handles at the beginning and end of the marker to correspond with the frames whose path you want to preview. Pick up and move the entire marker by dragging the playback head to a new location.

The Onion Skin buttons at the bottom of the timeline give you four different ways to display the Onion Skins. From left to right, the Onion Skin buttons are described here:

- **Onion Skin**   Click this button to view the animation path as a dimmed image. This option does not enable you to modify the Onion Skins on previous frames, as it serves the purpose of indicating the path. Only the current frame can be modified (see Figure 9-3).

- **Onion Skin Outlines**   Click this to display the Onion Skins in outline form (see Figure 9-4). As with the Onion Skin button, only the current frame can be modified with this selection.

- **Edit Multiple Frames**   This button displays the Onion Skins as opaque art and enables you to edit all frames within the confines of the Onion Skin marker. You can also use Edit Multiple Frames to move a frame sequence or frame sequences on several layers. To move multiple layers to another position on the timeline using Edit Multiple Frames, follow these steps:

  1. Lock or hide layers you don't want to move.
  2. Click the Edit Multiple Frames button.

Onion Skin

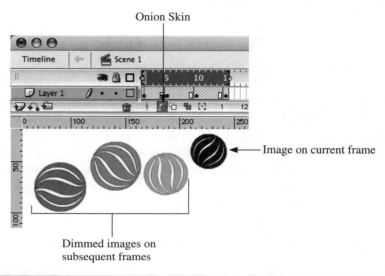

Image on current frame

Dimmed images on
subsequent frames

FIGURE 9-3   The Onion Skin button is turned on—notice the Onion Skin marker spanning
a frameset at the top of the timeline.

9

Onion Skin Outlines

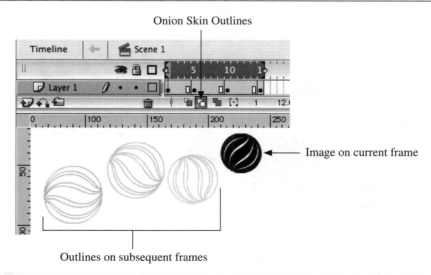

Image on current frame

Outlines on subsequent frames

FIGURE 9-4   The Onion Skin Outlines button is turned on to depict the path of an animation
in outline form.

3. Drag the Onion Skin over frames in the group you want to move.

4. Select Edit | Select All Frames (CTRL-ALT-A on Windows/OPT-CMD-A on the Mac).

5. Drag the timeline animation somewhere else (see Figure 9-5).

■ **Modify Onion Markers**   Click this button (see Figure 9-5) to modify the Onion Skins' display. The selections from the pop-up menu are as follows:

   ■ **Always Show Markers**   This displays a hollowed-out marker even when the Onion Skins feature is turned off.

   ■ **Anchor Onion**   This locks the Onion Skin marker in its current position. Select this to prevent the Onion Skin marker from moving when you move your playback head throughout the frames. In regular mode, the Onion Skin marker follows the path of the playback head position.

   ■ **Onion 2**   This displays two frames on either side of the selected frame.

   ■ **Onion 5**   This displays five frames on either side of the selected frame.

   ■ **Onion All**   This displays all frames on either side of the selected frame.

Turn off Onion Skins by clicking the buttons again. The buttons act as toggle switches. The Onion Skins settings in Flash enable you to pinpoint the path of an animation. This is an important and timesaving tool when you create graphics in motion.

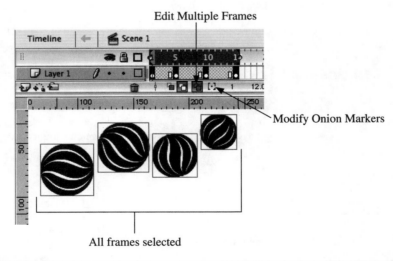

FIGURE 9-5   The Edit Multiple Frames button enables you to easily edit objects on multiple frames.

 *Locked layers do not display Onion Skins.*

Conclusion

In this chapter, you learned that you use the timeline, keyframes, and frames to animate in Flash. Specifically, you honed in on the concept of frame-by-frame animation. You learned how to apply the concept of keyframes by changing content on a ticking-clock exercise. Finally, you explored the power of Onion Skins and how to use them to preview frame content when building an animation.

In the next chapter, you will expand upon your knowledge of animation, keyframes, and frames by learning another way to create motion graphics. You'll study the various timeline effects, which allow you to quickly create some commonly used animated techniques. You were introduced to timeline effects in the first chapter of this book. Now you'll delve deeper into this wonderful new feature in Flash.

9

Chapter 10

Streamline Animation Using Timeline Effects

How to…

- ■ Use timeline effects
- ■ Understand the Effects group
- ■ Add timeline effects to movies

Animation is what takes your Flash movie to the next level. When you animate with Flash, you add sizzle to the steak. As you learned in the previous chapter, in an animation you use keyframes to specify major event changes and regular frames as content holders between keyframes. Keyframes are used with what have for years been the staples of Flash animation: motion tweening and shape tweening, which will be covered in Chapters 11 and 12, respectively. Keyframes are also essential to an exciting animation feature that was introduced with Flash MX 2004: *timeline effects*.

When you add a timeline effect to an object, Flash 8 takes care of adding the necessary frames to pull off the effect. However, you still need to know how to add a keyframe to signify the point in the movie where the effect occurs. Chapter 9 covers the basics of working with frames and keyframes in great detail, so you should review that chapter if you need a little practice in creating keyframes and using the associated keyboard shortcuts. Learning the shortcut keys will help you speed through the process of making complex, multilayered animations.

Understand Timeline Effects

You can add timeline effects to any object in your movie: text, shapes, groups, graphic symbols, bitmap images, and bitmap symbols. When you add a timeline effect to an object, Flash creates a layer for the effect and transfers the object to that layer. The effect name becomes the default name for the new layer. If the timeline effect involves animation, the proper number of frames is added to the timeline to pull off the effect.

Some of the timeline effects look similar to animation effects you could create in early versions of Flash, while other effects are not animated but do apply an effect to an object. For example, you can add a drop shadow to an object in your movie by using a timeline effect. You can also use timeline effects to transform objects, duplicate objects, and so on. Figure 10-1 shows a couple of objects to which timeline effects have been applied. In this figure you see the Explode effect applied to an object, and the Expand effect applied to text.

After you apply a timeline effect to an object, the original object becomes part of the effect. It will be listed as a symbol in the document's Library, and an Effects folder will appear in the Library as well. The new symbol acquires the effect name; however, the symbol is not nested in the Effects folder, which means you can access it quickly if you need further instances of the effect in your movie. If you use an effect more than once, Flash 8 appends the effect name with the next available number: Explode 1, Explode 2, and so on. You can create an instance of a timeline effect symbol by selecting the symbol to which the effect has been applied and dragging it to the stage.

The Effects folder may be broken down into subfolders if an effect requires it. For example, the Explode effect creates a subfolder that contains the individual pieces into which the object explodes.

FIGURE 10-1   You can use timeline effects to animate objects.

The following illustration shows the Library after the Explode timeline effect has been applied to an object.

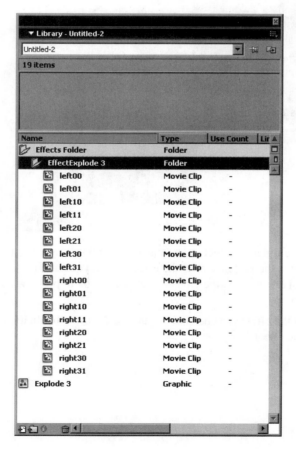

Add Timeline Effects

As mentioned previously, you can add a timeline effect to any object in a Flash 8 movie. If you add a timeline effect to a movie clip, Flash 8 nests the effect within the movie clip. Each timeline effect has its own dialog box that you use to fine-tune the effect to suit the movie in which it appears. To add a timeline effect to an object, follow these steps:

1. On the stage, select the object, group, text object, symbol, or bitmap to which you want to apply the effect.

2. Right-click (Windows) or CTRL-click (Mac) and, from the context menu, choose the timeline effect you want to apply, as shown in the following illustration.

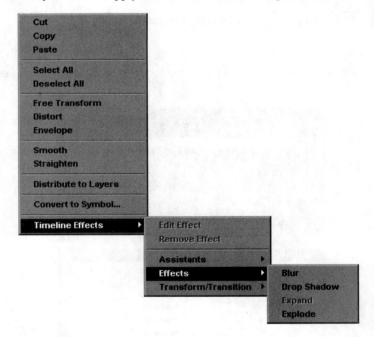

3. After you apply a timeline effect to an object, a dialog box opens with the effect's default parameters. Adjust the parameters of the effect to suit your movie. As you modify the parameters of an effect, click the Update Preview button to preview the effect with the current parameters.

4. Click OK when the effect is as desired. Figure 10-2 shows the dialog box for the Drop Shadow timeline effect.

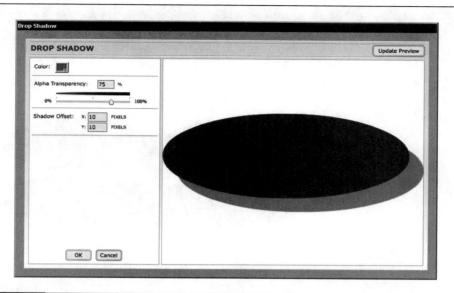

FIGURE 10-2   Each timeline effect has a unique dialog box.

As you saw in the context menu in the previous section, the timeline effects are divided into three groups: Assistants, Effects, and Transform/Transition. When you move your pointer over a group, a drop-down menu lists the available effects. If an effect cannot be applied to the object you have selected, it is dimmed out. For example, the Expand effect is only for text or a group of objects.

Use Timeline Effects from the Assistants Group

When you choose a timeline effect from the Assistants group, Flash 8 assists you in performing a task. You have two effects available from this group: Copy To Grid and Distributed Duplicate.

Use the Copy To Grid Timeline Effect

You use the Copy To Grid timeline effect to copy a selected object, symbol, or graphic to the grid. When you choose this timeline effect, you determine the number of copies by specifying the grid size and spacing. To apply this effect to an object, follow these steps:

1. Select the object to which you want to apply the effect. Right-click (Windows) or CTRL-click (Mac) and then choose Timeline Effects | Assistants | Copy to Grid from the context menu. The Copy To Grid dialog box appears, as shown next.

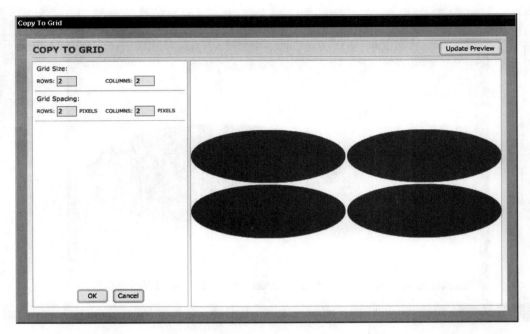

2. Accept the default grid size or enter different values in the Rows and Columns fields.

3. Accept the default grid spacing or enter different values in the Rows and Columns fields. This value is the spacing between rows and columns as measured in pixels.

4. Click the Update Preview button to preview the effect with your settings.

5. Click OK to apply the effect to the selected object. Alternatively, you can repeat any of the previous steps and choose different options or enter different values if the effect is not suitable for your movie.

Use the Distributed Duplicate Timeline Effect

When you apply the Distributed Duplicate timeline effect to a selected object, symbol, or graphic, you specify how many duplicates are made and how they are distributed across the stage. You can scale, rotate, and determine the opacity of the duplicates. To apply the Distributed Duplicate timeline effect, follow these steps:

1. Select the object to which you want to apply the effect. Right-click (Windows) or CTRL-click (Mac) and then choose Timeline Effects | Assistants | Distributed Duplicate from the context menu. The Distributed Duplicate dialog box appears, as shown next.

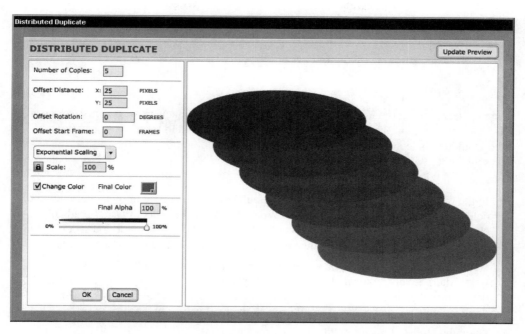

2. Accept the default number of copies or enter a different value in the Number Of Copies field.

3. Accept the default Offset Distance or enter different values in the Offset Distance X and Y fields. These values are the distance in pixels each duplicate is offset from the previous duplicate.

4. Accept the default Offset Rotation or enter a different value in the Offset Rotation field. This value is the number of degrees each duplicate is rotated relative to the previous duplicate.

5. Accept the default Offset Start Frame value or enter a different value in that field. If you accept the default value of 0, the duplicates appear as soon as the effect appears in the movie. If you enter a value greater than 0, that number of frames will play before the next duplicate appears.

6. Accept the default Exponential Scaling percentage or enter a different value in that field. This value is the percent by which each duplicate is scaled up or down relative to the size of the previous duplicate. Enter a value greater than 100 to increase the size of each duplicate or less than 100 to decrease the size of each duplicate. By default, each duplicate is scaled proportionately. Note that you can also choose Linear Scaling from the drop-down list.

NOTE *When you click the Lock icon, the X and Y scaling fields appear. Enter different values in these fields to scale the object disproportionately.*

Did you know?

Cartoon Animation

Before the advent of computer animation, cartoonists had to create a separate illustration for each frame of a cartoon. The cartoonist would often draw the main frames of the cartoon, which would be the equivalent of the keyframes in computer animation, and the cartoonist's understudy would draw the in-between frames.

7. In the Change Color section, accept the default color for the final duplicate or click the color swatch to select a different color. When the effect is applied, Flash 8 gradually changes the color of each duplicate, the final duplicate being the color you specify. If you do not want the duplicates to change color, deselect the Change Color check box.

8. Accept the default Final Alpha value or enter a different value in the Final Alpha field. Alternatively, you can drag the Final Alpha slider to select a value. This setting determines the opacity of the final duplicate. Flash 8 changes the opacity of each duplicate by an equal percentage to arrive at the final value you specify.

9. Click the Update Preview button to preview the effect.

10. Click OK to apply the effect to the selected object. If the effect is not suitable for your movie, you can repeat any of the previous steps and choose different options or enter different values.

Use Effects from the Effects Group

When you want to add some special effects to a Flash movie, you can do so with timeline effects from the Effects group. You can apply any of the following effects to an object, symbol, or bitmap: Blur, Drop Shadow, Expand, or Explode. All of these effects are animated with the exception of the Drop Shadow effect.

Use the Blur Timeline Effect

When you apply the Blur timeline effect to a selected object, symbol, or bitmap, an aura emanates from each object in the selection. You can specify the number of frames used to pull off the effect and the size of each blur. To apply the Blur effect, follow these steps:

1. Select the object to which you want to apply the effect. Right-click (Windows) or CTRL-click (Mac) and then choose Timeline Effects | Effects | Blur from the context menu. The Blur dialog box appears, as shown in the following illustration.

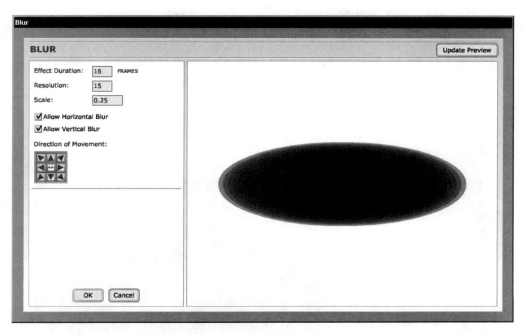

2. Accept the default number of frames or enter a different value in the Effect Duration field.

3. Accept the default resolution value or enter a different value in the Resolution field. This value determines how many blurs appear in each frame.

4. Accept the default scale value or enter a different value in the Scale field. This value determines the amount by which each blur is scaled. The default value of .25 increases each blur to 25 percent of its size from the preceding frame.

5. By default, the effect applies horizontal and vertical blur. Deselect either option to apply blur in only one direction.

If you deselect both Allow Vertical Blur and Allow Horizontal Blur, the effect looks like a flashing light.

6. By default, the Blur effect originates from the center of the object or selection and expands concentrically. Click a square in the Direction Of Movement grid to change the direction of movement.

7. Click the Update Preview button to preview the effect.

8. Click OK to apply the effect. You can repeat any of the previous steps and choose different options or enter different values if you decide the effect is not suitable for your movie.

Use the Drop Shadow Timeline Effect

When you want to make an object or text appear as if it is floating above the stage, you can do so by applying the Drop Shadow timeline effect. When you apply the Drop Shadow effect to an object, you can determine the shadow offset as well as the shadow color. To apply the Drop Shadow timeline effect to an object, follow these steps:

1. Select the object to which you want to apply the effect. Right-click (Windows) or CTRL-click (Mac) and then choose Timeline Effects | Effects | Drop Shadow to open the Drop Shadow dialog box, as shown in the following illustration.

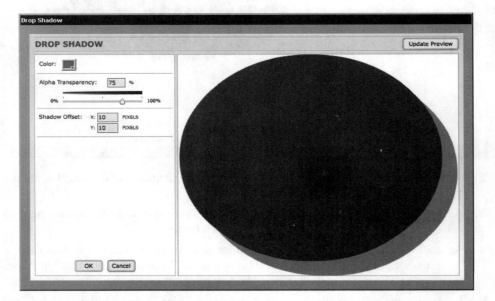

2. Accept the default color or click the Color swatch to choose a different color for the shadow.

3. Accept the default Alpha Transparency or enter a different value in the Alpha Transparency field. Alternatively, you can drag the Alpha Transparency slider to determine this value. Select a low value for a subtle shadow that allows more of the background color or underlying objects to show through, or a high value to create a pronounced shadow that shows little of the background.

4. Accept the default Shadow Offset values or enter different values in the X and Y fields. These values determine the distance in pixels that the shadow extends from the original object.

5. Click the Update Preview button to preview the effect.

6. Click OK to apply the shadow to the object. If the effect is not suitable for your movie, you can repeat any of the previous steps and choose different options or enter different values.

Use the Expand Timeline Effect

You can use the Expand timeline effect on a group of objects or a word. The effect is not available if you select a single object such as an oval or rectangle; in fact, the effect is grayed out if you select a single object and choose Timeline Effects | Effects. However, you can use the effect to animate a single letter. The effect works on a single text object but not a single graphic object. When you apply this effect, the text objects expand. You can also modify the effect to squeeze the objects or make the text objects expand and then contract. This effect works well to animate text objects. When you apply the effect, you can specify the number of frames used to pull off the effect, the direction of movement, and the amount the objects are offset during each frame of the animation. To apply the Expand effect, follow these steps:

1. Select the text object to which you want to apply the effect. Right-click (Windows) or CTRL-click (Mac) and then choose Timeline Effects | Effects | Expand from the context menu to open the Expand dialog box, shown next.

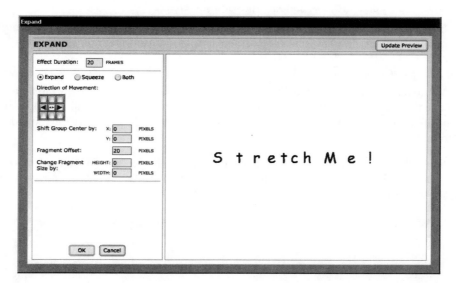

2. Accept the default value for Effect Duration or enter a different value. This value determines the number of frames used to pull off the effect.

3. By default this effect expands the objects. Click the Squeeze radio button to compress the objects, or click the Both radio button to expand and then contract the objects.

4. Click a square in the Direction Of Movement grid to determine the direction in which the objects move. By default the effect occurs from the center out. Click the left square and the effect moves from right to left, or click the right square and the effect moves from left to right. The upper and lower rows of squares are not available for this effect.

TIP   *For an interesting variation of this effect, apply it to vertical text.*

5. In the Shift Group Center By section, accept the default value of 0 or enter different values in the X and/or Y fields. The value determines the distance in pixels that the objects are offset during the effect.

6. Accept the default Fragment Offset value or enter a different value in that field. This value determines how far the objects expand from one frame to the next. If you accept the default Effect Duration of 20 frames and the default Fragment Offset of 20 pixels, the effect expands or contracts the objects by 400 pixels during the course of the effect.

7. In the Change Fragment Size By section, accept the default Height and Width values of 0 or enter different values. This value determines how much the height and width of each object change during the effect.

You can create an interesting animation by entering negative values in the Height and Width fields.

8. Click the Update Preview button to preview the effect.

9. Click OK to apply the effect. You can repeat any of the previous steps and choose different options or enter different values if the effect is not suitable for your movie.

Use the Explode Timeline Effect

If you want to disintegrate a selected object, symbol, or bitmap, you can easily do so by applying the Explode timeline effect. When you apply this effect, you can specify the direction from which the effect occurs, as well as fragment size, rotation, and so on. To apply the Explode effect, follow these steps:

1. Select the object to which you want to apply the effect. Right-click (Windows) or CTRL-click (Mac) and then choose Timeline Effects | Effect | Explode from the context menu to open the Explode dialog box shown in the following illustration.

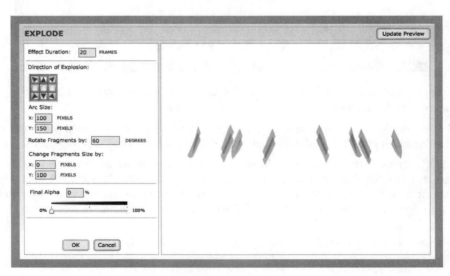

2. Accept the default Effect Duration of 20 frames or enter a different value in that field. This value determines the number of frames used to complete the effect.

3. Click a square in the Direction Of Explosion grid to determine the direction in which the fragments move after the object explodes.

4. In the Arc Size area, accept the default X and Y values or enter different values. When the effect is played in a Flash movie, the object fragments follow an arc in the direction of the explosion. The Arc Size values determine the height and width of the arc.

5. In the Rotate Fragments By section, accept the default value of 60 degrees or enter a different value. This value determines the number of degrees by which each fragment is rotated.

6. In the Change Fragments Size By section, accept the default values or enter different values in the X and/or Y fields. The Explode effect breaks an object into 16 pieces. The values you enter in the X and Y fields determine how much the width and height of each piece is changed during the effect duration.

7. Accept the default Final Alpha of 0 or enter a different value in that field. Alternatively, you can select a value by dragging the Final Alpha slider. This value determines the opacity of the fragments on the effect's final frame. The default value of 0 renders the objects invisible at the end of the explosion.

8. Click the Update Preview button to preview the effect.

9. Click OK to apply the effect. If you decide the effect is not suitable for your movie, you can repeat any of the previous steps and choose different options or enter different values.

10

Use Effects from the Transform/Transition Group

In the Transform/Transition group of the Timeline Effects menu, you'll find an effect you can use to transform objects, symbols, and bitmaps with mathematical precision and an effect you can use to simulate a video transition. You can control either effect by determining whether the effect is applied equally across all frames of the animation or whether the effect begins slowly and ends quickly, or vice versa.

Use the Transform Timeline Effect

When you apply the Transform effect to an object, symbol, or bitmap, you can change the object's, symbol's, or bitmap's size, make it spin, move it to a different position, and more. You can specify the effect duration in frames and change the color and opacity of the object during the animation. To apply the Transform effect to an object, follow these steps:

1. Select the object, symbol, or bitmap to which you want to apply the effect. Right-click (Windows) or CTRL-click (Mac) and then choose Timeline Effects | Transform/Transition | Transform from the context menu to open the Transform dialog box shown next.

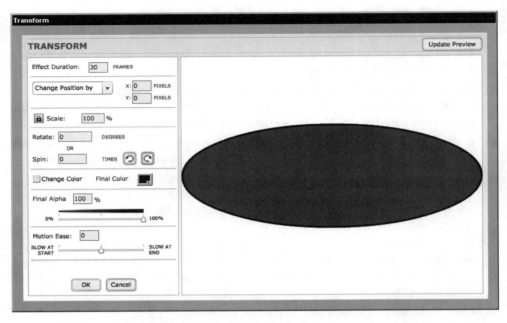

2. Accept the default Effect Duration of 30 frames or enter a different value in that field. This value determines the number of frames used to pull off the effect.

3. To change the position of an object by a given number of pixels, enter values in the X and/or Y fields. Alternatively, click the down arrow to the right of Change Position By and choose Move To Position from the drop-down menu. If you choose this option, the values you enter in the X and Y fields will designate the coordinates of the stage position to which you want the object to move.

4. To change the size of the object, enter a value in the Scale field. Enter a value less than 100 to decrease the size of the object or greater than 100 to increase the size of the object. This scales the object proportionately. To scale the object disproportionately, click the Lock icon and X and Y fields become available. These fields enable you to enter different values for the X and Y scale of the object.

5. To rotate the object, enter a value in the Rotate field. This value is in degrees. Alternatively, you can enter a value in the Spin field. This value is the number of times you want the object to spin while the effect occurs. When you enter a value in either field, Flash 8 enters the correct value in the other field. For example, if you enter 360 for rotation, Flash 8 enters a value of 1 in the Spin field. Alternatively, you can enter a value for the number of times you want the object to spin, and Flash will supply the value for the Rotate field.

6. Click the Rotate Clockwise or Rotate Counterclockwise icon to specify the direction in which the object rotates.

7. To change the color of the object during the course of the effect, click the Change Color check box and then click the Final Color swatch to choose a color from the pop-up palette. This determines the color the object will have when the effect concludes. The

transition from the object's original color to its final color is applied gradually on each frame of the effect.

8. Accept the default Final Alpha value of 100 percent (opaque) or enter a different value to make the object become transparent as the effect occurs.

Enter a value of 0 for Final Alpha and the object disappears on the last frame of the effect.

9. To modify the speed at which the effect begins and ends, enter a value between –100 and 100 in the Motion Ease field. Enter a value less than 0 to have the animation begin slowly but end quickly, or a value greater than 0 to have the animation begin quickly and end slowly. Alternatively, you can drag on the slider below the Motion Ease field to specify a value.

10. Click the Update Preview button to preview the effect.

11. Click OK to apply the effect. You can repeat any of the previous steps and choose different options or enter different values if the effect is not suitable for your movie.

Use the Transition Timeline Effect

When you apply the Transition timeline effect to an object, the object fades in or fades out. This is similar to transition effects you see in movies, where a scene fades in or fades out. You can specify the duration of the transition and the manner in which the transition occurs. This timeline effect works well with any object and is excellent when used with text or bitmap images. To apply the Transition effect, follow these steps:

1. Select the object to which you want to apply the effect. Right-click (Windows) or CTRL-click (Mac) and then choose Timeline Effects | Transform/Transition | Transition from the context menu to open the Transition dialog box shown in the following illustration.

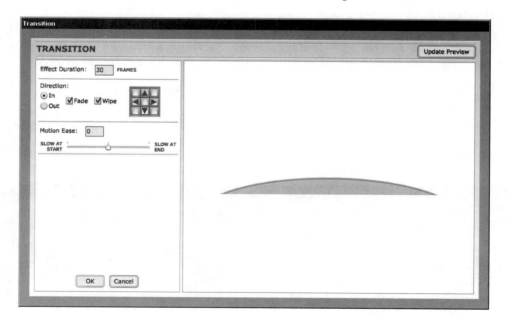

2. Accept the default Effect Duration of 30 frames or enter a different value in this field. This value represents the number of frames that elapse as the effect occurs.

3. Accept the default direction for In or click the Out radio button. By default, Flash 8 will apply a fade and a wipe to the object. The Fade option gradually increases (fades in) or decreases (fades out) the object opacity. The Wipe option gradually reveals (wipes in) or hides (wipes out) the object. Deselect either option to apply only one transition effect to the object.

4. Click one of the arrows in the direction grid to determine the direction from which the effect occurs.

5. To modify the speed at which the effect begins and ends, enter a value between −100 and 100 in the Motion Ease field. Enter a value less than 0 to have the animation begin slowly but end quickly, or a value greater than 0 to have the animation begin quickly and end slowly. Alternatively, you can drag on the slider below the Motion Ease field to select a value.

6. Click the Update Preview button to preview the effect.

7. Click OK to apply the effect. You can repeat any of the previous steps and choose different options or enter different values if the effect is not suitable for your movie.

Preview and Modify Timeline Effects

When you use other forms of Flash animation, you can preview the effect within the authoring window by scrubbing the playhead across the frames. You can preview a timeline effect in this manner. However, the only way to make sure the effect is applied in the desired manner is to test the movie by choosing Control | Test Movie.

Edit an Effect

If, after previewing a movie, you decide that a timeline effect isn't playing as you'd envisioned, you can edit the effect. When you edit the effect, you can enter different values and choose different options to modify the effect to suit your movie. You can edit an effect as follows:

1. Select the object to which you have applied the effect you need to edit.

2. Right-click (Windows) or CTRL-click (Mac) and choose Timeline Effects | Edit Effect from the context menu to open the effect's dialog box. Alternatively, you can open the Properties Inspector and click the Edit button in the Effect section, as shown in the following illustration.

3. Enter the desired values and/or choose different effect options.

4. Click the Update Preview button in the effect's dialog box to preview the effect with the new settings.

5. If the preview is acceptable, click OK to apply the effect; otherwise, repeat steps 3 and 4 until the effect previews as desired.

Remove an Effect

If, after testing a movie with a timeline effect, you decide that your movie would look better without the effect, you can remove the effect at any time. To remove an effect from an object, follow these steps.

1. Select the object from which you want to remove the effect.

2. Right-click (Windows) or CTRL-click (Mac) and choose Timeline Effects | Remove Effect. Flash 8 removes the effect from the object.

Conclusion

In this chapter, you learned to animate and apply effects to objects using the Flash 8 timeline effects feature. You learned how to apply effects to objects, modify effect parameters, and edit effects. You also learned how to remove effects from objects. In the next chapter, you'll learn how to animate objects with motion tweening.

10

Chapter 11

Incorporate Motion Tweening into Your Design

How to...

- Make a simple motion tween
- Tween with multiple keyframes
- Change size, rotation, skew, and color on a motion tween
- Tween symbols on multiple layers
- Control frames and frame sequences in a motion tween
- Adjust tweened objects with the Properties Inspector
- Create a motion guide
- Use a mask layer with a motion tween

With frame-by-frame animation you manually change objects on each frame of a movie. Frame-by-frame animation is tedious work and may not be appropriate for complex animations that require smooth motion. When you require smooth animation, motion tweening is the appropriate choice. If you are creating an animation in which you are transforming one shape into another, shape tweening is the logical choice. Shape tweening, the topic of the next chapter, is also referred to as *morphing* one object into another.

When you *tween* an object in Flash, you determine the object's position and other attributes on keyframes, and the software mathematically generates a sequence of frames, known as *in-between frames*, between two keyframes. The farther apart the keyframes are on the timeline, the smoother the movement will be. In contrast to frame-by-frame animation, tweening takes the guesswork out of the gradual transition of an object between two keyframes. In Flash, you can choose either frame-by-frame or tweening animation, depending upon the requirements of your project.

Understand Motion Versus Shape Tweening

Tweening in Flash is a standard animation technique, and it comes in two forms: motion and shape. Although both methods of tweening are based on the same concept, their applications and purposes are quite different. In fact newcomers to Flash animation are sometimes puzzled as to which animation type to use in a movie.

In a very simple animation, it may not matter whether you use motion or shape tweening. However, when animations become more sophisticated, your selection will indeed matter. This is why it's important that you understand the similarities and differences between the two animation types. *Motion tweening*, as the name implies, is used primarily to affect the motion of an object over time. As such, it can be used on editable objects, grouped objects, symbols, and text. *Shape tweening*, on the other hand, is used to change the shape of an object and can only be used on editable objects. Shape tweening is often used for morphing and otherwise changing the separate elements of editable shapes. Even though you can perform motion tweening on editable objects, you cannot morph the shape; you can only animate motion, size, rotation, and skewing.

There are many areas of overlap between the two types of tweening, and these definitions don't address the subtleties of these powerful tools. For example, both shape and motion tweens can be used to change the position of an object and the object's color, scale, rotation, and skew, though the same actions may produce drastically different results. With practice, you will get a firm understanding of both forms of tweening and instinctively understand which one to use to create compelling, eye-catching animations. This chapter focuses on all aspects of motion tweening, and Chapter 12 examines shape tweening.

Make a Simple Motion Tween

Before learning to make a motion tween, you need to understand some basic rules. As stated previously, a motion tween can be used on editable and grouped objects, symbols, and text. If you want to tween an object's color and opacity in a motion tween, the object must be a symbol. (Graphic symbols and buttons are covered in Chapter 8, and movie clip symbols are discussed in Chapter 13.)

In its simplest form, a motion tween moves an object from point A to point B over a given number of frames. Motion tweening basically involves five steps:

1. Creating a keyframe at the point in your movie where your animation begins.

2. Creating and selecting an object group or symbol.

3. Creating a keyframe where the animation ends.

4. Modifying the object's position and other parameters on the last keyframe.

5. Selecting a frame in between the two keyframes and then creating a motion tween by right-clicking (Windows) or CTRL-clicking (Macintosh), and then choosing Create Motion Tween from the context menu.

After successfully creating a motion tween animation, a symbol appears on the timeline, as shown in Figure 11-1.

The procedure used to create the motion tween shown in Figure 11-1 is detailed here:

1. Create a simple object on the first frame of the main timeline, and either group the object or make it into a graphic symbol or movie clip. By default, a keyframe will appear on frame 1, Layer 1. This will serve as the first point in the animation you are about to create. If you want the animation to begin at a different point in your movie, select the frame on which you want the animation to begin, and press F6 to convert it to a keyframe.

2. Create a new keyframe on Layer 1 farther on down the timeline where you want the next change in your animation to occur. Select the frame and then choose Insert | Timeline | Keyframe or press F6. In Figure 11-1, the ending animation keyframe was created on frame 6. After you create the new keyframe, a span of frames appears between the keyframes, as shown in the following illustration.

11

3. With any in-between frame selected, right-click (Windows) or CTRL-click (Macintosh) and choose Create Motion Tween from the pop-up context menu. Alternatively, you can choose Insert | Timeline | Create Motion Tween. When you create a motion tween, frames are automatically generated between the two keyframes (in this case between frames 1 and 6, as shown next), and a right-pointing arrow appears on a light-blue background

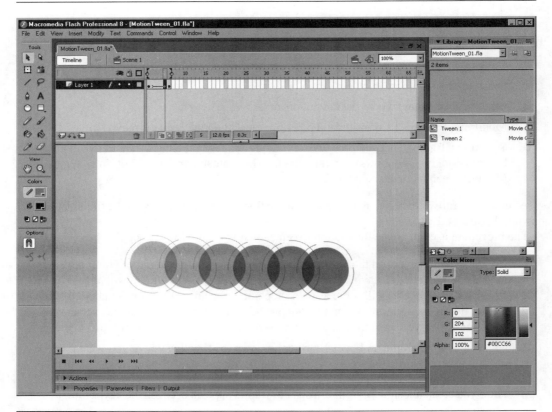

FIGURE 11-1 Motion tweening a grouped object

to indicate a motion tween. You can also add a motion tween by selecting an in-between frame and then choosing Motion from the Tween menu in the Properties Inspector.

4. With the last keyframe selected, drag the object to another location on the stage to change its position. Make any additional changes such as scaling, rotating, or skewing the object.

5. Press ENTER or RETURN to test the movie in the timeline to see the gradual transition of the object between the two keyframes.

To convert an existing object into a symbol for use in a motion tween, click the object and select Modify | Convert to Symbol or press F8, which opens the Convert To Symbol dialog box. Select the behavior of the new symbol (Movie Clip or Graphic) and click OK. The object is now a symbol, stored in the Library. A symbol can be tweened in the same way that you tween an editable object or group of objects, with the exception that you can change the symbol's color in a motion tween animation. You do this by selecting the graphic symbol on one of the animation keyframes, choosing Tint from the Color menu in the Properties Inspector, and selecting the color to which you want the object to change. This cannot be done on a group of objects.

Add Frames to a Motion Tween

If you play back an animation with six frames, such as the movie we looked at previously in Figure 11-1, you will notice that the motion is choppy and the animation ends rather quickly. This occurs because Flash has only four in-between frames in which to interpolate the animation. With the default movie frame rate of 12 frames per second, this animation lasts for less than half a second. This is fine if you're creating a simple animation, or if you intentionally want to create an animation with herky-jerky motion. If, however, your goal is to create smooth motion, you can do so by adding more in-between frames, or by creating an animation with sufficient keyframes in the first place.

To add more in-between frames, click an in-between frame in your motion tween animation. If you've enabled Span Based Selection in the General section of the Preferences tab, press CTRL (Windows)/CMD (Mac) to select a frame in the middle of the tweened keyframes. Once an individual frame is selected, press F5 to add a frame. Each time you press F5, another frame will be added. Alternatively, you can select multiple frames and then press F5 to create a like number of frames and speed up the process. For example, if you select three frames, every time you press F5, three frames are added to your animation.

11

Enhance a Motion Tween with Multiple Keyframes

In Figure 11-1, the object travels in a single line, from one keyframe to another. This creates limited movement and is, quite frankly, boring. You can create a more compelling animation by inserting additional keyframes into the animation and changing the direction of the object on each keyframe.

In Figure 11-2, the position of an object has been changed several times by adding keyframes to the animation. To add a keyframe to an existing frame sequence, select an in-between frame (hold down CTRL in Windows/CMD on the Mac if Span Based Selection is enabled) and then click F6 to add a keyframe. To extend an animation, add a keyframe farther up the timeline by selecting a blank frame and then pressing F6. This extends the length of the current frame sequence and gives you another opportunity to further animate the object. You also can extend the length of an existing frame sequence by clicking the last keyframe and dragging it to its new position.

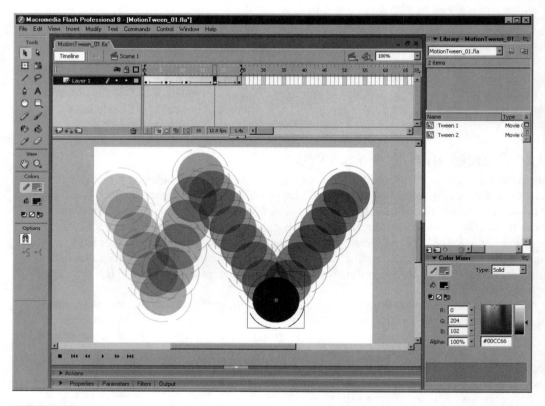

FIGURE 11-2   Adding additional keyframes can add interest to a motion tween animation.

Figure 11-2 is an alternate version of the animation shown previously in Figure 11-1. In the alternate version, three new keyframes were added, and on each keyframe the object was moved to a different position to create the illusion of a ball bouncing up and down. If you click the Onion Skin button (shown next) you'll find it easy to go back and change the object on any keyframe because you can preview each frame of the animation. When you're using Onion Skins for the purpose of viewing each frame of an animation, as was done in Figure 11-2, it's important to drag the Onion Skin markers to span all the frames of the animation, as shown next. Otherwise, you won't see Onion Skins on each frame of the animation.

Onion Skin frame markers

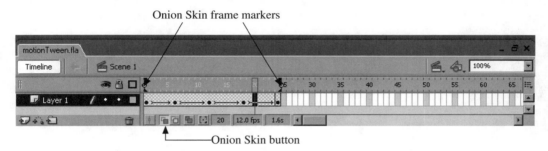

Onion Skin button

Scale, Rotate, Skew, and Change Color with a Motion Tween

In the previous examples, only the position of the object was changed. To add additional interest to your animations, you can use any of the transformation tools or menu commands (Modify | Transform) to change your object, and then animate the change with a motion tween. To apply a transformation to a motion tween, select a keyframe in the animation, select the object, and then modify it using one of the transformation tools, as outlined in Chapter 5.

Figure 11-3 shows a circle whose position, skew, opacity, and size are modified while in motion. The Onion Skin feature is used to make it easy to preview the object on each frame of animation. On frame 6, the object is scaled to 50 percent of its original size and skewed with the Free Transform tool. On frame 18, the scale is reduced to 25 percent of the original. To scale an object in a motion tween animation, click the keyframe you want the transformation to occur on, select the object, and then scale the object to the desired size. When the animation is played, the object gradually changes size between keyframes. In this figure, the opacity of the ball is also changed. Changing the opacity and color of an object is discussed next.

Change the Color of a Tweened Symbol

When an object is made into any kind of symbol, you can use a motion tween to animate the color and opacity of the object. In Figure 11-3, the object opacity changes from opaque to partially transparent and back to opaque again. You change the opacity (alpha) of a symbol as

11

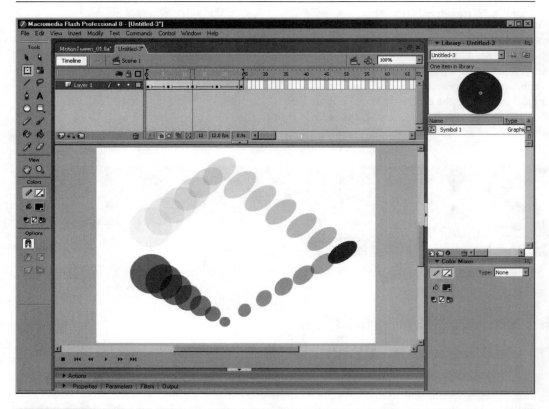

FIGURE 11-3   Scaling and skewing an object in motion

well as the other color settings of a symbol in the Color menu in the Properties Inspector, as shown in the following illustration.

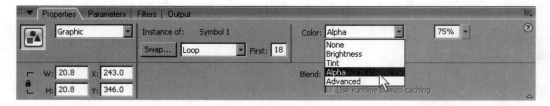

To animate the color of a symbol, select the symbol in a keyframe and then use the Properties Inspector's Tint or Advanced settings to change the symbol's color. To change the opacity of an object, open the Properties Inspector and choose Alpha from the Color list. You can either use the vertical slider to pick an Alpha percentage or type the desired percentage in the Alpha text box.

Refer to Chapter 8 for a detailed description of the color settings available for symbols in the Properties Inspector. You can create some interesting motion tween animations when you change the color characteristics of a symbol.

Create a Motion Tween with Graphic Symbols on Multiple Layers

You can create an almost never-ending variety of motion tween animations when you use the Flash tools and the Properties Inspector features. Figure 11-4 shows an example of a motion tween on multiple layers, where the position and size of bus and car symbols have been transformed. When the animation is played, it appears as though the vehicles are moving toward you. There are five graphic symbols on the stage, and each object resides on its own layer. Layers stack upon each other in order of display; objects on upper layers eclipse objects that appear directly beneath them on lower layers. For example, the street layer is under the bus and car layers. Examining this movie step-by-step will help you learn the process of creating a tween animation on multiple layers.

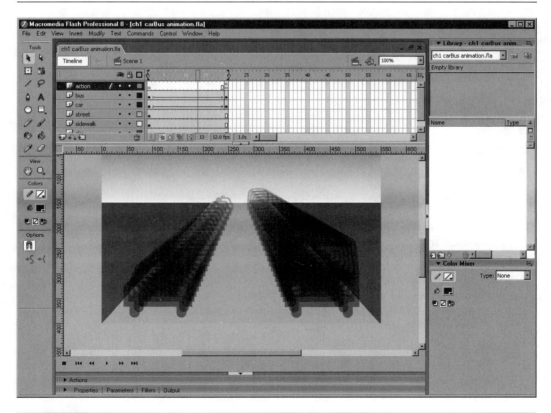

FIGURE 11-4   A separate layer is used to animate each symbol.

It's important to understand that the following example of a motion tween animation is fairly rudimentary. When you become more experienced with the drawing and animation tools, you'll find that the most efficient way to work is to convert most of the objects in your movies to symbols. In fact, nesting symbols within symbols can often be the most efficient way to animate. Also, many of your tweened animations will be contained within movie clips, each on its own timeline, which makes it easy to edit every aspect of the symbol. Before you learn how to do this, though, you have to understand how to create a motion tween animation in the main timeline first.

Deconstruct a Multilayer Movie That Uses Motion Tweens

First, you should always plan your animation, as was done for the movie we're about to deconstruct. Sketch all of the keyframes of the animation on a piece of paper to get an idea of the actions you want to have occur at each point in the movie. This will help you figure out how many layers you'll need. It will also help you determine the stacking order of the layers. Sketching an animation is also known as *storyboarding*.

It's a good idea to name layers and symbols to reflect the nature of the object that resides on the layer. For example, in Figure 11-4, the car symbol is called "car," as is the layer. The logical naming of symbols and layers is especially important if other people will be working on your project or if you'll update the project from time to time. When you name symbols and layers in a logical manner, there's no mistaking the purpose of each layer or its objects. The layers in Figure 11-4 are named (from the top layer to the bottom):

- Action
- Bus
- Car
- Street
- Sidewalk
- Sky

The following steps went into creating this multilayer animation:

1. After the layers and symbols were created, the first frame in the sidewalk layer was selected and the sidewalk symbol was dragged from the Library onto the stage. The symbol is a rectangle with a fill and no stroke.

2. After the sidewalk was in place, frame 1 of the street layer was selected and the street symbol was dragged from the Library onto the stage. The street was created with the rectangle tool. The Free Transform tool was used to make the beginning of the street narrow to give perspective to the scene.

3. Once the street was created, frame 1 of the sky was selected and the sky symbol was put in place. The sky is a simple rectangle with a gradient fill.

4. Frame 1 of the bus layer was selected and the bus symbol was dragged from the Library onto the stage. (The bus and the car were drawn with the Pen tool.) The process was repeated and the car symbol was positioned on frame 1 of the car layer. The car and the bus symbols are the only objects that are animated. The goal was to make the bus and the car appear as if they're moving toward the viewer. This effect involves changing the position and the scale of the bus and car symbols.

5. With all the elements in place, a motion tween was applied to the in-between frames on the bus and car layers. The bus symbol was tweened first. With the bus object selected, a keyframe was inserted in frame 20. This keyframe is where the final movement in the animation occurs. The process was repeated on the car layer.

6. A motion tween was created by selecting a frame in between the keyframes, right-clicking in Windows/CTRL-clicking on the Mac, and choosing Create Motion Tween from the context menu. A black arrow with a light blue background appeared on the in-between frames to indicate a successful motion tween.

7. Finally, the bus and car symbols were changed in frame 20 on their respective layers. With the bus object selected in frame 20, the bus was moved to the bottom of the stage onto the street. The process was repeated with the car. The paths of the bus and car conform to the forward perspective of the street. Enlarging the scale of the two objects creates the illusion of objects moving forward in space. In frame 20, the scale of the car and bus symbols was enlarged to approximately 400 percent in the last keyframe of both the bus and car layers. If you were to play back the movie with the Controller, the bus and car would appear to move forward in space and time.

Motion tweening on different layers can also be used to make objects appear behind or in front of one another. If you were to transpose the position of the bus and car in frame 1 of their respective layers (placing the car to the right and the bus to the left), they would cross paths somewhere in the middle, and the bus would block out the car at that point. Layering also can be used for hiding objects underneath one another during the span of a motion tween animation.

Control Frames and Frame Sequences in a Motion Tween

Once you've created a movie with several layers and tweens, there's always a possibility that the movie will need editing. Even the smallest revision can create a domino effect, which may change the entire flow of the movie. This is why housing your animation sequences in movie clip symbols is an efficient manner in which to work. It's a lot easier to edit each individual tweened animation in a movie clip symbol than it is to edit several complex tweens on the main timeline. A detailed discussion of movie clip symbols appears in Chapter 13, but for now, let's consider a revision of a tweened animation on the main timeline.

You have several methods to choose from when you need to modify frame sequences and move keyframes around. This is helpful because, as often as objects in a movie need to be changed, the actual frames themselves may also need to be moved. Sometimes the timing of objects being animated on different layers may need to be revised, too.

Let's return to the previous example of the tweened car and bus movie shown in Figure 11-4. There are many ways to modify this movie. For starters, let's suppose your client wants to change the timing of the animation so that the car moves a split second after the bus. Instead of redoing the entire animation, you could move the car frame sequence forward on the timeline, perhaps beginning it on frame 10, so that the car is introduced after the bus. However, if you only made that change and played the movie back, all the other elements would disappear from the stage in frame 21, and the client wouldn't be happy with that outcome.

To prevent the other objects from disappearing when the movie is played, you can add frames to all other layers up to frame 30, where the car frame sequence now ends. To do so, click frame 30 of each layer and press F5. This fills in the frames to the last frame on the selected layer. If the last frame is a regular frame—as it is on the unanimated sky, street, and sidewalk layers—you can select the frame, press CTRL (Windows) or CMD (Mac), and drag the frame to increase or reduce the frame span. When you use either one of these techniques on a layer with animation, such as the top tweened layer called "bus," it only adds blank keyframes. On a tweened layer, use CTRL-click (Windows)/CMD-click (Mac) on the tween and press F5 until you reach frame 30. This will enable you to add additional frames to each layer in a motion tween sequence.

Copy and Paste Frames

If you need to copy a keyframe, frame, or frame sequence to another layer, you easily can do so in Flash. Copying frames leaves the selected frames in place and places a copy of the frames on the clipboard. A copy of the frame sequence can be pasted at any time during your Flash session, unless of course you copy something else to the clipboard.

You can copy a frame sequence or an individual frame by selecting the frame (or frame sequence), right-clicking (Windows) or CTRL-clicking (Mac), and then choosing Copy Frames from the context menu. Alternatively, you can press CTRL-ALT-C (Windows)/OPT-CMD-C (Mac). Click the first frame to which you want to paste the copied frames, right-click (Windows) or CTRL-click (Mac), and then choose Paste Frames from the context menu. Alternatively, you can press CTRL-ALT-V in Windows or OPT-CMD-V on the Mac. A duplicate of the frame sequence appears. If you're copying and pasting a tweened frame sequence, make certain that the last keyframe is in the selection; otherwise, a dashed line will appear indicating that the tween is broken.

Frames can be cut from a timeline by selecting the frames and then choosing Edit | Timeline | Cut Frames. Alternatively, you can press CTRL-ALT-X in Windows or OPT-CMD-X on the Mac. Choosing this command removes the frame selection from the timeline and places a copy on the clipboard. You can then paste the frame selection into another layer or to another position in the timeline by choosing Edit | Timeline | Paste Frames. You can also paste frames from the clipboard into another Flash movie, or for that matter, into a new movie clip symbol.

Reverse a Frame Sequence

When you reverse a tweened frame sequence, it goes in the opposite direction. Figure 11-5 is an illustration of a simple bouncing ball that has one frame sequence that makes the ball appear to go up and a reverse frame sequence that makes the ball appear to go down, simulating the flowing

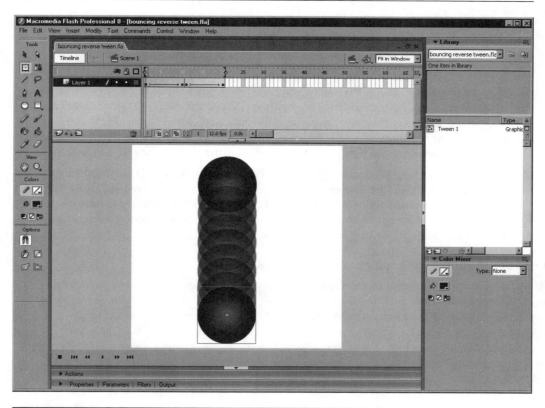

FIGURE 11-5 You can create realistic animation sequences by reversing frames.

motion of a bouncing ball. This simple ball animation is a good example of how you can save time using Flash features. Instead of creating a new motion tween to reverse the ball's direction, you can copy, paste, and then reverse the tween animation to quickly achieve the same result.

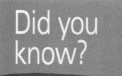

Editable Objects and Tweens

In previous versions of Flash, you could not apply a motion tween to an editable object. This has all changed in Flash 8. When you apply a motion tween to an editable object, you can animate the object's movement, rotation, size, and skew. However, you cannot morph the shape into a different object. To accomplish that task, you need the tried-and-true shape tween, which is the topic of the next chapter.

Here's how you can reverse a sequence of tweened frames:

1. Create a motion tween animation using the steps outlined previously.

2. Select the tweened frame sequence, right-click (Windows)/CTRL-click (Mac), and then choose Copy Frames from the context menu.

3. Select the next frame after the frames you just copied, right-click (Windows) or CTRL-click (Mac), and then choose Paste Frames from the context menu. If you scrub the playhead over the frames, the movement of the object will seem strange because the motion abruptly returns to the beginning of the loop when it reaches the first frame of the pasted sequence. You can easily fix that by reversing the second frame sequence.

4. Select the new frame sequence, right-click (Windows) or CTRL-click (Mac) and choose Reverse Frames from the context menu. This reverses the selected tweened frame sequence. Now, when you test the movie, the object that you animated goes one direction and then does an abrupt about-face. Alternatively, you can reverse selected frames by choosing Modify | Timeline | Reverse Frames.

Convert In-between Frames to Keyframes

Reversing frames on a tween can be a little quirky. Sometimes, reversing tweened frames on more complex animations actually disengages the tween, and when the reversed frame sequence is played it appears to have no motion tween. Other times, the reversed frames don't play correctly, and what you see is not the reverse of the copied frames, but confusing motions and unsyncopated transformations. To avoid problems like these, you can convert your copied motion tween frames into keyframes *before* you reverse the order of the frame sequence. Do this by selecting the entire span, right-clicking (Windows) or CTRL-clicking (Mac), and choosing Convert

Copying Keyframes

You can copy a keyframe and paste it to another location in the same frame sequence by selecting a keyframe and ALT-dragging in Windows/OPT-dragging on the Mac. This makes a duplicate keyframe. In addition, objects can be copied and pasted into place on the object's current layer or onto another layer. To do this, select the object and select Edit | Copy (or CTRL-C in Windows/CMD-C on the Mac). Then select a new frame in the layer into which you want to paste the object and choose Edit | Paste In Place (CTRL-SHIFT-V in Windows/ CMD-SHIFT-V on the Mac). This can be a real timesaver if you place a frame sequence on a layer and then decide later that you need to move it or replicate it.

to Keyframes from the context menu. Alternatively, you can choose Modify | Frames | Convert to Keyframes. Once you've converted the tweened frame sequence into keyframes, select all the keyframes, right-click (Windows) or CTRL-click (Mac), and choose Reverse Frames from the context menu. This is a foolproof way to reverse a complex motion tween animation and have it play properly.

Not only can you reverse movement when you convert tweened frame sequences to keyframes and then reverse the frames, you can also reverse tweened transformations and the color effects on a tweened symbol.

Figure 11-6 shows a cartoon of a chicken whose wings are flapping up and down. The wings flapping up and down were created using the methods outlined in the previous paragraph. As you can see in the right wing and left wing layers in the timeline, the keyframes after frame 15 are the reverse of the motion tween sequence on frames 1 through 15.

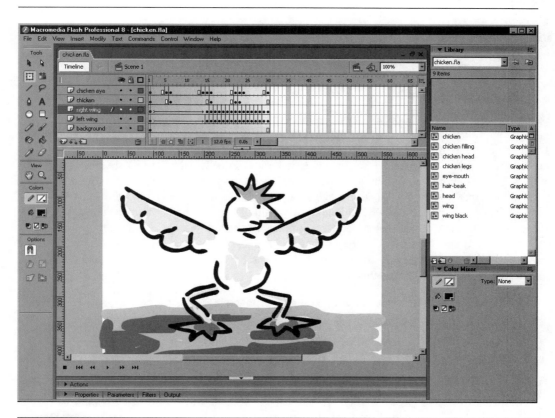

FIGURE 11-6 You can create comical animations by reversing frames.

Animate Objects with Properties Inspector Effects

You can use settings from the Properties Inspector in a motion tween animation. Grouped graphics and symbols can be customized with rotation effects, and you can modify the manner in which the animation occurs by changing the way it eases in and out. The Rotate feature can create special effects like the spinning of an object, and the Ease feature lets you determine whether an animation begins quickly and ends slowly, or vice versa. For example, a car accelerates gradually as it overcomes inertia. If you want to create an animation of an accelerating car, you begin (ease in) the animation slowly and end it (ease out) quickly.

Use the Properties Inspector to Rotate a Graphic

When you create a motion tween animation and use the Free Transform Rotate tool to rotate an object, your options are somewhat limited. For example, you cannot use the tool to get an object

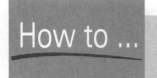 **Create Blank Keyframes**

Sometimes in your animation you want an object to appear and disappear, to achieve a certain effect. Intermittent display of an object makes it appear as though it's being lit by a strobe light. You can achieve this quite easily by adding blank frames, but not on a tweened sequence. (If you try to create a blank keyframe in a tweened frame sequence, it will break the tween.)

A good example of this technique would be a frame-by-frame sequence of photographs that creates the Flash equivalent of a slide show. The photos would be displayed for three to five seconds and interspersed with one or two blank keyframes before the next photo is displayed. This produces a flickering effect similar to an old movie.

There are many other reasons to use blank keyframes. For example, you may want an object to appear in one part of an animation and disappear in another. To create blank keyframes within a set, follow this procedure:

1. Select a frame or frames in a frame sequence that is not tweened.
2. Right-click (Windows) or CTRL-click (Mac) the frame(s) you want to be blank, and choose Convert To Blank Keyframes from the context menu.

When you create blank keyframes, they become placeholders in the frame sequence. You can leave them blank if this is the effect you are after, or you can add different objects to the blank keyframes, thus converting them to regular keyframes. Converting regular frames to blank keyframes maintains the original length of the animation.

to spin for one rotation, spin for a given number of rotations, or spin continuously. However, you can use the Properties Inspector to adjust the rotation of a tweened object and create some very interesting effects (see Figure 11-7). You can automatically set and customize the rotation of an object so it will appear as if it were spinning. You can also cause an object to be oriented to a specified path, which is discussed in the next section. You can align an object to a path only if you are using motion tween animation.

Let's consider an example of how you might put this feature to use. In Figure 11-8, the little hand of the clock graphic spins clockwise in position when the movie is tested. A tweened rotation is applied to the little hand. Let's quickly review the process of how to create this effect.

The clock in Figure 11-8 was created on three layers: the "ticks" layer, the "little hand" layer, and the "big hand" layer. The only element that is animated is the little hand graphic symbol on the little hand layer. This symbol was created with a reference point (the object's center of rotation) located at the bottom center of the symbol; when the rotation is applied to the symbol, the bottom of the little hand remains static while the tip of the hand rotates.

The little hand motion-tween animation continues to frame 40. With a frame in the tween selected on the little hand layer, the Properties Inspector was displayed (as shown previously in Figure 11-7). In the Rotate section, CW (clockwise) was chosen and the number 3 was typed in for the Times setting.

If you follow these steps, you can make an object rotate clockwise three times each time the frame sequence loops. If you enter a higher value in the Rotate Times setting without changing the number of frames in the sequence, the object will appear to rotate faster. You can also select CCW (counterclockwise) as a rotation direction. If you have modified an object in a keyframe with the Free Transform Rotate and Skew tool, Rotate will be indicated as Auto in the Properties Inspector.

Use the Properties Inspector to Ease In and Out

You adjust the ease in the Properties Inspector to control the manner in which an animation begins and ends. You can specify the Ease value by entering a number from −100 to 100 in the

11

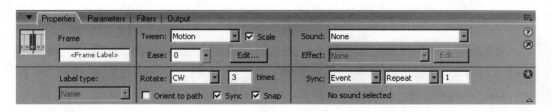

FIGURE 11-7   You can precisely control the number of rotations an object makes with the Properties Inspector.

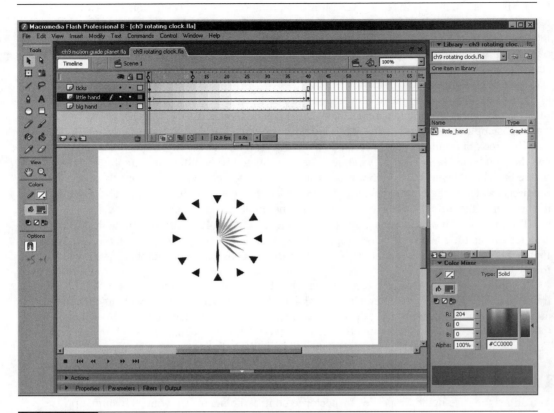

FIGURE 11-8 You use the Properties Inspector to control rotation in a motion tween animation.

text box or by clicking the triangle to the right of the text field and then dragging the Ease slider up or down, as shown in the following illustration.

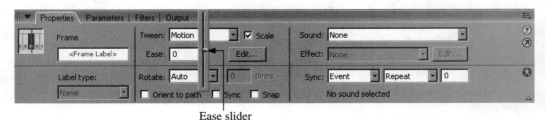

Ease slider

To make a motion tween animation start slowly and speed up at the end (ease in), select a value between −1 and −100. To make the tween begin quickly and end slowly (ease out), select a value between 1 and 100.

Flash 8
Professional

How to Create a Custom Ease In/Ease Out

If you own Flash Professional, you can create a Custom Ease In/Ease Out by clicking the Edit button next to the Tween menu in the Properties Inspector. This opens the Custom Ease In/Ease Out dialog box shown in the following illustration. The default interpolation between frames is linear, unless you ease the animation in or out as defined in the last section. The Custom Ease In/Ease Out dialog box displays a diagonal line (no ease in or out) or a curve if you've entered an Ease value. The horizontal legend (Frames) in the dialog box shows frames, while the vertical legend (Tween) shows the percentage completed of the tween. To modify the manner in which the animation eases in and out, you click the desired positions on the curve to add points. Each point has two tangent handles similar to Bézier points on a path. Click and drag the tangent handles to change the manner in which the animation eases in and out. Click the Play button to preview the animation on stage.

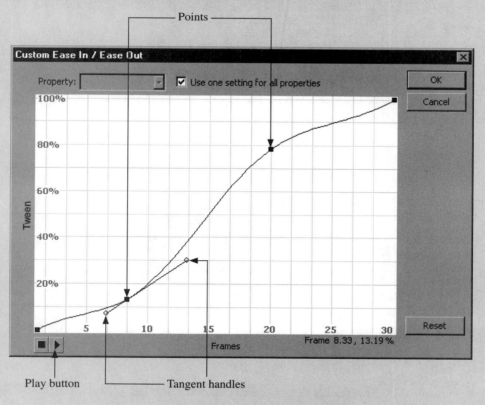

11

Animate on a Guided Path

For the most part, regular tweening involves a linear movement. Sometimes you may need an object to follow a complex path, such as an arc or a circle. You can't accomplish this with a regular motion tween, but you can have an object follow a predefined path that you create using one of the Flash drawing tools. You do this by creating a path on a guide layer and then creating a motion tween animation on a guided layer where an object follows the path.

Figure 11-9 shows an example of a motion tween animation where an object follows a path on a motion guide layer. The little planet is tweened and follows a motion guide to revolve around the bigger planet. If the little planet was tweened with a frame-by-frame animation,

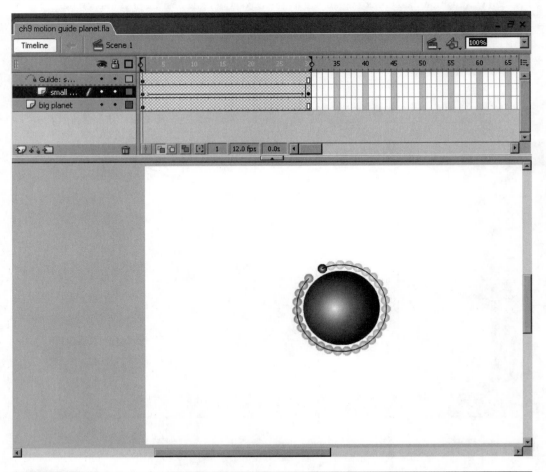

FIGURE 11-9   You add a motion guide to animate an object along a path.

it could take hundreds of keyframes to accomplish this. Creating copious keyframes is very time consuming, and you probably have better things to do with your time.

When you want an object to follow a curved path, the perfect solution is to create a motion tween animation where the object follows a motion guide. The little planet in the example in Figure 11-9 was attached to an oval motion guide to create the illusion of its rotating around the big planet. Let's take a look at how you can create a similar animation.

> **NOTE**   *Motion guides are invisible when the movie is played back.*

Create a Motion Guide

A motion guide consists of a path that's drawn on a guide layer. You can create a motion path using the Pen, Pencil, Line, Brush, Circle, or Rectangle tool. If you use the Circle or Rectangle tool to create a motion path, use the Eraser tool to open the path, thus creating a beginning and end for the path. To create a motion guide, follow these steps:

1. In our example (Figure 11-9), the small planet resides on its own layer, as does the big planet. They are placed on different layers so that they will animate correctly. Assuming that all your layers and graphics are in place for the animation you are about to create, you are ready to create the motion guide. Select the object that will follow the motion guide, and click the Add Guide Layer button at the bottom of the Layers section of the timeline. Alternatively, you can right-click (Windows) or CTRL-click (Macintosh) the layer that contains the object that will follow the motion path, and then choose Add Motion Guide from the context menu. A Motion Guide icon will appear on the new layer, along with the name of the layer that is being guided. Note that the layer being guided is beneath the motion guide layer and indented slightly to the right in the Layers section, as shown in the following illustration.

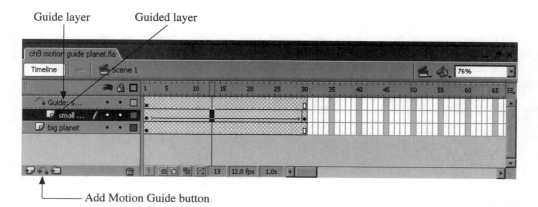

2. Select the motion guide layer and draw the guide. In the planet example in Figure 11-9, the Oval tool was selected for this purpose with a stroke of blue and with no fill. A motion guide can be any stroke color, as it is not seen when the movie is published. In fact, if you choose a contrasting color the path will be easier to distinguish. In the example, an editable oval was drawn as a guide to extend the parameters of the big planet.

3. A motion guide has to have a beginning and an end to which you can attach the guided object on the keyframes. To make the oval work as a motion guide, a small piece of the guide oval was erased using the Eraser tool. If you use the Oval or Rectangle tool to create your path, it does not have a beginning or end. Use the Eraser tool to create a gap in the path, thereby creating a beginning and end.

4. It's a good idea to lock the motion guide layer so you don't accidentally select and move it while aligning the guided object to the ends of the guide. Lock the guide by clicking the Lock button on the motion guide layer.

5. Determine how many frames your animation will be, and then extend the motion guide and stationary layers to the ending frame by selecting that frame and pressing F5. In the example, the layers were extended to frame 30. Doing this assured that the motion guide and the big planet would be available for the duration of the animation.

6. When you have all the components in place, select the first keyframe on the guided layer, select the object, and align it to beginning of the path. A hollow circle will appear in the object as you near the beginning of the path, indicating that the object will snap to the path when you release the mouse button. It will be easier to snap the symbol to the path if you drag it by its registration point, especially when you're aligning a small symbol to a path.

7. Press F6 to create a keyframe at the last frame, and then align the object to the end of the path.

8. Select a frame between the keyframes on the guided layer, right-click (Windows) or CTRL-click (Mac), and choose Create Motion Tween from the context menu.

When you choose Control | Test Movie, Flash plays the movie in another window, and the motion guide is invisible, just as it will be when you publish the movie. When you want to preview the movie in authoring mode, click the eye icon on the motion guide layer to render the motion path invisible. Then you can test your animation by pressing ENTER or RETURN.

If your motion guide path is very complex, you'll have to place additional keyframes for your object to follow to create a more realistic animation. To do so, click a frame within the frame sequence where you want to add the new keyframe and then press F6. Reposition the object on the new keyframe so that it aligns to the path. When the movie plays, the object accurately follows the path and you have a more realistic animation.

Use the Properties Inspector to Tweak Motion Guide Animations

Sometimes when an object follows a motion guide, the object needs to bend and turn in the direction of the path in order for it to appear properly. For example, if you created a car and it was following a path to simulate a winding road, the animation wouldn't look real if the front of the car didn't turn in the direction of the path. In Flash, you can easily have an object follow a path by using the Orient To Path option in the Properties Inspector. To orient a tweened object along a path, click one of the in-between frames and in the Properties Inspector, check the Orient To Path check box.

Other Properties Inspector options that apply to motion guides include Sync (synchronize) and Snap. Select Sync if you're using an animated graphic symbol and the total number of frames within the symbol doesn't equal the number of frames it will occupy on the timeline. Checking the Snap check box, as shown in the following illustration, ensures that the object's reference point will snap to its path. Select this option if your object appears to be veering off the path when you preview the animation.

To unlink a guided layer from a motion guide path, drag the layer above the motion guide. It then becomes a regular layer. To link an unguided layer to a motion guide path, drag the layer beneath the motion guide and follow the steps in the previous section to align the layer symbol to the path.

Use a Mask Layer with a Motion Tween: A Tutorial

The number of effects you can create with tweened objects is limited only by your imagination. In addition to the techniques discussed in this chapter, you can combine effects that have been covered in previous chapters with motion tweening. In this tutorial, a mask is tweened. You can apply this basic recipe to other projects and create many interesting animations.

In Figure 11-10, a mask is used to create the illusion of water running through a word. The word "water" is static on the top layer, which is named "text layer," and a bitmap picture of water reflections on the surface of a swimming pool moves in a continuous loop from left to right in the background, giving the illusion of rippling waves on the surface of a lake. When you create a mask, it's like looking through a porthole that is in the shape of the mask. The process for creating a motion tween animation that is revealed through a mask is as follows:

1. As always, plan out the movie before you begin. Determine how many objects and layers you'll need. Remember to give your objects and layers unique names so that you can easily identify them. Determine the duration of the movie, or the duration of the animation if this is part of a movie.

2. Create and name the first layer and type a word. This will become the mask layer. In this example, the word "water" was typed and made editable by being broken apart (choose Modify | Break Apart from the menu or press CTRL-B in Windows/CMD-B on the Mac).

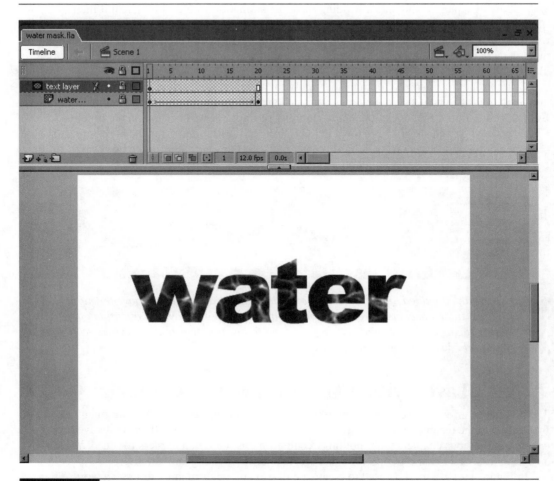

FIGURE 11-10   A mask can be used to act as a window to an animation on a lower layer.

Choose this command again because the first time you use the Break Apart command it breaks the word down into individual letters. The second time you apply the command, the letters are converted to editable vector shapes. The text would still work as a mask if you didn't break it apart. However, breaking text apart into vector shapes ensures that there won't be any font conflicts if your intended audience does not have the font you used to create the text mask installed on their computers.

3. Create a second layer, as in the example, and name it. Make sure the second layer is below the text layer. Import an image into this new layer. This will be the masked layer, or the layer that is masked out. The water image in this example is a PICT file, but you can import an image saved in most popular image formats into Flash.

4. Convert the imported picture to vector objects by clicking the image and choosing Bitmap | Trace Bitmap. In many cases, this will help reduce the size of the image.

5. Convert the image into a graphic symbol by selecting Modify | Convert to Symbol (F8).

6. The water image on the water layer was duplicated three times. All copies were then aligned end-to-end, grouped, and then the group was converted into a graphic symbol. When the masked image loops, it looks like the water is flowing continuously behind the word. To create a long series of duplicated bitmaps like the one in the example, drag an instance of the masked symbol to the masked layer (in this case, it's called the "water" layer). For the tile effect to work properly, the bitmap you use must also be a seamless tile. In other words, the left side of the bitmap must mirror the right side. When you duplicate and align a seamless tile, it is just that, *seamless*; you can't tell where one tile ends and another begins. When you use this technique in your own animations, the sum of the seamless tiles should be long enough to accommodate the entire word. Note that the water tile bleeds off the right edge of the stage so that a break won't occur in the masked image (water) during the tweening (see Figure 11-11).

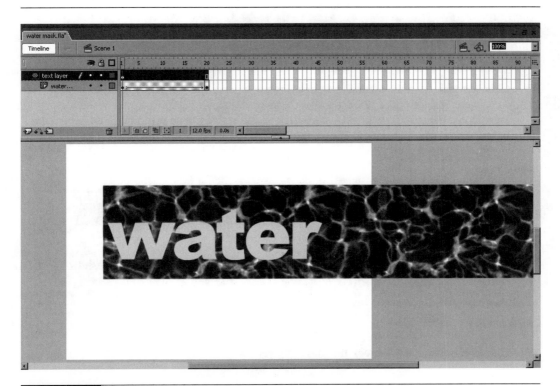

FIGURE 11-11 You can tile an image to make it animate as an endless loop.

7. To apply the mask, right-click (in Windows) or CTRL-click (on the Mac) the layer icon in the text layer to display the context pop-up menu, shown next.

8. Choose Mask from the menu. The Layer icon now turns into an oval-shaped icon with a checkered background, indicating that the layer contains a mask. Conversely, the water layer icon turns into a checkered pattern background with a turned-up corner. Both icons can be seen in the next illustration. The masked layer must always reside under the mask layer.

Mask layer

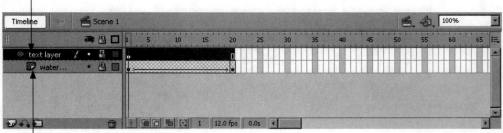

Masked layer

9. Click the Lock icon to unlock the masked layer.

10. The masked layer (the water image in the example) now needs to be tweened. Remember: the word stays static while the bitmap moves. Click a frame in the masked layer to create the second keyframe (F6). In our example, frame 20 is selected. On the text layer, add enough frames so the text mask is visible until frame 20 by clicking this frame and pressing F5 or by choosing Insert | Timeline | Insert Frame.

11. Reposition the bitmap image on the first and last keyframes so the image appears to move from left to right. You may have to go back and tweak the position of the image after previewing the movie to achieve the desired result. Click the in-between frames, right-click (Windows) or CTRL-click (Mac), and then choose Create Motion Tween from the context menu.

12. Lock the mask and masked layers. You must lock the masked layer in order to preview the effects of the mask while working in authoring mode.

If you press ENTER or RETURN to play the movie on the timeline, you won't see anything happen. By default, the results of a mask are not visible on the Flash stage unless you lock the mask layer. To test the movie, do one of the following:

- ■ Select Control | Test Movie. This publishes the movie and displays it in another window.
- ■ Click the Lock button in both the mask and masked layers and then press ENTER or RETURN. Note that if you create a mask that masks multiple layers, you must click the Lock icon on each masked layer in order to preview the effects in authoring mode.

Locking the layers enables you to see and test the mask in authoring mode. Remember to unlock the layers if you need to further edit the animation.

Conclusion

Once you get the feel for it, motion tweening can add some wonderful diversity to your Flash movies. In this chapter you learned the basics of creating a motion tween animation and how to constrain a motion tween animation to a path. You also learned to modify the speed with which the animation begins and ends by specifying the Ease value. In the next chapter, shape tweening is presented in detail. When you master frame-by-frame animation, motion tween animation, and shape tween animation, your animator's toolkit will contain all the necessary goodies to create compelling animations for your Flash movies.

Chapter 12

Use Shape Tweening to Animate

How to...

- Create a shape tween
- Use a shape tween with multiple keyframes
- Modify properties of a shape tween
- Tween on a multilayer movie
- Morph between objects
- Apply shape hints
- Set shape tween properties
- Organize your timeline

As discussed in Chapter 11, motion tweening works only on editable objects, graphic symbols, or grouped objects. In fact, the very name "motion tween" implies that its primary use is to change the motion of an object over time. In contrast, shape tweening can be applied only to editable objects and is primarily used to change the shape of one object into another.

You can use a motion tween to change the size, skew, rotation, color, and position of an object. The same properties can be altered with a shape tween, and often with a different and unexpected outcome. The reason motion tween and shape tween animations appear different is that when you change the rotation and skew of an object with a motion tween, the object is addressed as a whole entity, whereas when you change the rotation and skew of an object with a shape tween, the object is perceived as an editable shape instead of a whole entity. Thus, with a shape tween, the individual edges of the editable shape with many facets can transform separately from the object as a whole, causing a shape tween to yield different results from a motion tween. For example, if you are using a shape tween to transform a star shape into a rectangle, the tip of each star is a point that Flash takes into account when changing the shape into a rectangle. Motion and shape tweening can perform similar functions, but they serve different purposes.

Because of the malleable nature of editable objects, shape tweening is used for morphing objects. *Morphing* occurs when one shape transforms into another shape. In addition, color can be tweened easily on an editable object. This effect won't work with a motion tween unless, of course, the tweened object is a symbol and you modify the symbol's properties.

Now you have some idea of how motion and shape tweening can generate different results. Once you get a feel for tweening, you will better understand when it's appropriate and effective to use a particular method.

Create a Shape Tween

You can create a shape tween that changes the position of an object. However, the method you use to create a shape tween animation is slightly different from the method you use to create a motion tween animation. Not only that, but if you only want to animate the change in position of an object, you should opt to use a motion tween. With that in mind, let's consider how to make a simple shape tween where the position, shape, and color of an object change over time, as shown here.

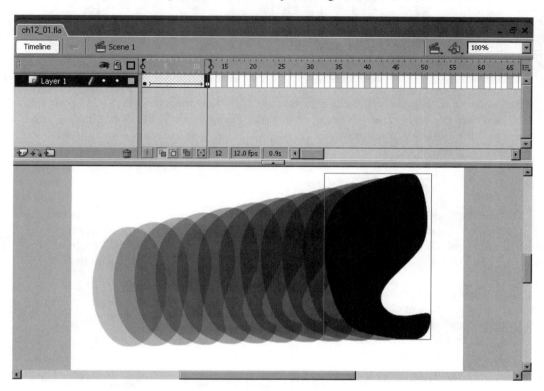

To create a simple shape tween animation, follow these simple steps:

1. Create a keyframe and then draw or import an editable object on the stage.

2. Determine the number of frames for your animation, select the ending frame, and press F6 to convert it to a keyframe.

3. With the last keyframe selected, move the object to another position on the stage.

4. Change the object's fill color.

5. Click the frames in between the two keyframes and select Shape from the Tween pop-up menu in the Properties Inspector, as shown in the following illustration.

Tween menu

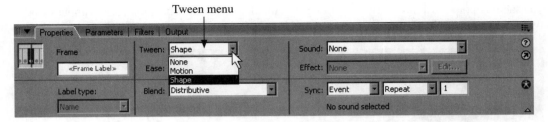

6. Notice that the frame sequence in the timeline now has a green tint with a right-pointing arrow in it, as shown next. Now, when you play the movie back, the shape changes position and color over time.

At face value, shape tweening doesn't look much different from motion tweening, other than the fact that you create a shape tween from the Properties Inspector and the in-between frames are a different color on the timeline. But as we move through this chapter, you will begin to see how you can use shape tweening for some compelling effects you can't achieve with motion tweening.

Let's take a look at the following example. Figure 12-1 shows an animated gradient background. The gradient colors change during the course of the animation, creating a pulsating color effect. This technique can be done only with a shape tween because the colors have to be editable in order to change in time.

To create a shape tween gradient animation, follow this procedure:

1. Create a keyframe and then, on the stage, create a rectangle over the area in which you want the gradient to appear. Fill the rectangle with a colorful gradient. (Gradients are discussed in Chapter 5.)

2. Determine the length of your animation, select the ending frame, and press F6 to convert it to a keyframe.

3. Click a frame between the keyframes and select Shape from the Tween pop-up menu in the Properties Inspector.

4. Create additional keyframes between the first keyframes you created. Make as many as you want depending on how many times you want the object to cycle through new colors. Note that when you create a new keyframe, the green background and right-pointing arrow appear, indicating a shape tween. Creating the tween first and then adding the keyframes is the expedient way to create a shape tween animation.

5. Return to each keyframe and change the gradient. You can also change the angle, size, and position of the gradient on each keyframe.

6. Test the movie and you'll see the color gradually transform in a kaleidoscopic effect.

For a different effect, experiment with radial and liner gradients when using this technique.

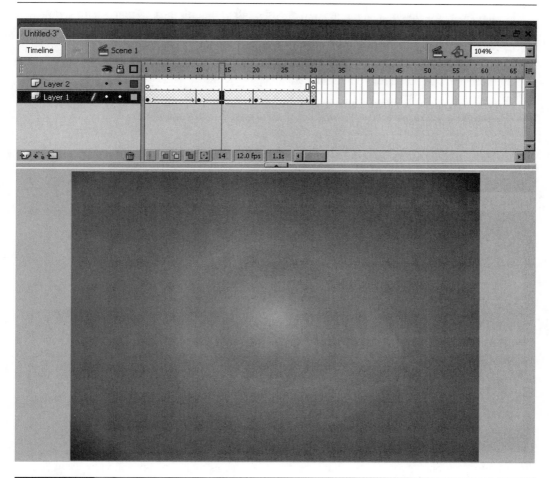

FIGURE 12-1   You can animate gradient colors with a shape tween.

12

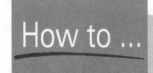How to ... **Add a Stop Action to the Timeline**

If the continuous looping of a movie is not appropriate, you can add a Stop action on the last frame in the timeline, which disables the default action of replaying the movie from frame 1. To add a Stop action to your movie, follow these steps:

1. Create a new layer and name it Action. Although you don't have to place actions on a separate layer, it's much easier to edit frame actions if they appear on a separate layer.

2. Select the last frame of your movie and press F6 to convert it to a keyframe. You cannot assign an action to a regular frame.

3. Press F9 to display the Actions panel. In the right portion of the panel (the Actions list), type **stop();** exactly the way you see it here. Your screen will look like this:

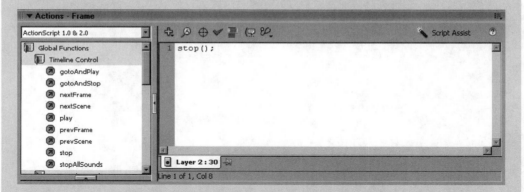

When you test your movie, the animation will stop when it reaches the last frame. In Chapter 16, you will learn how to create ActionScript to control the playback of frames on the main timeline.

Transform an Object's Shape

As mentioned previously, you can use the Free Transform tools on a shape tween just as you do on a motion tween. The difference between a shape and motion tween becomes obvious when you add rotation and skewing to a shape tween.

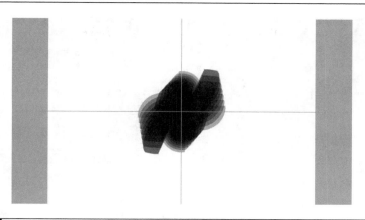

FIGURE 12-2   You use a shape tween to morph one shape into another.

Figure 12-2 shows a shape tween of an object with three keyframes. The beginning and ending keyframes are identical, but in the middle keyframe the object has been skewed and rotated. When the animation is played, the object appears to morph into something different in the in-between frames. In fact, around frame 7, the object appears as a shapeless blob, momentarily losing all visual connection to the original object.

Distinguish Between a Shape Tween and a Motion Tween on a Multilayer Movie

12

Grouped, editable, or symbol objects are easy to edit in a motion tween, but you can't take advantage of the features available to shape tweens, such as morphing. Placing objects on separate layers can easily resolve the difficulty of working with editable objects in shape tweens. You can easily edit these elements by going to the layer the object resides on and then applying the desired edits. Let's compare the same multilayer, tweened graphic as a shape tween and as a motion tween and see what kinds of different results we get.

Figure 12-3 represents a four-layer shape tween, with frame 16 selected. When the in-between frames are examined, you can see that shape tweening causes radical transformations on each layer, returning each object to its original state on the last keyframe.

There are several changes taking place over the course of the shape tween animation in Figure 12-3. The word "eye" resides on the top layer. The Break Apart command has been applied to the text object to convert it to editable vectors. The object's alpha, rotation, and width properties are changed throughout the tween, which causes the text object to appear almost as if it's inside out.

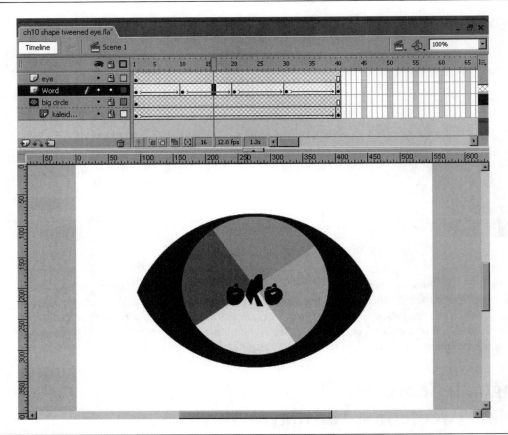

FIGURE 12-3 You can easily edit a shape tween animation created with multiple layers.

The same word rotated in a motion tween with nearly identical settings would appear to rotate on a center axis, as shown in Figure 12-4. Notice the difference between frame 14 in this figure and frame 16 in Figure 12-3.

In the motion tween, the four sections of the masked background rotate from a center axis, whereas in the shape tween, the sections separate and distort like the colored pieces of glass in a kaleidoscope.

Both movies were created with the same objects, but in Figure 12-3 the moving objects are animated with a shape tween, and in Figure 12-4 the moving objects are grouped and each group is animated with a motion tween. Because the characteristics of each animation method are different, the animations look different, even though in each case the same objects were used.

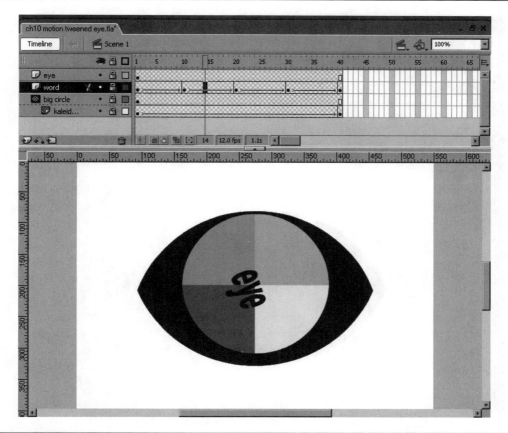

FIGURE 12-4   The animation in Figure 12-3 with a motion tween applied to the word layer

It's interesting and helpful to compare the two types of tweening to understand the depth of each method. Both methods have their special applications. You also can combine both methods of tweening on different layers in a movie to reap the benefits of both shape and motion tweening.

Deconstruct a Multilayer Shape Tween

To help you better understand the concept of shape tweening and the power of a multilayer tween, in this section you will dissect a multilayer movie in which only shape tweens are used. Figure 12-5 represents a multilayer movie on which two of the layers are animated with a shape tween. We looked at this movie previously, but now let's consider how it was made. There is also a mask used in this movie, and the masked object is tweened and conforms to the shape of an eye.

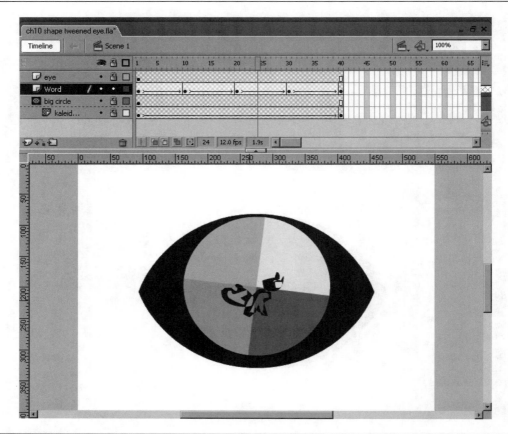

FIGURE 12-5   You use multiple layers when you need to create complex shape tween animations.

Use the following steps to create this movie or re-create a similar effect on another movie:

1. Create the four layers, naming and ordering them as follows:
    - eye
    - word
    - big circle
    - kaleidoscope

2. Select the eye layer and create an object that resembles the shape of an eye. The eye provides a framework, with a hollowed-out pupil, for two overlapping tweens.

3. Select the word layer, type the word **eye**, set the properties of the text, and then center it within the pupil part of the eye on its own layer. Because these objects reside on separate layers, the editable objects won't get tangled up in one another. The text also needs to be editable to work as a shape tween. To make it so, select the text and break it apart (Modify | Break Apart). Remember, you must apply the Break Apart command twice. The first time you apply the command, the word is separated into individual letters; it is the second application that converts the letters into editable vector objects.

4. Select the big circle layer. This layer contains a circle that represents the pupil in the center of the eye, and it acts as the mask for the last layer, kaleidoscope. If the mask didn't exist, the kaleidoscope animation in the background of the pupil would just appear as four rectangles sitting on a layer behind the eye and, as such, would not connect to the pupil. So, to create this effect, make a colored circle and use the edge of the pupil on the eye layer to determine the approximate circumference of this circle.

5. The masked layer, kaleidoscope, consists of four identical boxes framed together in the shape of a big rectangle, as shown in the following illustration.

6. Each rectangle has a different color, so the movement resembles big pieces of confetti in a kaleidoscope, shifting and morphing as the center twirls. Make these boxes with the Rectangle tool. You can easily duplicate the rectangle three times by selecting the first rectangle, pressing CTRL-SHIFT (Windows) or OPT-SHIFT (Mac), and then dragging the shape. Release the mouse button when the first duplicate is aligned, and then repeat to create two more rectangles. Holding down SHIFT constrains motion along the axis on which you are dragging. Once all four rectangles are aligned appropriately (into one big rectangle), center this new big rectangle over the mask (the big circle).

7. Select the big circle layer, right-click (Windows) or CTRL-click (Mac), and choose Mask from the context menu to mask the big circle layer. When a mask is applied to a layer, the Layer icon turns into a blue oval icon with a checked pattern. The layer beneath the mask layer becomes the masked layer. Masked layer icons are represented in the timeline with an indented layer icon, filled with a checked pattern. By default, the mask and masked layers are locked, which enables you to preview the mask in authoring mode. To edit objects on the mask or masked layer, click the Lock icon to unlock the layer.

12

8. Select frame 40 of the word and kaleidoscope layers and press F6 to convert them to keyframes, and press F5 on frame 40 of the eye layer and the big circle layer to extend the regular frames on these layers for the duration of the animation.

9. The word and kaleidoscope layers are all set for tweening. Select an in-between frame on the word layer and in the Properties Inspector, choose Shape for the Tween type. Repeat this for the kaleidoscope layer.

10. After the shape tweens are established, add keyframes to the word and kaleidoscope layers on frames 10, 20, and 30.

11. With keyframe 10 selected on the word layer, reduce the width of the word to approximately 50 percent and align it to the same center reference point it occupied in frame 1.

12. Select keyframe 20 on the word layer. Because the keyframes were created before any changes were made to the word object, it looks the same as it did on keyframe 1. Choose Modify | Transform | Flip Vertical to rotate the word object 180 degrees in keyframe 20, as shown here.

13. Select the object on keyframe 30, and then choose Modify | Transform | Rotate 90° CW.

14. Click the Lock icon to lock all layers except the kaleidoscope layer. Locking a layer prevents you from inadvertently selecting and moving objects on that layer.

15. Select the four rectangles on the kaleidoscope layer, and use the Free Rotation tool to rotate the four rectangles together to different angles on keyframes 10, 20, 30, and 40. The movie is now complete.

When the movie is played back (Control | Test Movie), instead of the objects on the word and kaleidoscope levels rotating as complete objects, individual pieces of each shape transform into different shapes while rotating. Some shapes intersect their own paths during the course of the animation, causing an outline effect. The resulting movie looks completely different than it would if it used motion tweening instead of shape tweening.

Morph Between Objects

Shape tweening is often used to create a morphing effect in an animation. Unlike motion tweens, which treat an object as a whole entity, shape tweens enable you to transform one object into another.

When you morph one object into another, the transformation that takes place is determined by the original shapes and by any changes you apply on keyframes that you add between the first and last keyframe. Morphing in Flash enables you to create an animation in which you morph one object into another—an oval into a rectangle, for example. What's more, you can scale, skew, rotate, and change the color of the original shape to further enhance the morph effect.

Figure 12-6 displays a square outline that morphs into a triangle, then into a circle, then into a swirl on frame 40, and finally disappears—leaving a blank scene for a second. On frame 41, the shapes gradually reappear on stage from left to right. On frame 41, the editable objects are replaced by graphic symbols, and they are motion tweened in steps of five framesets each,

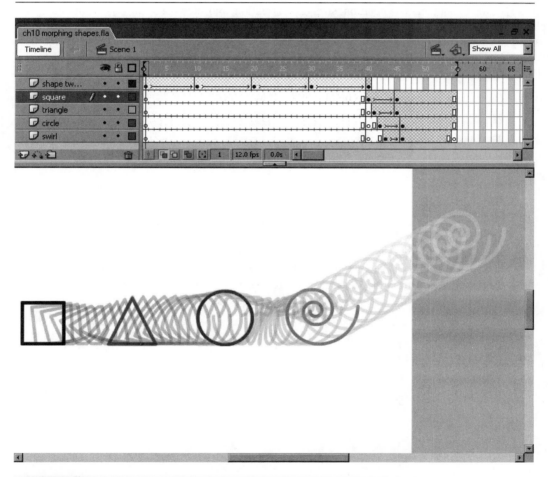

FIGURE 12-6   You can create compelling animations when you combine motion tweening and shape tweening in the same document.

12

one frame apart. This movie plays for about four seconds but packs a powerful impression on its viewer in a short period of time. It's a very simple movie and a good example of how simple images are often more effective than complex images in morphing.

Morphing does require planning and discretion to work successfully. This technique can produce undesirable results when not used correctly.

Deconstruct a Movie That Uses a Morph Effect

The process of morphing is different from that of an everyday shape or motion tween. A regular tween involves gradually changing the properties of an object from one keyframe to another. Morphing is different because it involves gradually changing one object into another object from one keyframe to another. The position, size, color, rotation, and skew also can vary from one object to a completely different object. In Figure 12-6, the shape of the object changes, as well as its position and color on keyframes up to keyframe 30, when the swirl flies off the stage. To thoroughly understand the process of morphing an object with a shape tween, let's examine the steps required to create the animation shown in Figure 12-6:

1. Create five layers and name them in the following order:
   - shape tweens
   - square
   - triangle
   - circle
   - swirl

2. The first layer, shape tweens, contains the majority of the contents of the movie. On keyframe 1, you will create all four shapes (square, triangle, circle, and swirl), put them into place, and align them. Choose View | Grid | Snap to Grid to make it easy to align and distribute the shapes on the stage. Begin by selecting the Rectangle tool. Press the SHIFT key to constrain the shape to a square. Position the square on stage, and then in the Properties Inspector, change the stroke to three pixels.

3. Make a simple triangle outline shape with the same stroke, and place it to the right of the first shape.

4. Create a circle outline and a swirl shape to the right of the triangle, as shown here.

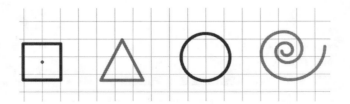

5. Choose Window | Design Panels | Align to display the Align panel (shown next) if you want to distribute the objects evenly. To align, select all objects and click one of the vertical Align options (the bottom, center, or top icon) and one of the horizontal Distribute icons to distribute the objects evenly.

6. With all four shapes in place, add a keyframe to frame 40 in the shape tweens layer and add a shape tween using the methods outlined in the "Create a Shape Tween" section, earlier in this chapter.

7. Convert frames 10, 20, and 30 to keyframes by selecting the frames and pressing F6. With all the tweening and elements in place, the movie will begin to take shape when objects are systematically eliminated from each keyframe, creating the illusion of one object morphing into another.

8. Working backwards, select keyframe 40 on the shape tweens layer and drag the swirl object off the stage to the upper-right corner. This makes the object fly off the stage after the circle transforms into the swirl. With frame 40 selected, delete the other three objects to the left (square, triangle, and circle).

9. With keyframe 30 selected, leave the swirl in place and delete the square, triangle, and circle.

10. With keyframe 20 selected, delete the square, triangle, and swirl, leaving this keyframe to highlight the circle, as shown in Figure 12-7.

11. Repeat the process on keyframe 10 by deleting the swirl, circle, and square, and again on keyframe 1, deleting all objects to the right of the square.

12. At this point, when the movie is played back, each simple shape transforms into another, and between keyframes 30 and 40, the swirl flies off the stage.

13. In the balance of the movie from frame 40 on, the shapes from Layer 1 are eliminated completely. They are replaced by a graphic symbol of a square, triangle, circle, and swirl on their subsequent layers. These graphic symbols were copied from the previously created editable shapes that were used on the first layer to create the morph. By frame 55, all the objects have gradually reappeared in the identical position from which they were originally morphed in frames 1 through 30, as shown in the timeline in Figure 12-7.

12

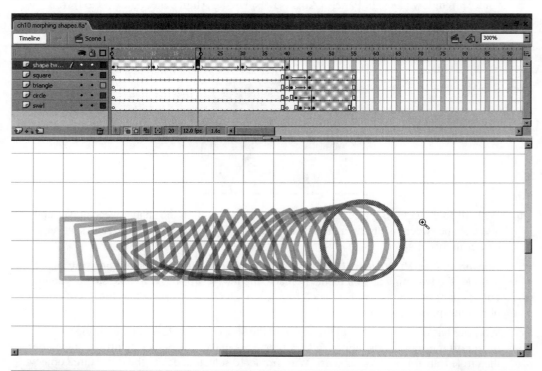

FIGURE 12-7 You systematically delete objects to complete the shape tween part of the animation.

Apply Shape Hints to Your Morph

When you morph from one object to another, the in-between frames often transform in an unpredictable way, especially if the objects are complex. If you were to scrub the playhead over the in-between frames from left to right, the object on the end keyframe of your animation would appear to gradually take shape from the first frame to the last. The manner in which objects morph is a default Flash algorithm, but you can change the way Flash morphs an object by applying shape hints. *Shape hints* on a morph identify key points on the beginning object and the end object. A shape hint on one object corresponds to the one marked with the same identifying letter on the other object.

The position of these shape hints as key tweening points is crucial to the outcome of the morph. They serve as a roadmap for the morph, determining what direction the points will travel to arrive at the shape's final destination. Just as with a road map, there are many different ways to get to your destination. Shape hints provide markers to help you get there and, on the way, provide different scenery, depending on which path they take.

You, the designer, use shape hints to achieve the desired outcome of your shape tween animations. If you don't like the way your shape is morphing in Flash, you can edit the position of shape hints on either or both shapes until the morph animation meets your expectations. Shape hints are an important feature of serious morphing. The ability to control the hints can mean the difference between the object appearing as a shapeless blob on in-between frames or as an object your viewers can readily identify. Your goal as a designer is to give your viewing audience visual clues to help them determine what the final shape looks like. Shape hints are your means to this end.

Shape hints are indicated as letters (from *a* to *z*) contained in small circles. You can place up to 26 shape hints on an object. To control the shape hints on a shape tween, click an object in a keyframe and select Modify | Shape | Add Shape Hint (CTRL-SHIFT-H in Windows or CMD-SHIFT-H on the Mac). A hint letter appears in the center of the object on both keyframes in the animation. The first hint is always designated by the letter *a*. Shape hints have a magnetic attraction, snapping to the edge of your object. Drag the hint to the desired point on the first object. To add more hints, repeat this process. In Figure 12-8, three additional hints were added and positioned on the circle.

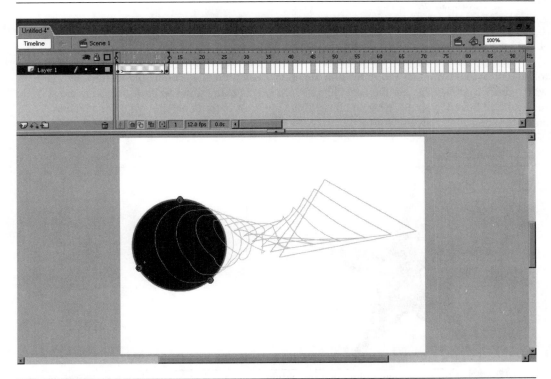

12

FIGURE 12-8 You add shape hints to designate key points on both shapes in your animation.

After positioning the shape hints on the first object, select the keyframe that designates the end of the animation. All of the shape hints for the second shape are stacked on top of each other. Move the shape hints to the desired position on the second shape. Shape hints are most successful if placed in a logical, clockwise order, starting from the top left of the object as a reference point. Otherwise, unpredictable results will occur. In Figure 12-9, a star transforms into a rectangle. The shape hints on the star (*a*, *b*, *c*, *d*, and *e*) are placed clockwise from the top left around five points of the star.

The corresponding shape hints (*a*, *b*, *c*, and *d*) on the rectangle in the last keyframe are also placed clockwise from the upper-left corner, making the star flawlessly morph into a rectangle in the last keyframe.

When you move the hints from different points on your object, you can preview the path of the shape hints on each frame of the animation if the Onion Skin feature is enabled.

Right-click (Windows) or CTRL-click (Mac) a shape hint to reveal a context menu that enables you to add a shape hint, remove the selected shape hint, remove all shape hints, and show shape hints.

To remove shape hints, click the object and select Modify | Shape | Remove Shape Hints. All shape hints will disappear.

Shape hints are easy to tweak if they don't meet your expectations. It's simple to go back to the first or last keyframe and reposition the hints. Each time this is done, the manner in which one shape morphs into the next changes. Do this as many times as necessary to achieve the desired effect. If you place shape hints at logical points on both objects, your shape tween animation performs flawlessly.

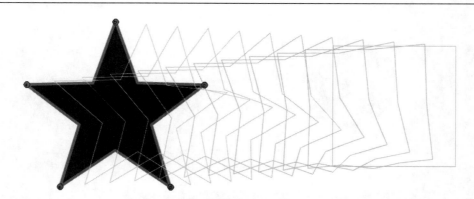

FIGURE 12-9 You place shape hints in alphabetical order in a clockwise direction.

Set Shape Tween Properties

Like motion tweens, shape tweens can be assigned parameters. When the in-between frames of a shape tween are selected, the Ease and Blend settings become available in the Properties Inspector.

The Ease setting is based on the same premise as easing on a motion tween. Tweening from one keyframe to another doesn't give you much control over the speed at which an object begins or ends its transformation. Easing in and out gives you control over the speed at which the object begins and ends its transformation. You can enter a value from −100 to 100 in the Ease text box or click the triangle to the right of the field and use the Ease slider, as shown in Figure 12-10.

To make a shape tween animation begin slowly and end quickly, select a value between −1 and −100. To make a shape tween animation begin quickly and end slowly, select an ease value between 1 and 100.

The Blend settings become available when an in-between frame of a shape tween animation is selected and the Properties Inspector is displayed. Select Distributive or Angular from the Blend menu, as shown in the following illustration. When Distributive is chosen, the shape tween will smooth out edges in a tween. When Angular is selected, hard, straight edges and lines will maintain their integrity throughout a tween. Like the Ease parameters, the Blend settings are applied to the in-between frames of a shape tween.

The Custom Ease feature in Flash Professional is not available for shape tween animations.

Blend menu

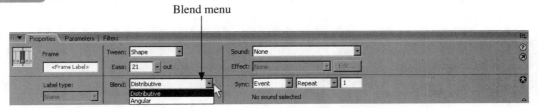

Shape tweening can also be combined with other types of animation to create dynamic effects. Good planning always remains a key ingredient with a shape tween; without it, your results can be unpredictable.

FIGURE 12-10 You can specify the Ease value by using a slider.

Organize Your Timeline

Once you know how to create complex, multilayer animations, you will appreciate the tools Flash offers to help you organize your timeline. In Flash, you can create labels and comments on frames in the timeline, as well as named anchors. None of these features actually appears in the movie on playback. They are simply tools to help you identify keyframes in a timeline that contain key events such as the start of an animation. Comments are particularly useful if multiple users are working on your Flash file. They give you a chance to explain to each colleague what's happening on a particular keyframe. Tools like this are vital in multilevel, time-based applications.

Let's take look at each one specifically to see what it does and how you apply it:

■ **Labels**   These are little messages you type in the Properties Inspector while a keyframe is selected. Keyframe labels help you identify the purpose of a keyframe and subsequent frames. In addition, you can refer to labels when you apply frame actions with ActionScript. (ActionScript will be covered in Chapters 15 and 16.)

To create a frame label, do the following:

1. Click a keyframe in a frame sequence and in the Properties Inspector, click in the Frame text box.

2. Type in a name. The name appears next to the keyframe you selected, to the right of a red flag icon in the timeline. If there are not enough frames adjacent to the keyframe to which you've assigned a label, the label will be truncated.

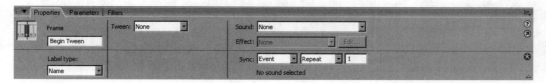

■ **Comments**   These are descriptive text notations that you can add to a frame sequence. Comments are often used when an element or condition enters a frame in the timeline. In a complex movie with multiple developers, comments on a timeline are a common sight. You can also use comments when you create ActionScript. More information on comments and how to create ActionScript and use them in the Actions panel is provided in Chapter 15. To make a comment on a keyframe in the timeline, follow these steps:

1. Click a keyframe, open the Properties Inspector, and in the Frame box, type your comment, as shown here.

2. Click the triangle to the right of the Label Type field and choose Comment from the drop-down list. The comment appears in the frame sequence after two forward slashes. The following illustration shows a timeline to which a label and comment have been added.

 *You can also insert a comment by typing two forward slashes (//) in the Properties Inspector Frame field, followed by your comment. After you press ENTER or RETURN, Flash recognizes the text as a comment.*

■ **Named anchors**   Named anchors provide an easy way for viewers to use the Forward and Back buttons in their web browsers to navigate in your movie. To convert a frame label into a named anchor, simply select Anchor from the Label Type drop-down list, as shown here.

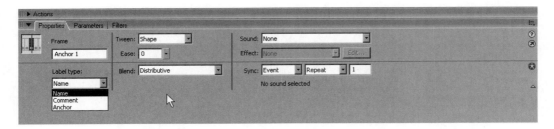

Named anchors will work only for viewers whose browsers are equipped with the Flash Player version 6 or later plug-in.

12

Conclusion

In this chapter, you learned to create compelling animations using the Flash shape tween feature. You learned how to animate the changing of a shape's characteristics and how to morph one shape into another. You also learned to control how the transformation takes place by adding shape hints to each shape. In the next chapter, we will jump right into buttons and movie clips. Once you master these integral Flash symbols, you'll be well on your way to mastering Flash.

Chapter 13

Grasp the Concept Behind Buttons and Movie Clips

How to…

- Make a single-state button
- Make a complex multistate button
- Add sound to a button
- Add simple effects to a button
- Change the behavior of a symbol
- Understand movie clips in Flash
- Create an animated movie clip
- Make an animated button from a movie clip

As you learned in previous chapters, symbols help bring order to the chaos of movie creation. After you add a symbol to the document Library, you can use multiple symbol instances, which reduce your movie's file size. Symbols, as you'll recall, come in three types: graphic, button, and movie clip. Graphic symbols and buttons are discussed in Chapter 8, as are many of the rules that apply to all symbols. For example, all symbols are stored in the Library, and you can create multiple instances of any symbol, which help reduce the file size of the published movie. This is a great benefit when you consider the size of some movie clips, especially those with video. By creating multiple instances of the movie clip, you instruct Flash to create a duplicate of the symbol from the information in the document Library. This is what reduces the file size of the published movie. In this chapter, we'll explore some of the more advanced techniques you can use for buttons, and you'll get a good working knowledge of how to create movie clips.

Explore the Power of Buttons and Movie Clips

A movie is defined as *interactive* when a viewer can respond to the movie and make choices that change the viewing experience. Interactivity not only makes a web site more engaging, it encourages the viewer to participate in the ongoing process, thereby keeping him or her on your site longer.

A good example of simple interactivity is the hyperlink. A hyperlink in an HTML document is an example of interactivity in its simplest form. The process of clicking a hyperlink to open a different web page gives the viewer the opportunity to interact and experience more of the site. Although links to HTML documents and SWF files are easy to make, you can create far more sophisticated types of interactivity in Flash. When you add interactivity to a Flash movie, you generally use buttons, movie clips, or both, in some capacity.

For example, you can use ActionScript interactivity to create a button that can change a movie clip's properties—such as size, position, rotation, or color—when a viewer clicks the button. You can also program a button to start and stop a movie clip, render a movie clip invisible, and much more. Buttons can also be nested in movie clips to create special effects for games, e-commerce applications, and interactive web sites. You use ActionScript or behaviors to add interactivity to buttons and movie clips. But before you can use ActionScript to supercharge your buttons and movie clips, you must first understand the mechanics of creating them.

Both buttons and movie clips are considered objects and, as such, can be assigned properties, methods, and event handlers. The *properties* of a button or movie clip instance are the characteristics of the object, such as color, height, and so forth. *Event handlers* are triggers that are used to execute ActionScript when an event occurs such as a viewer of your movie pressing a button. *Methods* are used in ActionScript. For example, if you create a movie clip that is a container for ActionScript to retrieve the date from the host computer, you create an instance of the Date object in the movie clip and use the getMonth method of the Date object to get the current month.

Objects, methods, and events are all part of the framework of ActionScript, the Flash scripting language. ActionScript, which can be quite extensive and complex, is discussed in Chapters 15 and 16. For now, we will concentrate on the basics of making buttons and movie clips. You need a solid understanding of how to create these objects before you pursue adding any enhanced interactivity to these symbols with ActionScript.

Create a Single-state Button

Buttons in Flash can range from simple to extremely complex, and they are limited only by your imagination. They don't all have to look like the classic push buttons seen on so many web sites and in the Flash button common library. In fact, many buttons in Flash don't look like buttons at all.

The ability to choose when ActionScript, or a behavior you've applied to a button, occurs, makes it possible for you to create custom-designed navigation menus that have elements popping out in the movie whenever and wherever you want. For example, you can program the buttons so that interactivity occurs when users roll a mouse over a button, click a button, or release the mouse button after a button click. You can also use bitmaps, sounds, and movie clips on your button timeline. You can make buttons that have no visible contents and exist only to allow you to take advantage of the scripting available on a button object. You can also use invisible buttons as hot spots for Flash games. You learned how to create a basic multistate button in Chapter 8, but before you can take advantage of any of the more advanced capabilities just outlined, you need to know a little more about buttons.

The button you created in Chapter 8 is an example of just one of the many kinds of buttons you can create in Flash. There will be many instances, for example, when you don't need the actual button to be interactive on the Over and Down states. You might just need a clickable button to perform an action on a frame or a movie clip. In a situation like this, you only need to use the Up frame, and the creation process is as follows:

1.   Select Insert | New Symbol (CTRL-F8 on Windows/CMD-F8 on the Mac).

2.   In the Create New Symbol dialog box, select the Button behavior, give the button a name, and click OK. On the Up frame, add or make a graphic, as shown next. If you want to define the active area, select the Hit frame, press F7 to convert it to a blank keyframe, and copy the graphic from the Up frame and paste it in the Hit frame.

13

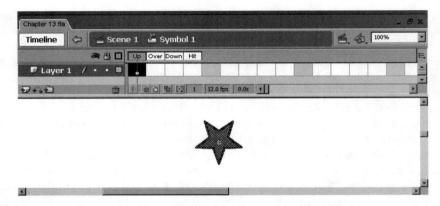

3. Exit Button Editing mode either by clicking the Scene icon in the upper-left corner or by clicking the blue Back arrow to the left of the Scene icon.

With a simple button, you don't have to add frames for the states you don't need (Over and Down). Any graphic in the Up frame is sufficient to make a button work. You can create a simple button anytime you need a button as a trigger for ActionScript.

Make an Invisible Button

You can create an invisible button when you want an area of the stage to be interactive but don't need to display an actual graphic. You can assign ActionScript to a button even if it's not visible. To make an invisible button, create a regular button, but leave all frames blank except for the Hit frame. The Hit frame is necessary because the target area must be defined in order for the button to be operable. First, create a button symbol and then, in Symbol Editing mode, select the Hit frame and press F6 to make it a keyframe. Use one of the drawing tools to define the target area for your invisible button.

Invisible buttons are useful when you have large blocks of text that you want viewers to read. Place an invisible button on a layer underneath the text with a target area slightly larger than the text box. Program the button to advance the movie to another frame when it is clicked.

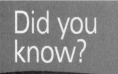

Hit Areas

It is not absolutely necessary for you to indicate a hit area. If you elect not to do so, Flash assumes the object on the Up state represents the target area of the button. It's a good idea to use the Hit frame when you create a small button or an unusually shaped button, though. This gives viewers a bigger target area.

Create Complex Multistate Buttons

When you create a button that uses more than one frame, you create a multistate button. You're probably used to looking at multistate buttons that change color and shape slightly when you position your cursor over them or click them. But in Flash, multistate buttons don't have to be limited to the same graphic transforming on different states. You can get extremely creative with buttons by using different graphics for each state and adding sound and animation. When you create complex buttons, you'll find that it's easier if you work with additional layers. Let's explore some techniques you can use to create interesting buttons to make your movies stand out from the crowd.

Use Different Graphics on Each Button Frame

If you're thinking out of the box, you'll see that there's no reason a button always has to display the same graphic for each button state. Changing the graphic on different button frames is easy in Flash. Figure 13-1 shows the graphics used for a multistate button's Up, Over, and Down frames. When the movie loads, the button appears as an image of two fish. When a viewer moves the cursor over the fish, the button icon turns into a goat. When the viewer clicks on the button, the icon turns into a man pouring water.

This button is much like the one in Chapter 8, only this has different images instead of different views of the same image on the Up, Over, and Down states. Swapping graphics for each button state exhibits a simple form of interactivity because the button responds to mouse events and adds interest to your Flash production. Although a button that swaps images may not wow viewers, you can expand on this technique by adding sounds to buttons or by using animated movie clips in the Over and Down frames. When you create buttons with sound and motion, you take your Flash movies to the next level.

13

Up   Over   Down

FIGURE 13-1   You add visual interest to a button when you use different graphics on each state.

If you're creating a different graphic for a button frame, press F7 to create a blank keyframe. When you create a multistate button, you can also use the Onion Skin feature to see what the graphics on the other button frames look like.

Test a Button

You can't test a button in Authoring mode (when you're actually creating a Flash movie). Flash is set with this default behavior so that you will be able to select and move the button while you are working with it. After you have created a button, you can move on to the next phase of creating your movie; however, it's a good idea to make sure the button functions properly before pressing on.

There are a few ways to test buttons. If the button selected in the Library is multistate (uses more than the Up frame), a play button will appear in the upper-right corner of the Library thumbnail preview, as shown in the following illustration. Click this button to see the changes on each button frame. If you have included a graphic on the Hit frame, the graphic will appear in the Library preview.

You can also test buttons in Authoring mode by enabling them, as discussed in Chapter 8. After selecting this command, you'll be able to interact with the button on the stage. When you are done testing the button, choose Control | Enable Simple Buttons and you can go back to the business of editing your movie as you'll now be able to select and move buttons. You'll recall from Chapter 8 that when buttons are enabled in movie editing mode, you can't move or modify them the way you ordinarily would while editing a movie. You can select the button by dragging a marquee around it with the Selection tool and then move it by pressing your keyboard arrow keys. However, your best bet is to select the Enable Simple Buttons command again to disable buttons prior to editing or moving them.

You can also select Control | Test Movie to test your button. When you choose this command, Flash publishes the movie as an SWF file and opens it in another window. The buttons will be fully active in this mode. When you use the Test Movie command, you're able to preview and test the movie in a manner closer to what your intended audience will experience.

Add Sound to a Button

You can easily expand on a multistate button by adding a short sound to the Over or Down frame. You can import your own sound for a button or use a wide selection of short sounds that you can find on the Internet. If you download sounds from the Internet for use in your Flash movies, make sure you're not violating any copyright laws. Many Flash resources on the Internet provide sounds that you can use for your movies. Make sure you read any EULA (End User Licensing Agreement) the web site owners have posted.

When you add sounds to a button, you involve another of your viewers' senses. You can make the button sound like a real click, a beep, or anything your imagination can conjure up. When you add sound to a button, choose a sound that is short in duration and has a relatively small file size. Since Flash plays button sounds in their entirety, a long sound might mix with other sounds that play after the button is clicked, and the montage of sounds may confuse your viewers. Now that your creative juices are stirring, let's discuss how to add sound to a button.

When you want to add a sound to a button, choose a short sound that's less than two seconds in duration. After you import the sound into the document, it resides in the document Library, which means you can create instances of the sound as needed without increasing the file size of the published movie.

To add sound to a button on the Over and Down states, follow these steps:

1. Create a button following the steps outlined previously. Make sure you have keyframes on the Over and Down frames.

2. Choose File | Import | Import to Library to open the Import To Library dialog box.

3. Choose the desired sound file and then click Open to add the sound to the document Library.

4. While still in Button Editing mode, choose Window | Library. Alternatively, you can press CTRL-L (Windows) or CMD-L (Mac) to display the Library.

5. You can add a sound to any button frame except the Hit frame. The most logical frames on which to play sounds would be the Over and Down frames. If you place a sound on the Up frame, it plays when the viewer moves the cursor over the button, just as it would do if you placed the sound in the Over frame.

13

6. Select the Over keyframe and drag a sound to the stage. Select the Down keyframe and drag a different sound to the stage. The following illustration shows different sounds placed on the Over and Down keyframes.

7. Test the button by choosing Control | Enable Simple Buttons or Control | Test Movie, and then interacting with the button to make sure the sounds play as desired.

 *When you create buttons with multiple graphics and sounds, it's a good idea to create a separate layer for each item. To create a new layer while creating a button, click the Insert Layer button near the bottom of the timeline window. Alternatively, select the first layer, right-click (Windows) or* CTRL*-click (Mac), and then choose Insert Layer from the context menu.*

Add Simple Effects to a Button

The following is an example of how you might construct a simple navigational menu in Flash. The buttons in this menu aren't used or constructed as typical buttons on a web page. Since buttons are objects on their own timelines with simple ActionScript assigned to them, let's see how we can use buttons to create an interesting navigation menu.

Figure 13-2 shows a linear navigation bar. When the user positions the cursor over a topic ("what's new," "archives," "glossary," or "resources"), a graphic that looks like a paintbrush stroke appears in the background of the button in focus. This effect is created with a button that is empty on the Up frame. The actual topic is not a button; it's a text object. The button with the empty Up frame resides on a different layer on the main timeline and has a single layer with an empty Up frame, a brushstroke in the Over frame, and a rectangle larger than the brushstroke

FIGURE 13-2   You can use interactive buttons on navigation bars.

that resides in the Hit frame. The brushstroke graphic appears when a user interacts with the buttons. Empty button states are often used to achieve effects like this. You'll learn how to use ActionScript to make useful interactive buttons in Chapter 16. The following steps show you how to create a simple navigation bar similar to the one in Figure 13-2.

1. Gather your assets. When you create a navigation bar similar to the one in this example, you should always gather your assets before you build the button. In fact, it's a good idea to plan any complex Flash movie out before you launch Flash. In the case of this example, the maze graphic was imported from Illustrator. The curly bracket was created in Flash, as was the navigation bar structure. Finally, all elements were converted into symbols. In this case, the objects were converted to graphic symbols. However, if you wanted to include additional interactivity such as an animation of the maze or other elements, you would use movie clip symbols instead of graphic symbols.

2. With all the assets organized in the Library, construct the layers. For this example, set up and name the layers in the main timeline in the following order:

   ■ topics

   ■ static_art

   ■ buttons

3. On the static_art layer, you create the navigation bar. In this example, with the document Library open, instances of the curly_bracket, graphic_line, and maze objects were dragged to the stage on the static_art layer. The maze and graphic_line objects were positioned and aligned, as shown in Figure 13-2. The curly_bracket instance was duplicated three times (select the object and press SHIFT-CTRL in Windows/SHIFT-OPT on the Mac while dragging the curly_bracket). The purpose of holding down SHIFT is to constrain the horizontal position of the curly_bracket instance while duplicating it. Each release of the mouse button creates a duplicate instance. A reasonable distance was approximated between these duplicate curly_bracket instances, and then they were all aligned and evenly spaced using the Align panel (Window | Align).

4. On the topics layer, use the Text tool to create the text. In the example shown, the words were typed in as four separate text blocks (what's new, archives, glossary, and resources). The Align panel (Window | Align) was used to align each text object with its corresponding curly bracket.

5. When everything else is in place, create the button. In this example, the paintbrush (swish) button was created. A graphic symbol named "swish" was created, and an instance was added to the button's Over frame. The button's Up frame is blank, so for all intents and purposes, the button is invisible when the movie loads.

6. Add another keyframe to the Hit frame. On this frame, a rectangle slightly larger than the graphic was created. The Back button was clicked and the new button was added to the Library. As you know, after a button is created, it is stored in the document Library for future use, as shown in the following illustration.

13

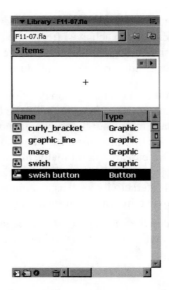

7. With the button symbol selected, drag an instance of your button onto the stage and center it over the first topic (text object). Because the button's Up frame is blank, the symbol instance appears as a light-blue rectangle. This blue rectangle indicates the Hit area on a button with an empty Up frame. When the movie plays, and the button loads, the light-blue rectangle will not be visible. Duplicate the button instance and align it to the remaining topics on the navigation bar.

When the navigation bar is tested and you move your cursor over a topic, the button graphic appears. Nothing happens when the button is clicked because no ActionScript has been added to the button. Generally, you use a button to navigate to another HTML page, load an SWF file, or navigate to a keyframe in the current timeline or a movie clip timeline. In Chapter 16, we'll explore applying ActionScript to buttons.

Understand Movie Clips in Flash

As mentioned many times throughout this book, movie clips are independent movies that have their own timelines. Because they are symbols, movie clips possess many of the attributes common to all symbols. For example, movie clip instances can be used as many times as needed in a movie without affecting the file size. They can also be assigned instance names so that you can use ActionScript to communicate with the instance from other symbols or timelines.

Just because a movie clip has a timeline doesn't mean it must contain animation. A movie clip can be a static graphic occupying a single frame or it can be a full-fledged animation, similar to what you would create on the main timeline. Movie clips can also be used as containers for ActionScript. Movie clips can also serve as targets into which other movies are loaded.

Movie clips can be controlled by buttons, frame actions, and other movie clips, and vice versa. They can communicate with each other and reside within other movie clips or on different levels. A movie clip is always one of the most scriptable elements in a Flash movie. In this section, you'll learn the basics of creating movie clips. Once you understand how to make a movie clip, you can move on to more advanced applications such as creating ActionScript to change the properties of a movie clip.

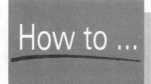

How to ... Change the Behavior of a Symbol Instance

As mentioned in Chapter 8, one of the many cool features in Flash is the ability to change the behavior of a symbol on the fly. You can actually change a button instance to a graphic or a movie clip with the click of a button. When you change the behavior of a symbol instance, that instance can have limited access to the properties associated with the newly assigned behavior. For example, if you change a symbol instance from button to graphic, the button instance no longer responds to a user's mouse click and behaves just like a regular graphic symbol. If you change a symbol instance from button to movie clip, the symbol can now be scripted as if it were a movie clip. Of course, the symbol instance doesn't have a movie clip timeline, but you can use ActionScript to communicate with the symbol just as you would with any other movie clip. To change the behavior of a symbol, do the following:

1. Select an instance of a symbol on the stage.

2. Choose Window | Properties to access the Properties Inspector.

3. In the Behavior pop-up list, select the desired behavior, as shown in the following illustration.

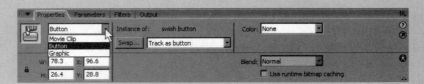

Now, when you select the object, the new behavior will be noted in the Properties Inspector. If you're changing a symbol instance to a button, additional selections become available for this behavior type, as shown here:

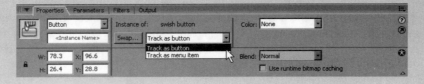

13

The two options are described here:

- **Track As Button**   This selection is used for a standard single button and is the default.
- **Track As Menu Item**   This selection is used if you're creating pop-up navigational menus that have several selections within a defined area that can have mouse events attached to them.

Also in the Properties Inspector is a Swap button, which enables you to swap one instance of a symbol with another. For more information on swapping symbols, refer to Chapter 8.

Also as mentioned in Chapter 8, you can assign an instance name to a button by using the Properties Inspector. An *instance name* is a special name you give an instance so you can refer to it with ActionScript. When you assign a name to a symbol instance, you can specify the target path to the symbol instance and use ActionScript from within a movie clip to communicate with the named instance. To give a button an instance name, select the button and in the Properties Inspector, type a name for the button in the <Instance Name> field, as shown here, and then press ENTER (Windows)/RETURN (Mac).

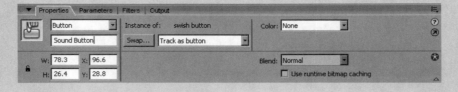

Plan Your Movie Clip

Throughout this book, organization is stressed as a key element in a successful Flash movie. More than any other element, movie clips demand extra planning and attention for movies of a medium-to-complex nature. As you will see, when you start adding actions to movie clips, your task as a Flash designer becomes more complex.

An instance of a movie clip takes on a unique role in Flash. You can refer to one in a script if you give the instance a name. You name an instance the same way you name a button instance, by typing a name in the <Instance Name> field in the Properties Inspector.

A movie clip instance is identified in a script by its instance name and its location in your movie. Since movie clips can be nested in other movie clips, you can communicate with movie clips on multiple timelines within timelines. In Flash, the path of a movie clip can be either absolute or relative. An *absolute* path is the complete path to an instance, which includes the level where it is located. There are ways you can refer to these levels in ActionScript, including _level, _root, and _parent. A *relative* path refers to an instance in relation to the instance it's talking to. If you've worked with HTML, this will all seem familiar to you. In other words, when you create a script that references movie clips with unique instance names, you can refer to the instance by its name and by its location in either absolute or relative terms.

A movie clip can be called from any level in the current movie or other movies, or from a different movie that you've loaded into the current movie. For now, let's simply address how to make a movie clip.

Examine the Main Timeline Versus the Movie Clip Timeline

To understand how timelines and movie clips function, let's consider the following example. Figure 13-3 shows two animated pictures that appear to be identical. The picture on the left is a static graphic symbol that has been animated on the main timeline. The identical picture on the right is a movie clip. The timeline in the movie clip is identical to the animated graphic on the main timeline.

Notice in the main timeline that you can see the animated frames on the animated graphic layer. On the layer with the movie clip (animated movie clip layer), only one frame is occupied on the main timeline because all animation takes place on the movie clip's timeline. The movie clip is a self-contained animation occupying one keyframe on the main timeline. You can use as many instances of your movie clip as needed in your production. Now that you understand the difference between a movie clip and a timeline animation, let's take a look at how to construct an animated movie clip.

Create an Animated Movie Clip

The example shown in Figure 13-4 is a simple multilayer movie clip in which the words "movie clip" are animated. This example demonstrates the importance of organizing assets before building your movie clip. With a bit of organization, creating movie clips becomes a much simpler task.

13

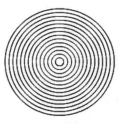

**Animated
graphic symbol
on main timeline**

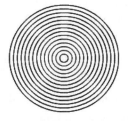

**Animated
movie clip on
its own timeline**

FIGURE 13-3   An movie clip animation occupies a single keyframe on the timeline.

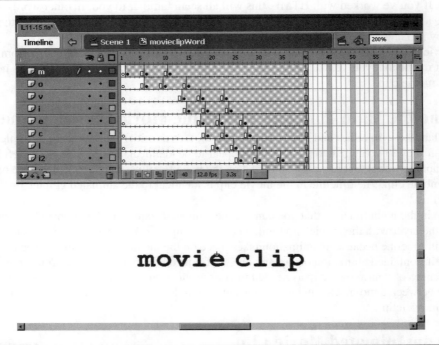

FIGURE 13-4 Organization is paramount, even when you're creating a simple animation in a movie clip.

Let's talk about what happens in this short movie clip. When the animation plays, the words "movie clip" appear letter by letter as if being typed. The animation stops on its last frame because a Stop action has been added to this frame. On a lower layer, a shadow of the words appears. This shadow is another animated movie clip nested inside the main movie clip's timeline.

Creating a complex multilayer movie clip animation can be a daunting task. To better understand how the process works, follow these steps to create this example.

1. Create a new symbol by choosing Insert | New Symbol or by pressing CTRL-F8 (Windows) or CMD-F8 (Mac).

2. Give your symbol a name and select Movie Clip as the behavior.

3. Type a word or words. For this example, the words "movie clip" were typed.

4. Break the words apart into separate letters by choosing Modify | Break Apart.

5. Convert each letter to a graphic symbol by selecting it and then pressing F8. Give each symbol a unique name and remember to choose the Graphic behavior. Note that you can create new symbols while working in Movie Clip Editing mode.

6. Select all the letters and then choose Modify | Timeline | Distribute to Layers. Alternatively, you can right-click (Windows) or CTRL-click (Mac) and choose Distribute To Layers from the context menu. This command takes the selected letters and distributes each to its own layer. When you animate the movie clip, you'll understand the importance of assigning each symbol its own layer.

7. Create a keyframe for frame 5 on each layer. The quickest way to do this is to select frame 5 on the top layer and then SHIFT-click frame 5 on the bottom layer. Press F6 and the selected frames are converted to keyframes.

8. Repeat the process in step 7 to add keyframes to frame 10 on all layers.

9. Return to the letter symbols on frames 1 and 5, and jumble the letters around a little, as shown in the following illustration:

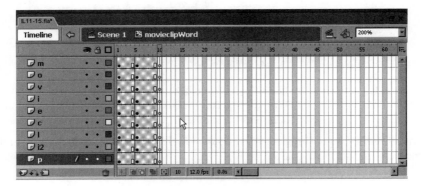

10. If you scrub the playhead over the timeline, you'll notice that everything happens at the same time. The goal was to create an animation in which each letter appeared separately, like a typewriter typing. In the final movie clip, the frames are staggered so that the letters appear individually. Select frame 1 for the second letter in the animation. Then, while holding down SHIFT, click frame 10. This selects the entire frame span.

11. Drag the frame span five frames to the right. Repeat this for the remaining letters in the animation, as shown in the following illustration.

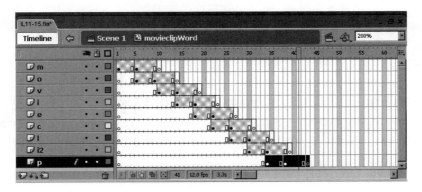

13

12. To get all the letters to remain on the stage at the end, add frames on all layers to line up with the last frame in the timeline. To do so, click the frame in the "i" layer of the animation just above the last frame in the last layer, SHIFT-click the same frame in the "m" layer of the animation, and then press F5. The timeline should look like the one shown here:

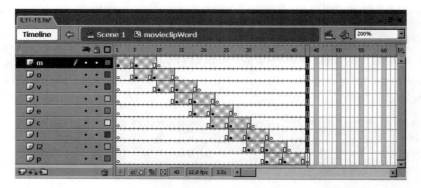

13. Exit Movie Clip Editing mode, drag an instance of this movie clip onto the stage, and test the movie. You'll notice that it loops continuously. To make the movie clip only loop once, we need to add a Stop action to the movie clip timeline.

14. Return to Movie Clip Editing mode by double-clicking either the icon in the Library or the movie clip instance on the stage.

15. Add a new layer to the top of the movie clip timeline and name it "action."

16. Open the Actions panel by choosing Window | Development Panels | Actions or by clicking F9.

17. Select the last frame on the action layer and press F6 to convert it to a keyframe. You can add a frame action only to a keyframe.

18. In the Actions window, enter the following exactly as you see it:
stop();

NOTE   *ActionScript is case-sensitive. When you add an action such as the Stop action, the word should be light blue in color. If it is black, you have incorrectly entered the action.*

19. Close the Actions panel and test the movie. Now when the movie clip plays, it will stop on the last frame.

Make an Animated Button from a Movie Clip

Buttons can be made from vector art, bitmaps, and photos, as well as movie clips. A movie clip instance can be nested on the Up, Over, or Down frame of a button. You can also nest buttons in movie clips.

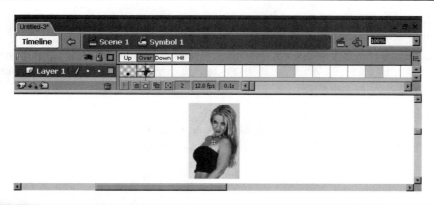

FIGURE 13-5   You can add movie clips with image sequences to a button frame.

Figure 13-5 depicts a button that has an animated JPEG sequence in the Over frame. When the viewer positions the mouse cursor over the picture, the animated JPEG sequence begins to play. When the mouse is off the picture, the animation stops. When the viewer clicks the picture, a still JPEG image replaces the picture on the Up position.

With a little creativity, there are many interesting effects you can achieve by combining buttons and movie clips. Let's review the process that was used to make this button:

1. The still pictures were exported as a JPEG sequence from a video-editing program and imported into Flash.

2. The JPEGs were all converted to movie clip symbols and given unique names. Although the JPEG sequences don't have to be movie clips, it's easier to go back in later and apply effects if they are already movie clip symbols.

3. Another movie clip was created and named walk_mc. In Movie Clip Editing mode, the movie clip JPEG sequence was reconstructed, frame by frame, on the first layer. To do so, a keyframe was added to each frame, and each movie clip of the JPEG sequence was dragged onto a frame until the whole movie clip sequence was completed. When the frame-by-frame JPEG sequence animation was completed in the movie clip timeline, Movie Clip Editing mode was exited.

4. A button was created and named.

5. On the button timeline, keyframes were added to all four states.

6. On the Up and Down frames, two of the JPEG sequence still movie clips were added to the appropriate keyframes.

7. On the Over state, the movie clip named walk_mc was added to the keyframe.

13

8. The Hit frame is blank for this button. You could put a rectangle in this frame to designate the hit area, but it's not necessary because the graphic in the Up frame is large enough to define the button target.

9. Button Editing mode was exited, and an instance of the button was dragged onto the stage to test the movie. When the mouse is moved over the button, the animated movie clip plays.

You can create an interactive button that piques viewer curiosity by combining image sequences and movie clips in the appropriate button frames in this way. You can also easily add sound to either a button state or the JPEG movie clip sequence.

Conclusion

In this chapter, you learned more about how to create buttons and movie clips, the basic objects for interactive Flash movies. You learned to create simple buttons, as well as multistate buttons. You also learned how to create self-contained animations in the form of movie clips, and how to combine movie clips and buttons to create viewer interest. In the next chapter, you'll explore behaviors, yet another feature you can use to create compelling Flash movies.

Part IV

Lay the Groundwork for Flash Interactivity

Chapter 14

Use Behaviors to Create Interactive Movies

How to...

- Add behaviors to movie clips
- Add behaviors to buttons
- Use behaviors to control sounds

If you want to add interactivity to your movies but are a little timid when it comes to learning how to code ActionScript, you'll love behaviors. You can use behaviors to make buttons perform certain tasks when clicked. For example, you can create a simple button and then use a behavior to load a sound from the Library. If ActionScript seems a bit daunting, you can make your movies behave just the way you want with behaviors.

In this chapter, you will learn how to use behaviors to make your Flash movies do some pretty cool stuff. You'll learn how to apply behaviors to movie clips and buttons, how to control sounds with behaviors, and how to use behaviors to load external files and web pages. If your Flash movie's misbehaving because you can't quite get it to do what you want, it won't be after you learn how to use behaviors.

Understand Behaviors and How They Work

Behaviors can be described as "ActionScript to go." You simply select an object that you want to make interactive and then add the appropriate behavior. You may have to fill in a blank or two—providing the URL you want associated with a behavior, for example—but that's about it. Flash 8 Basic or Flash 8 Professional does all the smoke and mirrors stuff, such as creating the ActionScript to make the behavior work. When you test the movie, presto, the object behaves!

Behaviors are not a substitute for ActionScript. You can do far more if you learn ActionScript. However, behaviors are a quick, down-and-dirty way to make your movie interactive. You can add behaviors to movie clips, buttons, and keyframes, the same objects to which you can apply ActionScript.

You can also use a behavior on an instance of a graphic symbol. However, when you do, Flash will display a dialog box (shown here) telling you that the instance will be converted to a symbol to which behaviors can be applied.

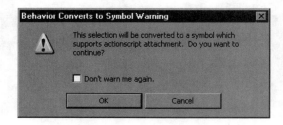

Understand Events

When you assign a behavior to an object, you determine which event triggers the behavior. An event occurs when a user interacts with the object to which the behavior is assigned. For example, when a user passes the pointer over an object, an On Roll Over event occurs. When you work with behaviors, you can choose any of the following events as the trigger for the behavior:

- **On Drag Out**   The behavior occurs after the user clicks the object to which the behavior is applied and then rolls off the object while still holding the mouse button.
- **On Drag Over**   The behavior occurs after the user clicks the object, rolls off the object, and then rolls over the object while holding down the mouse button.
- **On Key Press**   The behavior occurs when the user clicks the key you specify.
- **On Press**   The behavior occurs on the down stroke of a mouse click on the object.
- **On Release**   The behavior occurs on the release of a mouse click on the object.
- **On Release Outside**   The behavior occurs when the user clicks the object and releases the mouse button beyond the target area of the object.
- **On Roll Out**   The behavior occurs when the user moves his mouse over the object and then beyond the target area.
- **On Roll Over**   The behavior occurs when the user moves his mouse over the object target area.

Add Behaviors to a Movie

When you decide to add a bit of interactivity to a movie but don't have the time to cook up a long ActionScript, you can assign a behavior to an object or keyframe. For example, with behaviors you can duplicate a movie clip, change its stacking order on the stage, and much more. When you assign a behavior to an object, you determine the event that triggers the behavior, as discussed in the previous section. When you assign a behavior to a keyframe, no event is needed because the behavior occurs when the movie reaches the keyframe. The behaviors displayed in the Behaviors panel will reflect the object to which you are assigning the behavior. In other words, the actions listed for a movie clip are different from those listed for a keyframe, a graphic symbol, or a button.

14

Assign a Behavior to an Object

You can assign a behavior to an object such as a button or a movie clip to cause the object to behave in a certain manner. (Remember, if you want to communicate with a movie clip or button, you must give the movie clip instance a unique name.) You can add a behavior to an object at any time by following these steps:

1. Select the object to which you want to apply the behavior.
2. Choose Window | Behaviors. The Behaviors panel appears. Alternatively, you can press SHIFT-F3 to display the Behaviors panel.

3. Click the plus sign (+) to display the behavior groups.

4. Move your pointer over a behavior group to display the available behaviors, and click the behavior you want to apply, as shown here.

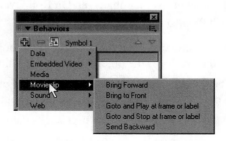

You can assign more than one behavior to an object. For example, to a button you can assign one behavior that duplicates a movie clip and another that plays a movie clip.

Choose a Behavior Event

When you add a behavior to a button or movie clip, the default event that triggers the behavior is On Release. In other words, the behavior occurs when the user releases the mouse button after clicking the object to which the behavior is applied. To choose a different behavior event, follow these steps:

1. Assign a behavior to an object as outlined previously. After you assign a behavior to an object, two columns will appear in the Behaviors panel: Event and Action.

2. To change the current event, click the event and then click the down arrow that appears to the right of the current event.

3. Choose a new event from the drop-down list, as shown here.

Apply a Behavior to a Keyframe

Another excellent use for behaviors is to assign them to keyframes. When you assign a behavior to a keyframe, the behavior occurs when the keyframe is played. Of course, you can mix behaviors on buttons and keyframes. For example, you can add a behavior to a button that causes a certain frame to be played when the button is clicked, and then have another behavior occur when the frame is reached. To assign a behavior to a frame, follow these steps:

1. Select the frame to which you want to assign the behavior.

2. Press F6 to convert the frame to a keyframe if it is not already one. Like actions, behaviors can be assigned only to keyframes. While the Behaviors panel will be more than happy to let you assign a behavior when you've selected a regular frame, the behavior will be applied to the closest previous keyframe in the timeline.

3. Choose Window | Behaviors. Alternatively, you can press SHIFT-F3 to open the Behaviors panel.

4. Select the behavior you want to apply to the keyframe from the drop-down list. Notice that you have fewer behaviors to choose from when you apply a behavior to a keyframe.

After you add the behavior to the keyframe, it will appear in the Action column of the Behaviors panel. In the Event column, the word "None" appears, as shown here, which indicates that the behavior has been assigned to a keyframe, and the button and movie clip events do not apply.

Arrange the Order of Behaviors

When you assign multiple behaviors to an object or keyframe, the behaviors execute in the order in which you add them. Of course, in the case of buttons, the events take precedence over the behavior. For example, behaviors assigned to the On Roll Over event occur when a user rolls a mouse over the button. If you have multiple behaviors assigned to an event, the behaviors assigned to the event occur in the order in which they appear in the panel.

14

If while testing the movie you find that the behaviors aren't occurring at the right time, you can rectify this by changing the order in which the behaviors execute. To arrange the order in which behaviors occur, follow these steps:

1. Select the object to which you have assigned the behaviors.

2. Choose Window | Behaviors to display the Behaviors panel, which lists all behaviors assigned to the object.

3. Select the behavior whose order position you want to change. Depending on where the selected behavior appears in the Behaviors panel, the Move Up button, Move Down button, or both will be active, as shown next.

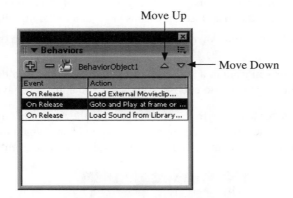

4. Click the Move Up button to move the behavior up the list. When you move a behavior up, it executes before behaviors listed beneath it. Click the button as often as needed to move the behavior to the desired position in the list.

5. Click the Move Down button to move a behavior down the list. When you move a behavior down, it executes after behaviors listed before it, except as mentioned previously when you have multiple events assigned to a button. In this case, the event has priority, and the behaviors assigned to each event execute in the order you specify. Click this button as often as needed to move the behavior to the desired position in the list.

6. Choose Control | Test Movie to preview the object with the rearranged behaviors to ensure that the behaviors execute in the desired order.

Delete a Behavior

After you preview a movie, you may decide that your production would be better without certain behaviors you've assigned to objects or keyframes. You can delete a behavior at any time by following these steps:

1. Select the object or keyframe from which you want to delete a behavior.

2. Choose Window | Behaviors. The Behaviors panel appears.

3. Select the behavior you want to remove.

4. Click the Delete Behavior button, which looks like a minus sign (−). The behavior is no longer assigned to the object or keyframe.

Communicate with Symbol Instances

Remember that you must give an instance a unique name if you want to be able to use a behavior or action to control it. You can name a symbol instance in the Properties Inspector by typing a name in the <Instance Name> field.

When you assign a behavior to a button symbol and want the behavior to control a movie clip or an embedded video, you choose the desired behavior from the Behaviors panel, and the dialog box associated with the behavior appears. Within the dialog box, you will find the target paths to all instances of symbols in your movie. Click the instance name that you want to control with the behavior. Remember, you can choose a relative path or an absolute path to the symbol, as shown here. For more information on target paths, refer to Chapter 13.

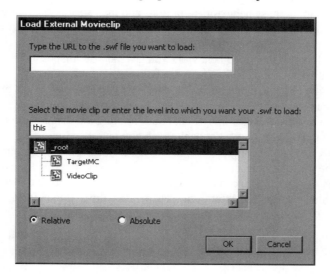

The dialog box for a behavior includes the target paths to all movie clip instances, whether or not you've given them unique names. If you attempt to use a behavior to communicate with a symbol that has no instance name, Flash displays the warning box shown here.

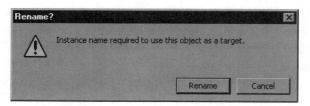

14

When you see the Rename? warning dialog box, click Rename to display the Instance Name dialog box shown here. Enter a unique name for the instance and click OK. Flash assigns the name to the symbol instance. The instance name appears in the Properties Inspector and the Movie Explorer, and you can now refer to the instance with other behaviors or with ActionScript.

Use Embedded Video Behaviors

If you have embedded videos in a Flash movie, you can control them through the use of behaviors. You can use behaviors to play, stop, pause, rewind, fast-forward, hide, or show a video. As a rule, you apply these behaviors to buttons and then specify the embedded video instance you want the behavior to control. In fact, you can create a custom controller for an embedded video by creating custom button symbols and then applying the desired behavior to the buttons. Table 14-1 shows the video behaviors you have at your disposal. These behaviors can be selected from the Embedded Video menu in the Behaviors panel.

At first glance, some of these video behaviors may seem unnecessary. Let's explore a few uses for these behaviors.

Suppose you want to create a Flash movie that does nothing but display video clips. You could begin by creating a different layer for each video clip and then importing the clips to the stage. By default, all videos are displayed and played. If you attempt to create a movie with multiple videos on the same keyframe, all of the clips will play at the same time and you'll have a mess on your hands. However, you can use behaviors on the first keyframe in the movie to stop each video and hide each video. After giving each video clip a unique instance name, you

Behavior	Description	Required Parameters
Play Video	Plays an embedded video	Instance name of the target video clip
Stop Video	Stops playing a video	Instance name of the target video clip
Pause Video	Pauses the video on the current frame	Instance name of the target video clip
Rewind Video	Rewinds the video for a specified number of frames	Instance name of the target video clip and the desired number of frames to rewind the clip
Fast Forward Video	Advances the video a specified number of frames	Instance name of the target video clip and the number of frames to advance the clip
Hide Video	Hides the video, even if it is playing	Instance name of the target video clip
Show Video	Displays a hidden video	Instance name of the target video clip

TABLE 14-1   You Can Control Embedded Video Clips with Behaviors.

can create a navigation bar with the name of each video clip in the form of a button symbol. You could then use behaviors to show and play the associated video clip when a button is clicked. You could also cover the eventuality that another video clip is playing by adding the proper behaviors to the button to stop and hide the other video clips in your movie.

Use Movie Clip Behaviors

If you've got any degree of interactivity in your Flash movies, you also have movie clips in them. When you use ActionScript, movie clips can perform some pretty neat tricks. However, if you're not yet adept at ActionScript, you can still get your movie clips to jump through hoops by assigning behaviors to them. Table 14-2 lists the behaviors you can use to control movie clips. You can assign these behaviors to movie clip events from the Movieclip menu in the Behaviors panel.

Behavior	Description	Required Parameters
Bring Forward	Moves an existing movie clip to the next level in the stacking order	Instance name of the target movie clip
Bring to Front	Moves an existing movie clip to the top of the stacking order	Instance name of the target movie clip
Duplicate Movie Clip	Creates a duplicate of a movie clip	Instance name of the target movie clip, plus the distance in pixels to offset the duplicated clip from the xy position of the original
Goto and Play at Frame or Label	Advances the movie to a specified frame on the main timeline or a movie clip timeline, and plays the movie	Instance name of the target movie clip and the frame to play, or the frame number or label on the _root timeline
Goto and Stop at Frame or Label	Advances and stops the movie at a specified frame on the main timeline or a movie clip timeline	Instance name of the target movie clip and the frame on which to stop, or the frame number or label on the _root timeline
Load External Movieclip	Loads an SWF file into an existing movie clip	Path to the SWF file and instance name of the movie clip
Load Graphic	Loads a JPEG image into an existing movie clip	Path to the JPEG file and instance name of the movie clip
Send Backward	Moves an existing movie clip one step lower in the stacking order	The instance name of the target movie clip
Send to Back	Moves an existing movie clip to the bottom of the stacking order	The instance name of the target movie clip
Start Dragging Movieclip	Makes it possible to drag a movie clip	The instance name of the target movie clip
Stop Dragging Movieclip	Cancels the current drag behavior	None

14

TABLE 14-2   You Can Use Behaviors to Control Movie Clips in Your Flash Productions.

After you've seen the available behaviors for movie clips, you're ready to start adding interactivity to your Flash movies. Many of the behaviors are self-explanatory, while others have multiple uses. A full dissertation on the possible use for each behavior is beyond the scope of this book. Experiment with the behaviors by assigning them to buttons or movie clips.

The logical object to use for each behavior is often dictated by what occurs after the behavior is executed. For example, if you wanted to use a behavior to advance to and play or stop at a specific frame on the root timeline or in a movie clip, you'd assign the behavior to a button. However, you could use a keyframe as the trigger for a behavior that navigates to a specific point in your production. Experimenting with the behaviors is the easiest way to master these tools and come up with some interesting effects.

But, like everything else in Flash, behaviors do require a bit of forethought. For example, when you load a graphic or an external movie, where do you put it? The obvious answer is in a movie clip, but do you want the movie clip to be visible when nothing's displayed in it? Probably not. Read on.

Create a Target Movie Clip

When you load a movie or graphic into Flash, it is loaded into the same level as the base movie. When content loads into the same level as the base movie, all of the previous content is replaced. If this is what you want to have happen, you need to do nothing other than choose _root (in Absolute mode) or this (in Relative mode) as the target movie clip into which you want the movie or graphic loaded.

However, if you're loading movies of different sizes, or if you want to give the user the option of choosing which movie to play, you must create a movie clip that will serve as the target into which the external movie or graphic will be loaded. The movie clip doesn't need any graphic content (such as a border); it just needs to have an instance name and it must exist in your movie. To create a target movie clip, follow these steps:

1. Choose Insert | New Symbol to open the Create New Symbol dialog box. Alternatively, you can press CTRL-F8.

2. Select the Movie Clip behavior, name the movie clip, and then click OK. You do not need to create any content for the movie clip. It is merely a location into which you load other content such as published movies or JPEG images.

3. Click the current scene button or the blue arrow to exit Symbol Editing mode. Your new movie clip is added to the document Library.

4. Choose Window | Library to open the document Library.

5. Select the movie clip you just created and drag it to the spot where you want external graphics or movie clips to appear when they load.

TIP   *Set up a vertical and horizontal guide where you want the target movie clip to be located. When you drag the clip close to the guides, it will snap to the intersection of the guides.*

6. Choose Window | Properties to open the Properties Inspector.

7. Enter a name for the movie clip in the <Instance Name> field, and then press ENTER (Windows) or RETURN (Mac). Your target movie clip is now ready to receive external content.

The beauty of an empty target movie clip is that you can load content of any size into it. The upper-left corner of the graphic or movie clip you load into the target movie clip aligns to the target movie clip's registration point.

Load a Graphic or Movie into a Target Movie Clip

The ability to load external content into a Flash movie makes it possible for you to create quick-loading, low-bandwidth interfaces. The trick is to create an interface with nothing but a navigation bar and a target movie clip. Of course, you may want to spiff it up a bit with an animated text banner.

After the interface loads, your viewers use menu selections to load external content into a target movie clip. For example, if you want to create a Flash movie to display video clips, you would begin by creating an empty target movie clip on your interface. Remember that the target movie clip has no content and does not need to be sized. It is merely a locator for the content that is loaded into the interface. Position the target movie clip within your interface, and remember that the upper-left corner of the movie you are loading into the target loads at the registration point of the target movie clip when the specified event occurs. You would then create a Flash document for each video clip that is the same size as the video you want to display. Import the video clip following the steps outlined in Chapter 7, and publish each video clip movie as an SWF file. On your interface, create menu buttons for each video you want to display and then use the Load Graphic (to load a JPEG image) or Load External Movieclip behavior to load content into the target movie clip. If all of the external content you're loading is the same size, you can create a symbol with a nice border for the content using the drawing tools. Remember to put the border symbol on a layer above the target movie clip so that it's visible after the content loads. To load content into a target movie clip, follow these steps:

1. Create a target movie clip and position it where you want the content to load, as outlined in the previous section. Remember that the upper-left corner of the content loads from the target movie clip's registration point. Therefore, if you're creating a border for the content, make sure to position the target movie clip in the upper-left corner of the border. What you need to do next depends on the content you want to load into the target movie clip. The following steps show how to load an external movie previously published as an SWF file.

2. Create the button that will load the external file when a viewer clicks it.

3. Select the button.

4. Choose Window | Behaviors to open the Behaviors panel.

5. Click the Add Behavior button and choose Movieclip | Load External Movieclip. The Load External Movieclip dialog box appears.

14

6. Enter the name of the movie in the URL field. Be sure the movie resides in the same folder as the movie you are creating.

7. Select the target movie clip into which the external movie clip will load, as shown next.

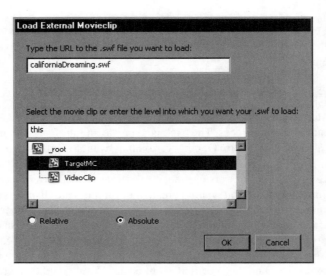

8. Click OK to finish assigning the behavior to the button.

9. Choose Control | Test Movie. After Flash publishes the movie and displays it in a new window, click the button. Your external movie clip should load into the target movie clip.

You can flesh out the production by using the Load External Movieclip behavior on other buttons to load different content. For that matter, you can assign the Load Graphic behavior to other buttons to load still images of the JPEG format into target movie clips. You don't have to worry about unloading the movie. As soon as a viewer clicks a different button, different content is loaded in the target clip.

Create a Drag-and-drop Movie Clip

If you want to give your viewers something to play with, you can create a drag-and-drop movie clip. Actually, you can use a drag-and-drop movie clip for more than play. You can create a navigation menu in a movie clip and, with the Drag Movie behavior, give viewers the option to move the menu to a different position. To create a drag-and-drop movie clip, follow these steps:

1. Create a new movie clip using the methods outlined in Chapter 13.

2. Drag the movie clip from the document Library and position it on the stage.

3. Choose Window | Properties to open the Properties Inspector.

4. Name the movie clip instance.

5. With the movie clip still selected, choose Window | Behaviors.

6. Click the Add Behavior button and choose Movieclip | Start Dragging Movieclip to open the Start Dragging Movieclip dialog box, shown next.

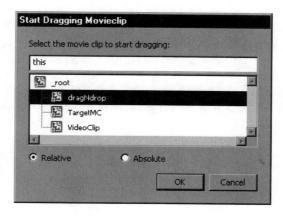

7. Click the movie clip's name in the dialog box to select it.

8. Click OK. Flash associates the movie clip with the behavior.

9. In the Behaviors panel, click the default On Release event and then choose the On Press event from the drop-down menu.

10. Choose Control | Test Movie. Flash publishes the movie and plays it in another window.

11. Move your cursor over the movie clip. Notice that the cursor becomes a pointing hand indicating that the movie clip can be clicked.

12. Click the movie clip and drag it to the desired position.

After you start moving the clip, you'll notice that the movie clip still stays stuck like glue to your pointer, even when you release the mouse button. In order to stop this magnetic attraction, you need to return to Movie Clip Editing mode and add the Stop Dragging Movieclip behavior to the symbol as follows:

1. With the movie clip selected, open the Behaviors panel, if it's not already open.

2. Click the Add Behavior button and choose Movieclip | Stop Dragging Movieclip. Flash opens a dialog box explaining what the behavior does.

3. Click OK to apply the behavior to the movie clip. In this case, you don't need to change the event since the default event is On Release, which will cause the movie clip to cease and desist its magnetic attraction when the mouse button is released.

4. Choose Control | Test Movie.

14

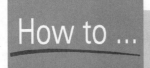 **Create a Funny Face Game**

Many vector illustration programs such as CorelDraw have vector drawings of face frames, eyes, noses, mouths, moustaches, and so on. Or, if you're really artistic, you can create your own face silhouettes and parts in your favorite illustration application. You can use these to create the Flash equivalent of a Mr. Potato Head game. Create a new movie and import a face frame into the movie. You can import Adobe Illustrator AI and EPS files, or FreeHand FH or FT files. Position the face silhouette on the stage and create a new layer for the face parts. Convert each face part to a movie clip symbol, and then use the Start Dragging Movieclip and Stop Dragging Movieclip behaviors to turn these into drag-and-drop movie clips. When you publish the movie, your viewers will be able to mix and match the facial parts to create funny faces.

When you test the drag-and-drop movie clip now, it latches onto the cursor as soon as you click the movie clip. You can drag the movie clip anywhere, and then drop it by releasing the mouse button.

 *By default, the Behaviors panel floats in the workspace. You can dock the panel in the Panel window on the right side of the interface.*

Control Sounds with Behaviors

You can also use behaviors to control any sound you have imported to the document Library. You can load a sound from the Library, load a streaming MP3 sound, play a sound, stop a specific sound, or stop all sounds. As a rule, you'll assign a behavior to control sound with a button. When the button is clicked, the sound is played, loaded, or stopped.

Add Linkage to Library Items

When you are going to control a Library item with ActionScript or behaviors, the item needs what is known as *linkage*. When you add linkage to a Library symbol such as a sound file, an image file, or a movie clip, you can access the asset with ActionScript without having to create an instance of the object on the stage. When you create linkage, you create an identifier for the Library item, which you would then use in behaviors or ActionScript to create the link from the script to the Library object.

To add linkage to a Library object, follow these steps:

1. Choose Window | Library to open the document Library.

2. Select the item for which you want to create linkage.

3. Right-click (Windows) or CTRL-click (Mac) and choose Linkage from the context menu. The Linkage Properties dialog box appears.

4. Click the Export For ActionScript check box. By default, the Export In First Frame option is selected, and the Identifier name for the object is the filename (for an imported object such as a sound or image file) or symbol name, as shown here. When you create ActionScript or use behaviors for an item in the document Library, accept the option to export in the first frame. This enables you to access the object with ActionScript or behaviors right after the movie fully loads.

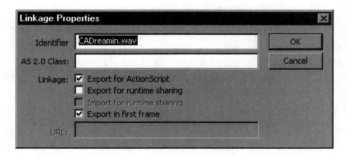

5. Accept the default identifier or enter a different name. If you're using the item in ActionScript, you're better off sticking with a short identifier that's easy to remember, as you'll have to type the identifier when creating your script.

6. Click OK to close the Linkage Properties dialog box. The Library item can now be accessed with ActionScript or behaviors.

Load a Library Sound

If you import a sound into the document Library, you can use a behavior to load the sound. When the sound is loaded, it plays. You can assign the behavior to a button or a timeline keyframe. When you assign the behavior, you also create an instance name for the Library sound, which enables you to further manipulate the sound with behaviors. The Library sound that is loaded with the behavior must have linkage properties, as outlined in the previous section. To load a Library sound, follow these steps:

1. Select the keyframe or object to which you want to assign the behavior.

2. Choose Window |Behaviors to access the Behaviors panel.

3. Click the Add Behavior button and choose Sound | Load Sound from Library. The Load Sound From Library dialog box appears.

14

4. In the top text field, enter the linkage identifier for the sound you want the behavior to load.

5. In the second text field, enter an instance name by which you want to refer to the loaded sound. You can use this instance name to play the sound on demand or stop the sound with other behaviors.

6. Deselect the Play This Sound When Loaded option if you do not want the sound to play when the event that triggers the behavior occurs. As a rule, you'd want this option enabled if the sound you're loading functions as background music for your movie. However, if you were assigning the behavior to a button, you would deselect this option and reference the instance name you assigned to the Library sound, which enables your viewers to play the sound on demand when the button is clicked.

7. Click OK. If you've assigned the behavior to a button or movie clip, accept the default On Release event or choose a different event.

When the movie is published, the sound loads when the keyframe to which you assigned the behavior plays or the event associated with the object occurs.

After you load a Library sound, you can use the Start Sound behavior to play the sound when a button is clicked or when a different keyframe in the movie plays. Once the sound starts

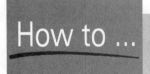

How to ... Create a Flash Documentary

You can create a Flash movie with narration for images in your movie. For example, if you're creating a Flash movie with images from the American Civil War, you can include documentary-style narration to accompany each image. Record the narration using a sound editing application, and export the narration in a sound format supported by Flash. Import each narration clip to the document Library, and create linkage and a unique identifier for each narration clip. On the first frame of your movie, use the Load Sound From Library behavior to load each sound into your movie. Make sure you deselect the Play This Sound When Loaded option. To finish your documentary production, create an invisible button large enough to cover each image that will have accompanying narration. Assign the Start Sound behavior to each invisible button and enter the instance name for the sound you want to play. Use the default On Release event for the behavior and the narration will play when the button is clicked. As the button is invisible, create some text instructions at the start of the movie telling viewers to click the image to play the narration.

playing, you can stop it with the Stop Sound behavior. Typically, you'd assign these behaviors to a button, but you could assign them to a keyframe. When you assign either behavior to an object, a dialog box appears in which you enter the instance name you entered when you used the Load Sound From Library behavior. The illustration here shows the Play Sound dialog box.

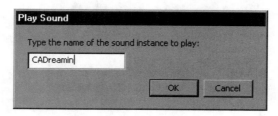

If you add a background sound to your movie you can create a button to stop the background sound from playing. Create the button and then assign the Stop All Sounds behavior to it. When the button is clicked, all sounds currently playing, including the background soundtrack, stop.

Use Behaviors to Navigate

You can also use behaviors in lieu of ActionScript to advance to different parts of your movie or open a web page. There are three behaviors that can be used for navigation: Goto And Play At Frame Or Label, Goto And Stop At Frame Or Label, and Go To Web Page.

Go to a Frame

If you're new to Flash and haven't quite mastered ActionScript, you can refer to the upcoming chapters for an introduction to ActionScript. However, if you have a movie that you need to get up and running right away and part of your interactivity involves advancing to different frames in the document, you can use behaviors to perform this task. To navigate to a frame, follow these steps:

1. Select the button or object that will be the trigger for the behavior.
2. Choose Window | Behaviors.
3. Click the Add Behavior button and choose Movieclip | Goto and Play at Frame or Label or Goto and Stop at Frame or Label. Your choice of behavior depends on whether you want the movie to continue playing when the behavior advances the movie to a frame, or whether you want it to stop. The following illustration shows the Goto And Play At Frame Or Label dialog box. All instances of movie clips are displayed in the dialog box. You can navigate to a movie clip by clicking its instance name. To navigate to a frame on the main timeline, click _root.

14

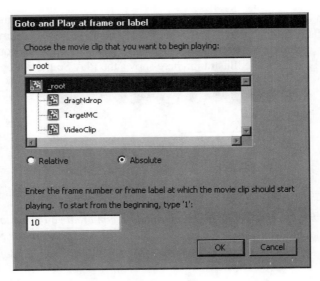

4. Enter the label name or frame number to which you want the movie to advance when the behavior executes. Remember if you enter a frame label, it must be spelled correctly or the behavior won't execute. Unlike ActionScript, frame labels are not case sensitive.

5. Click OK to assign the behavior to the object.

If you're assigning the Goto And Play At Frame Or Label behavior to buttons that will navigate to specific frames, assign the Goto And Stop At Frame Or Label behavior to the first frame of the movie.

Go to a URL

When you create an HTML document, you can create hyperlinks to other web pages. You can also do this in Flash. Prior to Flash MX 2004, the only way you could navigate to a web page was with the getURL action. Now you can use a behavior to open a web page. Just follow these steps:

1. Select the object to which you want to apply the behavior. Remember that you can apply a behavior to a keyframe, button symbol, or movie clip symbol.

2. Choose Window | Behaviors to open the Behaviors panel.

3. Click the Add Behavior button and choose Web | Go to Web Page. The Go To URL dialog box opens. Macromedia has included an example of the proper formatting for a URL in the URL text box.

4. Enter the URL for the web page you want to open when the behavior executes, as shown in this illustration.

5. Click the triangle to the right of the Open In field and choose one of the following:

- "_self" loads the web page in the same frame or window as the Flash movie.

- "_parent" loads the web page in the window of the frame that contains the Flash movie. If the frame is not nested, the web page loads in a full browser window.

- "_blank" loads the web page in a new browser window.

- "_top" loads the web page in a full browser window and removes any frames associated with the web page in which the Flash movie is embedded.

6. Click OK to exit the Go To URL dialog box.

Conclusion

In this chapter, you got your first taste of Flash interactivity with behaviors. You learned how to use behaviors to go to frames, play embedded video clips, and load external movie clips. You learned to apply behaviors to buttons, keyframes, and movie clips. You also learned to make target movie clips that function as containers for external media that you load with behaviors. In the next chapter, you'll get an introduction to ActionScript.

14

Chapter 15

Use ActionScript to Create Simple Interactivity

How to...

- Understand the basics of object-oriented programming
- Understand objects, classes, methods, and properties
- Use the Actions panel
- Get up and running with ActionScript
- Assign actions to a keyframe
- Create button events
- Use variables
- Understand the scope of variables
- Work with strings and expressions
- Use operators to change the value of variables
- Manipulate strings with operators and escape sequences

In the previous chapter, you received an introduction to the simple Flash interactivity that you can achieve with behaviors. As powerful as behaviors are, they are only the tip of the iceberg. In this chapter you'll get an introduction to ActionScript, Flash's powerful scripting language. ActionScript is similar to JavaScript. ActionScript can be the basis for such sundry tasks as creating menu navigation, loading content into a Flash production, and navigating to keyframes, or you can use ActionScript for more compelling projects such as games, shopping carts, forms, and much more. If you have ever done any programming with a language like JavaScript, you have a solid foundation on which to build your knowledge of ActionScript.

If you've used Flash previously, you'll find some changes in ActionScript. The release of Flash MX 2004 marked the introduction of ActionScript 2, which contains some powerful new features and actions. Unfortunately, a full dissertation of ActionScript 2 is beyond the scope of this book. In this chapter, you'll learn the basics to get up and running.

The introduction of ActionScript 2 was troubling for some designers. Instead of using the old tried-and-true parameters panes to flesh out an action, designers had to manually enter each parameter, which meant an intimate knowledge of the ActionScript language. This left many designers out in the cold when it came to adding interactivity with ActionScript. Fortunately, the Flash 8 Basic and Professional Actions panel sports a button labeled "Script Assist." Click the button and the familiar parameters panels from Flash 4, 5, and MX appear.

Before we examine the Actions panel and create some basic scripts, we'll review some basic concepts of object-oriented programming. This will provide you with a framework from which to efficiently produce error-free ActionScript.

Understanding Interactivity and ActionScript

When a movie is interactive, users control the flow or direction of the movie through their choices and selections. You can use ActionScript to program many different outcomes for an interactive movie, depending on the choices your viewers make. When you create Flash movies that give your viewers different options, they control the experience. This is the core to interactivity and the genius behind a Flash designer's clever use of ActionScript.

A non-interactive Flash movie runs in a linear fashion from beginning to end. Interactive Flash movies are different, because there is no specified order in which viewers experience the movie. An interactive Flash movie is similar to a web site. Users don't typically read every word or visit every linked page on a web site. Instead, they navigate to the pages that pique their interest them by making choices from the site's navigation menus. Each menu choice is a hyperlink, which serves up a web page when clicked. One visitor to a baseball team's web site may seek out scores or news, while another visitor may go directly to a story about a favorite player. With interactive media, users are in charge of their experience.

Understand the Basics of Object-Oriented Programming

Before we jump into ActionScript, we need to examine the framework of object-oriented programming languages. High-level object-oriented programming has been around for a long time and is becoming more prevalent in regard to web programming languages. It's critical that you understand the basic concepts behind object-oriented programming in order to get an idea of how ActionScript works.

Perhaps the best way to explain object-oriented programming is to explain what it is not. Years ago, before object-oriented programming was popularized, programmers used a method known as *structural* or *procedural* programming. In structural programming, the code was executed in a specific order, designated by the programmer. By contrast, object-oriented scripting languages do not execute commands in a specific order. Different modules of code are triggered by different events. For example, when a user clicks a button, this is an event that causes the programmer's code associated with the button to execute.

ActionScript is an object-oriented scripting language in which there is a heavy emphasis on code structure and organization. ActionScript code is organized into objects and modules. As an example, when you create ActionScript for a button, you are creating a small snippet of code (*module*) that executes when the button (*object*) is clicked. ActionScript code is very similar to JavaScript code and is based on the same ECMA-262 specifications as JavaScript. These specifications, published by the European Computer Manufacturers Association (ECMA), are contained in a document that defines the rules and parameters of the ActionScript and JavaScript languages. In fact, the two languages share a similar context. In this regard, if you're a JavaScript veteran, but are just now exploring the power of Flash and ActionScript, you'll become a proficient ActionScript programmer in no time.

15

Understand Classes, Objects, Methods, and Properties

Objects, classes, methods, and properties are the building blocks of object-oriented programming. These terms are all related, and you will find that understanding their hierarchy is one of the keys to understanding ActionScript.

ActionScript beginners are often surprised to discover that they have been creating objects since they first began using Flash. In fact, everything created in a movie is an object. Rectangles, imported bitmaps, and text items in a Flash movie are all individual objects. In fact, each individual frame and layer, and the movie itself, can be considered an individual object. You can also create your own objects using ActionScript code. For example, you can create an instance of the Date object that is used to retrieve the current date and time information from the user's computer.

Objects are identified by unique names and are also referenced by their location on a particular level. An object exists within a hierarchy in a movie and is called on not only by its established unique name but also by its location within the hierarchy. Objects may remain static through one part of the movie but change later. The Movie Explorer provides a graphical representation of your movie and the objects within it. The Movie Explorer presents this information in a format that looks similar to an outline, as shown in Figure 15-1. You can access the Movie Explorer by choosing Window | Explorer.

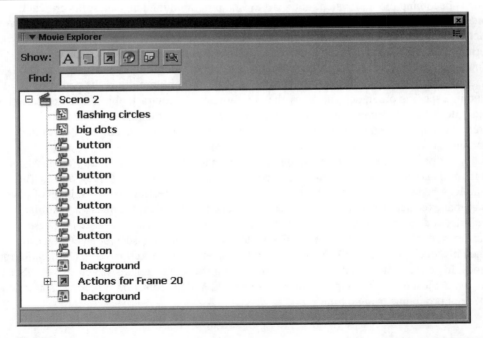

FIGURE 15-1   You use the Movie Explorer to view a graphical representation of objects in your movie.

Objects have *properties*. Properties describe objects. Think of properties as elements that make an object unique. For example, text objects have many properties that you set using the Properties Inspector. When creating a text box, you can set the font face property, which controls the style of the font, or the text color property, which determines the color of the text within the text box.

Many object properties are accessible through ActionScript code. For example, you can position an object within a movie by modifying its _x and _y properties, or change the height of an object by modifying its _height property.

A *class* describes everything there is to know about an object. You can think of a class as information that defines an object's properties, methods, and event handlers. Properties such as height, width, and position can be included in a class. The methods describe what you can achieve using ActionScript with an object. For example, the getMinutes method of the Date object retrieves the current minute of the hour from the host computer, the computer playing the Flash movie.

A class can be thought of as an object that makes other objects. When a class creates an object, that object is known as an *instance* of the class. To put this in easy-to-understand terms, let's look at the Date object. The Date object is an integral part of ActionScript that contains methods that retrieve the current date and time from the host computer. Before you can use any of the methods of the Date object, you have to create an instance of the object in your Flash movie. The following code shows the creation of an instance of the Date object:

```
myDate=new Date();
curHour=myDate.getHours();
curMintues=mydate.getMinutes();
```

The first line of code creates an instance of the Date object, while the second and third lines of code are using methods of the Date object (getHours and getMinutes) to retrieve the current hour and minute from the host computer. In Chapter 16 you'll dissect ActionScript that adds the date and time to a Flash movie.

The core actions within ActionScript have not changed much from Flash MX 2004 to Flash 8. However, there are new ActionScript groups and a plethora of new actions. A few of the actions from previous versions of Flash have been *deprecated*, which is fancy lawyer talk for saying that the Flash designers have created a better mousetrap. The old mousetrap is still functional, but the friendly programmers that created Flash 8 suggest that you learn the latest action, because the deprecated actions may be dropped from future versions of Flash. If you are an experienced ActionScript user, you will probably agree that this version is the most intuitive and powerful yet. The new Script Assist feature takes a lot of the drudgery out of hand-coding ActionScript. This powerful new feature will benefit ActionScript veterans and beginners alike. In the upcoming sections, you'll learn how ActionScript is used to add interactivity to your Flash productions.

15

Use the Actions Panel

When you need to create ActionScript for a button, keyframe, or movie clip, the Actions panel takes center stage. In the default panel setup, the Actions panel is docked with the Properties Inspector, directly beneath the stage. You can change this so that the Actions panel floats in the workspace. If you float the Actions panel, it remains in that position until you decide to dock it or revert to the default panel layout. The Actions panel can be accessed through these methods:

■ Choose Window | Actions.

■ Press F9.

■ If the title bar is displayed in the workspace but the panel itself is closed, click the word "Actions" to open the panel. Click Actions again to collapse the panel. Alternatively, you can click the right-facing arrow to open the panel. The right-facing arrow becomes a down arrow when the panel is open. Click the down arrow to close the panel.

Figure 15-2 shows the Actions panel displaying a simple script that loads a movie when a button is clicked. Notice that the title bar is labeled "Actions – Button," indicating that the actions being coded will occur when the button is released. Since you can also create ActionScript for buttons and movie clips, the title bar changes to reflect the object you have selected. Before you begin writing a script, make sure the Actions title bar displays the proper object.

If you're new to Flash, the first time you open the Actions panel you may think you've opened Pandora's box. There's quite a bit going on in this panel, as you can see in Figure 15-2. Notice that the panel is divided into three parts. The split window on the left contains the Actions books and shows all of the scripts within the movie. The large window on the right side of the panel is the Script pane, and shows the script for the currently selected object or keyframe. You create ActionScript in this pane by doing one of the following:

■ Manually type the code in the Script pane.

■ Click the Add Action button, select an ActionScript group, and then select an action.

■ Open one of the Actions books and drag an action into the Script pane.

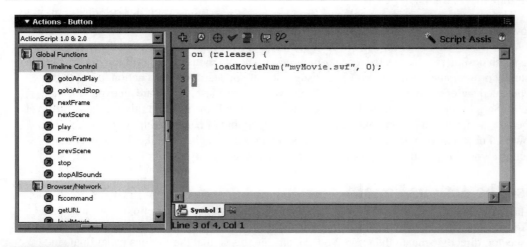

FIGURE 15-2   The Actions panel contains your toolkit to add interactivity to your movies.

- Open one of the Actions books and double-click an action.
- Open one of the Actions books, right-click (Windows) or CTRL-click (Mac) an action, and then choose Add To Script from the context menu.

When you add an action to the Script pane or manually enter enough code, Flash displays code hints. *Code hints* show you the parameters that must be entered in order for the code to properly execute. The following illustration shows the code hints that appear when you type **on** followed by a left parenthesis.

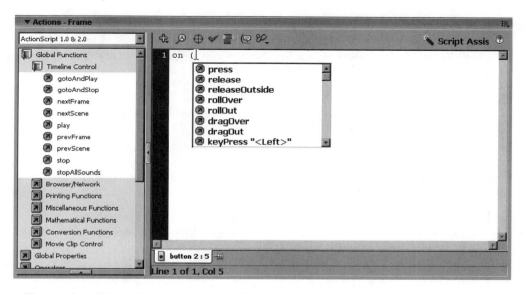

The previous illustration is an example of a drop-down menu of code hints. When you add other actions, such as the gotoAndPlay action to a script, code hints appear in the form of a tooltip, as shown next.

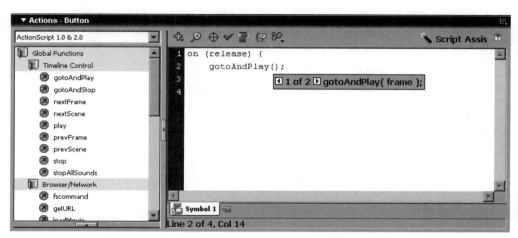

15

You'll learn to create scripts for buttons, keyframes and movie clips in the upcoming "Add ActionScript to Your Movies" section.

Use the Actions Panel Options Menu

Like most panels in Flash 8, the Actions panel has an Options menu that you use to invoke various commands related to the panel. You open the Actions panel Options menu by clicking the icon on the right end of the Actions panel title bar. The following commands appear on this menu:

- **Pin Script**   This option pins the script on which you are currently working so that it is displayed when you select other keyframes or objects in the movie.

- **Close Script**   Choose this command to unpin a pinned script when the object or keyframe to which the script is assigned is selected.

- **Close All Scripts**   This unpins all pinned scripts.

- **Go To Line**   This option quickly navigates to an indicated line number in the code. This can be especially useful for very long code snippets.

- **Find And Replace**   This command finds a particular string and then replaces it with another string entered by the ActionScript programmer. It can be used to replace variable names within code or specific passages of text. If the case-sensitive option is selected, the new text must have the same case as the old.

- **Find Again**   This command finds the next instance of the string of characters entered in the Find And Replace dialog box. The command is dimmed out until you after you invoke the Find And Replace command.

- **Auto Format**   When this is selected, the code will be formatted according to the Auto Format Options section of ActionScript Preferences, which are also accessed from the Options menu.

- **Check Syntax**   This checks the code for errors and lists any errors found so that they can be corrected.

- **Show Code Hint**   This option displays a code hint in the Script pane for an action you enter. For example, when you click the gotoAndPlay action, you have two available code hints that cover the available parameters for the action: one that prompts you for the frame label or number, and another that prompts you for the scene number as well as the frame label or number. Note that if you've labeled a frame or named a scene, you must enter the label or name in the proper case; otherwise, your ActionScript will fail.

- **Import Script**   This selection enables you to import an ActionScript text file in the AS format into the Script pane.

- **Export Script**   This option exports the script currently displayed in the Script pane as an ActionScript (AS) file. This feature is useful for archiving code that you may want to examine or use again later, or for easily transporting a script between machines.

- **Print**   Use this option to output only the code in the Script pane to the printer.

- **Script Assist**   This option displays parameters panes for each action you select, which eliminates the need for manually entering parameters. You can achieve the same result by clicking the Script Assist button.

- **Esc Shortcut Keys**   When this option is selected, the ESC key combinations for actions will be displayed next to the actual actions when you open the Actions panel or click the Add Action button.

- **Hidden Characters**   This option displays hidden characters in the Script pane, such as the carriage return character that signifies a new line of code is to follow.

- **Line Numbers**   This toggles the line numbers on and off in the code window. The line numbers have no function in the code. You use them as a visual aid when writing a script.

- **Word Wrap**   This option causes long lines of code to wrap in the Script pane, which enables you to view all of the code without having to scroll.

- **Preferences**   The Preferences option displays the Flash Preferences dialog box. Click ActionScript to set preferences for the Actions panel, such as fonts, font colors, font size, and text indentations. Click the Auto Format section to specify how Flash auto-formats ActionScript.

- **Help**   This option displays Flash 8 Help.

- **Group Actions With**   This option displays a submenu that enables you to choose a panel with which to group the Actions panel.

- **Maximize Panel**   Use this option to display the Actions panel at maximum size.

- **Close Actions**   Use this command to close the Actions panel. Note that this command is only available if you've grouped the Actions panel with another panel.

- **Rename Panel Group**   Use this command to rename the panel.

- **Maximize Panel Group**   This maximizes the size of the panel.

- **Close Panel Group**   Use this to close the panel group.

TIP   *When you are writing a script for a keyframe, you may notice that the script disappears from the Actions panel when you select a different frame on the timeline. If you want the script you are working on to remain visible in the Actions panel when you select another frame or object, click the Pin ActiveScript button at the bottom of the Script pane. To unpin the script, click the button again.*

15

Get to Know the Actions Toolbox

The Actions Toolbox comes loaded with a plethora of icons that look like books. Within these books you'll find the available actions, operators, functions, and properties for Flash 8. After you click a book icon, you can select an action. Depending on the book you open, you may find several sub-books, which may contain more sub-books or actions. An action, function, method, or property is represented by a circle with a diagonal arrow.

There are an awful lot of actions books in the Actions panel, more than you'll probably ever use. The good news is that you don't need to know every action in every actions book in order to add interactivity to your Flash movies. The easiest way to learn ActionScript is to crawl before you walk and learn the actions you need to add a desired effect to your Flash movie. At times you may have a hard time remembering in which book a particular action resides. Fortunately, the designers of Flash 8 have included an Index book at the bottom of the actions books list. Open the Index book and you can scroll through every action, function, property, and method you have at your disposal. And believe us, there are a lot of lines to scroll through.

If you select an action from the Index book, you may need other actions from the book in which the selected action resides. For example, if you select the getMinutes method of the Date object, you may need to include other methods of the Date object in your script. When you select a listing from the Index, you can quickly navigate to the original book in which the listing appears by right-clicking (Windows) or CTRL-clicking (Mac) and then choosing Show Original from the context menu.

A complete reference of each and every actions book is beyond the scope of this book. In upcoming chapters, you'll receive information about particular actions books and actions as they relate to the topic of discussion. To cut down on the number of steps, the instructions in this book will provide the path to an action, rather than instructions to "click this book, then click this sub-book," and so on. For example, to find the gotoAndPlay action, which resides in the Timeline book, which is a sub-book of the Global Functions book, you'll be told to "click Global Functions | Timeline and add gotoAndPlay () to your script." Remember, you can add an action to a script by double-clicking the action, dragging and dropping it into the Script pane, or by right-clicking (Windows) or CTRL-clicking (Mac) the desired action and then choosing Add To Script from the context menu.

Get ActionScript Help

ActionScript can be confusing, especially when you're creating your first script. If you don't format your code correctly or define an action's parameters properly, your script will fail. To view a description of an action from the Actions panel, complete with an example, select the action for which you need help and then right-click (Windows) or CTRL-click (Mac), and choose View Help from the context menu. After choosing either method, you'll see the information in the Help panel, as shown next. For the purpose of this illustration, the Help panel has been enlarged. You can also access ActionScript help by choosing Help from the Actions panel Options menu.

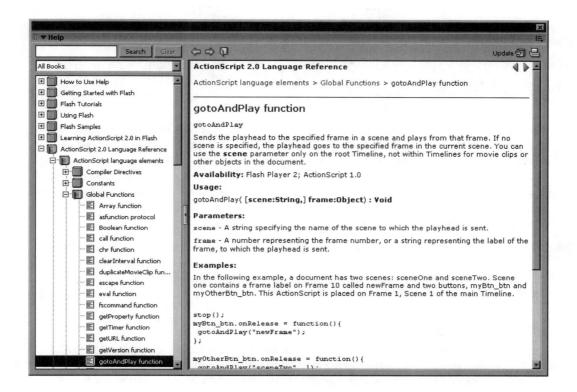

Add ActionScript to Your Movies

ActionScript is relatively easy to learn if you approach the language in a logical manner. The remainder of this chapter and Chapter 16 will provide you with basic information about how to add interactivity to your Flash movies with ActionScript. This information is designed to get you up and running with some basic techniques, as well as provide you with the framework for understanding and using popular actions and properties. This book does not cover all the actions associated with ActionScript—the topic is simply too broad and warrants a book of its own. However, in the remaining sections of this chapter, you'll receive an ActionScript primer. In upcoming chapters, you'll receive a few cookbook recipes you can add to your Flash movies.

15

Assign an Action to a Keyframe

When you add an action to a keyframe, it's generally to control the flow of a movie. Typically you'll use frame actions to stop a movie or advance the movie to a designated frame. Assigning an action to a keyframe in Flash is a surprisingly simple process. When a keyframe contains an action, a small cursive letter *a* is placed in the appropriate frame in the timeline, as shown in the following illustration. When you create actions for keyframes, it's a good idea to create an action layer and use this layer for all actions assigned to keyframes.

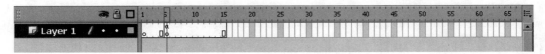

To assign an action to a keyframe, click the desired keyframe and choose Windows | Actions. Select the desired action from the applicable actions book and add it to the script using one of the methods outlined previously. Many of the actions you'll assign to keyframes can be found by clicking Global Functions | Timeline Control, where you'll find actions such as gotoAndPlay, which you use to advance the movie to a keyframe and play the movie from that frame forward, or gotoAndStop, which advances the movie to the desired keyframe and halts the movie. Actions you assign to a keyframe occur as soon as the keyframe is reached.

If you select a regular frame and open the Actions panel, you can still create a script. However, the script will not be assigned to the frame if it is not a keyframe. When you select a normal frame and create a script, the script will be assigned to the closest previous keyframe in the timeline.

Assign an Action to a Button

When you add an action to a button, the action is executed based on the event you associate with the button. These events are the same as the events you specify when you assign behaviors to a button, as discussed in Chapter 14. For example, if you assign the loadMovie action to a button, the action loads an external SWF movie into the current movie. You can choose the event that triggers the ActionScript that loads the movie. If you want the movie to load when the user releases the mouse button, choose the On Release event. The kicker is that you must manually enter the event that triggers the ActionScript, unless you use Script Assist. Without Script Assist, you must enter the event with the proper syntax in order for Flash to recognize it as an event; otherwise, your code will fail. The proper syntax for the most commonly used button events are described in the "Understand Events" section of Chapter 14.

The behaviors presented in Chapter 14 are designed for those with little or no experience with ActionScript who want to add interactivity to their movies. While behaviors are powerful, they are just the tip of the iceberg when it comes to Flash interactivity. You can replicate any behavior using ActionScript, and more. For example, with the Load External Movieclip behavior, Flash creates ActionScript similar to what you can do with the loadMovienum or loadMovie action. However, with ActionScript, you can specify additional parameters, such as the level into which the movie loads. Behaviors are cut and dried. If they suit your movie, you can use behaviors to add interactivity. However, when you need to create an effect similar to a behavior but with a few subtle differences, you need to use ActionScript. Adding basic ActionScript to your designer's toolkit lets you take your first steps toward becoming a developer. When you start assigning basic ActionScript to your buttons, your viewing audience will notice.

Flash does, however, give you a helping hand in the form of a *code hint*. As soon as you type the word "on" follow by an opening parenthesis, Flash displays the events shown in the following illustration. Click the event to choose it, and then type a closing parenthesis.

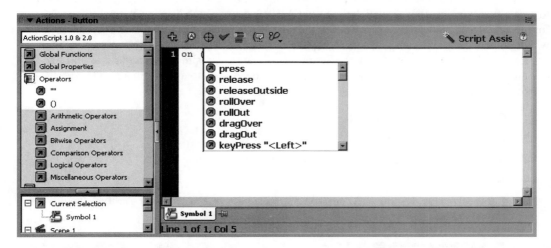

After entering the event that will trigger the code, follow these steps to complete a button script:

1. Click inside the Script pane and type an opening curly brace: {. A curly brace precedes a group of actions. All actions end with a closing curly brace.

2. Press ENTER (Windows)/RETURN (Mac). This wraps the code to a new line.

3. Press TAB. This step is optional. However, if you indent associated lines of code, it will be easier to figure out the flow of your ActionScript.

4. Select the action(s) that will execute when the associated event occurs. When you add an action to your script from an actions book, Flash automatically inserts a semicolon, which indicates the end of a line of code.

5. If the action you added requires additional information in order to properly execute, a code hint appears. If so, enter the requested information, place your cursor at the end of the line, and then press ENTER (Windows)/RETURN (Mac) to advance to the next line. Continue adding actions to your script as needed to pull off the desired effect. For most button scripts, you'll only be entering a few lines of code.

6. Type a closing curly brace to signify the associated actions' end. The following example shows a script that will advance the movie to frame 5 and play the frame when the button is released.

```
on (release) {
    gotoAndPlay(5);
}
```

15

Using Script Assist

If you're not a hard-core programmer and feel intimidated by the thought of manually entering code, you'll love the new Script Assist feature in Flash 8. Instead of having to rely on code hints to create functional scripts, you click the Script Assist button, which displays parameter panes for the action you are using. In many cases, the parameters panes contain drop-down lists from which you choose the desired object to complete the code.

Let's look at an example of how the Script Assist feature can simplify your task as a Flash designer. The following scenario uses the goto action to navigate to a frame in a movie with the help of Script Assist.

1. Create a new Flash document.

2. Create a simple button.

3. Select the fifth frame and press F6 to convert it to a keyframe.

4. Select the first frame.

5. Choose Window | Actions. Alternatively, you can press F9 to open the Actions panel shown next.

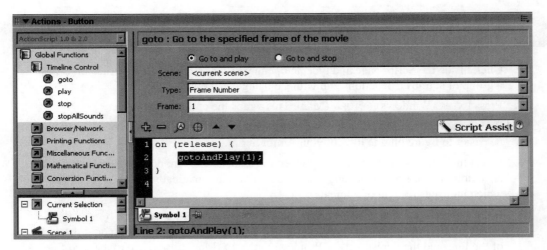

6. Click the Script Assist button.

7. Click Global Functions | Timeline Control, and then add the stop action to your script.

8. Select the button.

9. Click Global Functions | Timeline Control, and then add the goto action to your script. The Go To And Play radio button is selected by default. When the action executes, the movie jumps to the specified frame and plays. The other option goes to the specified frame and the movie stops playing until further input from the user. Notice that Flash has added "on (release)" to the script, as shown next. The means that the action will execute when the button is released. To change the event that triggers the goto action, move your

cursor over the first line of script, and the parameters pane changes to reveal a check box for every event associated with a button.

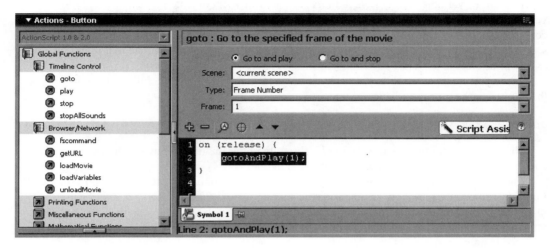

10. Click the Scene down arrow and choose the scene in which the desired frame appears from the drop-down list. If you have any named scenes in your movie, they appear on this list.

11. Click the Type down arrow and choose an option from the drop-down list. If the action will advance the movie to a frame you have labeled, choose Frame Label.

12. Type the desired frame in the Frame field. Alternatively, you can click the Frame down arrow and choose a frame that you have labeled from the drop-down list. For the purpose of this exercise, type **5** in the Frame text field.

13. Choose Window | Actions to close the Actions panel.

14. Choose Control | Test Movie to publish the document in another window.

15. Click the button. The movie advances to frame 5, loops back to frame 1, and stops. If you were creating a real-world movie and wanted the viewer to see something you'd placed on frame 5, you'd add the stop action to frame 5, which of course is already a keyframe.

Now wasn't that a lot easier than manually entering code? Thanks to the Script Assist button, ActionScript is now available to those of you who are "code challenged."

Keep Track of Things: Variables and Operators

Variables are common elements in all programming languages. Variables can either contain information that is stored in memory, or they can be placeholders for information that will be stored in memory and used later in your production. When you add variables to a Flash movie, it's like giving Flash a memory. The simplest use of a variable is the Input Text box. The variable name you associate with the Input Text box is used to store the information entered by viewers of your Flash movie. For example, you could use a variable in an Input Text box to store the

15

viewer's name and then retrieve the name at a future point in the movie to greet the viewer or congratulate the viewer on winning a Flash game.

The name "variable" really says it all: A variable is a script object that has the ability to vary. In other words, you can declare a variable at the start of a Flash movie and the information contained in the variable can change as the movie progresses. You can use variables to tally scores in Flash movies or keep track of a viewer's purchases for a Flash movie that functions as an online store.

When you create a variable, you assign a value to it. For example, the following code assigns the value 3 to the global variable *apples*:

```
apples=3;
```

The value 3 will remain stored in *apples* throughout the life of the movie unless you create code that changes the value at a later point in the movie.

Naming variables within Flash is fairly simple. However, unlike in previous versions of Flash, variable names are now case sensitive, meaning that *APPLE* and *apple* cannot be used interchangeably and be understood as the same variable in Flash. A variable name must be one uninterrupted string, and reserved words—predefined ActionScript commands—cannot be used as variable names.

TIP

It is a good idea to give your variables meaningful, easily recognizable names in your movie. Years ago, some programming languages forced programmers to use one- or two-letter combinations as variables. If you can recognize what the purpose of a variable is simply by looking at its name, it will make it easier to track down problems within the code later. However, you should strive to keep the variable name as simple as possible. Many times an ActionScript will fail because the programmer misspelled a variable when referring to it in a later frame of the movie.

Set the Scope of a Variable

Variables can be local or global in scope. As you might guess, a global variable is available throughout the life of the movie. You can access it in frame 1 and frame 1000. A local variable, on the other hand, is recognized only within one statement in ActionScript. It is enclosed in the curly braces you have seen generated in the code window. Outside of that statement, the local variable cannot be accessed.

To set a global variable in the Actions panel, type the variable name in the Script pane followed by an equal sign (=) and then the value of the variable. As a rule, you set a global variable on the first frame of your movie. As mentioned previously, make sure you create an actions layer for all frame actions. Doing so will save you hours of frustration if your script doesn't perform as expected. When you create an actions layer and religiously use the layer for all frame actions, you'll quickly be able to find all of your frame actions, which are designated by a cursive lowercase *a* on the timeline.

Understand Strings and Numeric Data

When you declare a variable in ActionScript, you create a variable name and value and indicate whether or not the variable is an expression. An expression can be a value that can be used in a mathematical computation, or an expression can be a mathematical computation that computes the values of other variables using mathematical operators such as the addition or multiplication operand. If you do not declare a variable as an expression, it is string data, which are alphanumeric characters used to display information such as a person's name or a street address. Incorrectly declared variables are a major source of errors in ActionScript, since strings and expressions are processed differently in the code.

When you create a variable and set it to a numeric value, you can use the variable in computations—for example, to tally a score for a game. There are two types of data in Flash: *text data* (also known as *string data*) and *numeric data*. You were introduced to string data in the description of the Input Text box. The data entered in an Input Text box can be used to form greetings in a Flash movie, identify a user, and so on. When you want to create a variable that contains string data, the data must be surrounded by quotation marks. The following code would assign a string to the variable *prezName*:

```
prezName="Millard Fillmore";
```

When string data is made up of alphabetical characters, it is known as *string literal data*. You can also have numbers in string data. For example, when you need to identify a person's address, you add numeric characters to the string data. Consider the following:

```
streetAddress="555 Goldenrod Lane"
```

Numeric data serves a different purpose in ActionScript. Numeric data can be a simple numeric value or several values connected by operators, which is known as an *expression*. When you create a variable and enter a numeric value that is not surrounded by quotation marks, Flash recognizes the data as numeric data. The following shows some examples of variables:

```
//Variable sets the value of Apples to 3
Apples=3;
//Variable sets the PlayerScore to 27000
PlayerScore=27000;
//Variable HighScore is set equal to the value of the variable
PlayerScore
HighScore=PlayerScore;
//Variable mainCourse is string literal data
mainCourse="Spaghetti"
//Variable sauce is string literal data
sauce="Marinara sauce"
//Variable Dinner is set equal to the text data from the variables
mainCourse and sauce
Dinner= mainCourse + sauce
```

NOTE   *When you see // followed by text in ActionScript, the text following the slashes is a comment. Comments are not recognized as ActionScript code and serve as a reminder as to what the ensuing lines of code are all about.*

15

In the last example, the variable *Dinner* is actually an expression that combines the contents of values from two string literal variables: *mainCourse* and *sauce*. When you combine two string literal values, you are concatenating data. You'll learn how to manipulate string data in the upcoming "Manipulate String Data" section of this chapter.

Use Operators to Manipulate Values

In the previous sections, you have already seen several examples of operators at work. Operators tie variable names and values together. The most common operator is =, which is often called an *assignment* operator because it assigns a value to a variable name. What makes variables powerful is the way they can be manipulated with operators. Other common operators include + (the addition operator), * (the multiplication operator), – (the subtraction operator), and / (the division operator). Some ActionScript users also frequently use ++ and –– (the increment and decrement operators, respectively). Here is an example of several operators in action:

```
//Take the value of Apples and add it to itself. Doubles the value
of Apples
Apples=Apples+Apples;
//Divides the value of Apples by 15
Apples=Apples/15;
//Subtracts one from the value of Apples
Apples--;
```

In the next script, which also uses operators, the multiplication operator (*) is used. The * operator in this script is used further to define the value of a variable. The variable z is set to the value of an expression: *x+y*2. In addition, a Trace action is added to the end of the script to trace the results of the expression that sets the value of the variable *z*. The Trace action helps you test a script to make certain it's working correctly. This is particularly helpful if you cannot see the results of your script when you test the movie, as is the case in the following script. If the trace doesn't return the value you expect, you need to go back and modify your ActionScript until the trace returns the expected result. Follow these steps to practice using variables and expressions in your Flash work.

1. Choose Windows | Actions to access the Actions panel.

2. Click the first frame of the timeline and then click in the Script pane of the Actions panel.

3. Type in the following script exactly as you see it:
   ```
   x=3;
   y=4;
   z=x+y*2;
   trace(z)
   ```

4. To see the results of the multiplication script from the Trace action, test the movie (CTRL-ENTER in Windows/CMD-ENTER on the Mac). An output window will appear with the correct calculation. In this case, the calculation yields a number of 11 based upon the preceding script.

After you test the movie, you see that the value of z is 11, even though you've used the addition operator before the multiplication operator. This is because mathematical expressions exhibit what is known as *operator precedence*. The multiplication operation was performed before addition because the multiplication operand has precedence over the addition operand. If you want the values of x and y to be added before being multiplied by 2, you would modify the expression by placing parentheses (also known as brackets) around the operation that adds the values of x and y, which would modify the code for the previous example as follows:

```
x=3;
y=4;
z=(x+y)*2;

trace(z)
```

Now the value of z equals 14, because the value of x plus y (7) is multiplied by 2, whereas in the original example, the value of y is first multiplied by 2 before being added to the value of the variable x. When you create expressions, keep the following operator precedence in mind: Operations in brackets have precedence over division, which has precedence over multiplication, which has precedence over addition, which has precedence over subtraction. Little did you know you'd have to remember high school math when you decided to become a Flash ActionScript guru.

Although the preceding script is just a small sampling of how variables and operators can work together, you can begin to see what powerful tools variables and operators are in ActionScript. Now let's take a look at some other basic concepts.

Manipulate String Data

Manipulating string data is one of the trickier tasks in any programming language. Even though expressions are used to manipulate both string data and numeric data, this is where the resemblance ends. When you create an expression to manipulate numeric data, the expression computes the values of variables to attain another value. When you create an expression to manipulate string data, you combine string data from other variables to create different string data. Consider the following example:

```
streetNumber="555"
streetName="Goldenrod Lane"
streetAddress=streetNumber + streetName
```

In the preceding example, the values of the *streetNumber* and *streetName* variables are recognized by Flash as string data because each value is in quotation marks. The variable *streetNumber* is numeric literal data, while *streetName* is text literal data. The variable *streetAddress* is set equal to an expression, which combines the value of the *streetNumber* variable with the value of the *streetName* variable, yielding string data in the form of a street address. However, the way the expression now reads, the result would be 555Goldenrod Lane. Adding a space before the value in the variable *streetName* will rectify this:

```
streetName=" Goldenrod Lane"
```

15

Another way you can get the *streetAddress* variable to display correctly is by adding a string literal character in your expression as follows:

```
streetAddress=streetNumber + " " + streetName
```

In the previous examples, the variable *streetAddress* combines the string data of *streetNumber* and *streetName* to create a recognizable street address. This is known as *string concatenation*. It is accomplished through fairly simple code—the two variables would be added together using the + operator, which not only is the addition operator but also is the concatenation operator. A blank space surrounded by quotation marks was added to the expression so that the street address wouldn't be jumbled together. You can use the blank space in lieu of adding a space to a variable, such as the variable *streetName* in this example. Doing so enables you to use the variable *streetName* in other areas of your movie where a space does not need to precede the text data.

There are some characters that are not reproducible within a string. For example, a string may need a carriage return, but you can't include one by typing a carriage return between the quotes in the variable declaration. Instead, you must use an *escape sequence*. An escape sequence allows you to insert characters that you otherwise could not use in a string. An escape sequence is preceded by a backslash character. Some common escape codes include the following:

- **\f** inserts a form feed.
- **\r** inserts a carriage return.
- **\"** inserts double quotes. This is necessary because if you typed the quote directly, it would be considered part of the string declaration syntax.
- **\t** inserts a tab character.

Any escape sequence can be included in a string through concatenation. In the following example,

```
TopEightiesBands= "Journey" + "\r" + "Flock of Seagulls" + "\r" +
"Mister Mister";
```

a carriage return would be placed between Journey, Flock of Seagulls, and Mister Mister, displaying each on a separate line.

Conclusion

In this chapter, you received your first taste of Flash's powerful ActionScript language. You learned how to navigate the Actions panel and navigate through the actions books. You also learned the ins and outs of object-oriented programming. You learned the power of variables, how to create them, and how to combine their values in the form of an expression. In the next chapter, you'll learn how to use some of the common Flash actions to add interactivity to your movies. You also learned how to simplify ActionScript through the use of Script Assist.

Chapter 16

Add Advanced Interactivity with ActionScript

How to...

- Use ActionScript to navigate the timeline
- Use the loadMovie action
- Modify a movie clip with ActionScript
- Use ActionScript to add the time to a movie

In the previous chapter, you learned how to use the Actions panel and were introduced to a bit of ActionScript theory. Now it's time to take that knowledge to the next level and learn how to use ActionScript in a movie. In this chapter, you'll learn how to use some of the most popular actions to add interactivity to your movies. Some of the actions may seem similar to the behaviors discussed in Chapter 14, but they have more power and give you additional control.

In this chapter, you'll expand on your knowledge of navigating the timeline by learning to use the Timeline Control actions. You'll learn to load external media into different levels without erasing the existing content. Another topic of discussion is how to convert a mild-mannered movie clip into a superhero by changing its properties. And, as if that weren't enough interaction for one chapter, you'll also learn how to use the Date object to add the date and time to your Flash productions.

> **NOTE** *The new Script Assist feature is used in all examples shown in this chapter.*

Navigate the Timeline with ActionScript

In Chapter 14 you learned to use ready-made ActionScript known as behaviors to navigate the timeline. While this is all well and good, there will be times when you need to navigate the timeline from within an ActionScript that is assigned to a button or a frame in the timeline. For example, in a Flash game, you can create ActionScript that tallies a player's score. After the player scores a certain number of points, you can use a conditional statement in conjunction with the gotoAndPlay action to advance the player to another scene in the movie.

When you navigate with ActionScript, you often reference timelines in different movie clips. For that matter, you reference different movie clips with many forms of ActionScript. In the upcoming sections, you'll learn how to target the desired movie clip and how to use the Timeline Control actions.

Learn About Targets

As discussed previously, when you want to communicate from the main timeline to a movie clip timeline or from one movie clip timeline to another, you communicate to a named instance. This is similar to navigating on the Internet. A web page has a URL (the target) that can be accessed from a link on another web page. In Flash, the target can be accessed from a keyframe, a button, or another movie clip. When a specified event occurs, the action executes with respect to the specified target.

When you drag a movie clip symbol from the document Library onto the stage, you create an instance of the movie clip. As mentioned previously, when you name an instance of a movie clip, you create a target that you can address with ActionScript. You use the Properties Inspector to name a movie clip instance.

When you create ActionScript that needs to reference a target, you can find all the instances of movie clip and button symbols used in your movie in the Insert Target Path dialog box. To access the Insert Target Path dialog box, click the Insert Target Path button in the Actions panel, as shown next. The ActionScript in this image is assigned to a button but will cause a movie clip named myClip to move to the x coordinate of 350 when the button is released.

Insert Target Path button

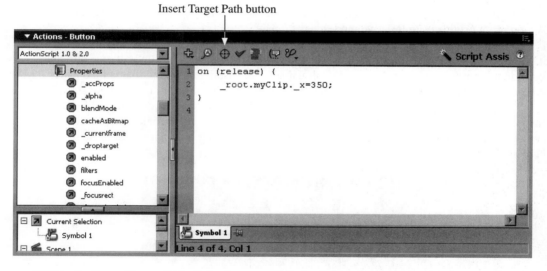

Within the Insert Target Path dialog box you'll find a listing for every button or movie clip instance in your movie. There are two modes in which you can address a target instance: Relative or Absolute. For more information on Relative and Absolute modes, see Chapter 14. The next illustration shows the Insert Target Path dialog box as used in Absolute mode. Notice the reference to the _root timeline.

16

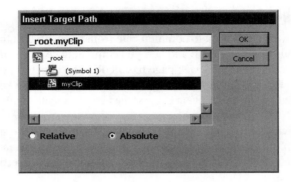

When you create ActionScript within a movie clip that references that movie clip, you use Relative mode to target the clip. When you select the clip from within the Insert Target Path dialog box, the word *this* (which is also known as an *alias* in programmer-speak) is all that appears in your script to reference it, which, loosely translated, means that the ActionScript refers to *this symbol*. As you gain more experience with ActionScript, you'll end up with movies that have movie clips nested within movie clips. When this is the case, you can communicate between the nested movie clips using Absolute mode, and refer to the clip from which the ActionScript originates in Relative mode.

Even if you don't use Script Assist while creating ActionScript, Flash 8 is very forgiving if you forget to name an instance of a movie clip. Every instance of a button or movie clip that you add to your movie is listed by its default name in the Insert Target Path dialog box. When you select an instance that does not have a unique name, Flash 8 displays the warning shown next. When you see this warning, you can rename the movie clip without opening the Properties Inspector by clicking the Rename button. Doing this opens the Rename dialog box, which enables you to give the symbol instance a unique name by typing the desired name and then clicking OK.

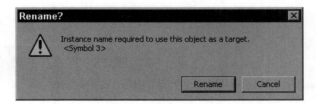

Use Timeline Control Actions

Now that you know something about targets, let's examine the actions you can use to navigate the timeline. These are similar to some of the movie clip behaviors discussed in Chapter 14, but Timeline Actions give you more flexibility than movie clip behaviors.

Use the gotoAndPlay and gotoAndStop Actions

You use the gotoAndPlay action when you want to advance the movie to a different frame and play the frames that follow when an event occurs. You use the gotoAndStop action when you want to navigate to and stop at a specific frame of the movie. Normally you assign these actions to a button, but you could also use them on a keyframe. When you use the gotoAndPlay action, you need to give Flash some information: either the frame to which you want to navigate or the frame and scene to which you want to navigate. The following steps show how to use these actions in conjunction with a button:

1. Select the button to which you want to apply the action.

2. Press F9 to open the Actions panel.

3. Click the Script Assist button.

4. Click Global Functions | Timeline Control to add the goto action to your script. The Script pane of the Actions panel reconfigures, as shown next. By default, the Go To And Play radio button is selected. If you want the action to cause the movie to go to and stop at a frame, click that radio button.

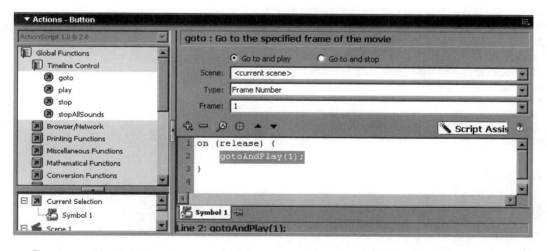

5. Accept the default scene parameter (<current scene>), or click the Scene down arrow and choose an option from the drop-down list. If you have any named scenes in your movie, they are shown on this list.

6. Accept the default type parameter (Frame Number) or click the Type down arrow, and then choose an option from the drop-down list. If you have followed good ActionScript practice and labeled all of the frames in your movie, choose Frame Label from the drop-down list.

16

7. Type the desired frame number in the Frame text field. Alternatively, click the Frame down arrow and choose an option from the drop-down list. On this list, you'll find the names of all frames you have labeled.

8. Close the Actions panel.

When you need to navigate to the next or previous frame, you can easily do so by choosing that option from the Type drop-down list when using Script Assist. You can use ActionScript to advance to the next scene or previous scene by choosing <next scene> or <previous scene> from the Scene drop-down list.

Stop or Play a Movie

You can stop a movie dead in its tracks using the Stop action, or play it using the Play action. Even though these are relatively simple actions, you can use them to add a good deal of interactivity to your Flash movies. For example, the Stop and Play actions form a dynamic duo when you need to create a drop-down menu. Another use for these actions arises when you want the viewer to read or look at something that you have displayed on a frame. You assign the Stop action to the frame that contains the content. On the same frame, you'll have a button that, when clicked by the viewer, will cause the movie to play again.

The ActionScript for these actions is relatively simple. You'll find these actions in the Actions panel Timeline Control book. As these actions have no parameters, you may find it simpler just to type the action in the Script pane rather than opening the Timeline Control book. Remember that ActionScript is case sensitive. The following shows the proper syntax for the Stop and Play actions.

```
play();
stop();
```

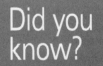

About Parentheses and ActionScript

If you're new to programming, you may wonder what the purpose of parentheses is in ActionScript. Parentheses are added to notify the Flash Player what parameters are associated with a particular action, or in the case of a button, what event triggers the ActionScript. Action parameters are signified by opening and closing parentheses. In the previous example, the two parameters for the action are the scene and frame. The release event that triggers the ActionScript is signified by opening and closing parentheses as well.

Load External Media

In Chapter 14, you learned to use the Load External Movieclip behavior to load content into a Flash movie. The behavior works flawlessly when you load content into a target movie clip. However, when you load content into a Flash movie, you must specify how the content is to be loaded. When you work in Script Assist mode, adding the loadMovie action enables you to specify the desired level into which the movie is loaded. The parameters pane for this action does yeoman's work enabling you to load the movie into either a target or a level. When you work without Script Assist and want to load external movies into a level, you use the loadMovieNum action and follow the code hint prompts to manually enter the movie name, the level into which the movie is loaded, and the method by which variables are sent. If you are loading the movie into a target movie clip without using Script Assist, you use the loadMovie action and follow the code hint prompts to manually enter the movie name, the target into which the movie is loaded, and the method by which the variables are sent.

Understand Movie Levels

A Flash movie can have up to 99 levels. If you're familiar with image-editing applications, levels are similar to layers. When you first create a Flash movie it resides on level 0, the root level. When you import external media such as a JPEG image or a Flash movie into a higher level, the movie background is invisible, because the content on the higher level eclipses all content beneath it on lower levels.

One way you can use levels is to create a base movie with nothing but a banner and buttons that load additional content. This gives you a quick-loading movie. When you create the Flash movies that will load into the base movie, you arrange all of the content so that the navigation buttons and header on the base movie are still visible. You can then program the buttons in the base movie to load external media (other SWF files or JPEG images) into a higher level. If you program each button from the base movie to load content into the same level, there's no need to unload the movies. Whenever a new movie is loaded into a level, it erases the previous content in the level.

Use the loadMovie Action

You can use the loadMovie action (loadMovieNum when working without Script Assist) to load Flash SWF movies or JPEG images into a specific level. When you use the loadMovie action, you specify the level into which the content is to be loaded. The following steps illustrate how to use the loadMovie action with a button.

1. Select the button to which you want to assign the action.

2. Press F9 to open the Actions panel.

3. Click the Script Assist button to switch to Script Assist mode.

4. Click Global Functions | Browser Network and then double-click the loadMovie action to add it to your script.

16

5. In the URL field, type the name of the movie you want to load. You can also load a JPEG image by referring to it by its filename.

6. Accept the default location option (Level) and type the level into which you want to load the movie, as shown next.

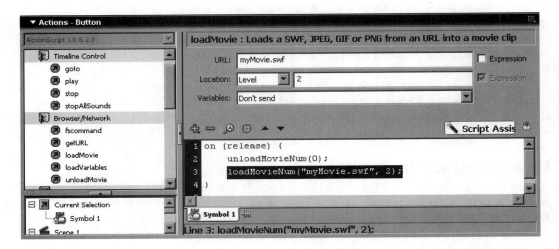

Use the unloadMovie Action

If you load a movie into a level in which a movie is already playing, the next movie that you load will play in its place. However, when you are working with multiple levels, you may have the need to clear a level or two when loading new content. To do this you use the unloadMovie action as follows:

1. Select the button that will be used to load new content into the movie.

2. Press F9 to open the Actions panel.

3. Click the Script Assist button to switch to Script Assist mode.

4. Click Global Functions | Browser Control and then double-click the unloadMovie action to add it to your script.

5. Accept the default location (Level) and type the level from which the movie will be unloaded, as shown next.

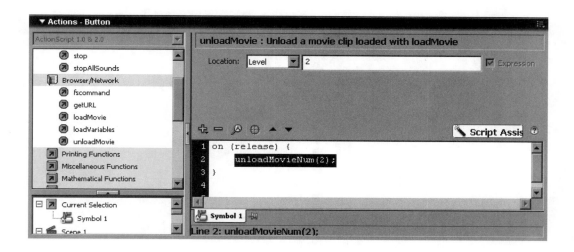

Modify Movie Clip Properties

You can use ActionScript to put a movie clip through its paces. When you want to animate an object with ActionScript, it's not the same as motion tweening or shape tweening. You can use ActionScript to move an object from point A to point B and increase its size, but there is no transformation. When the action executes, the change happens when a button is clicked or when a keyframe is reached. If you use the default movie frame rate of 12 fps, the action executes during the time span of a single frame, which, if you do the math, is 1/12 of a second. A button click causes the ActionScript to execute at the same speed.

However, if you need to make extensive alterations to several movie clip objects during the course of a movie, motion tweening and shape tweening bloat the file size terribly. In this regard, you're better off using ActionScript when you need to make wholesale modifications to movie clip properties, as you would when creating a Flash game. When creating a game or eye candy, designers commonly nest a graphic symbol in a movie clip and then use ActionScript to control the movie clip. Nesting symbols are covered in Chapter 8.

When you nest a graphic symbol in a movie clip, you can control all of the properties of the nested graphic symbol with ActionScript. You can move the object to specific coordinates on the stage, scale the object, control its opacity, and more. Remember, when you address a movie clip from another movie clip, the timeline, or a button, the movie clip must have a unique instance name. In the upcoming sections, you'll learn how to modify a movie clip using some of the more common properties. To view all of the movie clip properties you can modify, open the Actions panel and click ActionScript 2.0 Classes | Movie | Movie Clip | Properties to reveal the properties shown here.

16

Scale a Movie Clip

You can use ActionScript to scale a movie clip. You can change a movie clip's x scale, y scale, or both. When you scale a movie clip, you enter a value that is a percentage of the movie clip symbol's original size. The following steps show how to scale a movie clip when a button is clicked. In this section, you'll also learn how to copy lines of script and then alter them to achieve the desired result.

1. Create a movie clip in which an object such as a rectangle or oval is nested.
2. Drag the movie clip on stage and use the Properties Inspector to name the instance.
3. Create a button symbol and drag it on stage.
4. Select the button.
5. Press F9 to open the Actions panel.
6. In the left window of the Actions panel, click ActionScript 2.0 Classes | Movie | Movie Clip | Properties and then double-click _xscale to add the property to your script.
7. In the Expression field, type an equal sign (=) after _xscale and enter the value to which you want the object scaled. To increase the _xscale, enter a value larger than 100; to decrease it, enter a value less than 100. For the purpose of this exercise, enter a value of 150.

8. Click the Script Assist button to exit Script Assist mode.

9. Select the not_yet_set text and then click the Insert Target Path button to open the Insert Target Path dialog box, shown next.

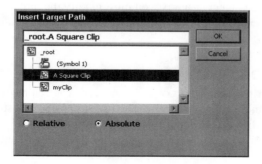

10. Select the named instance of the movie clip whose properties will change when the button is clicked.

11. Click the Absolute radio button and then click OK.

12. Select the line of code you just completed by dragging your cursor over it.

13. Right-click (Windows) or CTRL-click (Mac) and choose Copy from the context menu.

14. Position your cursor after the semicolon that signifies the end of the line of code you just copied, and press ENTER (Windows) or RETURN (Mac) to advance to the next line.

15. Right-click (Windows) or CTRL-click (Mac) and choose Paste from the context menu. You could have manually entered the code, but this is quicker since all you have to do is change the *x* to *y*.

16. Select the *x* in the line of code you just pasted and type *y*. Your Script pane should resemble the following illustration.

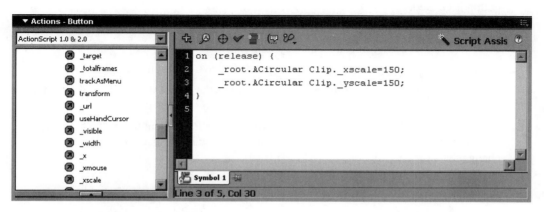

17. Choose Control | Test Movie. When you click the button, the object increases in size by 50 percent.

Note that the movie clip only increases in scale the first time you click the button. When you click the button again, the movie clip scale does not increase. That is because the action specifies that the object is to be increased to 150 percent of its *original* size. After you have clicked the button once, the object is the specified scale value, and subsequent clicks will have no effect. In order to repeatedly modify an object property, you must modify the movie clip in increments, a task that you'll learn in the upcoming "Modify a Movie Clip Incrementally" section of this chapter.

Move a Movie Clip

You can also use ActionScript to change an object's position. You can move the object to a given coordinate on the stage or move it incrementally. The following steps illustrate how to move a movie clip to a given position on the stage when a button is clicked.

1. Create a movie clip in which an object such as a rectangle or oval is nested.
2. Drag the movie clip on stage and use the Properties Inspector to name the instance.
3. Create a button symbol and drag it on stage.
4. Select the button.
5. Press F9 to open the Actions panel.
6. In the left window of the Actions panel, click ActionScript 2.0 Classes | Movie | Movie Clip | Properties and then double-click _x to add the property to your script.
7. In the Expression field, type an equal sign (=) after _x and enter the coordinate to which you want to move the object.
8. Click the Script Assist button to exit Script Assist mode.
9. Select the not_yet_set text and then click the Insert Target Path button to open the Insert Target Path dialog box.
10. Select the named instance of the movie clip whose properties will change when the button is clicked.
11. Click the Absolute radio button and then click OK.
12. Select the line of code you just created by dragging your cursor over it.
13. Right-click (Windows) or CTRL-click (Mac) and choose Copy from the context menu.
14. Position your cursor after the semicolon that signifies the end of the line of code you just copied, and press ENTER (Windows) or RETURN (Mac) to advance to the next line.
15. Right-click (Windows) or CTRL-click (Mac) and choose Paste from the context menu. You could have manually entered the code, but this is quicker since all you have to do is change the *x* to *y*.
16. Select the *x* in the line of code you just pasted and type **y**.

17. Change the y value to the coordinate to which you want to move the object. The following illustration shows code that will move a movie clip to x=350, y=150 when the button is clicked and then released.

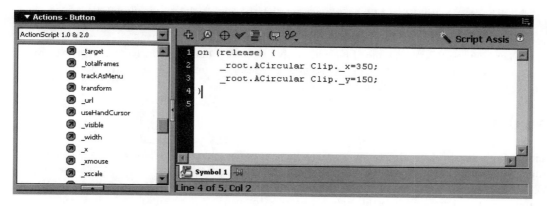

18. Choose Control | Test Movie. When you click the button, the movie clip moves to the specified coordinates.

Rotate a Movie Clip

Another movie clip property you can transform with ActionScript is rotation. You can rotate a movie clockwise by entering a value between 0 and 180, and counterclockwise by entering a value between 0 and −180. To rotate a movie clip when a button is clicked, follow these steps:

1. Create a movie clip in which an object such as a rectangle or oval is nested.

2. Drag the movie clip on stage and use the Properties Inspector to name the instance.

3. Create a button symbol and drag it on stage.

4. Select the button.

5. Press F9 to open the Actions panel.

6. In the left window of the Actions panel, click ActionScript 2.0 Classes | Movie | Movie Clip | Properties and then double-click _rotation to add the property to your script.

7. In the Expression field, type an equal sign (=) after _rotation and enter the number of degrees you want the object to rotate. Enter a value between 0 and 180 to rotate the movie clip clockwise; between 0 and −180 to rotate the clip counterclockwise.

8. Select the not_yet_set text and then click the Insert Target Path button to open the Insert Target Path dialog box.

16

9. Select the named instance of the movie clip whose properties will change when the button is clicked.

10. Click the Absolute radio button and then click OK.

11. Choose Control | Test Movie. When you click the button, the movie clip moves to the specified coordinates.

When you test this movie, the clip rotates only on the first button click. To rotate a clip again and again, you have to rotate the clip in increments, which will be explained in the "Modify a Movie Clip Incrementally" section of this chapter.

Modify Movie Clip Opacity

If you want a movie clip to fade away when a button is clicked, you can make it happen by modifying a movie clip's alpha property, which changes the opacity of the movie clip. When you modify the clip's alpha property, you specify a value between 0 (invisible) and 100 (opaque). A value between 0 and 100 causes the movie clip to exhibit a degree of transparency; the object being more transparent as the value gets closer to 0. To change a movie clip's opacity when a button is clicked, follow these steps:

1. Create a movie clip in which an object such as a rectangle or oval is nested.

2. Drag the movie clip on stage and use the Properties Inspector to name the instance.

3. Create a button symbol and drag it on stage.

4. Select the button.

5. Press F9 to open the Actions panel.

6. In the left window of the Actions panel, click ActionScript 2.0 Classes | Movie | Movie Clip | Properties and then double-click _alpha to add the property to your script.

7. In the Expression field, type an equal sign (=) after _alpha and enter the desired value.

8. Select the not_yet_set text and then click the Insert Target Path button to open the Insert Target Path dialog box.

9. Select the named instance of the movie clip whose properties will change when the button is clicked.

10. Click the Absolute radio button and then click OK.

11. Choose Control | Test Movie. When you click the button, the movie clip becomes more transparent.

Modify a Movie Clip Incrementally

In the previous examples, you learned how to cause an object's properties to be modified when a button is clicked. However, this type of change is not very interesting. If you want to give your viewers something to play with, or if you want to create a game, you'll need the ability to modify one or more properties with each click of the mouse.

To modify a movie clip by a certain increment every time a button is clicked, you use the plus (+) or minus (–) sign after the movie clip property you want to modify, followed by the equal sign (=) and the value by which you want the property to increment. For example, if you wanted to increase the _xscale property for a movie clip instance named Line by 15 percent, you would enter the following code:

```
_root.Line._xscale+=15;
```

To decrease the scale of the same movie clip by 20 percent, you would enter the following code:

```
_root.Line._xscale-=20;
```

You can incrementally change the other properties discussed in this chapter by creating code similar to the previous examples. The following lines of code increment the _x property of a movie clip by 5 pixels. When you increment the _x property by a positive value, the movie clip moves from left to right; when you increment it by a negative value (known as *decrementing*), the clip moves from right to left. Note that if you put the following two lines of code in a script, they'd cancel each other out and the clip wouldn't move.

```
_root.Line._x+=5;
_root.Line._x-=5;
```

Experiment with the other examples in this chapter to explore the power of incrementally changing an object's properties.

Apply ActionScript to a Movie Clip

In the previous sections on ActionScript, you learned to apply actions to buttons and timelines. As you know, keyframes have no events; any associated ActionScript executes when the Flash Player plays the keyframe. Buttons have unique events that correspond with the user's interactions. When you assign ActionScript to movie clips, you can choose from events unique to movie clips. The default event for a movie clip is load, which executes any attached ActionScript code when the movie clip loads.

16

Many of the movie clip events are associated with data or key strokes, which is advanced ActionScript and therefore beyond the scope of this book. There is, however, an event that goes hand in hand with modifying object properties. The event is known as enterFrame. In an earlier section you learned that you can move a movie clip in increments along the x or y axis. In the previous examples, a button click was required to accomplish that property change. Wouldn't it be cool if you could create a movie clip that starts animating itself? You can, if you change the right property and use the enterFrame clip event. When you assign the enterFrame clip event to ActionScript, the ActionScript code that follows occurs every time the movie clip frame is played. And if you put your ActionScript in a one-frame movie clip, the enterFrame event assures that the script executes whenever the movie clip is visible on the stage. For an example of the power you can harness using ActionScript in a movie clip with the enterFrame event, follow these steps:

1. Create a small circle about 20 pixels in diameter.

2. Press F8 to convert the circle to a symbol, and choose the movie clip behavior.

3. Press F9 to open the Actions panel.

4. Click the Script Assist button to enter Script Assist mode.

5. In the left window of the Actions panel, click ActionScript 2.0 Classes | Movie | Movie Clip | Properties and then double-click _x to add the property to your script.

6. Position your cursor after _x and type +=3.

7. Click the first line of code and then click the EnterFrame radio button, as shown next.

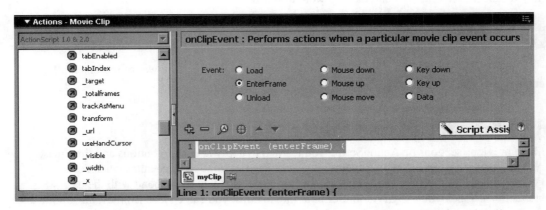

8. Click the second line of code and move your cursor over the not_yet_set text and then click the Insert Target Path button.

9. Select the named instance to which you want to apply the code and also the Relative radio button, as the code will be applied to the movie clip itself.

10. Click OK to exit the Insert Target Path dialog box. Your Actions panel should resemble the following.

11. Choose Control | Test Movie. The movie clip should start moving of its own accord. Is it magic or is it ActionScript?

Even though a "magic" movie clip looks pretty cool the first time you see it, it ceases to keep your interest after a few seconds. I mean, after all, who wants to watch a sluggish circle crawl across the stage? You can change this by using one of the methods of the Math object to create a random number. To modify your magic movie clip so that the motion is random, follow these steps:

1. Select the movie clip you just animated.

2. Press F9 to open the Actions panel.

3. Move your cursor over the second line of script and then delete the number 3.

4. In the left window of the Actions panel, click ActionScript 2 Classes | Core | Math | Methods and then double-click Random to add it to your script. Your Actions panel should look like the following illustration.

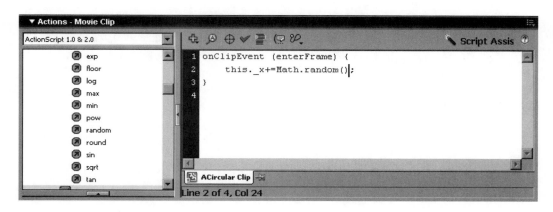

16

5. Type an asterisk (*) followed by the number 7. This, combined with the Random method of the Math object, generates a random number between 1 and 7. Line 2 of your ActionScript should look as follows.

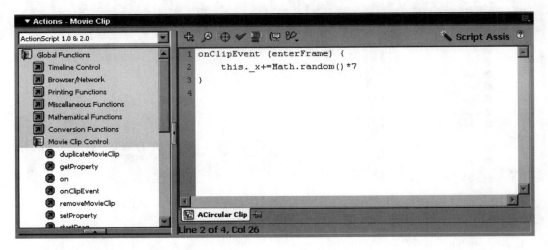

6. Choose Control | Test Movie.

Now when the movie clip starts moving the motion is random, kind of like a stuttering effect. This looks much better than the original movie clip animation. But wait, there's more.

A movie clip doing the stutter step in a straight line, while more interesting than the previous animation, will quickly lose your viewer's interest. To make the stutter step movie clip an "all singing and dancing" movie clip, you can modify a few more properties, and of course you'll want them to be modified in a random matter. To spice up your movie clip animation, follow these steps:

1. Select the movie clip you just animated.

2. Press F9 to open the Actions panel.

3. Place your cursor after the semicolon (;) in the second line of code, press ENTER (Windows) or RETURN (Mac), and type the following lines of code:

```
this._y-=Math.random()*7;
this._alpha=Math.random()*70;
this._xscale=Math.random()*150;
this._yscale=Math.random()*350;
```

NOTE *You could enter this code in Script Assist mode, but it would be a bit tedious as you'd have to switch back and forth between Script Assist and Normal mode to enter the target path. Another way you could work would be to select the second line of code, right-click (Windows) or CTRL-click (Macintosh), and then choose Copy from the context menu. Then paste the code to the next line as outlined previously, and change to property being modified and the value.*

4. Remember to end each line of code with a semicolon and then press ENTER (Windows) or RETURN (Mac) to advance to a new line.

5. Choose Control | Test Movie.

Now you're getting somewhere. Your circle movie clip is now doing the Flash boogaloo, and the great thing about it is that the motion is not predictable. If you analyze the code you just created, you can see the _x and _y properties of the movie clip are incrementing randomly with a value between 1 and 7. The _alpha property (opacity) is changing randomly to a value between 1 and 70. Can you say "flashing light"? To top it off, the _xscale and _yscale properties of the movie clip are changing randomly by different amounts. Now how cool is that?

The only thing about our shucking and jiving, stuttering movie clip is that one is the loneliest number. To add some real pizzazz to your production, you'll want a whole brigade of these dudes hopping about in your movie. You could duplicate the original several times. But the economical way to do this is to convert your animated movie clip to a symbol. That's right, a symbol within a symbol. So, before moving on to the next section, follow these steps:

1. Select the animated movie clip.

2. Press F8 to open the Convert To Symbol dialog box.

3. Name the new symbol, choose the movie clip behavior, and then click OK to exit the Convert To Symbol dialog box. Your animated movie clip is added to the document Library.

Did you know?

Understand the Random Method of the Math Object

16

The Random method of the Math object generates a random number between 0 and 1. Multiplying this by a value results in a random value between 1 and the value. When you use the Random method of the Math object, you can multiply it by any value to suit the Flash movie you're working on. For example, use this._x=Math.random()*550 to generate a random value between 1 and 550 the default width of the stage.

When you convert a movie clip with ActionScript, you've created modular ActionScript. You can use this movie clip in any other scene or frame of your movie. For that matter, you can use the movie clip in another movie by opening the document and dragging the symbol from one document Library to another. Before you finish this exercise, open the document Library, select the animated movie clip symbol you just created, and drag several copies of it onto the stage. When you test the movie now, you've got a bunch of circles moving about, and each movie clip looks different because the properties are changing randomly. You could create an interesting animation by creating a couple of variations of this clip that use different colored objects, and by specifying that the _x and _y properties of a few clips decrement, which will make them move in the opposite direction.

Deconstruct a Movie Clip That Displays the Time

In Chapter 15, you were introduced to Flash objects, properties, and methods. To give you an idea of how they work, this section will deconstruct a movie clip in which the Date object retrieves the current time from the user's computer. You'll also get a primer on how conditional statements work.

Use ActionScript to Display the Time of Day

The source file (timeClip.fla) for the upcoming sections can be found at www.osborne.com. The code and text box that display the date and time are nested within a movie clip, which means that the time movie clip is modular. You can use it in any Flash movie by opening the Library for the timeClip.fla file in Flash and then dragging the movie clip into the document Library of the movie you want to use it in. The ActionScript for the timeClip movie clip is shown in the following example:

```
mydate = new Date();
hours = mydate.getHours();
minutes = mydate.getMinutes();
seconds = mydate.getSeconds();
// Calculate value of AMorPM variable before changing hours variable to
compensate for military time
if (hours<12) {
    AMorPM = "AM";
} else {
    AMorPM = "PM";
}
// At midnight military time =0
if (hours<1) {
    hours = 12;
}
```

```
if (hours>12) {
    hours = hours-12;
}
if (minutes<10) {
    minutes = "0"+minutes;
}
if (seconds<10) {
    seconds = "0"+seconds;
}
current_time = hours+":"+minutes+":"+seconds+" "+AMorPM;
```

The first line of code specifies the clip event that must occur in order for the following lines of ActionScript to execute. The enterFrame event is used so that the Flash Player continually executes the ActionScript and the time is updated as the movie plays. If the Default Load event were used, the Flash Player would display the time at which the movie clip loaded and that's it.

The second line of code creates an instance of the Date object. Remember, to create an instance of the Date object, you first create a variable, then type the equal sign (=), and then in the left window of the Actions panel, click ActionScript 2.0 Classes | Core | Date and double-click new Date() to add it to your script.

Use Methods of the Date Object

After creating an instance of the Date object, you use methods of the Date object to pluck information from the host computer. Lines 3 through 5 of the code retrieve the current time information from the host computer. This code is repeated here so you can examine it in detail.

```
hours=mydate.getHours();
minutes=mydate.getMinutes();
seconds=mydate.getSeconds();
// Calculate value of AMorPM variable before changing hours variable
to compensate for military time
```

Although the code looks a tad complex when you examine it as a whole, it's really quite simple. The *hours* variable is set equal to the current value of the getHours method of the Date object. Because the instance of the Date object is called *mydate*, this precedes the method and is separated by a dot. When you need to create code like this, you first type the variable name. In this case, *hours* is used because the variable will retrieve the current hour from the host computer. After entering the variable name, you type an equal sign and the instance name of the Date object followed by a dot (.). To add the getHours method to the script, click ActionScript 2.0 Classes | Core | Date | Methods in the left window of the Actions panel, and then double-click getHours to add the method to your script. The *minutes* and *seconds* variables retrieve the current minute and second from the host computer and are created in a similar manner; name the variable and then choose the proper method to retrieve the desired data.

16

ActionScript uses the military method of telling time. Midnight is 0 hour. The last line of the previous code is a comment to remind the programmer why the following lines of code were created. In the next section, you'll dissect the conditional statements that convert the time from 24-hour military time to the 12-hour clock that your viewers are accustomed to seeing.

Add Conditional Statements

When you add a conditional statement to ActionScript, you put a fork in the road. While the following section does provide an explanation of the conditional statements used in our sample script, it is by no means a complete discussion of conditional statements and their use in Flash movies.

When you add a conditional statement to your script, the script code that will execute next depends on the outcome of the conditional statement. If the statement evaluates as true, the code that follows is executed; if not, a different line of code is executed. Consider the following lines of code from our example:

```
if (hours<12){
        AMorPM="AM";
}else{
        AMorPM="PM";
}
// At midnight military time =0
if(hours<1){
        hours=12;
}
if(hours>12){
        hours=hours-12;
}
if(minutes<10){
        minutes="0"+minutes;
}
if(seconds<10){
        seconds="0"+seconds;
}
```

The first conditional statement begins with the *if* action, which you will find in the Conditions/Loops book, which is a sub-book of the Statements book. The statement within parentheses sets the variable *AMorPM* to AM if the variable *hours* is less than 12. If the variable *hours* is not less than 12 (i.e., greater than or equal to 12), the next line of code is evaluated. This begins with the *then* action, which is also found in the Conditions/Loops book. The ActionScript associated with the *then* action again executes when the first statement evaluates as false. So if the hour is greater than 12, it's PM.

The next set of conditional statements corrects for military time. If the variable *hours* is less than 1, it's past midnight but before 1:00 in the morning. If the variable *hours* is greater than 12, 12 is subtracted from 24-hour time.

The last two conditional statements keep things neat and tidy by adding a zero to the variables *minutes* and *seconds* so that the clock displays two digits when the value is less than 10.

Display the Time

The final line of code displays the time. A variable is created to concatenate the previous variables into the time of day. The code is shown next. The variable *current_time* is set equal to the variables *hours*, *minutes*, *seconds*, and *AMorPM*. Two colons and a space are added to format the time properly. Notice the quotations marks that signify that these items are string data. For more information on concatenation and string variables, refer to Chapter 15.

```
current_time = hours+":"+minutes+":"+seconds+" "+AMorPM;
```

Displaying the time in the movie is the easy part. The Text tool is used to create a dynamic text field, which is given the variable name *current_time*. Remember, you associate a variable name with a dynamic text field by entering the desired variable name in the Properties Inspector Var field, as shown in the following illustration.

Use the Trace Action

When you're working with variables that are not displayed on screen, you have no idea whether the variables are holding the correct data or not. You can rectify this situation by tracing a variable. You do this by using the Trace action. You can also use the Trace action to display a message. The following steps show you how to trace a variable that is constantly changing. In this case, you'll be tracing the value of variables that are set equal to properties of a movie clip.

1. Create a circle and then press F8 to convert it to a symbol.
2. Choose the movie clip behavior, name the symbol, and then click OK to exit the Convert To Symbol dialog box.
3. Open the Properties Inspector and name the movie clip instance *Circle*.
4. Select the movie clip and then press F9 to open the Actions panel.
5. Type **onClipEvent** and an opening parenthesis.
6. After you type the parenthesis, Flash displays code hints for movie clip events.
7. Click enterFrame and then type a closing parenthesis.

16

8. Type an opening curly brace and then press ENTER (Windows) or RETURN (Mac) to create a new line.

9. Type **xProp=this._x;** and press ENTER (Windows) or RETURN (Mac) to create a new line.

10. Type **yProp=this._y;** and press ENTER (Windows) or RETURN (Mac) to create a new line.

11. In steps 9 and 10 you created two variables and set them equal to movie clip properties, in this case the _x and _y properties of the movie clip. Because you've specified the enterFrame clip event, the values of these variables constantly update.

12. In the left window of the Actions panel, click Global Functions | Miscellaneous Functions, and then double-click Trace to add it to your script.

13. After you add the action to your script, your cursor will flash between the parentheses. Flash prompts you with a code hint to enter a message. At this point, you can type a message as a quoted string to display it when the code executes. When you want to trace a variable, as you're doing in this example, type the name of the variable with no quotes. Type **this.xProp** between the parentheses. Type a semicolon after the closing parenthesis and then press ENTER (Windows) or RETURN (Mac) to create a new line.

14. Add the Trace action to your script again, only this time type **this.yProp** between the parentheses. Type a semicolon after the closing parenthesis and then press ENTER (Windows) or RETURN (Mac) to create a new line.

15. Type a closing curly brace. Your code should look like the following:

```
onClipEvent(enterFrame){
        xProp=this._x;
        yProp=this._y;
        trace (this.xProp);
        trace (this.yProp);
}
```

16. Close the Actions panel and then press SHIFT-F3 to open the Behaviors panel.

17. Click the Add Behavior button and then click Movie Clip | Start Dragging Movieclip. The Start Dragging Movieclip dialog box appears.

18. Click the circle icon and then click OK.

19. Click the default On Release event and choose Press from the drop-down list.

20. Click the Add Behavior button and then click Movie Clip | Stop Dragging Movieclip. This adds the Stop Dragging behavior to the movie clip. Accept the default Release event.

21. Choose Control | Test Movie. Flash publishes the movie and plays it in a different window.

As soon as Flash publishes the movie, the Output window appears and notes the values of the *xProp* and *yProp* variables. Click the movie clip and drag it around the stage. Notice that the values update continuously. Using the Trace action in this manner can help you debug a Flash game in which the values of variables are constantly updated when a movie clip moves. The only problem after the values initially appear is that you have no way of knowing which value is which. You can correct this problem by concatenating a quoted string message with the value of the variable. To concatenate a message with a variable value, you would modify steps 12 and 13 in the previous list of steps by typing the message you want to appear as a quoted string, typing the plus sign (+) and then typing the variable you want to trace, as shown in the following code. Notice the space after the word "is." This is so the message and variable value won't run together in the Output window.

```
onClipEvent(enterFrame){
     xProp=this._x
     yProp=this._y
     trace ("The x position is " + this.xProp)
     trace ("The y position is " + this.yProp)
}
```

Now when you test your movie and start dragging the movie clip, the Output window displays the message and the variable value, making it easier for you to keep track of what's happening as the variable values update, as shown in the following illustration. Note that the values in the illustration you see here are all the same, because the movie clip cannot be dragged at the same time the computer is capturing the screenshot for this illustration. When you follow these steps and drag the movie clip in Flash, the values update in real time.

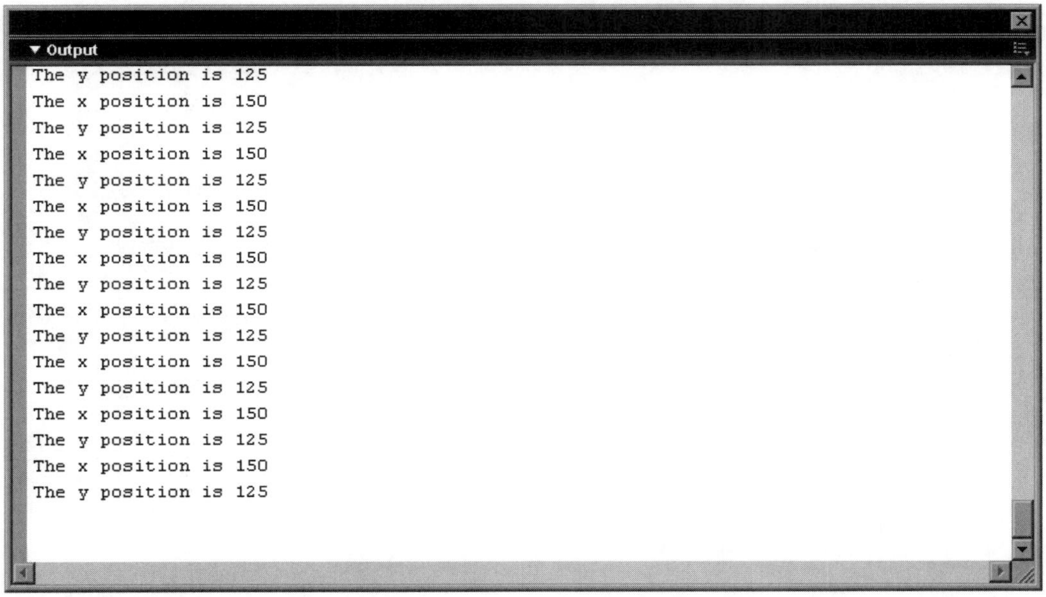

16

 *To clear all messages from the Output window, click the Options menu button in the upper-right corner of the window and choose Clear from the drop-down menu.*

Conclusion

In this chapter, you learned to use basic ActionScript to add interactivity to your movies. You learned how to use actions from the Timeline Control book for navigation, how to load external content using the loadMovie action, and how to modify a movie clip by changing its properties. You also learned how to assign actions to movie clips and choose the event that triggers the action. And you learned how to trace the values of variables using the Trace action. In the next chapter, you'll learn how to use some of the Flash components to add another level of interactivity to your movies.

Part V

Embellish and Publish Your Flash Movies

Chapter 17

Use Flash Components

How to...

- Work with Flash components
- Use the Components panel
- Use the Component Inspector
- Use the TextArea component
- Use the ScrollPane component
- Use the Window component
- Use the Flash Video Components (Professional Only)

Flash 8 Basic and Professional offer yet another way for you to add interactivity to your Flash movies: components. Components can be used to work wonders in the hands of developers, yet many designers shy away from them because of the ActionScript involved. And indeed, many components involve a great deal of ActionScript and are beyond the scope of this book. However, a few are useful and don't involve copious amounts of ActionScript. The components covered in this chapter will give you an introduction to the interactivity they can add to your Flash productions.

In this chapter, you'll learn how to use the Components panel and the Component Inspector. These panels act in tandem; you use one to add the desired component to a document and the other to modify the component's parameters. In the final sections of this chapter, you'll learn to use components to display text in a scrolling text box, display images in a scrolling pane, and display external content in a window.

Understand Components

Flash components are prebuilt objects that can be used to perform various common tasks, such as displaying a large amount of text in a small space and using the scrolling text box component to enable viewers to view all of the text with the aid of a scroll bar. If you're proficient at ActionScript, you can create objects such as scrolling text boxes from scratch. If, however, you're not proficient at creating UI (user interface) objects from scratch or have a limited knowledge of ActionScript, you can use a component to achieve a desired result.

Flash 8 Basic ships with one component group whereas Flash 8 Professional has five groups. In a nutshell, a component is a movie clip with adjustable parameters. If you're familiar with the Smart Clip from Flash 5, a component is the equivalent in Flash 8. You can download additional components from the Macromedia Exchange (http://www.macromedia.com/cfusion/exchange/index.cfm). At this URL you'll find a list of Macromedia applications. Follow the link to the Flash Exchange and you can download components created by Macromedia and other Flash authors.

You'll need the most current version of the Macromedia Extensions Manager to install downloaded components. You can download the Macromedia Extensions Manager at the following URL: http://www.macromedia.com/exchange/em_download/. After installing the Macromedia Extensions Manager, all you have to do is double-click a downloaded component or extension and the Extensions Manager will install the component for you.

Use the Components Panel

When you want to add a component to a document, you use the Components panel. Within the Components panel, you'll find the components that ship with the version of Flash 8 you own, as well as any components you've downloaded from Macromedia's web site. Components are organized into groups in the Components panel. If you own Flash Basic, you'll see only one group of components: User Interface. If you own Flash 8 Professional, you'll have five groups of components from which to choose: Data, FLV Playback–Player 8, FLV Playback Custom UI, Media–Player 6-7, and User Interface, as shown here. Note the plus sign (+) to the left of each group name, which indicates the group is collapsed. Click the plus sign (+) to expand the group and see all available components from within the group. The User Interface component group in Flash Basic is a subset of the Flash Professional User Interface component group.

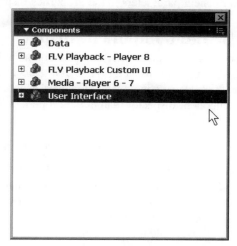

To add a component to a document, follow these steps:

1. Choose Window | Components. Alternatively, you can click the Components title bar if the panel is currently displayed in the workspace.

2. If you have more than one group of components in the panel, you may have to expand the group to select the desired component. If necessary, click the plus sign (+) icon to the left of the group's name to expand the group.

3. Select the desired component and drag it into the document. When you release the mouse button, the component appears on the stage.

After adding a component to a Flash document, you can adjust the component parameters in the Parameters tab of the Properties Inspector. The following illustration shows the Properties Inspector with the Parameters tab open, as configured for the TextArea component. Notice the icon with an arrow pointing at an angle. If you're proficient at ActionScript and the component uses ActionScript, click this icon to edit the code.

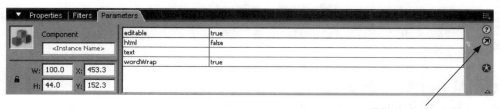

Edit ActionScript icon

17

If you're going to refer to the component with ActionScript from another object in your movie, such as a button or movie clip, you must give the component a unique name, as you would for a regular movie clip symbol instance. You can handle this task while adjusting the component parameters in the Properties Inspector.

Use the Component Inspector

You can set a component's parameters in the Properties Inspector, but you can also set them in the Component Inspector. The parameters available in the Component Inspector vary depending on the selected component. However, generally you will have more parameters available in the Component Inspector than in the Properties Inspector. To set a component's parameters using the Component Inspector, follow these steps:

1. Select an instance of a component in the document on which you are working.

2. Choose Window | Component Inspector.

3. Click the Parameters tab. Shown here is the Component Inspector as configured for the TextArea component. If you compare this with the Properties Inspector illustration in the previous section, you can see the additional parameters the Component Inspector has available for this component.

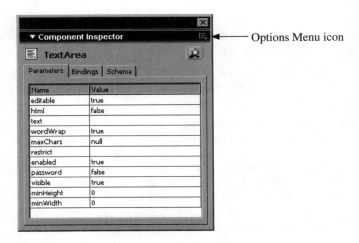

Options Menu icon

 *To receive help on a component, click the Component Inspector's Options Menu icon and choose Help On Component to display help for the component whose parameters you are editing.*

Learn About Live Preview

When you launch Flash 8, a feature called Live Preview is enabled by default. Live Preview lets you preview components in authoring mode as they will appear in the published movie.

For example, if you use the Button component in a document and change the label parameter, the new label will be displayed. If you use a component such as ScrollPane that loads external media, the media will not be displayed in Live Preview, but any other parameter changes you make will be displayed instantly. This illustration shows a Button component whose title was changed as displayed in Live Preview mode.

> My Button

If you prefer, you can disable Live Preview by choosing Enable Live Preview from the Control menu. When you first open the menu, Enable Live Preview has a check mark next to it indicating that Live Preview is enabled. When you select this option to disable Live Preview, the check mark disappears. This illustration shows what the Button component looks like when Live Preview is disabled. Notice that all you see is the component's bounding box; the label and graphic items are no longer displayed.

Use the TextArea Component

If you need to stuff a lot of text into a small space, the TextArea component is the solution to your dilemma. The TextArea component includes a scroll bar that viewers can use to scroll through the text. You control the width and height of the text window. To add a TextArea component to your document, follow these steps:

1. Choose Window | Components. The Components panel opens.

2. If necessary, click the plus sign (+) to the left of the User Interface component group to expand the group, select the TextArea component, and drag it to the desired position on the stage.

3. Select the Free Transform tool and size the component to suit your document. Remember, you can also use the Free Transform tool to move the component if necessary. Alternatively, you can open the Properties Inspector and enter values in the applicable fields to size and position the component.

4. Open the Properties Inspector and click the Parameters tab to reveal the parameters, as shown next.

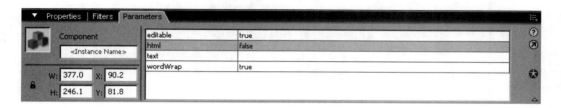

17

5. To modify a parameter, double-click the current parameter option to reveal a drop-down list. Click the desired parameter option to choose it. For the TextArea component, you can modify the following parameters:

- ■ **Editable** Choose True (the default) to make the text editable in a web browser; False will make the text uneditable.

- ■ **Html** Choose True if you want to be able to apply HTML 1.0 tags to format the text. For example, Title will boldface the text. The default value is False.

- ■ **Text** This field is blank when you click the Parameters tab. This is where you type in the text you want to display, along with any necessary HTML tags if you've enabled the HTML parameter.

- ■ **wordWrap** The default value is True, which wraps text to the next line when it reaches the end of the TextArea component as it is currently sized. Choose False to display the text as a single line with a horizontal scroll bar that viewers can use to scroll through the line of text.

6. If you have Live Preview enabled, the instance of the component on the stage will update after you finish editing a parameter.

7. Choose Control | Test Movie. Flash publishes the movie and plays it in another window. This illustration shows a TextArea component being tested.

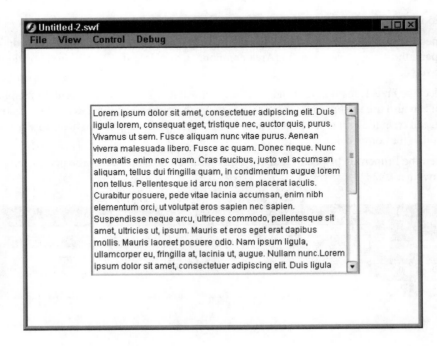

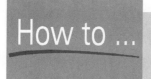

The Text field in the Parameters tab is very small. If you're going to stuff a lot of text into a TextArea component, you're better off creating your text in a word processing application, where you'll be able to see all of it at once. It will also be easier to add HTML tags and edit the text after creating it. As an added bonus, you can spell check the text. (Although Flash 8 has a spell checker, the spell checker will not detect misspelled words in a component.) After the text is the way you want it, select it all and then choose CTRL-C *(Windows) or* CMD-C *(Mac). In Flash, place your cursor inside the Text field in either the Parameters tab of the Properties Inspector or the Text field in the Component Inspector, and then choose* CTRL-V *(Windows) or* CMD-V *(Mac) to paste the text into the field.*

Use the ScrollPane Component

If you need to display a large photograph in a Flash document or several images stitched together as a single image, your best bet is the ScrollPane component. When you use this component, the image is displayed in a scrollable window. The image can be much larger than the window; users will view hidden areas of the image by scrolling with the scroll bars. You can also use this component to display an SWF movie in a scrollable window. You can control the size of the component,

How to ...   Create a Scrolling Slide Show

There are a lot of recipes for scrolling slide shows, but most of them rely heavily on ActionScript. With a little bit of editing in an image-editing application such as Macromedia Fireworks MX, you can combine several images, optimize them for your Flash document, and then display them in a ScrollPane component, which means, "Look, Ma, no ActionScript!"

The first step in creating your scrolling slide show is to assemble your images in your favorite image-editing application. Resample the images so they are all the same size. If you're working with landscape digital images, 320×240 pixels is a good size. If you own an application such as Macromedia Fireworks MX or newer that features batch processing, you can resample all of your images at once.

After resampling your images, create a new document that is large enough to contain a composite of all of the images. For example, if you have ten images that are 320×240 pixels each, create a new document that is 3,200×240 pixels in size. Arrange your images end to end in the new document, as shown next.

(Continued)

17

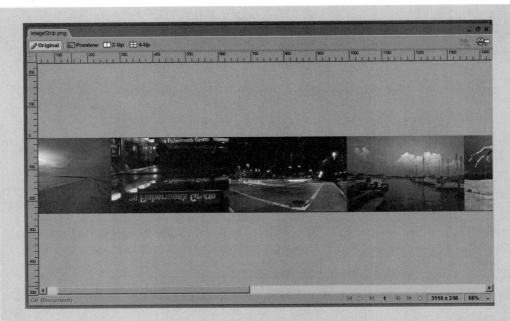

Your next step is to export the document as a JPEG file. Compress the composite image for web delivery. If you're using Macromedia Fireworks, you can display the original and the optimized image using the 2-Up preview, as shown next. Compress the images so that they still look crisp, while striving for a compact file size.

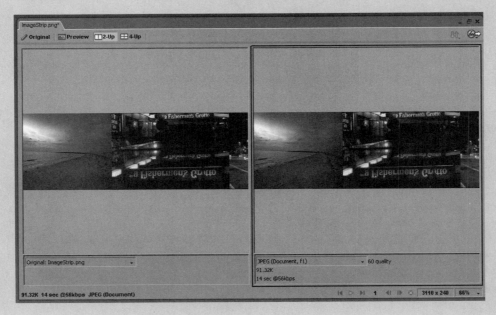

Launch Flash 8 and create a new document. Choose a background color and other embellishments that enhance your scrolling slide show. Add a ScrollPane component to the document as outlined in the previous section. Open the Properties Inspector and size the component to fit one image from your slide show, adding 16 pixels to the height to accommodate the horizontal scroll bar. If each image was 320×240 pixels before you assembled them into a single image, you'd size the ScrollPane component to 320×256 pixels. Click the Parameters tab and specify the parameters to suit your document as outlined in the previous section. For a scrolling slide show, set ScrollDrag to false and vScrollPolicy to off. The following illustration shows an example of a scrolling slide show.

the amount to scroll the content, and whether users can drag the content with a mouse click. To add the ScrollPane component to a document, follow these steps:

1. Choose Window | Components. The Components panel opens.

2. Select the ScrollPane component and drag it to the desired position on the stage.

3. If necessary, click the plus sign (+) to the left of the User Interface component group to expand the group, select the Free Transform tool, and size the component to suit your document. Remember that you can also use the Free Transform tool to move the component if necessary. Alternatively, you can open the Properties Inspector and enter values in the fields to size and position the component.

17

Add 15 pixels to the height of the component if a horizontal scroll bar will be visible, and 15 pixels to the width if a vertical scroll bar will be visible. This accommodates for the size of the scroll bar and ensures the content you are loading into the ScrollPane component will not be clipped.

4. Open the Properties Inspector and click the Parameters tab to reveal the parameters, as shown next. Alternatively, you can modify parameters by choosing Window | Component Inspector.

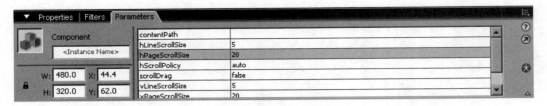

5. Modify the following parameters:

■ **contentPath**   Enter the path to the content you want to load in the component. The path can be a relative path to an SWF or JPEG file or a path to a file at another web site. If the file is in the same folder as the Flash movie, enter the filename plus extension, such as *myMovie.swf*.

■ **hLineScrollSize**   This parameter specifies how many units (pixels) the content scrolls when the user clicks a horizontal scroll bar arrow button. The default value is 5.

■ **hPageScrollSize**   This specifies how many units (pixels) the content scrolls when the user clicks the horizontal scroll track. The default value is 20.

■ **hScrollPolicy**   This option specifies whether or not the horizontal scroll bar is displayed. The default value, Auto, displays the bar when the horizontal content exceeds the boundary of the component instance as currently sized. Your alternative choices are On and Off.

■ **scrollDrag**   This specifies whether users can click and drag to move the content or not. The default value of False disables scroll dragging; True enables it.

■ **vLineScrollSize**   This parameter specifies how many units (pixels) the content scrolls when the user clicks a vertical scroll bar arrow button. The default value is 5.

■ **vPageScrollSize**   This specifies how many units (pixels) the content scrolls when the user clicks the vertical scroll track. The default value is 20.

■ **vScrollPolicy**   This option specifies whether or not the vertical scroll bar is displayed. The default value, Auto, displays the bar when the vertical content exceeds the boundary of the component instance as currently sized. Your alternative choices are On and Off.

6. If you have Live Preview enabled, the component will update after you set each parameter; however, you will not be able to preview the content until you test the movie.

7. Choose Control | Test Movie. Flash publishes the movie and displays it in another window. Test the component to make sure the scroll bars function as desired and that the content loads and displays properly. If the content does not load, make sure you have entered the correct filename and path. Remember, you must include the filename extension.

Use the Window Component

If you need to display an SWF movie or a JPEG image in a Flash document, you can use the Load External Movieclip behavior to load the content into a target movie clip. Or you can take the path of least resistance and put the Window component through its paces. When you use the Window component, you can size the window to suit your media, display a title, and include a Close button. To add the Window component to a document, follow these steps:

1. Choose Window | Components. The Components panel opens.

2. Select the Window component and drag it to the desired position on the stage.

3. Open the Properties Inspector and enter values in the W and H fields to size the component for the media you will load into the window. Be sure to add 25 pixels to the H value to accommodate the height of the title bar.

4. Click the Parameters tab to reveal the parameters. The only available parameter for this component in the Properties Inspector is Title. This parameter determines the text that is displayed in the component's title bar. Enter the desired title for the component.

5. Choose Window | Component Inspector, as shown next, to reveal additional parameters for the component.

17

6. Modify the following parameters:

- ■ **closeButton**   This specifies whether a Close button is displayed on the right side of the title bar. Double-click the default False option and click True to display a Close button on the title bar.

- ■ **contentPath**   Enter the path to the content you want to load in the component. The path can be a relative path to an SWF or JPEG file or a path to a file at another web site.

- ■ **title**   Type the title you want displayed in the component title bar.

7. If you have Live Preview enabled, you'll be able to see the component update on the stage after you specify a parameter. You will not, however, be able to view the content that will load into the component.

8. Choose Control | Test Movie. Flash publishes the movie and displays it in another window. While you are testing the movie, make sure that the window is sized properly so that none of the content is clipped. The following illustration shows a Window component into which a JPEG image has been loaded.

Use the FLV Playback–Player 8 Component

If you're certain that your audience will have Flash Player 8 as the plug-in for Flash content, this component is an excellent way to display Flash video. When setting up the component, you can choose from a wide variety of skins and determine which controls will be available for your users.

The most basic controller enables your viewers to pause the video and mute the sound, whereas the all-singing-and-dancing version of the component enables viewers to pause, play, fast forward, or rewind the video, in addition to being able to control the volume of the video. To use the FLV Playback–Player 8 component, follow these steps:

1. Use the Flash 8 Video encoder to encode a video file into the .flv format.

2. Upload the video to your host server.

3. Create a new Flash document that is the same size as your video.

4. Choose Window | Components to open the Components panel.

5. Click the plus sign (+) to the left of FLV Playback–Flash Player 8, and then drag the FLV Playback component into the document, aligning the component to the upper-left corner of the document.

6. Open the Properties Inspector and click the Parameters tab to reveal the component's parameters, as shown next.

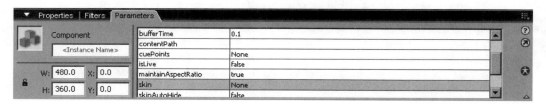

7. Accept the first and second parameters, which cause the video to auto-play and rewind when finished playing. Alternatively, click the default parameter (True), click the down arrow to the right of the parameter, and choose False from the drop-down menu.

Flash 8 Professional — Use Flash Video Components

Flash Professional ships with three component groups that enable you to provide your viewers with controls with which they can view video. These components are ideal for the Flash video experience in that they enable you to create a Flash movie with a controller that links to a Flash .flv file that is streamed into the Flash movie from a web server. The type of controller you choose depends on your audience and how much control you want to supply them. You can choose from components that play .flv files using the Flash 8 Player, or using the Flash 6 or 7 Player.

17

8. Click the default autoSize parameter (False), click the down arrow to the right of the parameter, and choose True from the drop-down menu. This causes the parameter to resize to the dimensions of the .flv video.

9. Click the contentPath parameter and then click the magnifying glass icon to reveal the Content Path dialog box.

10. Enter the path to the .flv file you just uploaded to your server, as shown next. Accept the default parameters to match source FLV dimensions and to download the FLV. Note that you must be connected to the Internet for Flash to access the .flv video.

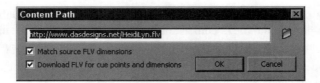

11. Click OK. Flash gets the information from your server and resizes the component to the source media.

By default, this component does not use a skin. If all you need is an envelope with which to play back your FLV file within a Flash document, you can publish the file and upload the SWF file to your server. If, however, you want to supply controls for your viewers, follow the upcoming steps.

12. Click the skin parameter and then click the magnifying glass icon to reveal the Select Skin dialog box shown next.

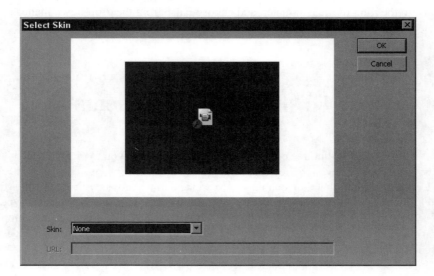

13. Click the Skin down arrow and choose the desired option from the drop-down list. After you choose a skin, the image in the dialog box updates to reveal what the controller looks like and what controls are supplied with the controller. There are two versions of each controller: one that displays the controller over the video and another that displays the controller externally.

14. Click OK to apply the selected skin.

15. Choose Control | Test Movie to test the movie in another window. The following illustration shows the component with an external controller.

16. After testing your movie, publish the movie. When you publish a movie with a component that uses a skin, Flash creates an SWF file for the movie, an SWF file for the skin, and an HTML document into which the SWF file is embedded as an object. Upload these files to your server. Make sure they're all in the same folder on your server.

17. If you don't have the luxury of working with this component while you have a live Internet connection, save the file immediately after creating it. Make sure your .flv video resides in the same folder as the FLA file. Instead of typing the path to the FLV file on your server in step 10, click the folder icon and select the FLV file that will be associated with the component. This enables you to test the movie on your local machine. After you publish the movie, upload the movie SWF file, the skin SWF file, the HTML document into which the SWF file is embedded, and the .flv video file to your server. Make sure these files are all in the same folder.

17

Use the Media–Player 6-7 Media Playback Component

If your audience does not have the Flash 8 Player installed on their computers, you should use the Media–Player 6-7 component. This component enables streaming playback of an .flv video file. Users can control the experience by holding their cursors over the playback bar to reveal a controller that enables them to pause, play, or rewind the video, in addition to being able to control the volume of the clip. If you are using this component to play video with the Flash 6 Player, the .flv video must reside on a Flash Communications server. To use the Media–Player 6-7 Playback component, follow these steps:

1. Use the Flash 8 Video encoder to encode a Flash.flv video.

2. Upload the video to your host server.

3. Create a new Flash document that is the same size as your video.

4. Choose Window | Components to open the Components panel.

5. Click the plus sign (+) to the left of FLV Playback–Flash Player 8 and then drag the FLV Playback component into the document, aligning the component to the upper-left corner of the document.

6. Open the Properties Inspector and size the component to that of your video.

7. Click the Parameters tab to reveal the component's parameters. Note that this component has no editable parameters in the Properties Inspector.

8. Click the Launch Component Inspector button to reveal the component's parameters in the Component Inspector, as shown next.

9. Enter the URL to the .flv video file you uploaded to your server.

10. Click the Use Preferred Media Size check box. This option sizes the video to the component so that the video appears within the component window.

11. Close the Component Inspector.

12. Choose Control | Test Movie. The movie is published and plays in another window, as shown here.

Where to Go from Here

As mentioned at the start of the chapter, a detailed dissertation of each and every component is beyond the scope of this book. If after reading the previous sections you are intrigued by the possible uses for components, you can expand on the knowledge you've gained in this chapter and find other uses for the components covered here. After you've mastered these components, you can delve into the other components in the Components panel. Experimentation and practice are the keys to mastering every facet of an application. If you get stumped with some of the components, log onto the Internet and visit the Macromedia Developer Center (www.macromedia .com/devnet/) and read what other designers and developers are doing with components. Note that you can also extend Flash 8 by clicking the Extend Flash link in the Flash 8 startup menu, if you still have it enabled.

17

Conclusion

In this chapter, you received an introduction to components and how to use them in your Flash movies. You learned how to use the Components panel to add components to your movies. You also learned how to use the Component Inspector and the Parameters tab of the Properties Inspector to modify component parameters to suit your movies. In addition, you learned how to use three of the most popular components. In the next chapter, you'll learn how to optimize and publish your Flash productions.

Chapter 18

Test and Publish Your Flash Movies

How to...

- Optimize your Flash production
- Test your production
- Use the Bandwidth Profiler
- Debug a movie
- Publish your movie
- Create a Flash projector

After you have created a compelling Flash production with animated graphics, navigation menus, and all the other Flash bells and whistles, it's time to share your production with the world. You do so by publishing the movie and uploading it to your or your client's web site. But before you rush headlong into publishing the movie, you have a few more steps to take.

First, you should optimize your movie to make sure it's the smallest file size possible. Then you should test the movie to make sure everything's performing as you'd envisioned. If you've got ActionScript in your movie, you should also debug the movie. When you are assured that everything's working perfectly, you can publish the document and upload it to the web site's server.

In this chapter, you'll learn how to perform the final tasks necessary prior to publishing and uploading a movie to a web site. You'll learn how to preview your movie in Flash and in a web browser, and how to analyze your movie frame by frame using the Bandwidth Profiler. Another important task you'll learn about is how to debug your movie. In the latter part of the chapter, you'll learn how to export and publish your movie in a variety of formats. You'll also learn how to create a standalone executable file of your movie.

Optimize Your Movie

When you publish a movie, Flash combines all of its elements into a single SWF movie. When the HTML document in which the SWF movie is embedded is accessed from a user's web browser, the SWF movie streams into the user's browser and begins to play as soon as enough data has downloaded to play the first frame of the movie. As the author of the Flash movie, you should strive to keep your content as compact as possible. Much of this is done beforehand by optimizing images in an image-editing application or by specifying export settings from within Flash. However, there are some other things you can do to further optimize your movie before you publish it. Consider the following opportunities before you publish your production:

- *Whenever possible, group graphic objects or symbols.* Grouped items are treated as a single item by the Flash Player and therefore will download more efficiently.

- *Whenever possible, use tweening instead of frame-by-frame animations.* Tweened animations will result in smaller file sizes. If you have movie clips in your production that are frame-by-frame animations, convert them to tweened animations if possible.

■ *Convert all graphics to symbols when possible.* When you create instances of symbols, the Flash Player refers to the document Library to create the symbol, resulting in a smaller file size for the published movie. You may not be able to do this during the final stages of a project, but you should keep this in mind while creating a Flash project.

■ *Optimize all bitmap graphics.* You can optimize each bitmap by selecting it in the document Library and then choosing Properties from the context menu to open the Properties dialog box. As a rule, you can apply more compression to small bitmaps that are displayed for a short period of time as they don't have as much detail as large bitmaps. You can also globally set image quality for all bitmaps in the Publish Settings dialog box.

■ *Do not embed fonts unless it's absolutely necessary.* When you embed fonts, you increase the file size of the document. If you stick with system fonts (serif or sans), the movie will display properly on most systems and with most popular browsers. If you must use fancy fonts for ornamental elements such as headers, convert the characters to vector graphics by choosing Modify | Break Apart. (Remember that you need to apply this command twice to text objects to convert characters to vector graphics.)

■ *Limit your use of components, since they can bloat the file size.*

■ *Whenever possible, do not exceed the default movie frame rate of 12 fps.* A higher frame rate results in smoother playback but increases the file size. The only exception is when you're including full-motion video in a movie. In this case, do not exceed a frame rate of 15 fps for streaming Internet content. If you're creating a Flash movie with video content that will be played from a CD, you can specify a frame rate of 30 fps.

■ *When creating graphic symbols for your production, shy away from multicolored gradients if at all possible.* While they're lovely to look at, they increase the file size of the published movie.

■ *Delete any unused objects from the document Library.* You can do this by opening the document Library and then choosing Select Unused Items from the Library Options menu. Flash highlights all unused Library items, which you can now delete by dragging them to the trash can icon or by pressing DELETE.

Test Your Movie

As you create your Flash production, you should keep several factors in mind: the intended viewing audience's Internet connection speed, the audience's browser of choice, the computer equipment likely to be used, the desktop size, and so on. Your best efforts will go to waste if the movie exceeds the viewing audience's available bandwidth.

As you create your Flash productions, you should always have the final phase of the project in mind. In other words: test, test, and then test again. You should test your production in authoring mode any time you make a major change. For example, when you write code for a button to play a frame of a movie clip, make sure that the button functions perfectly before you go on to the next phase. Testing during the creation process can save you hours of headaches during the final phases of your production. If you have a complex Flash production and one item isn't functioning perfectly, the problem could lie almost anywhere in the movie.

You should also get in the habit of naming everything in your productions. Give each symbol, frame, and scene a unique name. If your movie includes ActionScript, add comments when applicable and be sure to give meaningful names to symbols. It's also good practice to label keyframes and give meaningful names to scenes in your production. Naming objects, keyframes, scenes, and adding comments to ActionScript make it easy for you to debug your productions.

When you create a Flash production, your first line of defense for catching any potential problems is the Test Movie command. Invoking this command publishes your production as an SWF file and opens it in another window. When you preview a movie in this manner, it plays using the same Flash Player plug-in used to view Flash movies in a browser; however, when you use the Test Movie command, you have more options in the form of menu commands that appear after you invoke the command. You can examine your movie in detail to see the amount of data present on each frame of the movie, simulate how the movie will download when streaming into a browser at different connection speeds, and so on. These features will be covered in detail in upcoming sections.

Examine Movies with the Bandwidth Profiler

When you initially preview a movie using the Test Movie command, the movie plays in another window almost instantaneously. Of course, this is not what happens when your audience views the movie over the Internet. The movie data streams into the viewer's browser. When you author a Flash movie, you must be cognizant of the amount of data you're feeding into the bandwidth pipeline; otherwise, you run the risk of creating a movie that will halt while additional data downloads. You can safeguard against this by previewing your movie with the Bandwidth Profiler, shown in Figure 18-1.

To access the Bandwidth Profiler shown in Figure 18-1, follow these steps:

1. Choose Control | Test Movie. Flash publishes the movie and plays it in another window.

2. Choose View | Bandwidth Profiler to display the Bandwidth Profiler.

When you preview your movie using the Bandwidth Profiler, two windows appear above the window in which the movie is playing. The left window displays information about your movie. In the Movie section, you'll find the following information about your movie: dimensions, frame rate, file size, duration in frames and seconds, and preload time. In the Settings section, you can see the currently selected bandwidth setting. In the State section you'll see the frame currently being played, plus the amount of data contained in that frame.

In the right window, your movie is displayed as a graph. The manner in which the data is presented depends on the viewing mode you choose. When you launch the Bandwidth Profiler,

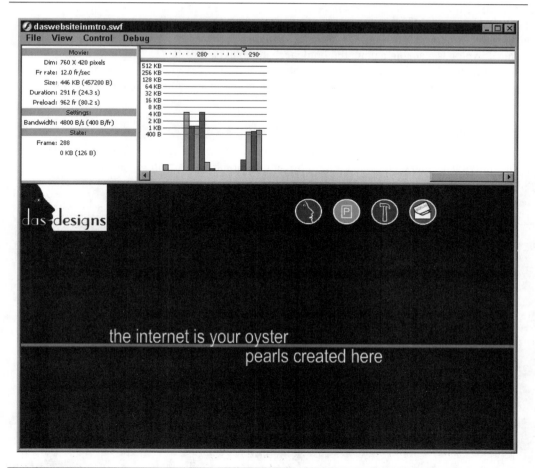

FIGURE 18-1 You can alleviate bandwidth problems when previewing your movie.

it opens in the mode most recently used. In Figure 18-1, the data is shown as a frame-by-frame graph. You also have the option of viewing the Bandwidth Profiler as a Streaming Graph. Both modes will be discussed in upcoming sections.

View the Bandwidth Profiler as a Frame-by-frame Graph

When you access the Bandwidth Profiler you can choose to view the data as a frame-by-frame graph by choosing View | Frame By Frame Graph. When you view the Bandwidth Profiler as a frame-by-frame graph, a vertical bar designates the amount of data for each frame, as shown previously in Figure 18-1. The amount of frame data is displayed as alternating vertical bars of light and dark gray. You can compare the height of the bar to the scale on the left side of the

18

graph to determine how much data will be downloaded when the Flash Player encounters the frame. At the bottom of the graph you'll see a red line. This designates the download setting you chose. If any frame's bar appears above the red line, the movie will halt at that frame until the data downloads, causing a potential bottleneck and playback issue. To gain information about an individual frame, click it. The information will be displayed in the State section of the left window. You'll learn more about download settings in the upcoming "Choose a Download Setting" section of this chapter.

View the Bandwidth Profiler as a Streaming Graph

To view the Bandwidth Profiler as a streaming graph, as shown in Figure 18-2, test the movie as outlined previously, and then choose View | Streaming Graph. In a streaming graph, frames that contain a small amount of data appear as several bars stacked on top of one another in a single

FIGURE 18-2   You can alleviate bandwidth bottlenecks by viewing the Bandwidth Profiler as a streaming graph.

time unit. Frames that contain a lot of data span several time units. Frame data is displayed as alternating bars of light and dark gray. To find out information about an individual block of data, click a bar and the amount of data is displayed in the State section of the left window. If several bars are stacked in a single time unit, click a bar to display the frame in the preview window. All of the information about the frame is displayed in the State section of the left window.

Choose a Download Setting

If you know the available bandwidth with which your intended audience accesses the Internet, you can choose this setting when analyzing your movies. When you choose a setting that matches your intended audience's download speed, the value next to the red line changes to indicate the selected bandwidth setting. This also changes the height of each bar in the graph. If you choose a higher download setting, each bar will be shorter, which signifies that the frames will load more quickly. If you choose a lower download setting, each bar will become higher, indicating that the data will take longer to load. To choose a download setting, select View | Download Settings and then choose one of the settings from the drop-down menu shown here.

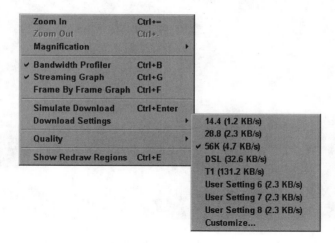

Simulate a Download

When you choose a specific download setting, you can experience the movie as your intended audience will by simulating a download. When you simulate a download, Flash streams the movie data according to the download setting you specify. To simulate a download, choose View | Simulate Download. As soon as you invoke this command, Flash starts streaming the movie according to the specified download setting. As the data streams, a green bar appears above the graph in the Bandwidth Profiler to show how many frames of data have loaded. A downward-pointing arrow indicates the frame currently being played. The arrow is stationary until enough data has downloaded to play the first frame. As you preview the download, pay careful attention

18

to the position of the arrow in relation to the green progress bar. If the arrow catches up to the green bar and then stops, the movie stops playing until enough additional data has downloaded to play the next frame. If this happens, you need to build a preloader, a device that displays text indicating that the data is loading. When you create a preloader, you create ActionScript that plays the preloader until enough data has downloaded to play the movie without stopping.

Build a Preloader

When you add a preloader to your Flash movie, you display a message to your audience letting them know that the main attraction is downloading and to "please wait." Preloaders run the gamut from simple text messages to intricate but quick-loading animations to keep your audience amused. This illustration shows a sophisticated preloader that features a progress bar and animated stars that follow the viewer's cursor.

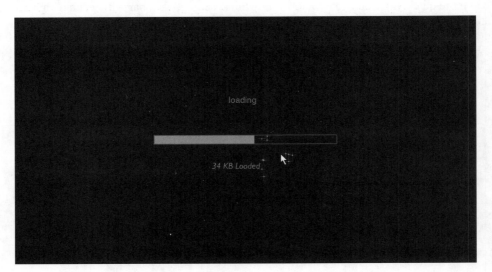

As you saw in the previous section, if your movie is not loading fast enough, your viewing audience will have to deal with a movie that halts on a frame. If the movie stalls on a frame and other parts of the movie, such as the soundtrack, have already loaded, the movie and soundtrack will be out of sync when enough data downloads for the movie to continue to the ensuing frames. You can solve these problems by adding a preloader to your movie as follows:

1. Test the movie.

2. Choose View | Download Settings and then choose the setting that reflects the speed with which your intended audience will access the Internet.

3. Choose View | Simulate Download.

4. As the movie downloads, pay careful attention to the position of the arrow that indicates the current frame being played.

5. Note the frame on which the arrow stops. Wait until the movie starts playing again. If the movie plays to the end without stopping, you've located the bandwidth bottleneck. If the movie stops on future frames, note the number of the last frame on which the movie stops. This is the amount of data that must be downloaded before the movie will play without halting. You're now ready to build your preloader.

6. Create a new scene and name it Preloader. Make sure the Preloader scene appears before scene 1 in the Scene panel. Here you will build a simple preloader that displays the message "Loading".

7. Create a new layer.

8. Type the word **Loading**. Make sure you use the serif or sans font. This ensures that your preloader will load almost instantaneously.

9. Create keyframes on frame 9 and frame 10.

10. Select keyframe 9 and then press F9 to open the Actions panel.

11. Enter the following code in the Script pane:

```
if( framesloaded>27){
        gotoAndPlay("1", 1);
}
```

12. The preceding code tells the Flash Player to go to scene 1 and play the first frame when 27 frames have loaded. Replace the number 27 with the number of the frame you determined is the bandwidth bottleneck plus 10 to cover the number of frames in your preloader. For example, if the movie halted on frame 56 during the simulated download, you'd tell the Flash Player to go to and play scene 1, frame 1, when 66 frames have downloaded.

13. Select keyframe 10 and open the Actions panel.

14. Enter the following code in the Script pane:

```
gotoAndPlay (1);
```

15. Choose Control | Test Movie and then View | Simulate Download. When the movie begins to play, you'll see your preloader. When the green progress bar in the Bandwidth Profiler reaches the frame specified in your ActionScript, the movie will begin playing, and if you've discovered the culprit frame causing the bandwidth bottleneck, the movie will play to conclusion without halting along the way.

Test the Movie in a Browser

When you test a movie using the Test Movie command, you can uncover any potential flaws in your production. However, you do not simulate your intended audience's experience. You can preview the movie in your system's default browser by choosing Preview | HTML. Alternatively, you can press F12.

18

Preview Your Movie in Different File Formats

Flash gives you tremendous flexibility when you are creating a production, and this flexibility continues when it comes time to publish the movie. In addition to publishing your production as a Flash SWF movie, you can also publish the movie as a QuickTime movie; export a single frame as a GIF, JPEG, or PNG image; and more.

The Publish Settings dialog box, which will be discussed in detail later in this chapter, allows you to select up to eight different file formats in which to publish your production. If you check all eight check boxes, viewers will be able to download your movie into any of those formats. The File | Preview menu reflects the choices you have made in the Publish Settings dialog box. To preview a movie in one of the formats you enabled, choose File | Preview and select the desired file format from the Preview list. After choosing a file format, the movie (or frame if you've selected a format that exports a single frame) is displayed in the default application your operating system associates with the export file type. For example, if you preview a movie you're exporting as a QuickTime file, the QuickTime Player launches and plays your movie.

Debug a Movie

Whether you're a programmer, web developer, or designer, you need to ensure that your movie plays properly and that the ActionScript executes flawlessly. If you can analyze what happens within your movie as it is playing, you stand a better chance of getting rid of the bugs in your movie before you upload the file to a web site or another destination. Fortunately, Flash supplies a tool with which you can debug your movies: the Debugger.

To debug a movie, choose Control | Debug Movie from the menu. This publishes the movie in another window and displays the Debugger window, as shown in Figure 18-3. Click the Continue button in the Debugger to begin playing and debugging your movie.

The status bar at the top of the Debugger window tells you the location of the movie you are debugging. If the location is remote, the status bar will indicate the URL. The window below the status bar displays all of the movie clips in your movie.

Notice the tabs just below the movie clip list in the Debugger window. These tabs are populated with values after you click the Continue button, which begins playing the movie. These allow you to further analyze individual elements in your movie to detect any glitches:

- **Properties** This tab allows you to view the properties and the values of properties of a selected movie clip and change them as the movie runs. To do this, click a movie clip in the top display list and, in the Properties tab, the values update. Double-click any of the active values in this tab, and then enter a different value to preview the effect it will have on your movie.

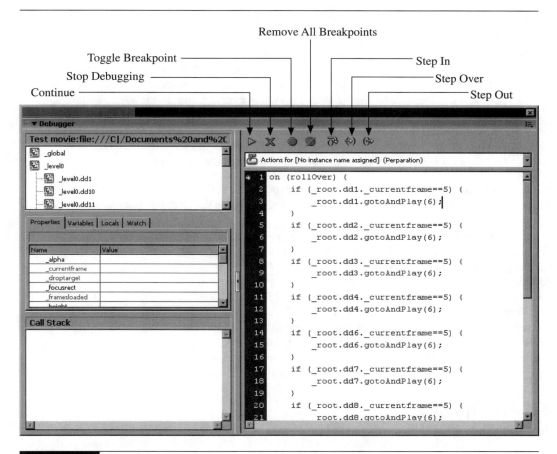

FIGURE 18-3   You debug a movie to test your ActionScript.

■ **Variables**   This tab allows you to view the variables and the values of variables on
a selected movie clip. Click the Variables tab to view variables associated with the
currently selected item from the display list. The variables update as the movie plays.
To see the effect a different value will have, double-click a variable value in this tab and
then enter a new value.

> TIP   *If the properties and variables are not visible, click the divider bar above Call Stack and
> drag down to reveal them.*

18

- **Locals** This tab displays the local variables used in the movie and the values of those variables.

- **Watch** This tab allows you to monitor certain variables closely. You can add variables to this list by selecting them in the Variables tab and then choosing Add Watch from the Debugger Options menu. Alternatively, you can select the variable, right-click (Windows) or CTRL-click (Mac), and choose Watch from the context menu. In the Variables tab, a blue dot appears to the left of a watched variable. To remove a variable from the Watch list, select the variable in the Watch list and choose Remove Watch from the Debugger Options menu. Alternatively, you can select the variable in the Watch list, right-click (Windows) or CTRL-click (Mac), and choose Remove from the context menu.

The Debugger window is useful from two perspectives. You can track and watch various pieces of your movie while previewing it, and you can debug a movie while it streams from a server.

To debug a Flash Player (SWF) file remotely, you must have published the file with the appropriate setting beforehand. To publish a remotely debuggable SWF file, select the Debugging Permitted check box on the Flash tab in the Publish Settings dialog box under Options. Then set a password in the box for this purpose. You will need to enter this password to access the SWF file from a remote computer to debug the file.

When viewing a Flash movie from a remote location, you can use the standalone Flash Player to debug, provided the movie has been published with the Debugging Permitted option selected, which causes an SWD file to be created. This file holds all the debugging information and must reside in the same folder as the SWF file if the remote debug is to work. For more information about debugging remotely, refer to your Flash 8 reference manual.

Set Breakpoints

In Figure 18-3, you will notice that there is a button in the Debugger window called Toggle Breakpoint. Breakpoints were introduced in Flash MX, and they allow you to set breaks in the script so that when you test the movie in the Debugger window the movie will stop where you inserted a breakpoint. Why would you want it to stop playing at a certain point? If your script contains complex variables, conditional statements, property changes, or math functions, you can pause the movie when the script that contains the element you want to check runs to make sure the script is performing as envisioned. Otherwise, the movie will continue playing and you have no idea whether the code is functioning as desired.

Breakpoints are set in the Actions panel and controlled in the Debugger. Although you can set a breakpoint in the Debugger, the logical course of action is to set the breakpoint in the Actions panel. To set a breakpoint on a line of code in the Actions panel, do the following:

1. If line numbers are not currently displayed in the Script pane, choose Line Numbers from the Actions panel Options menu.

2. Click a line of code on which you want to insert a breakpoint.

3. Click the Debug Options icon (which looks like a stethoscope) in the Actions panel to reveal a pop-up menu.

4. Select Set Breakpoints from the pop-up menu. Note that you can also remove breakpoints from this pop-up menu. To remove a breakpoint, select a breakpoint line and then select Remove Breakpoints from the pop-up menu.

You can also set a breakpoint by clicking to the left of a code line number.

5. In the Actions panel, a red stop icon appears next to each line of code where you've set a breakpoint, as shown next.

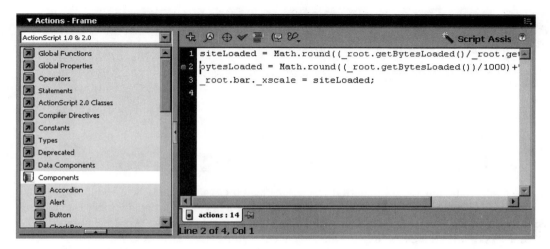

6. When you debug the movie by choosing Control | Debug, the Debugger appears immediately after Flash publishes the movie in another window. In the right window of the Debugger, an alert appears that reads, "The Flash Player is paused so that breakpoints may be adjusted. Click Continue to start the movie."

7. Click the Continue button to begin playing and debugging the movie.

8. As you play the movie in the Debugger window, the movie stops at the breakpoints you specified in the Actions panel. When you reach a breakpoint, you can use the various windows of the Debugger to analyze properties, variable values, and so on. The following illustration shows a movie halted at a breakpoint. However, no properties are displayed as a variable has not yet been selected.

18

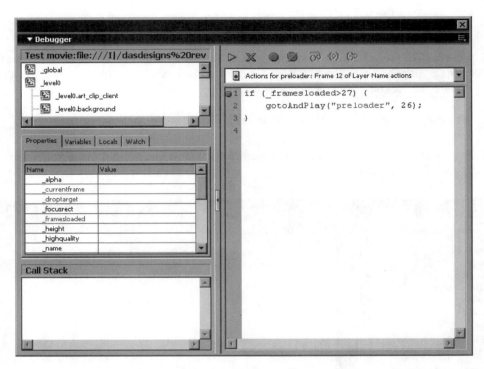

To continue to play the script until it reaches the next breakpoint, click the Continue button. To add another breakpoint in the Debugger window, select a line of code and click the Toggle Breakpoint button. You can remove all breakpoints by clicking the Remove All Breakpoints button. To skip over a breakpoint, click the Step Over button.

Note that when you add breakpoints in the Debugger they are active only for the current debugging section. This is also true when you remove breakpoints. When you exit test movie mode and return to editing your movie, the breakpoints are restored to what you set in the Actions panel. The only way to completely remove a breakpoint is to select it in the Actions panel, click the Debugger Options icon, and then choose Remove Breakpoint from the pop-up menu. To remove all breakpoints from a movie, click the Debugger Options icon and then choose Remove All Breakpoints from the pop-up menu.

As you click the Continue button to navigate through breakpoints in the Debugger, the current breakpoint icon (red stop sign) will contain a yellow arrow to indicate that it is the current breakpoint.

Use the Features in the Output Window

When you learned to use the Trace action in Chapter 16, you saw the Output window in action. The Output window serves many other uses. When your ActionScript code contains an error, the Output window alerts you and even tells you which frame the ActionScript resides on and which line of code is in error. It also prompts you as to the type of error. The Output window is a tremendous ally, especially when you're learning ActionScript. Armed with the information from the Output window, you can exit testing mode and view the errant line of code in the Actions panel.

List Objects and Variables

There are additional ways to use the Output window to gather data on a movie in movie testing mode. When a movie is playing, you can choose Debug | List Objects or Debug | List Variables. When you choose the List Objects command, the Output window appears displaying a list of the objects in your movie, with their respective levels and paths. This gives you the opportunity to make sure that the targets are addressed properly. When you choose the List Variables command, all of the variables in your movie are listed in the Output window, as shown next. The Output window displays the value of the variable at the time you invoked the List Variables command but does not update in real time. However, the list is useful in that it will give you the value of all of the variables at a given point in time.

```
▼ Output

Variable _level0.instance50.vol = 75
Movie Clip: Target="_level0.instance50.pan_control"
Variable _level0.instance50.pan_control.value = 50
Movie Clip: Target="_level0.instance50.pan_control.graph"
Button: Target="_level0.instance50.pan_control.graph.instance51"
Variable _level0.instance50.pan_control.graph.instance51.scale9Grid = [getter/setter]
undefined
Variable _level0.instance50.pan_control.graph.instance51.filters = [getter/setter] [
object #14, class 'Array'] []
Variable _level0.instance50.pan_control.graph.instance51.cacheAsBitmap = [getter/setter
] false
Variable _level0.instance50.pan_control.graph.instance51.blendMode = [getter/setter]
"normal"
Variable _level0.instance50.pan_control.graph.instance51.tabIndex = [getter/setter]
undefined
Movie Clip: Target="_level0.instance50.volume_control"
Variable _level0.instance50.volume_control.value = 75
Movie Clip: Target="_level0.instance50.volume_control.graph"
Button: Target="_level0.instance50.volume_control.graph.instance52"
```

Export Your Flash Movie

After you've previewed the movie and ensured that it plays as envisioned, you are then ready to prepare the movie for its final destination. You do this by either exporting the movie or publishing it. Although exporting a movie is similar in nature to publishing a movie, it's important to understand the difference between the two. When you choose File | Export | Image, or File | Export | Movie, you have different options depending on the format you choose. You are limited to exporting the document in the format selected. To export the document in additional formats, you must run the command again. When you publish a movie, you have more options for each format. In addition, if you publish the document as a Flash movie, you can embed the movie within an HTML document. You can also simultaneously publish the movie in multiple formats with the click of a button, or a single menu command.

Exporting is fine for distributing an SWF movie or updating an SWF file embedded in an HTML page. Publishing, however, offers more options, especially when you're creating content for the Web or a multimedia production. When you publish a movie you use the Publish Settings dialog box, which is discussed in a later section, for exporting your files in multiple formats with an optional HTML file. You can also specify settings for each selected file format in this dialog box. The Export Movie dialog box and the Publish Settings dialog box each offers some options that are not offered in the other dialog box, so be sure to choose the method that is right for your movie.

There are two different ways you can export your movie: you can export single-frame images of your movie or you can export the entire movie and every frame associated with it.

Export a Single Frame

You would export a single frame if there's a static piece of art, such as a logo, that you want to use in another movie or a printed piece. To export a single frame from a multiframe movie, use the playhead to navigate to the frame you want to export and follow these steps:

1. Choose File | Export Image to open the Export Image dialog box.

2. Give the file a name and choose from one of the available file formats: .swf, .emf, .wmf (Windows only), .eps 3.0, .ai 7.0 and under, .dxf, .bmp, .jpg, .gif, or .png.

3. Navigate to the folder in which you want to save the file, and then click Save.

Export Your Movie

To export a movie, select File | Export Movie. This command is useful if you need to export a series of sequential frames for use in another program. For example, you could save a frame sequence in the PNG format and open each frame individually in FreeHand, Fireworks, or any other program that supports sequential files in the PNG format. Or you could export frames in the AI format and open each file as a frame sequence in Adobe Illustrator. The many different ways you can export sequential frames into other programs with the Export Movie command can be divided into three basic categories:

- The following file formats are available for saving your movie frames in sequential still frames: .wmf, .eps, .ai, .dxf, .bmp, .jpg, .gif, and .png.

- The following file formats export a movie in a movie format: .swf, .avi, .mov, and .gif (Animated GIF).

- The following file formats can be used to export sounds: .wav or .aif (Mac only).

Although there are many formats to choose from, most often you will be exporting your movie as an SWF file. During this conversion from FLA to SWF format, Flash will eliminate extra information, sounds, timelines, and bitmaps that are contained in the FLA file to compress the SWF file to the smallest file size possible. Sound and bitmap files are also automatically compressed, which also pares down the size of SWF files tremendously.

Fine-tune Your Export for Specific File Formats

When you export movies to different file formats from the Export Movie dialog box, after you have selected a format you'll see an additional dialog box that will prompt you for special information related to your chosen format. For example, if you are exporting a movie using the QuickTime (MOV) format, you would name the file and select .mov as the Save As Type selection in the Export Movie dialog box. Then an Export QuickTime dialog box will appear, as shown here, offering you further options for fine-tuning the file for the intended destination.

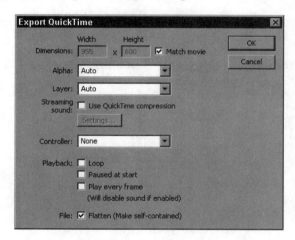

If you export a movie or an image from Flash for web delivery, you must write the HTML code to insert or embed the image/movie into an HTML document. Unlike the Publish command, the Export commands do not automatically generate an HTML file with your SWF file embedded in it. You will have to create the HTML document and HTML code to embed the file using a word-processing application, or a web-design application such as Macromedia Dreamweaver.

Specify Publish Settings

For a multimedia project that's bound for the Web or even for a self-playing projector file, you use the Publish Settings dialog box to set parameters for the published file. The Publish Settings dialog box offers a more comprehensive set of options than the Export boxes do, and it enables you to preview and select all the different settings from the same parent dialog box.

18

As discussed previously, you can publish to many different file formats in addition to the Flash SWF format, which enables you to target delivery of your production to an audience that might not have access to the Flash plug-in. This is easily accomplished with the Publish command, which affords you the ability to publish your Flash movie in up to eight different formats simultaneously. If desired, you can also generate an HTML document with the necessary code to embed your SWF movie.

To select a movie's publishing format, open the Flash document that you want to publish. Choose File | Publish Settings or press CTRL-SHIFT-F12 (Windows)/CMD-SHIFT-F12 (Mac). After you invoke the command, the Publish Settings dialog box appears with the Formats tab selected, as shown here.

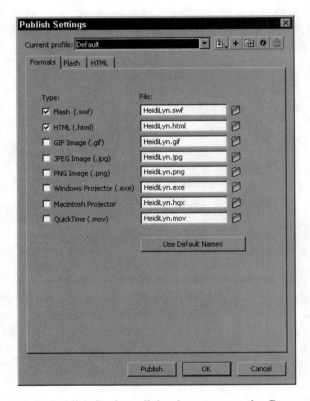

When you first open the Publish Settings dialog box, you see the Current Profile field at the top of the dialog box. This setting specifies the profile under which the movie will be published. The profile is determined by default, depending on the version of the Flash Player for which you are publishing the movie. For example, if you've created the document in Flash 8, the profile is Flash 8 Settings. You can create your own profiles, import profiles, and so on. For more information, refer to the Flash 8 Help panel.

From within the Formats tab, you can select each format in which you want to publish the file. After you select a format, another tab appears in which you can set publishing options for the format. To set options for a particular format, click its tab and follow the prompts.

There are eight file format choices in the Publish Settings dialog box: Flash (.swf), HTML (.html), GIF Image (.gif), JPEG Image (.jpg), PNG Image (.png), Windows Projector (.exe), Macintosh Projector (.hqx), and QuickTime (.mov). Publishing for each file format is covered in detail in the upcoming sections.

To fine-tune the settings for each format, you click the applicable tab and follow the prompts. When you first open the Publish Settings dialog box, the following tabs are selected by default:

- ■ **Formats**   From this tab you select the type of file formats in which you want to publish the document and assign filenames.
- ■ **Flash**   From this tab you specify settings for a Flash SWF movie.
- ■ **HTML**   From this tab you specify settings for the HTML document in which the Flash movie will be embedded.

TIP

The Publish and Publish Preview commands automatically generate filenames in the Publish Settings dialog box. You can specify a different filename by clicking the Use Default Names button on the Formats tab and then entering the desired filename for each format in which you publish the movie.

Although you don't have to publish your file as a Flash SWF movie or embed it in an HTML document, the designers of Flash assume that this is your intention, which is why these tabs appear by default. If desired, you can deselect either option by clicking the appropriate check boxes in the Formats tab.

After you have selected additional formats, the applicable tabs appear (or disappear if you decide not to publish a file in one of the default formats). The upcoming sections contain specific instructions for each file format.

Use the Flash Tab

When you open the Publish Settings dialog box, the Flash tab is selected by default. From within this tab, you can accept the default settings or fine-tune the settings to suit your Flash production. The Flash tab is shown in the following illustration.

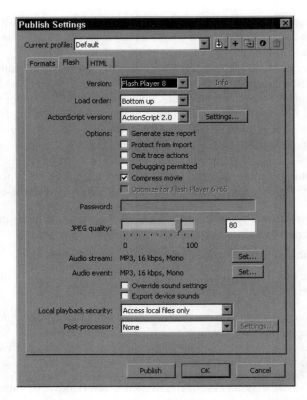

To specify settings for a Flash movie, click the Flash tab and set the following options:

- **Version** Choose the version of the Flash Player you are targeting. You can choose from versions 1 through 7. In Flash Professional, you can also publish a file that will play with one of the Flash Lite players, which are used to play Flash content on devices such as PDAs and cell phones. Note that if your movie contains ActionScript from a particular version of Flash and you publish the movie for an earlier version of the Flash Player, your movie may not play as desired.

- **Load Order** If you want to select the order in which Flash loads the layers of your movie, you can do so by selecting one of the following options from the Load Order pop-up menu. If playback on the Web is slow, Flash will start to display individual layers in the order specified.

  - **Bottom Up** This option loads the movie in a browser from bottom to top.

  - **Top Down** This option downloads and displays the top layer first and then continues down the page to the bottom.

- **ActionScript Version** Choose ActionScript 2.0 or ActionScript 1.0. If you open an FLA file created with a previous version of Flash, ActionScript 1.0 is selected by default. Select ActionScript 2.0 to update the file to the new ActionScript standard.

- ■ **Options**   The Options section includes the following check boxes:
  - ■ **Generate Size Report**   This option generates a text file when you publish the movie. The file supplies you with a detailed report about the size of each frame and the various events that take place in your movie.
  - ■ **Protect From Import**   This option prevents viewers from importing the SWF file into Flash and converting it into a source file.
  - ■ **Omit Trace Actions**   This option deletes any Trace actions in your movie when you publish the file. This option prevents the Output window from appearing when your published movie is viewed.
  - ■ **Debugging Permitted**   This option allows you to debug your movie from a remote location using a password.
  - ■ **Compress Movie**   Use this option to compress your movie using the SWF compression methods.
  - ■ **Optimize for Flash Player 6 r 65**   This option optimizes the movie for this version of the Flash Player.
- ■ **JPEG Quality**   You can globally adjust the JPEG quality by using a slider or by entering a value in the field from 0 (low quality) through 100 (high quality). Note that this setting will not override any changes you've made to a bitmap's properties in the Library.
- ■ **Audio Stream or Audio Event**   Use either one of these options if your sound is streaming or occurs with an event. You can select from MP3 (Compression), 16 Kbps (Bit Rate), or Mono. Note that monaural sound has no settings. When you click Set, the Sound Settings dialog box appears, offering you the following options:
  - ■ **Compression**   You can set the sound compression parameters for MP3 (the default), ADPCM, or Raw Format, or you can disable sound altogether.
  - ■ **Bit Rate**   Choose from the following bit rates: 8 Kbps, 16 Kbps, 20 Kbps, 24 Kbps, 32 Kbps, 48 Kbps, 56 Kbps, 64 Kbps, 80 Kbps, 112 Kbps, 128 Kbps, and 160 Kbps. Higher settings result in a higher quality of sound at the expense of a larger file size.
  - ■ **Quality**   You can choose from Fast, Medium, or Best. This setting determines the amount of time Flash will take to compress sound files. If you choose Medium or Best, as a rule the audio portions of your movie will sound better, but it will take Flash longer to publish the movie.
- ■ **Override Sound Settings**   This setting overrides all settings you specified in the sound's Properties dialog box from within the document Library.
- ■ **Export Device Sounds**   This setting is available in Flash Professional only and enables you to export sounds for a movie published for the Flash Lite 1.0 Player that will be played on devices such as cell phones and PDAs.

18

■ **Local Playback Security** This setting determines which external files the Flash Player allows to be played. From the drop-down menu, choose Access Local Files Only or Access Network Only.

■ **Post-Processor** This Flash Professional–only option enables you to choose any post processor installed on your system from the drop-down menu. After choosing a post processor, click the Settings button to set up the device for processing the document.

Use the HTML Tab

To embed your SWF file in an HTML document, select HTML from the Formats tab of the Publish Settings dialog box. Then click the HTML tab to display the HTML settings, as shown in Figure 18-4.

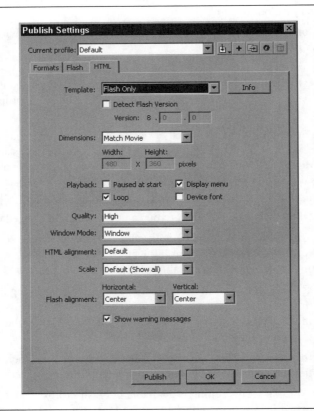

FIGURE 18-4 You use the HTML tab to fine-tune the settings for the HTML document in which your Flash movie is embedded.

This tab contains the following settings:

■ **Template**   Click the Template down arrow and you can select from several different templates. The template generated by your selection will provide a fill-in-the-blanks HTML page with the appropriate script generated for a particular outcome. When you select each template, you can click the Info button to view a description of the code that will be generated. For example, if you choose Image Map from the Template drop-down and then click the Info button, the following dialog box will appear.

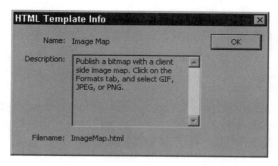

When you choose Flash Only (the default) from the Template pop-up menu, the template will use the OBJECT and EMBED tags to embed your Flash movie in the HTML document. By default, this format sets the background color of your web page to the same color as the background of your Flash movie.

■ **Detect Flash Version**   Click this box to embed code in the HTML document to detect which version of the Flash Player the user has installed on his or her system. If you choose this option, the Version field becomes available. The version of the Flash Player you select in the Flash tab is displayed followed by two blank fields. Enter the numbers for the subset of the Flash Player you want the HTML document to detect.

■ **Dimensions**   This option enables you to specify the movie's dimensions within the browser. The following selections are available in the Dimensions pop-up menu:

■ **Match Movie**   This selection matches the dimensions of the published movie to the size you specified when creating the FLA document.

■ **Pixels**   This option allows you to type in values within a range of 1 to 28,800 pixels for width and height fields that become available when you select this option.

■ **Percent**   This setting allows you to type in values within a range of 1 to 100 for width and height fields that become available when you choose this option. Note that you can also enter values larger than 100, although this is not advisable as any bitmap images in the movie will become pixilated when the movie is played. When you enter a value in either field, the other field does not update to resize the movie proportionately. Therefore, you should enter the same value in each field; otherwise, the movie will be distorted.

18

- **Playback** This section offers several playback choices for your movie:
  - **Paused At Start** This option allows your viewer to begin the movie by clicking a button you've programmed to play the movie. This option is useful if you want to display certain information on the first frame of the movie that you want users to read before the movie plays.
  - **Display Menu** Choose this option to give the viewer access to the full Flash context menu. If you deselect this option, viewers will not be able to choose playback options from the context menu.
  - **Loop** Select this option if you want the movie to start over again when it has reached its last frame.
  - **Device Font** This option enables Windows viewers to speed playback on their systems by substituting device fonts (sans or serif) whenever a Flash movie uses system-installed fonts from the viewer's computer.
- **Quality** This enables you to decide the quality setting used by the Flash Player to play your movie. If your viewing audience accesses the Internet with slow connection speeds or older computers, choosing a lower setting can speed up the playback of your movie. These choices will control smoothing of images and anti-aliasing of text and images in the Flash movie. The overall function of the Quality setting is to balance image quality with playback speed when the published movie is viewed. The following settings are available:
  - **Low** Flash will set anti-aliasing to off.
  - **Auto Low** Flash will begin playing back your movie with anti-aliasing off. If the Flash Player decides that the viewer's system and Internet connection can control the anti-aliasing without affecting movie playback, Flash will enable anti-aliasing.
  - **Auto High** Flash will enable anti-aliasing when the movie begins playing and disable it if playback issues occur.
  - **Medium** With this setting, you are at the 50-50 mark; the Flash Player handles minor anti-aliasing but will not smooth bitmaps.
  - **High** The Flash Player applies anti-aliasing to all graphics except animated bitmaps at this setting.
  - **Best** This option causes the Flash Player to apply anti-aliasing to all objects as the movie plays.

- **Window Mode**   The following settings are available for Window Mode:

  - **Window**   This is the regular default window mode that plays the movie in a rectangular window within the browser window.

  - **Opaque Windowless**   This option causes the Flash Player to hide all elements existing on the HTML page except the Flash movie.

  - **Transparent Windowless**   This option causes the Flash Player to display any elements on the web page that exist beneath areas of the Flash movie where there are no graphics. This option works for Windows Internet Explorer only and may hinder playback performance.

- **HTML Alignment**   The alignment selected will be added to the HTML template. Choose from the standard HTML settings of Default, Left, Right, Top, and Bottom.

- **Scale**   This option gives you four choices:

  - **Default (Show All)**   This option defaults to the user's browser settings.

  - **No Border**   This option scales the Flash movie to the specified area with no border. The movie is scaled proportionate to the original dimensions; however, some clipping may occur if you specify a scale or dimension that exceeds the user's desktop size.

  - **Exact Fit**   This scales the movie to the available browser area. Note that distortion may occur if the browser area is not proportionate to the dimensions of the movie.

  - **No Scale**   This option disables the user's ability to scale the movie.

- **Flash Alignment**   This option determines how the Flash movie is aligned within the application window. From Flash Alignment you can pick the Horizontal pop-up menu and choose from Left, Center, and Right. From the Vertical pop-up menu you can select Top, Center, or Bottom.

- **Show Warning Messages**   When you select this option, any problems or conflicts that occur when you publish your file will be brought to your attention; for instance, if you specify a tag setting such as alternate text for an image that doesn't exist.

Use the GIF Tab

GIF files are limited to a 256-color palette (indexed color). When you choose a GIF format, you need to define the color characteristics for the file in the lower section of the GIF tab, as shown in the following illustration. Also important to keep in mind is that if the Flash document you are publishing as a GIF file is comprised of bitmap images that have millions of colors, these will be interpolated to a 256-color palette, which will produce a large file, especially if your Flash movie is long.

18

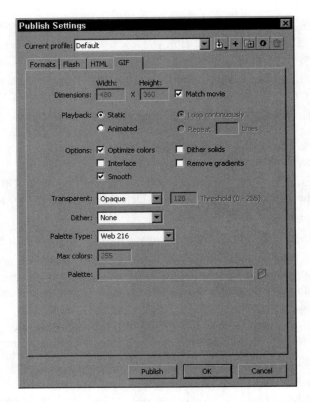

The following settings are available on the GIF tab of the Publish Settings dialog box:

■ **Dimensions** You can specify the width and height of the published file if you deselect the default Match Movie option that matches the dimensions of the published file to the dimensions of the Flash document.

■ **Playback** Choose from Static or Animated. If you choose Animated, you have the options Loop Continuously or Repeat, which plays the movie the number of times you enter.

■ **Options** In the Options section, you can specify the following:

■ **Optimize Colors** Selecting Optimize Colors will help reduce the colors in an image to make it fit within the 256-color parameters of the GIF format.

■ **Dither Solids** This option allows you to reduce the number of colors used in your image by replacing solid colors from the original file that aren't in the indexed palette with dithered colors. Dithered colors combine colors from the indexed palette to create a reasonable facsimile of the original color.

■ **Interlace**   When you choose Interlace, the resulting GIF file is revealed in stages as the file downloads. The end user's perception is that the file is downloading more quickly, when, in fact, interlacing increases or decreases file size in negligible increments.

■ **Remove Gradients**   If you select this option, gradients will be blended to a solid color to reduce the overall number of colors required to view your image. This option is very much like the Dither Solids box.

■ **Smooth**   When you choose the Smooth option, all graphics in your movie are smoothed to a vector-like appearance when the GIF file is published.

■ **Transparent**   This sets the transparency of the published file's background and determines how alpha settings are handled when the document is published as a GIF file. Choose Opaque to make the background a solid color, Transparent to make the background areas of the document transparent, or Alpha to set partial transparency. When you choose Alpha, you specify a Threshold value from 0 through 255. Lower values cause the background to become more transparent, while higher values cause the background to become more opaque. A setting of 128 is 50 percent transparency.

■ **Dither**   The Dither settings are None, Ordered, and Diffusion.

■ **Palette Type**   You can select from the following GIF-appropriate palettes:

  ■ **Web 216**   Choose this option to have the images in your document rendered with the standard web-safe palette.

  ■ **Adaptive**   Choose this option to have the file published with a palette of 256 colors derived from the images in your document. This option is appropriate if your intended viewing audience has computer graphic cards that are capable of producing a full range of color values.

  ■ **Web Snap Adaptive**   This option yields results similar to the Adaptive palette; however, colors that are close to the Web 216 palette snap to a color from that palette.

  ■ **Custom**   Choose this option to load a palette you have created specifically for the document you are publishing as a GIF file. You can create custom palettes in applications such as Macromedia Fireworks MX or Adobe Photoshop. When you choose this option, the Palette field is enabled.

■ **Max Colors**   This option becomes available when you choose Adaptive or Web Snap Adaptive in the Palette Type list. Enter the desired number of colors (a value from 0 through 255) in the text field. Specifying a smaller number of colors helps reduce the size of the overall GIF file. Image quality, however, suffers when you specify a small number of colors.

■ **Palette**   This option becomes available when you choose Custom in the Palette Type list and enables you to specify the custom color palette. For example, if you have created a custom palette in Fireworks or Photoshop, you can select it here and apply it to the GIF image you are creating. You can import a custom palette saved with the .act extension.

18

Use the JPEG Tab

When you export a movie in the JPEG format, it has millions of colors; therefore, JPEG is well suited to a movie that contains many bitmap images. The JPEG tab has relatively few options to be set, as you can see here:

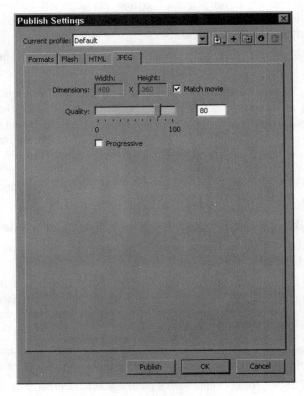

When you click the JPEG tab, you can set the following options:

- **Dimensions** You can manually set the width and height when you deselect the default Match Movie option.

- **Quality** Use the JPEG slider to adjust the compression of the published file. Alternatively, you can enter a value from 0 through 100 in the Quality field. Choose a high setting for the best quality images at the expense of a larger file size; choose a low setting for a small file size at the expense of image quality. Lower settings user higher compression, while higher settings use less compression.

- **Progressive** This is the JPEG equivalent of interlacing. If you check this box, a low-resolution image will appear when the file initially loads; as the file progressively loads, the image becomes clearer.

Use the PNG Tab

You can publish your Flash document as an 8 bit, 24 bit, or 24 bit with alpha PNG file. Since an 8-bit PNG file is similar to a file in the GIF format, the settings on the PNG tab of the Publish Settings dialog box are almost identical to those on the GIF and JPEG tabs when you choose this bit depth. You can also select filtering options for PNG files in this tab, as you can see in the illustration.

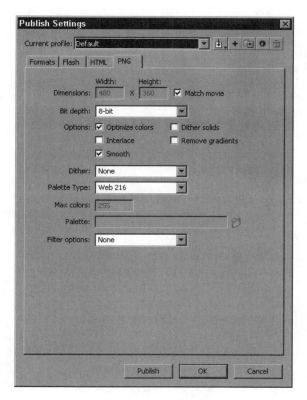

There are five filtering options in the Filter Options menu. These filters (Sub, Up, Average, Path, and Adaptive) perform a mathematical, line-by-line compression that helps reduce the size of the PNG file. When you choose 24-bit or 24-bit with alpha for the bit depth, the color options disappear because 24-bit has millions of colors. The other options still apply.

The PNG format provides most of the capabilities of GIF and JPEG in one format. The big difference is that, whereas the JPEG format uses lossy compression (i.e., color information is lost when the file is compressed), PNG file compression is lossless and will retain its quality over multiple generations.

18

Publish Projector Files

Projector files are primarily used for distributing movies on various media formats such as CD-ROM, DVD, desktop presentation formats, or e-mail. Projector files in Flash Player aren't cross-platform compatible. A projector file you create in a Mac format cannot be used on a Windows-based system, and vice versa. However, you can create projector files for both Windows and Mac platforms separately. Neither projector file setting generates a tab in the Publish Settings dialog box. You can select either format by choosing one of the following from the Formats tab.

- **Windows Projector**   Use this setting to create a standalone file that can be played by computers with the Windows operating system. The standalone file is an executable file that has the Flash Player bundled within. This is an excellent choice for multimedia applications that you are creating for CD-ROM and for a viewing audience that may not have the Flash Player installed.

- **Macintosh Projector**   Macintosh Projector files can only be viewed on the Mac. Again, this is a standalone executable file that contains the Flash Player.

Use the QuickTime Tab

The QuickTime movie format can be used both for web and disk presentations. QuickTime version 5 and later provides Flash with tracks in its architecture to help you take full advantage of sound and media in your Flash movie. In order to publish your movie in the QuickTime

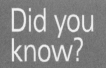

Did you know?   Flash Standalone Applications

Flash 8 is a powerful application that can be used to create applications, presentations, games, and more. However, when you create a standalone application and publish it as a Projector file, you cannot customize the player to make it appear as though you created a custom application. However, a company called Northcode (http://www.northcode.com) has developed an application known as SWF Studio, which is now in its third iteration. SWF Studio is a replacement for the Flash Projector, enabling you to create a standalone custom application. The application takes an SWF file and converts it to a projector, which you can customize with the various tabs present in the application. You can personalize the application by including an icon of your company logo in the title bar and displaying your company name, or for that matter, any other text that will fit in the title bar. You can download a trial version of the application at http://www.northcode.com.

format, you must specify Flash Player 5 in the Flash tab. The QuickTime tab of the Publish Settings dialog box is shown here:

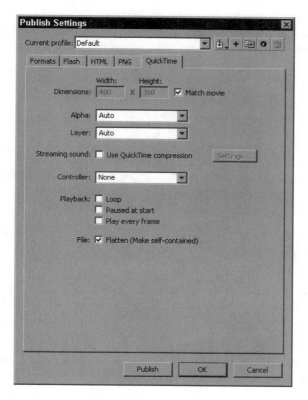

The following settings are selectable on this tab:

- **Dimensions** You can set the size of the movie in dimensions by entering new values for Width and Height after deselecting the Match Movie option, which matches the dimensions of the QuickTime movie to your original Flash movie.

- **Alpha** You can use this option to control the transparency of the background of your Flash track on top of QuickTime. You can select from these options:

  - **Auto** This setting causes the background of the Flash track to be transparent if there are any active tracks beneath the Flash track, or opaque if the Flash track is the only track.

  - **Alpha-Transparent** This option causes the background of the Flash track to be transparent, displaying any content on tracks beneath the Flash track.

  - **Copy** This makes the Flash track opaque, obscuring any content on tracks below the Flash track.

18

- **Layer**   You can decide where the Flash track lies in the stacking order of QuickTime tracks. Select from Auto, Top, or Bottom.

- **Streaming Sound**   Select this option to export streaming sound to a QuickTime sound track. After choosing this option, click the Settings button to reveal the Sound Settings dialog box shown next. Follow the prompts to select the desired compressor and other sound settings.

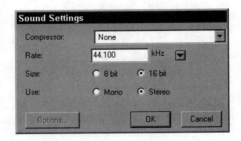

- **Controller**   You can select a QuickTime Controller interface for your QuickTime movie. Select from None, Standard, or QuickTime VR.

- **Playback**   The following Playback options are available for QuickTime movies:

  - **Loop**   This option causes the movie to play from start to finish and then loop back to the start. The movie continues playing as long as the QuickTime Player is open.

  - **Paused At Start**   This option will pause the movie before it starts playing. Users can then use the QuickTime Player controls to control playback.

  - **Play Every Frame**   This option plays every frame of the movie and does not drop frames to maintain time. Sound is not played when this option is selected.

- **Flatten**   Flattening makes a movie self-contained and eliminates references to external files. If you deselect this option and the external files are not present, the movie will not play.

Publish the Movie

After choosing the desired file formats, you're ready to publish the document in the specified formats. When you publish the document, Flash 8 creates a separate file for each format you select in the Formats tab. The files are published to the same folder in which you saved the Flash .fla file. You can publish the file by doing one of the following:

- Click the Publish button in the Publish Settings dialog box. After publishing the file, click OK to exit the Publish Settings dialog box.

- Choose File | Publish.

- Press F12.

Conclusion

In this chapter, you learned to optimize your Flash documents for publishing. You also learned to use the Debugger to find any ActionScript errors in your Flash documents. You learned to export your documents in a number of different formats and publish the document in a variety of formats. In the appendix that follows, you'll find information about where you can access Internet resources for Flash.

Appendix

Flash Resource Guide

Nowadays, Flash-driven sites are synonymous with good design practice. More and more designers, programmers, and web developers are using Flash to build web sites. Because Flash is so popular and so expansive in scope, there are many resources offered on the Web for Flash developers. If you are serious about learning Flash, you will probably need to turn to external resources at some point in your studies.

Keep in mind that many of these sites can be cross-referenced in other categories. In other words, if you don't find what you're looking for in one category, feel free to go to another. For example, a site recommended for sound loops might just as well contain tutorials on something else Flash-related. The purpose is to give you some initial direction, but you can find out additional information on these sites by poking around.

This appendix is a list of resources to help you keep your skills fine-tuned. Because Flash 8 is so new, some of the information in these resources may refer to older versions of Flash. Not to worry, though; Flash is still Flash regardless of the version number attached to it. If a resource relates to an older version, the information can generally be adapted to relate to the newer version. Also, by the time you read this book, the resources may very well have been updated. In either case, you are bound to find valuable information and inspiration when you browse through these links.

Training/Tutorial/Technical Sources

There is no shortage of free and fee-based Flash tutorials on the Web. At the time of this writing, Flash 8 tutorials are scarce because the program is relatively new. However, more and more Flash 8 tutorials and training tips go up on these sites every day, so keep checking back periodically for updated information. In the meantime, if you are new to Flash ActionScript, older tutorials might still be able to help you tweak your skills. And you certainly can use older source files to help you figure out some cool techniques you can achieve through scripting. Either the techniques will be accomplished the same way in 8, or you can easily research the "new and improved" way of doing a technique once you've identified what the effect you want to achieve is all about.

Many tutorials offer sample movies (source code) that can be downloaded. Unlike HTML, the source code of a Flash Player (SWF) file can't be viewed; unless you're a hacker (in which case, you wouldn't be reading this book), you need to obtain the FLA version (the original movie) of the file to see how it was made. Being able to view the code in a movie you really like is a great resource in itself.

The following sources currently are recommended for training and tutorials:

www.computerarts.co.uk   This Computer Arts site, which is the digital sibling of the print magazine, boasts news, product reviews, and extensive tutorials that cover all sorts of digital design programs, including a comprehensive assortment of learning tools for Flash.

www.ultrashock.com   Ultrashock is probably one of the most comprehensive resource sites on the Internet. It has it all: tutorials, user forums, downloadable .fla files, articles, games, cartoons, and an incredibly beautiful interface.

www.sonify.org Sonify is an often unheard-of resource for those interested in interactive audio for the Web, wireless applications, Beatnik audio and, of course, Flash. There are professional articles, tutorials, and discussion boards that cover a broad array of topics relevant to Flash and Flash development.

www.echoecho.com This site has a wealth of Flash tutorials from Flash basics to drawing, tweenings, and JavaScript. There is also a .fla archive with a collection of Flash movies that you can download that will show you how different effects are created.

www.senocular.com This site has Flash 8 tutorials available covering the new BitmapData, which, of course, allows direct bitmap manipulation at the pixel level. There's also a rather comprehensive FAQ for Flash questions that covers everything from working with a preloader to working with setInterval. There are links to many other Flash resources, forums, and Flash blogs.

www.popedeflash.com Pope de Flash is one of the leading sites for Flash and 3D. There are some outstanding tutorials, innovative open-source Flash/3D files, an extensive Flash/3D creator community, articles, news, promotions, and their very special Hit List, which covers the best of the best in Flash/3D.

www.swift3d.com If you're looking for real-world how-to techniques that use Swift 3D functions, this is a great site. This site also offers case studies showing how Swift 3D and Flash are used to solve advertising and marketing communications needs by companies through an elaborate case study presentation and the ability to view the company's completed web site. Be sure to check out TheFootDr.com and CoolNerd.org.

www.actionscripts.org This is a great site with many ActionScript tutorials for Flash 8. In addition, active Flash jobs are posted and are actually current openings! This site also contains current press releases and articles on the latest incarnation of Flash.

www.flash-mx.com This site is excellent for tutorials, source files, tips, and additional resources.

http://flash-creations.com This site by Helen Triolo has incredible and up-to-date tutorials on ActionScript syntax with step-by-step instructions, a specific lesson plan on creating a sample game, code snippets, sound files and sources, and a plethora of other online resources that are invaluable.

www.debreuil.com This site is excellent for ActionScript tutorials, specifically building object-oriented applications in Flash 5, and also offers downloads for TweenMx.

http://weblogs.macromedia.com/mesh/archives/2005/08/must_read_flash.cfm Mike Chambers' Flash platform developer web site has the latest information, tutorials, and tours of Flash 8 features.

www.communitymx.com This site has tutorials on JavaScript integration in Flash 8 and free content, including information on creating a video player in Flash 8 and a CSS case study about constructing a personal site using Flash 8. There are outstanding articles that relate to a programmer's look at Flash 8 and how to manage layouts in Flash 8.

www.flashstreamworks.com   This site is phenomenal. It contains everything, from downloads to broadband sites, to demos, resources, Flash streaming providers, and tutorials.

www.were-here.com   This site offers a myriad of tutorials for ActionScript and Swift3D, including tutorials that show you how to create mouse trails, arrays, drag-and-drop functionality, and dynamic text, as well as how to control a movie clip with a slider. Top tutorial items that have been added are related to the Zoom tool, vertical-scrolling menu, menu system, double-click windows, advanced buttons, playing music, ActionScript expressions, Date object, Tell Target button, and tweening motion guides. This is an excellent and well-respected source for free tutorials on the Web.

www.flashguru.co.uk   This site contains Flash examples with downloadable source files, and is probably best known for its Flash links that include tutorials, extensibility such as Flash Film Maker, Flfile API, JSAPI reference, etc. There are also some great Flash blogs such as Flash Magazine, Flaver, Fuel Games, Actionscript.com, Airtight Interactive, and Bit-101, and Playgrounds by the likes of Andy Foulds, Eric Natzke, Globz, Leo Geo, Levitated, and Limmy. This web site is chock full of incredible and useful stuff.

www.flashkit.com   Flashkit is another well-respected source for Flash tutorials on the Web. The scope of the Flash community is apparent on this site, with contributors from all over the world. This is a great place to exchange ideas and learn from one another.

http://www.animations.com   This site offers an extensive collection of editable Flash files with thousands of variables and options to enhance your projects. There are plenty of freebies and tutorials, from troubleshooting preloaders to tips for editing the Photo Scroller; however, there is a fee to join to have instant and unlimited access to downloads such as animations, interfaces, components, and tutorials.

www.lynda.com   Lynda offers Flash training in her books, her online site, and at her training facility in Ojai, California. Throughout the year she does numerous road shows all over the United States on Flash and other web-related topics. In addition, her site is packed with Flash tips, downloads, links, techniques, and many free resources including Lynda.com wallpaper, articles about color, inspirational web sites, tips, and resource links. There's also an educator's resources section that is dedicated to assisting the academic community that uses Lynda.com materials in the classroom.

www.flzone.net   This site offers tutorials, extensions, Flash files, and sounds, as well as demos and forums.

www.creativemac.com   This site offers tools and techniques for Mac users. There are tutorials available for many topics under the Mac umbrella, including Flash features and functions. This site is completely up-to-speed with the latest information on Flash 8, as well as project profiles which include case studies about how top producers use Flash. Additionally, be sure to check out their Mac Pro Sites ranging from Mac animation pro to Mac audio pro and Mac design pro. These links offer downloads of book and software reviews for members of that specific community.

www.juxtinteractive.com   This is an award-winning site with plenty of good design and a wealth of inspiration for would-be and experienced designers. Some of their new clients include Nestea Ice and Samuel Adams. Periodically, Juxt puts together training seminars offered on their site in Newport Beach, California. These training sessions are only for the truly advanced ActionScript developer. For more information on these seminars, contact them on their web site.

www.presstube.com   This site is an inspiration for all aspiring designers. There are a million incredible links to great stuff, plus an unbelievable number of animations to get your juices flowing.

Flash Animation

Animation, of course, is one of the main staples of Flash. The thing about Flash animation is that there are so many different ways you can create it. There are thousands of sites out there with great Flash animation, and here is a handful you can browse through to see how different designers utilize it.

www.coolhomepages.com   This web site demonstrates how everyone in the Flash community should become familiar with what is out there on the Web in terms of what other developers and designers are doing with the application. This site also offers galleries of some of the most interesting Flash work around, and it's a great source of inspiration and creative ideas to bring our projects to new levels of creativity and professionalism.

www.bestflashanimationsite.com   This site has the best Flash animation sites such as Corpse Bride, The Alias Experiment, Xbox 360, and Drachenboote.

www.melondezign.com   There is some very beautiful and hip Flash animation on this site. This is not exactly your run-of-the-mill kids' cartoon animation, but a very inspirational and innovative style of animation.

www.webmonkey.com   Webmonkey features great articles on all sorts of topics, targeted to all levels from beginner to advanced, concerning all things Flash.

www.mnh.si.edu/africanvoices   African Voices is a Smithsonian-sponsored web site that explores the objects that demonstrate Africa's striking beauty, history, and diversity.

www.desktopimage.com   Desktop Image is dedicated to providing the best free images for your desktop, most of them created in Flash.

www.djojostudios.com   This site specializes in web projects such as games, gadgets, simulations, and highly interactive web sites, all created with state-of-the-art tools, to help you produce Internet-ready content, while working towards low file sizes.

www.moccu.com   Moccu and its accompanying web site were created as a presence for outstanding web design and animation, bringing all forms of experts together: graphic designers, illustrators, animators, programmers, etc. This web site truly demonstrates its talent for game development and interactive storytelling, and uses Flash extensively.

www.rustboy.com   Rustboy is Brian Taylor's short film and accompanying web site, whose mission is to document the process of film production from concept through completion using Flash very creatively throughout.

www.yugop.com   This site uses Flash art, animation, and user interactivity in a very playful yet engaging way.

www.zanpo.com   Zanpo is a virtual city and online community. In this interactive world, you can chat with others, claim some territory, and build your own home . . . all working with Flash technology.

www.campchaos.com   Camp Chaos contains archived Flash cartoons, animations, movies, downloads, games, etc., and is inspiration for all of us.

www.curiousmedia.com   Curious Media, created by Randy Jamison, is an artistic playground of experimentation in animation. Eventually, the site will contain source code, files to download, and Flash community projects, but it's certainly worth exploring now.

www.hopbot.com   This is a well-designed site with plenty of artfully rendered animation. It uses an interesting combination of pictures, text, and random markings, and will show you some interesting things that can be done in Flash.

www.rooneydesign.com   This site offers great looping animation on a group of clever zoom transitions, as well as Flash games that range from Marble Match to Mr. VegHead Game, all created in Flash.

www.cartoonnetwork.com   If you are interested in animated cartoons in Flash, this site provides a cartooning extravaganza.

www.animfactory.net   At this software company, you can buy many animations created by a group of artists.

www.robertpenner.com   Robert Penner, a freelance Flash developer from Vancouver, Canada, offers a wonderful selection of web sites, animations, ActionScript-intensive Flash experiments, and news about the Flash community. His work and this site are very inspiring.

Audio

Since Flash is the ultimate in multimedia, it would be pretty boring if it weren't capable of incorporating sound. If you're new to Flash, you may need a little help figuring out where to go to get loops and sound effects. Although sound sources are just too numerous to mention, here are a few suggestions to get you pointed in the right direction:

www.soundshopper.com/   SoundShopper offers a broad range of music clips, loops, sound effects, and other audio elements for your Flash productions. You can try out and purchase any of these royalty-free sounds directly from the web site.

www.flashkit.com   Among its many tutorials, this site offers open source code and sound files that you can download. You can check out tutorials in which you import sound and create movie symbols, buttons, and actions. Tutorial source files are available for download on this site, too. Additionally, you can download sound loops for use in Flash projects. This site holds a huge library of royalty-free music loops.

www.were-here.com   This site offers a huge music loops section, which you can download for the Macintosh in AIF format or in WAV format for Windows.

www.webdevelopersjournal.com   The *Web Developer's Journal* web site is a great one, and the resources are endless. You can download multimedia Mac, PC, and SWF files and web development tools from this site. You can also download streaming media servers and MP3 search clients, such as CuteMX (a real-time MP3 search engine), Scour Exchange, and iMesh, where you can search for MP3 audio, video, and graphic files. There are looping and sampling software applications such as Fruity Loops, Hammerhead, Tuareg, Acid, and Electrifier Pro. Beatnik and MOD Play software are also available. The tutorials seem to cover only Flash 5 and older.

www.creativepro.com   You can find some great info here about Flash, including how to optimize your audio. This site also covers tutorials for Quark, Illustrator, and InDesign.

www.panic.com   You can download Audion (a MIDI-like application) from Panic, as well as graphical faces to use in your Flash web designs. Also, if you go into Audion 2 from the Panic site, you can learn how to handle all of your audio playing needs, all about MP3s, and how to stream network audio and encode, mix, edit, and so on.

Audio-editing Applications

There are many applications you can use for sound editing. If you are doing serious sound editing, the following applications probably won't meet all of your needs. But if you need something quick and inexpensive, these may be of help to you. Don't feel you need to limit yourself to these applications. Flash can import AIFF, WAV, and MP3 formats. You can walk on down to your local computer store, go to the sound applications software section, and try out some loops right off the shelf.

■ **Refill and Reason 3.0,** by Propellerheads, offers techno music-making at its best. Rebirth Refill recreates the original ReBirth drum sounds as well as offering a large number of Mods. Reason, an award-winning music production instruction, focuses on live playing and has unique features that present it as a solid choice to a hardware workstation synthesizer for composing, producing, or live playing. You can download a free trial version of both at www.propellerheads.se. This site also offers an outstanding selection of articles by product specialists in video clips demonstrating how the new features in the software work. There's also a section on tutorial video clips that take you through some of the features of their software.

- **Groovemaker 2.5** enables you to create hypnotic, nonstop professional dance tracks in real time. You can mix them, layer in some loops, and create a totally new remix. It offers MP3 expert compatibility and Mac OSX capabilities. The interface is space-age; and even if you don't like this kind of music, it sure is fun to play with the cool buttons and the synthesizer. Download a free trial version from www.groovemaker.com.

- **Acid Pro** by Sony Media Pictures is another loop-based music creation tool. Sound Forge 8.0 is also available from their web site: http://www.sonymediasoftware.com. Download a free trial version of Acid XPress from http://www.sonymediasoftware.com/download/freestuff.asp. You can find a plethora of information concerning Acid software at www.acidplanet.com. This site also offers numerous loops for download.

- **SmartSound Sonicfire Pro for Multimedia** and **Quicktracks for Adobe Premiere Pro** are inexpensive plug-in programs that come with prefab loops you can throw together in sort of a wizardlike fashion. Compared to the other applications, some of the loops are a little on the corny side. If you're in a hurry and need something quick and it doesn't have to be a Grammy Award–winning track, you can try this from www.smartsound.com. There is also a link to SmartSound case studies that should be reviewed; it helps users who have come to rely on their products to create soundtracks that add emotional punch to their products without requiring tremendous amounts of musical know-how. Basically, these case studies highlight ways the diverse creative-types out there continue to use SmartSound products.

- **Peak Pro 5** and **SoundSoap Pro** by Bias offer audio editing and processing on the Mac platform. These are easy-to-use and powerful programs that can export to many popular audio formats, including MP3, AVI, and WAV. This site offers a thorough set of documentation that you can download as PDF files for Peak, Peak Pro, SoundSoap, and Vbox. Check them out at www.bias-inc.com.

- **Audacity**, by Audacity Systems, is a free audio editor. You can record and play sounds, and import and export WAV, AIFF, Ogg Vorbis, and MP3 files. You can edit sounds using Cut, Copy and Paste, mix tracks, apply effects to your recordings, etc. Audacity has a built-in amplitude envelope editor, a customizable spectrogram mode, and a frequency analysis window for audio analysis applications. Several built-in effects include Echo, Change Tempo, and Noise Removal. All this is available at audacity.sourceforge.net.

- **SSEYO Koan** is a music-making technology that can accommodate audio interactivity, respond to or cue events in an interactive application, generate music in real time, and deliver high-quality, low-bandwidth audio files. Using the Koan audio engine with Flash can significantly enhance the audio interactivity of your movies. Visit www.sseyo.com for more information about Koan.

- **Beatnik** provides a way to deliver low-bandwidth music and sound effects. When it is used with Flash, projects are often referred to as *Flashniks*. Visit www.beatnik.com to learn more about the software, download the plug-in, and listen to Beatnik music.

Tips and Techniques

Flash ActionScript brains are abundant. It is through their designs and implied answers to technical questions that we will learn new techniques and further our knowledge as Flash designers and developers. So, whether it is to review techniques about loops, build ActionScripts, or create special text effects in Flash, the following designer sites should help you obtain most of the answers to your questions:

www.moock.org   This is Colin Moock's site. Moock is a well-respected Flash expert and author of *ActionScript MX, The Definitive Guide* (O'Reilly Press, 2002). If you haven't heard of him yet, you will, eventually. On his site, Colin offers answers to technical questions and inspiring examples from the popular to the obscure. In addition, there are very helpful ActionScript tutorials on this site.

www.flaxfx.com   Here you can create text effects for Flash in real time. Be sure to check out the samples at this site. It has 31 special-effects groups that can be tweaked using sliders and buttons to create a wide array of unique special effects.

www.macromedia.com   Of course, Flash's manufacturer, Macromedia, has a great site with lots of pertinent and helpful information. Be sure to look under Macromedia Flash Usability to find usability tips, downloadable source files, and guidelines with extensive hyperlinks to relevant and useful information. Also, check out the Flash gallery and "site of the day" section. There's also a Designer and Developer Resource section where they provide articles on writing maintainable code and designing for efficiency.

www.webtronik.com   This web site is in French but offers an incredible Flash portfolio by Sebastian Dupaul, with all types of tips and techniques.

Source Code

We could all use a little help now and then with scripting. Sometimes you will know that you want to create a particular effect, but you just won't know how to build it. If you can find something similar, and if the author has been kind enough to post the source code, then this may solve your problem. On these sites, you can search for open code for your Flash movies:

www.flashkit.com   This is probably the best Flash site around for viewing source files. In addition to great tutorials, this site contains a plethora of ActionScript source files in its Flash Arena section. With these resources you can learn how to create recordable movement with playback, avoid the pirating of your source files, work with time functions, and build text substrings, a progressive percentage preloader, buttons that load content into frames, and a virtual shopping cart.

www.were-here.com   This site offers a lot of source code available for downloading, from preloaders to shopping carts.

www.macromedia.com   Check out Macromedia's source code and guidelines, and take a look at the Development Center.

www.flashpro.nl   You can download Flash movies to view, along with 100 new effects and source files. If you click New Archives, there's a list of Flash materials. There's a Help section covering ActionScript techniques for beginners, games, and more. There is also a Review section that includes links to noteworthy sites. Additionally, there's always a featured ActionScript tutorial.

www.flashguru.co.uk   This site offers Flash samples with downloadable source files. Two tutorials worth checking out are those for collision detection and random function. Check out the resources at this site and the links to other Flash sites and projects.

Gaming Sites

Gaming in Flash has never been hotter—many gaming applications are now created in Flash. Here is a sampling of some interesting game sites. If this is your major field of interest, the following sites will give you some game inspiration.

www.Globz.com   This site contains many games that are beautifully executed. They are intelligent, hip works of art. This isn't your everyday arcade-style site. If you're interested in game design, you definitely want to check this one out.

www.rocketsnail.com   Many cool games await you on this site. You can license the use of their games to use on your site, too. Games on your web site could certainly draw more traffic to a site.

www.trygames.com   This site is the home of the Bug Factor, which is a very ambitious Flash game with professional illustration and animation created with Flash.

www.yenz.com   This site is the Secret Garden of Mutabor, which is a well-animated game site that is easy to navigate and play.

www.flashkit.com   This site offers many links to games developed in Flash.

www.titoonic.dk   This site is an unbelievable, highly playable game. It contains beautiful artwork, superior sound effects, and great animation.

Cartooning Applications

Flash designers interested in cartoon animations can purchase or download a trial version of Toon Boom Studio from www.toonboomstudio.com. Toon Boom Studio is a very cool cartooning application that you can use to create two-dimensional cartoons that export to SWF file format. You can also import Toon Boom SWF cartoons directly into Flash MX using the Toon Boom Studio Importer. Once they are in Flash, they can be made interactive.

Noteworthy Flash Movies

These sites are noteworthy because of their technical brilliance and use of design elements. Well-structured Flash sites always provide inspiration when you need to get your creative juices flowing.

www.macromedia.com/cfusion/showcase/index.cfm   This site changes every day. Having your work shown on this site is a real honor.

www.were-here.com   This site offers "design" links to many beautiful Flash sites for a plethora of creative ideas. There's also a "site check" location at this site that enables you to review other Flash sites people have created. By "reviewing" these sites, you can get some fresh ideas for your own Flash creations.

www.altpick.com   Art Mill shows incredible work in these interactive design sites, which are a testimony to magnificent design inspiration.

www.portfolios.com   You can view many designers' Flash portfolios on this site. Also, be sure to go into Folio Finder so you can review interactive portfolios created in Flash, as well as other interactive software. For the experienced gurus out there, you can set up your own portfolio to procure work.

www.creativepro.com   This site is for professionals. It holds some interesting links, such as a stock photography search, and it also offers a Personal Portfolio Hosting service.

www.secondstory.com   This site offers more than 40 interactive features on subjects ranging from the visual arts to music and history, all explored through a fabulous timeline of collected works. Again, if you're looking for inspiration, try this site.

www.heavy.com   This site offers great music and Flash animation.

www.pepsiworld.com   This site is all Flash and Shockwave; it's constantly updated, with great games as well, which keeps its perspective fresh and appealing to pop culture.

www.becominghuman.org   This site is a web documentary that traces the evolution of humans.

www.Colette.fr/index.php   This site offers outstanding examples of Flash cartooning and animation on an e-commerce web site. There are also excellent examples of streaming audio on Flash sites.

Flash Standalone Software

There are a few companies that create software that enables you to create standalone applications using the Flash Player. The following company includes a licensed version of the Flash Player.

http://www.northcode.com/home.php   Northcode features SWF Studio 3.0, which is an application that replaces the Flash Projector. You can use the software to create a custom application based on an SWF movie. The SWF Studio projector can be customized to include an icon of your company logo. You can also put your company name in the projector title bar and program an expiration date with the projector, after which date it will no longer be functional.

Flash Interface Design

Everyone is always looking for a great Flash idea. These sites are representative of outstanding Flash features with clever interfaces.

www.archpark.org.il   This site has an unbelievably brilliant timeline highlighting periods of time with crisp photography, Flash animations, and interactive maps. The site represents an archaeological attraction in Jerusalem.

www.philbrown.bc.ca   This outrageously designed site offers a true narrative experience that is fully balanced with the navigation of the site. It also utilizes liquid mask transitions.

www.fabrica.it/flipbook/   Flipbook! is an interactive Flash application that allows people to draw simple animations, save them to a gallery, and share them with other people via e-mail. This web site walks you through the steps towards creating your own flipbook. There's a great example of a site using server-side scripts to customize the users' own application from the Flash software and a FAQ that answers all your questions about how to work with Flipbook!.

Flash 3-D

Swift 3D v4.5 is an inexpensive standalone vector- and raster-based program that allows you to export in an SWF format, making it the ideal 3-D Flash companion. Electric Rain is the maker of Swift 3D, and on their site (www.erain.com) you can purchase Swift 3D and also check out what other designers created using Swift 3D and Flash. There are also great Swift 3D v4 tutorials and featured sites, as well as case studies and source files. You can also download a free demo tutorial.

Miscellaneous Resources

If you don't own Flash 8 yet, you can download a trial version from the Macromedia web site. This could be extremely helpful if you bought this book and you don't yet own Flash 8.

You will also find on the Macromedia site trial versions of Macromedia's Dreamweaver, Fireworks, FreeHand, Director, Contribute, and other programs. To evaluate these programs, you can download them from www.macromedia.com/downloads.

If you use other programs to create your vector or bitmap art or HTML, Macromedia's products are a wonderful complement to Flash. The interface on all these programs has a familiar look, as does the language used.

The Flash MX Player can be downloaded from this site, too. You might want to direct your Flash site visitors (those who don't have the correct Flash plug-in) to the Macromedia site to get the proper plug-in.

Flash Blogs

These sites offer archive links, Flash web development tips and techniques, articles, ActionScript code libraries, and experiments with Flash 8.

www.gskinner.com	www.Bit-101.com	www.Quasimondo.com
www.sephiroth.it	www.samuelwan.com	www.brajeshwar.com
www.danieldura.com	www.flazoom.com	www.flashguru.co.uk
www.newsfeed.fatorcaos.com.br	www.markme.com	www.joshdura.com
www.oscartrelles.com	www.impossibilities.com	www.hollowcube.com
www.fullasagoog.com	www.whatdoiknow.org	www.nuwance.com
www.moock.org		

Keep in mind that the Web is an ever-changing form of media and is constantly being updated. Although all the previous web sites and references were in existence at the time of this writing, some might be changed, gone, or rerouted by the time you arrive.

Index